PUBLIC LIBRARIES IN THE 21ST CENTURY

For James

Public Libraries in the 21st Century

Defining Services and Debating the Future

ANNE GOULDING
Loughborough University, UK

ASHGATE

Published by
Ashgate Publishing Limited
Gower House
Croft Road
Aldershot
Hampshire GU11 3HR
England

Ashgate Publishing Company
Suite 420
101 Cherry Street
Burlington, VT 05401-4405
USA

Ashgate website: http://www.ashgate.com

British Library Cataloguing in Publication Data
Goulding, Anne
Public libraries in the 21st century : defining services and debating the future
1. Public libraries - Great Britain - History - 21st century
2. Public services (Libraries) - Great Britain 3. Public services (Libraries) - Great Britain - Forecasting
I. Title
027.4'41

Library of Congress Cataloging-in-Publication Data
Goulding, Anne.
Public libraries in the 21st century : defining services and debating the future / by Anne Goulding.
p. cm.
Includes bibliographical references index.
ISBN 0-7546-4286-0
1. Public libraries--Great Britain. 2. Public libraries--Aims and objectives--Great Britain. 3. Libraries and community--Great Britain. 4. Public libraries--Great Britain--Administration. I. Title: Public libraries in the twenty-first century. II. Title.

Z791.A1G68 2006
074.441--dc22

ISBN-10: 0 7546 4286 0

Printed and bound in Great Britain by MPG Books

Contents

List of Figures

List of Tables

Acknowledgements

My thanks are due to the many who have assisted in the preparation and production of this work. Firstly, I would like to express my gratitude to the Arts and Humanities Research Board who awarded me a Research Leave Scheme award and to Loughborough University for granting me a year's study leave, giving me the time and opportunity to undertake the research on which this book is based. I also extend my thanks to my colleagues at the Department of Information Science at Loughborough University for covering my duties while I was on study leave. Perhaps most thanks should go to all those who gave so freely of their time and opinions in interview and discussion. Their interest and honesty ensured the fieldwork was stimulating and rewarding. I would also like to thank Rachel Spacey who provided me with valuable research assistance, especially with data preparation and analysis, and to Naheel Zaben for help with referencing and the bibliography. Finally, to all at Ashgate, many thanks for your patience.

PART 1
THE ENVIRONMENT

Chapter 1

Setting the Scene

Introduction

There are nearly 5,000 public library service points in the United Kingdom (Cipfa, 2004), 60 per cent of people hold a public library ticket, there are around 400 million visits to public libraries every year and 10 million people make a visit to a public library at least once a fortnight (Department for Culture, Media and Sport, 2004a). This scale of activity suggests that the public library service is a thriving and dynamic system, successfully supporting the literary, leisure, learning and cultural pastimes of the population. Many working within the public library field would confirm that the service is indeed prospering and operating effectively, albeit acknowledging that there are some problems which sometimes prevent public libraries being positioned at the heart of the intellectual and creative lives of the communities they serve. Certainly, a popular image of public libraries as down-at-heel, unwelcoming, uncomfortable places which have old and incomplete collections is enduring, often reinforced by media stereotypes and immoderate press reactions to published reports detailing declines in some of the more conventional aspects of public library provision. And there have been declines. Despite innovative initiatives, programmes and activities enabling public libraries to reach out to communities and engage those who have not in the past made good use of public library services, the statistics show a steady downward trend in the use of many of the core services provided by the public library service including book issues and visitor numbers, although the latter did show a slight increase for the first time in many years in 2002/3 (Cipfa, 2004).

This study takes stock of the public library service in the UK at a volatile time in its history. On the one hand, public goodwill towards the public library service remains strong, reinforced by government commitment since 1997 to improve standards and strengthen its contribution to important aspects of public policy. There is a good deal of optimism within the public library field that the service is raising its game and playing a significant role in achieving political priorities. On the other hand, reports of public libraries as 'a service in distress' (Culture, Media and Sport Committee, 2005, p. 3), 'sleepwalking to disaster' (Leadbeater, 2003, p. 13), 'due for renewal' (Audit Commission, 1997, p. 57) and 'losing their place in people's lives' (Audit Commission, 2002, p. 45) to the extent that they will be out of use by 2020 (Coates, 2004), suggest that, at the beginning of the 21st century, the service is at crisis point. The chapters which follow assess which of these accounts is most valid by analysing the current position of this valued public institution and its role in local and national life. The impact of recent policy initiatives directly targeted at public libraries is evaluated, as are broader developments in the public sector environment within which they operate. Examples of best practice in service delivery are explored as we consider the challenges and opportunities public library managers face in directing their services within an evolving social and policy environment and within shifting national and local priorities.

Developmental Factors

The following discussion does not attempt a full situational analysis of the public library service in the early years of the 21st century; that would require a separate study in itself. Rather, the key political, economic, social and professional developments raised by the representatives from the public library community interviewed for this study are clarified to set a context for the commentary which follows. This is only a brief overview that sets out to give an indication of the range of developments impacting on public library services and many of the issues are explored in more detail in subsequent chapters

Political Forces

The political forces impacting on the public library services in the United Kingdom are numerous and diverse because not only are public libraries a local government service having to respond to local political priorities, but they also have a national position as a statutory service. In many places in the discussion that follows, reference is made to the Government's agenda, often in relation to how public libraries can contribute to the achievement of government aspirations. This is in recognition of the fact that government policy is the key force driving changes to local public services and that to be part of the Government's plans, public libraries must respond positively to its priorities and vision in areas including education and lifelong learning, modernizing government, tackling social inclusion and strengthening communities. In fact, the ideological climate for libraries has improved as Westminster has already recognized the various ways in which public libraries contribute to wider government objectives on social inclusion, education, community development and ICT provision. Since Labour came to power in 1997, there have been two parliamentary debates on public libraries (Hansard, 2004a and 2004b) and two House of Commons Select Committee inquiry reports on public libraries, the first of which noted in its Conclusion:

> We can recollect few if any inquiries that have generated as many submissions to the Committee. That public interest reflects both the need for public library services and the high regard in which they are held by millions of people (Culture, Media and Sport Committee, 2000, para. 104).

The second inquiry reported early in 2005 and confirmed that public libraries are 'an important national resource' (Culture, Media and Sport Committee, 2005, p. 3).

It also found much to criticize, however, details of which are given throughout this book.

Political recognition of the value of the public library service does appear to be growing at a national level, therefore. It is important to remember, however, that as far as public libraries are concerned, 'national' does not mean UK-wide as, following devolution, the governing bodies of each of the home nations of England, Wales, Scotland and Northern Ireland are responsible for the provision of public library services to their own citizens[1].

Devolution Referenda on devolution for Scotland, Wales and Northern Ireland were key promises made in the Labour party's manifesto of 1997. During 1997 and 1998 referenda were held in Scotland, Wales and Northern Ireland. In Northern Ireland the referendum asked whether there was support for the Good Friday Agreement, which, alongside other important provisions on the constitutional future of Northern Ireland and power sharing, also provided for the establishment of a Northern Ireland Assembly with devolved legislative powers. Seventy one per cent voted in favour of the agreement. Elections for the Northern Ireland Assembly took place in June 1998, and the Executive took up its powers in December 1999 although it has since been suspended. In Wales and Scotland, the electorate was asked to vote on whether systems of devolved government should be established in the two countries. In Scotland, a clear majority (70 per cent) voted in favour while in Wales the result was much closer (50.3 per cent in favour). As a result, elections for a new Scottish Parliament and a new National Assembly for Wales were held on 6 May 1999 and devolved powers were formally transferred from the UK Government to the two devolved administrations on 1 July 1999. There are different levels of devolved responsibilities in the different home nations and there is no common pattern although all three new bodies have devolved responsibility for culture.

Although prior to devolution in 1997, both Scotland and Northern Ireland had separate library legislation and domestic Ministers (in the Scottish Office and Northern Ireland Office) responsible for public libraries, devolution has arguably strengthened the hand of the devolved administrations in their handling of public library issues and encouraged all four home countries to follow distinct paths in serving what are often quite different communities with very specific needs. The differences between public library services in the four home countries of the UK may not be very apparent yet but it is likely that as the separate assemblies and parliaments develop policies, priorities and agendas in this and other areas, divergence will become more evident, especially as cultural strategies are developed in Scotland, Northern Ireland and Wales. Scotland published its cultural strategy in 2000 (Scottish Executive, 2000) and Wales in 2002 (Welsh Assembly Government, 2002).

In recognition of the effects of devolution, Chapter 3 is titled 'National Agendas', the plural deliberately containing a double meaning – agendas because there are many national political developments impacting on public libraries and also in acknowledgement that the departments responsible for public libraries in the four home countries will be developing separate agendas for their public library services. The main focus of this book is mainly on English public libraries, however, primarily because of the better access to resources – printed, electronic and human. *Framework for the Future*, the Department for Culture, Media and Sport's (DCMS) long term strategy for public libraries in England was published in 2003 (Department for Culture, Media and Sport, 2003) and the implementation of the action plan to realize its recommendations has led to considerable activity under the direction of the Council for Museums, Libraries and Archives (MLA) for England. MLA is the development agency for museums, libraries and archives in England, advising government on policy and priorities for the sector.[2] There is no equivalent body for the other three home countries although for Wales, CyMAL (Museums, Archives and Libraries Wales) was established in 2004.[3] This is in a different position to the English MLA, however, as it is part of the Welsh Assembly; it is not a separate agency but a policy division of the Assembly, developing policy and giving policy advice directly to Ministers.

In Scotland and Northern Ireland there are no cross-domain bodies similar to either the English or Welsh models although both the SLIC (Scottish Library and Information Council)[4] and LISC(NI) (Library and Information Services Council Northern Ireland)[5] advise their respective governments on library and information issues and act as a focus for activity in the domain. At the time of writing, none of the three bodies in Wales, Scotland or Northern Ireland had published a strategy document for libraries similar to *Framework for the Future* although CyMAL has issued a prospectus outlining its roles, responsibilities and work programmes across the cultural sector of museums, libraries and archives (CyMAL, 2004). In Northern Ireland, *Tomorrow's Libraries*, was commissioned by the Department of Culture, Arts and Leisure for Northern Ireland (DCAL), 'to establish the current position of and to create an agreed future vision for, the service' but to date there appears to be little progress on the report's recommendations (Department of Culture, Arts and Leisure, 2002). The Scottish Executive has asked the SLIC to develop a standards and evaluation framework with the key themes of information, reading, access and community and also established a Cultural Commission to review existing cultural provision, including public libraries, and make recommendations for the future. The Commission published its final report in June 2005, recommending that the SLIC be re-constituted as the Library and Information Council of Scotland and continue its work on the establishment of national public library standards (Scottish Executive, 2005).

Because of the number of initiatives and publications as a result of *Framework for the Future*, the emphasis of this study is on English public libraries although references are made to the systems in the other three home countries where possible and when relevant. Representatives from the other three home countries were interviewed and their responses and comments give an indication of developments in Scotland, Wales and Northern Ireland.

Regional government New Labour's enthusiasm for constitutional reform did not stop at the creation of assemblies and parliaments for Wales, Scotland and Northern Ireland but also included plans for regional devolution for England. The creation of regional government in England was another commitment that the

Labour party made in its manifesto before it came to power in 1997. A government white paper published in 2002, *Your Region, Your Choice* (Office of the Deputy Prime Minister, 2002), defined the powers available to regional government, should any of the eight regions outside London choose to establish regional assemblies.. The assemblies would take over the roles and responsibilities of various bodies or quangos operating in the areas of: sustainable development; economic development; skills and employment; spatial planning; transport; waste; housing; health improvement; biodiversity; and, most importantly for public libraries, culture (Mulholland, 2004). Currently, all regions have unelected assemblies made up of local councillors, business and community leaders but to take over the powers envisaged for them by the Office of the Deputy Prime Minister (ODPM), the government department driving the regional agenda, referenda on whether to establish an elected assembly must be held. The first three of these were to be held in the autumn of 2004 but two were postponed following fears that the 'no' campaigns would prevail and the vote would be lost. In fact, the referendum that did go ahead in the North East of England returned a resounding 'no' to the concept of regional government, throwing the Government's regional devolution plans into turmoil.

There is certainly considerable opposition to regional assemblies, many feeling that an extra tier of government is an unnecessary and bureaucratic waste of money. Those in favour argue that elected assemblies would be democratically accountable to local voters, unlike the hotchpotch of appointed assemblies, consortiums, boards and regional government offices that is currently responsible for a whole host of issues at a regional level. Supporters also feel that the regions would gain an economic advantage if they had regional government and attract more investment from both UK and European parliaments. The main obstacle to regional government could be public apathy, however, as a vigorous public debate around regional government has yet to take off.

In the meantime, as far as public libraries are concerned, regional cultural consortiums have been created, regional cultural strategies have been formulated and Single Regional Agencies representing museums, libraries and archives have been established, all of which have implications for the operation and delivery of library services. Despite the stalling of referenda for elected regional assemblies, the Department for Culture, Media and Sport published a consultation paper in June 2004 setting out its approach on the role of elected regional assemblies in relation to the cultural sector (Department for Culture, Media and Sport, 2004b). It proposes that elected regional assemblies would be directly responsible for regional cultural consortiums, would prepare the regional cultural strategy and would have powers to provide funding for the Single Regional Agencies. The extent of regional cultural activity envisaged raises the question of whether library services should be provided on a regional basis to benefit from large, cross-sectoral partnerships, economies of scale and to counteract the effect of the local government review of the late 1990s which often split single large authorities into several smaller ones. Certainly, talk of 'fragmentation' and its downsides is prevalent but, initially, regional co-operation is considered vital to raise the profile of the cultural sector, encourage and support innovative service delivery and improve the sector's chances of accessing new sources of funding directed at the regions.

Public sector reform The Labour Party manifesto of 1997 promised to modernize local government and, duly elected, it published its plans in *Modern Local Government: In Touch with the People* (Department of the Environment, Transport and the Regions, 1998). Many of the elements of its reform agenda and how they have impacted on public libraries are discussed in detail in later chapters but, in essence, the Government was determined that local government should be more open, efficient and accountable, that services standards should be raised through a challenging performance management framework and the dissemination of good practice and that links between local councils and local people should be strengthened. Professor John Rouse explores New Labour's approach to performance and quality management in public services in a paper questioning how comfortably the Government's performance agenda sits with its claim to allow local public servants the freedom to deliver services as they see fit, providing those services show acceptable results (Rouse, 2001). In fact, he argues, the regulatory framework developed for local government continues a move towards 'centralized-decentralization' (Hoggett, 1996, p. 10) begun under previous Conservative administrations, driving out local autonomy and difference, which are increasingly regarded as deviations and cause for concern. As central government control over local government has tightened, so local development of services could become increasingly constrained as Whitehall expects to play a greater role in policy development. For public libraries in England, the DCMS established national 'offers' in *Framework for the Future* and instituted a performance management and standards regime in an attempt to improve quality and strengthen accountability, which can be seen as part and parcel of central government's efforts to modernize local government and raise standards in public service provision.

To support modernization, in July 2002 a statement of 'shared priorities' between local and central government was issued that identified seven priority areas in which both should focus their efforts to improve public services:

- Raising standards in schools;
- Improving the quality of life of children, young people, families at risk and older people;
- Promoting healthier communities;
- Creating safer and stronger communities;
- Transforming the local environment;
- Meeting local transport needs;
- Promoting the economic vitality of localities.

The challenge for all public services, including public libraries, is now to demonstrate how they help deliver these shared priorities. A study by PricewaterhouseCoopers (2005) funded by the Laser Foundation sought to establish the impact of public libraries on the shared priorities. The research found evidence of 'a clear and measurable contribution made by libraries to wider policy priorities at both local and national levels' (p. 6), particularly in the areas of services supporting education, children, health and older people.

Another development in modern public service delivery is the development of the concept of choice. The Prime Minister Tony Blair says he wants to update the 'paternalistic' and 'monolithic' 1945 welfare state with 'modern', consumer-orientated and devolved public services. The leaders of both main political parties seem keen to project themselves as champions of choice in public services although, as discussed in Chapter 4, some have questioned the validity of extending choice to public services and argue that many of the choices on offer are actually quite trivial. Primarily associated with health and education, the notion of consumer choice, individualism and competition characterizes the Government's approach to the public sector and all public services will have to respond as the Government seeks to push the key values of quality, accountability and choice into every area of the public sector.

An issue related to the quality of public services and the modernization agenda is the emphasis on 'joined-up' government, which Pollitt defines thus:

> "Joined-up government" is a phrase that denotes the aspiration to achieve horizontally and vertically co-ordinated thinking and action. Through this co-ordination it is hoped that a number of benefits can be achieved. First, situations in which different policies undermine each other can be eliminated. Second, better use can be made of scarce resources. Third, synergies may be created through the bringing together of different key stakeholders in a particular policy field or network. Fourth, it becomes possible to offer citizens seamless rather than fragmented access to a set of related services (Pollitt, 2003, p. 35).

The aim, therefore, is to ensure that public services and other agencies work together to make better use of resources and develop creative and effective approaches to problems and service delivery issues. In an attempt to free services from a 'silo mentality' that encourages them to perceive their work and activities in isolation to that of others working in related areas, the Government has been emphasizing partnership working to integrate services and address 'cross-cutting' issues and 'over-arching' themes. Although Pollitt suggests that there is little new about trying to co-ordinate policymaking and administration, joined-up government is certainly high up the Government's agenda and is being embraced at local government level as local authorities adopt partnership working as the best way of achieving corporate goals and tackling social issues. For public libraries, this means ensuring that partners both inside and outside local government understand what they have to offer and how they can contribute to cross-cutting agendas so that they can play their full role in the achievement of the local authority's plans.

The Knowledge-Driven Economy

Ideas around the knowledge-driven or knowledge-based economy are linked to and extend the concept of the Information Society, characterized by a high level of information use among the general public (Moore, 1999). In this vision, the development and use of communication and information technologies have stimulated huge changes in the organization of work and daily life, leading to a process of transition from a society and economy based on industrial wealth to one based on the exploitation and use of knowledge. According to the World Bank (2003):

> A knowledge-based economy relies primarily on the use of ideas rather than physical abilities and on the application of technology rather than the transformation of raw materials or the exploitation of cheap labour (p. 1).

Concerned that the UK must transform itself into a knowledge-driven economy to maintain or improve its global economic position, the Government published its competitiveness white paper in 1998 (Department for Trade and Industry, 1998). This sets out the economic framework for a successful economy, suggesting that the development and exploitation of the workforce's knowledge, skills and creativity will give the UK a global competitive edge. The success of the whole economy, not just individuals, is now considered to depend, as never before, on education and skills. If knowledge provides key competitive advantage, the creation and use of knowledge must be a priority. As a result, the demand for highly skilled workers has increased while that for unskilled or lower-skilled workers has declined (World Bank, 2003). Workers now require a good basic education enabling them to adapt and learn new knowledge and skills through retraining and lifelong learning.

Education and training have been top of the Government's concerns since the first New Labour administration came into power in 1997. Chapter 9 considers the Government's learning agenda and how public libraries are responding but the implication of a knowledge-driven economy in which the human and intellectual capital of skills and knowledge are the principal economic drivers is clear; education and learning must be priorities. The importance of learning skills is also evident in discourses of the knowledge-driven economy. The repercussion of an economic framework in which constantly updated knowledge is the principal input is that workers will need to keep on learning new skills and continually refresh their knowledge. The ability of workers to achieve this is often dependent on their capacity to learn. Lifelong learning skills are therefore stressed as key competencies, enabling individual workers to compete in a global economy (World Bank, 2003) and enabling individual economies to become and remain competitive.

For public libraries, the focus on learning and skills as fundamental to the prosperity of the nation must be a welcome one, concerned as they are with learning in its broadest sense. There is no doubting the Government's awareness of the need for education and lifelong learning and its commitment to raising standards in schools and upskilling the working population. As we will see in Chapter 9, though, there may be some differences of interpretation and understanding of the aim of education and learning with some in the public library community rejecting the Government's utilitarian view of learning as a tool for economic advancement (McCabe, 2001) in favour of a model which values learning as fundamental to social and personal, as well as economic, development.

Social Issues

The social changes that have taken place in the UK over the last couple of decades are extensive and only a brief overview of some of the most relevant for public library services can be given here. It is perhaps inevitable that individual readers will disagree with the range of issues chosen but these were the developments identified as most important by those interviewed.

Social exclusion Chapters 7 and 8 are devoted to neighbourhood renewal and how public libraries are responding to the Government's linked agendas on social exclusion and community development. The term 'multiple deprivation' is often used to characterize communities suffering from social exclusion where:

> …low incomes, unemployment, low educational attainment and attendance, poor health, poor housing and physical isolation come together. It is frequently characterized by a sense of stigma and hopelessness among people who suffer it, often manifested in alcohol and drug misuse, crime and fear of crime, long term sickness levels or poor parenting (Library and Information Services Council (Wales), 2003, p. 1).

Although the Government makes much of the strength of the economy, the UK still features near the bottom, if not at the bottom, of many of the European deprivation indicator tables including child poverty, workless households, adult literacy and numeracy, 18 year olds in education, teenage pregnancy, drug use and crime. The UK has one of the highest at-risk-of-poverty rates in the European Union, above the EU average and the highest rate for children aged under 15 (Eurostat, 2004). The Government has established a number of initiatives and cross-departmental units to encourage the kind of joined-up thinking discussed above in an attempt to tackle the UK's worst social problems. Units for social exclusion, neighbourhood renewal, rough sleepers, teenage pregnancy, and children and young people have all been set up while Sure Start links the Department for Education and Skills with the Department of Health to improve the health and well-being of pre-school children in deprived areas and Connexions, a youth service, offers a one-stop advice service for teenagers about education, training and employment.

As a result of its social policies, the Government claims that rough sleepers have fallen by two-thirds since 1998, the number of children excluded from school dropped by a third in 1999–2000, teenage pregnancy rates fell by 7 per cent in 1999 and one-and-a-half million children have been lifted out of poverty since 1997. There is evidence that child poverty has fallen, unemployment has dropped and youth offending rates have declined since New Labour came into office. Nevertheless, Britain remains a divided society and even those sympathetic to the Labour Government are critical of its lack of progress on creating a fairer, more equal Britain. The Blairite Institute for Public Policy Research (IPPR) reports that the gap between rich and poor has continued to grow since Labour came to power (Paxton and Dixon, 2004). The richest 1 per cent of the population has increased their share of national income from around 6 per cent in 1980 to 13 per cent in 1999. The wealthiest 10 per cent of the population now owns more than half the country's wealth, an increase from 47 per cent to 54 per cent over the past 10 years. At the other end of the socio-economic spectrum, 23 per cent of children in Britain lived in households earning below 60 per cent of median income in 2001, compared with just 5 per cent in Denmark, 10 per cent in Sweden and 14 per cent in Germany. Parental social class, gender and ethnicity still heavily influence life chances with people from a professional family background more than twice as likely to become professionals than those from a manual working class background, women more likely to live in poverty than men and 69 per cent of Pakistani or Bangladeshi individuals living in poverty in 2002/3, compared to 20 per cent of Whites.

The conclusion we can reach, then, is that although government policies and initiatives have started to address Britain's social problems, there is still a long way to go. The other important point to note is that society is not static. New issues arise and new communities add to the complexity of the social situation. The number of people living alone has increased, for example, not just among the older population where increased longevity has meant more single person households but also notably in the 25–44 age group. Twelve per cent of this group lives alone now compared with just two per cent in 1971 and the majority are men (Rikards et al., 2002). As Pahl notes, '[t]his general reduction in social support amongst a growing proportion of the population will be one of the most significant social changes of the next 15 years' (Pahl, 1999, p. 12) and will make demands on a range of public services. Similarly, immigration has added new elements to society and has raised the issue of how best to meet the needs of these new groups. The Government's policies on asylum seekers, for example, especially its dispersal policy, have been controversial and have required a response from local authority services.

For public libraries, the changing social landscape along with the demands for joined-up service delivery has meant that they have had to consider how their services can contribute to tackling social exclusion. This might involve reviewing and adjusting their collections, developing programmes or initiatives to promote lifelong learning and literacy, supporting access to local council and other services through e-government and other mechanisms and generally playing a part in community planning and development.

Lifestyles Although there might be a perception that Britain is a nation of television-watching couch potatoes who care little for other more demanding forms of entertainment, the 2002 General Household Survey shows that although television does play a large role in people's leisure activities (99 per cent had watched it during the four week reference period), the proportion of adults who said they listened to records or tapes increased steadily from 62 per cent in 1977 to 83 per cent in 2002 and between 1996 and 2002 there was no change in the proportion of adults who had read books (65 per cent) (Fox and Rikards, 2004).

Reading has enjoyed a high profile recently with the BBC's *Big Read* attracting large audiences and increasing the library lending and sales of books in the list of top 21 favourite books by 56 per cent and a massive 425 per cent respectively (BBC Press Office, 2003). Similarly, the book club on television chat show *Richard and Judy* has enjoyed the same success as its forerunner on Oprah Winfrey's US programme, its recommendations boosting sales and loans in a repeat of the 'Oprah effect'. It could be said, though, that these are merely capitalizing on a longer term trend of increasing interest in books and reading. According to consumer surveys, spending on books in Britain increased by more than £500 million between 1993 and 1999 and citizens in the UK spend more on books than any of their European counterparts (BBC News Online, 2002).

This should be good news for public libraries and, as discussed in Chapter 10, activities and initiatives in libraries have been successful in promoting users' engagement with literature and fiction. Countering this, however, there is a view that although people in Britain are reading more, they are also more acquisitive and many prefer to buy books rather than borrow them. Moore (unpub.) suggests that this cannot fully explain the decline in borrowing experienced by public libraries in the UK, however, as it is well documented that high levels of book purchase are usually associated with high levels of library use. Nevertheless, the abolition of the Net Book Agreement in 1994 enabled bookshops and supermarkets to sell books below their recommended retail price and adopt aggressive pricing strategies that meant that books were no longer considered a luxury item. Similarly, online bookshops like Amazon make ordering books quick, simple and possible from the comfort of your own home, convenient for the many who simply cannot find the time to visit either a bookshop or a library. Indeed, the growth of households with multiple earners, necessary for maintaining what is now considered an appropriate standard of living, has undoubtedly had its effect on families' leisure time with weekends often taken up with shopping or household chores, thus reducing the opportunity to spend time browsing in a library, especially if the library's opening hours do not suit. Shopping patterns have also changed with fewer people using town centres, preferring out of town retail developments. This can leave town centre libraries isolated.

The 'time poor' nature of many people's lives in Britain means that they are willing to buy convenience and although, as indicated above, the language of consumerism is controversial in public services there is no doubt that the increasingly consumerist attitudes of the British public have impacted on public services. Consumers are portrayed as demanding, sceptical, determined to get value for money, with high expectations of high quality products or services, intolerant of mistakes or delays, insistent on their 'rights' and vociferous when things go wrong. Public services have to adjust to working within this consumerist environment, especially as government rhetoric is promoting the notion of consumer choice and satisfaction as central to the reform of the public sector.

The Professional Environment

The profession does not exist in isolation and must respond to changes in the political and social environment such as those outlined above. The apparent public popularity of the public library service has already been noted and, as Froud and Mackenzie comment, across the UK libraries are often voted the most popular and valued council service (Froud and Mackenzie, 2002). That does not mean they can afford to be complacent, however, and they must continue to demonstrate how they can contribute and add value to local and national strategic objectives, working in partnerships to help deliver key priorities in the learning, inclusion and citizenship agendas. These national agendas inevitably raise questions for the public library profession and challenge it to consider how public library services can take advantage of the opportunities they present to provide new services or service delivery options while maintaining existing service offerings. Perhaps the key driver of change in the delivery of services, enabling public libraries to extend new services and functionality to users, has been Information and Communication Technology (ICT).

Information and Communication Technology Technological changes are often given a section of their own when environmental analyses are undertaken but here they are included in the consideration of professional developments to place them in the context of changes in the delivery of library and information services. ICT should be, after all, a tool and means to an end rather than an end in itself. Chapter 6 details the Government's policy objectives and public library developments in the area of ICT, focusing on how public libraries can play an important role in breaking down the digital divide by extending ICT use to socially excluded groups and individuals and also how they can support service improvement and development by helping deliver e-government services. The importance of the Internet as an information resource means that librarians increasingly define themselves in the context of an information society (Black, 2000) and government investment in the People's Network has enabled public libraries to explore the potential of ICT to deliver services which meet a host of policy objectives in the learning, social inclusion and citizenship areas. ICT is acknowledged as having a key role to play in learning through access to computer aided learning and as a way of finding information resources to support people's studies be these formal, informal, ICT-based or more conventional. Learning itself is perceived as fundamental to opening up people's opportunities and fighting social exclusion as it improves their employability and therefore their economic life chances (Library Association, 2001). Many in the public library profession would not reject this analysis but would perhaps temper this essentially functional view of learning with an appreciation of the wider benefits to be gained including the creation of, 'competences, confidence and skills which allow people to organize their lives, improve their quality of life, and engage with society' (SEMLAC, 2003, p. 31). The challenge now for public libraries is how they manage their ICT resources to ensure that they are effectively supporting people's learning activities, opening up opportunities to the socially excluded and enabling engagement with public services through e-government.

Leadership and advocacy The issues of leadership and advocacy for public libraries are often talked of in the same breath and are seen as being closely linked; strong leaders are needed to take services forward, speak with an authoritative professional voice and champion the cause of public libraries at local, regional and national levels. The effectiveness of leadership for the public library service in the UK has been scrutinized and frequently criticized in recent years, however, most contentiously in *Who's in Charge?*, a report written for the charity Libri by Tim Coates, a former managing director of bookshop chain Waterstone's (Coates, 2004). Published at the end of April 2004 just as interviews for this study were beginning, the report certainly made the fieldwork process lively. *Who's in Charge?* is essentially a polemic, designed to provoke a professional and public reaction and, to that end, it was very successful. The basic premise of the report is that unless public libraries do something drastic to arrest the fall in visitor and issue figures, there may be no libraries in ten or fifteen years' time. It recommends that local authorities should treble expenditure on books and reading material, increase opening hours by 50 per cent and institute a programme of library refurbishment and redecoration. While these suggestions are not controversial in themselves and many working in public libraries would wholeheartedly support their implementation, Coates' insistence that they can be achieved without increasing public library budgets but through savings made in reducing the number of staff involved in management and in streamlining acquisition processes, raised significant dissent within the profession.

The report sparked wide discussion, not just within the public library profession but also in the national media who picked up on the story. Several daily and Sunday newspapers ran columns by commentators looking back through rose-tinted spectacles to their library use as children and lamenting the demise of the public library service (see, for example, Hutton, 2004, Street-Porter, 2004). The report even provoked a debate in Parliament (Hansard, 2004b). Those involved with public libraries found much to criticize in the report as will become apparent in the many references to it in forthcoming chapters. Perhaps of most annoyance to many was that a report focusing on just one aspect of the public library service (the book lending role) and based on data from just one, not particularly representative public library service (Hampshire County Council), should gain so much media exposure when most of the good work underway in libraries goes unnoticed and unreported. Although some were philosophical, taking the view that any publicity is good publicity, the fact that they had to defend services to local authority managers and users left others feeling that they were on the back foot and in defensive mode when they wanted to be positive about service developments and initiatives. Commentators in the professional press and most of those interviewed for this book concede that *Who's in Charge?* does identify some serious issues that need to be tackled but also feel that its narrow focus, attachment to the retail model of provision and reliance on data from a single county council library authority means it is flawed as a meaningful piece of research. Interview participants also frequently pointed out that many of the issues it raised are already being addressed through *Framework for the Future* and its action plan (Department for Culture, Media and Sport, 2003).

In fact, *Framework for the Future* was one of the starting points for this study. Setting out the Government's vision of how public libraries in England contribute to a range of its political priorities, this document tells us a lot about how the Government views the service – its potential and the challenges that it must meet to ensure its survival and progress. *Framework for the Future* establishes what the Government claims is a long-term strategic vision for the public library service, establishing three key areas of activity which should be at the heart of its modern mission: the promotion of reading and informal learning; access to digital skills and services including e-government; and measures to tackle social exclusion, build community identity and develop citizenship. *Framework* was the subject of a House of Lords debate in March 2004, albeit a year after its publication. Opening the debate, Lord Harrison remarked that it was the first debate on public libraries for many years and although many speakers spoke with warmth about public libraries, several also made reference to the sparse attendance; it was budget day, however (Hansard, 2004a). Once again, though, the document was not without its critics within the profession and complaints about its lack of ambition were commonly made alongside regrets that there were no promises of extra funding to assist those library services perceived as failing. Three million pounds was allocated to MLA, for the implementation of the action plan arising out of *Framework*, however, and there has been progress on many of the items identified as requiring attention including work on the development of impact measures to demonstrate the contribution of libraries at local and national levels, a revision of the public library standards, the creation of a leadership development programme and draft workforce strategy, a review of public library stock procurement processes, the development of stock assessment and management tools and the initiation of a marketing strategy.

Marketing is seen as being closely linked to advocacy because only when libraries have a clear understanding of their role and value for each segment of their market can they be sure that they are delivering the services that their stakeholders want and require. The identification and articulation of core values and the formulation of key messages for different stakeholders is an important prerequisite for effective advocacy. It is also vital for successful promotional activities and interviewees often commented on the need for a professional promotional programme as there is a perception that many people are not aware of the range of services available from the public library. The majority were also in favour of a national programme, coordinated centrally and led by public relations professionals. In fact, a major promotional campaign is planned by MLA for late 2005 although it should be noted that this is subject to finding partners willing to contribute to its funding as resources always seem to be short in public library services.

Funding As the Local Government Association stated in its evidence to the 2000 Select Committee on public libraries, 'funding for public libraries has been historically precarious' (Culture, Media and Sport Committee, 2000, para. 10.1). Some blame this on the division of responsibilities at national level with the DCMS responsible for public library strategy, the ODPM responsible for the distribution of local government funds but the Treasury ultimately deciding how much should be spent on local authority services. Others feel that local authority officers and councillors do not appreciate the value of public library services and their role within the community and so do not provide them with adequate funds. Whatever the reason, the resources available to public library services declined over the late 1970s and into the 1980s and 1990s. A review of long term trends in public libraries in England by Nick Moore gives an excellent overview of the declining fortunes of public library services following what he calls 'the golden decade' of development following the 1964 Act (Moore, 2004, p. 41). The economic crisis of the mid-1970s led to cuts in local government expenditure and, at library service level, cuts to the book fund and staff establishment, both falling by about ten per cent between 1975/76 and 1980/81. Opening hours also fell dramatically, the number of service points open for more than 60 hours per week falling by over 60 per cent. Although overall expenditure did not necessarily fall, capital, staffing and resource costs all increased at a faster rate.

The 1980s were a gloomy time for public library funding with cuts to book funds, opening hours and staffing regularly reported (Black, 2000). Moore describes the stagnation that public libraries experienced through this period of retrenchment with expenditure growing but not enough to permit expansion (Moore, 2004). The number of qualified staff employed fell, although staff numbers rose overall, and opening hours continuing to fall, although the number of service points increased slightly. It is during this decade that the impact of cutbacks began to be reflected in borrowing statistics with the number of loans falling by nearly 15 per cent. Difficult times continued throughout the 1990s with closures and restricted access common. From steady state in the 1980s, the service began to experience serious decline (Moore, 2004). Economic uncertainty again meant public sector cuts. In the public library service, these fell most heavily on the materials budget, expenditure falling in real terms by 25 per cent over the decade. The number of staff employed also fell by nearly ten per cent with the bulk of cuts falling on the professional staff establishment. Perhaps unsurprisingly, the number of loans continued to fall.

In recent times, the public library standards have encouraged some local authorities to increase investment in their public library services although some geographical areas of the UK have fared better than others. Recent reports from Northern Ireland, for example, suggest there is a serious funding crisis there as budgets have been frozen, resulting in a real terms three per cent cut (BBC News Online, 2004). The Education and Library Boards look likely to respond with library closures, cuts to the book budgets and delaying maintenance work on buildings. Libraries throughout the UK have also been encouraged to engage in a competitive bidding culture and try to secure challenge funding to underpin service development. How sustainable these streams of income are, though, is a matter of considerable debate within the public library field.

The latest Cipfa public library statistics show that investment in libraries throughout the UK is at an all time high of over £1 billion (Cipfa, 2004) and yet many heads of service argue that this is not enough to make up for years of under-funding. Moore argues that expenditure should be £1.1 billion (at 2003 prices) in England alone if public library expenditure had grown at a comparable rate to GDP (Moore, 2004). In a briefing paper updating the figures in his *Cultural Trends* article, circulated in November 2004 in response to the announcement of the Select Committee Inquiry on public libraries, Moore reports that the level of expenditure in English public libraries increased markedly between 2000–01 and 2002–03 (Moore, unpub.). Total expenditure grew by 12.5 per cent in real terms with expenditure on staff growing by seven per cent and expenditure on books and other materials growing by five per cent. Moore comments that this growth marks the end of ten years of decline so that total expenditure has returned to levels last seen in 1990–91. He notes, though, that book expenditure is still only about three-quarters of the level for 1990–91.

Without substantial and continuous investment, the DCMS *Framework* vision is unlikely to be fulfilled and increasingly strained budgets and rising costs threaten development with Cilip Chief Executive Bob McKee blaming what he terms the 'dysfunctional division' between the DCMS and ODPM for the failure to address key funding issues within the public library sector (Cilip News, 2003, online resource). In June 2004, however, Lord Andrew McIntosh, then DCMS Minister responsible for public libraries, announced an extra £2m over the next two years to help raise the quality of library services and in July 2005 his successor David Lammy announced that the funding programme for library improvement was to be extended for a further two years, with £4 million of new money. When the first tranche of money was announced, however, Bob McKee warned that this sum would do little to address under funding in two key areas: books and buildings (Cilip News, 2004).

Summary

This brief overview of environmental factors relevant to public library services illustrates the extent to which the context within which they are operating has changed over the last decade. Policy developments, political interest and a variety of effectiveness and efficiency initiatives have, once again, thrown the issues of the nature and purpose of public libraries into sharp relief. Similarly, the changing and increasingly complex nature of UK society, ICT developments and new forms of entertainment all prompt a reassessment of whether the values and ideologies that sustained public libraries in the past are still relevant. At this complex time in their history, it is useful to reflect and explore how public library services are responding and perhaps redefining themselves as a result of the changing environment, changing attitudes and changing political priorities. The study reported in subsequent chapters aims to do just that.

The Study

The study is based on information from published and unpublished sources, supplemented by interviews with key stakeholders in the public library community including senior practitioners, policy makers and researchers. The intention is to explore the current position of this valued public institution by mapping the contemporary discourses surrounding issues of identity, social purpose, value, strategy and service facing the public library service in the United Kingdom. As outlined above, the context within which public libraries are operating has changed significantly over the last decade and the ideologies that public librarians and their supporters have used in the past to justify and legitimate the continued provision of public library services from the public purse may no longer be appropriate or relevant. Librarians and policy makers working within the public library sector are therefore confronting choices about the nature and purpose of the public library within society and exploring how to define that social role to justify its continued existence. The research reported here aims to expose and explore the philosophical and ideological arguments in the contemporary discourses of key stakeholders, focusing on the nature of the ideological arguments concerning the contemporary environment within which public libraries are operating, how this effects the social nature of the need for public library services and what public libraries ought to be, and are, doing to fulfil those needs.

Document Analysis

A literature/documentation search and analysis was undertaken to identify contemporary discourses, narratives and rhetoric surrounding the contribution of public libraries to UK society and the legitimating of the institution. Groups of statements that appeared to be regulated and have a coherence and force were identified as discourses (Scott, 1990). The analysis also explored the context within which these discourses were taking place and how they were influenced by the wider political, social and professional environment. The discourses identified were then discussed and explored in interviews with key stakeholders. The documents analysed were in published and unpublished format, both print and electronic.

Interviews

Fifty interviews or group discussion sessions with 61 people were undertaken in May and June 2004. In addition, the then Minister for Media and Heritage, Lord Andrew McIntosh, agreed to provide written responses to a list of questions. A list of all participants who agreed to be named is given in appendix 1. Those approached to participate were not randomly chosen but a 'purposeful' sampling method was employed which allows researchers to choose individuals or cases from which they can learn the most. Interviews were therefore undertaken with policy makers, strategists, senior public library practitioners and others with specific interests relevant to this study. Interviewees often also gave names of additional participants. The sample is not random, therefore, and the practitioners involved were often from library services known nationally as innovative and progressive, e.g. the authorities that were awarded Beacon Council status for Libraries as a Community Resource. It is acknowledged that the picture is skewed in favour of public library authorities with a positive story to tell about their own services. That is not to say, though, that they did not have valid comments to make on the full range of issues facing the public library service and often made the point that although their service was successful, there were others around them that were not.

Potential interviewees were approached by letter or email and those agreeing to participate were sent a list of questions in advance of the interview. The questions focused on areas of interest specific to the individual being interviewed although a set of standard questions applicable to a particular service or aspect of public library service provision was developed. A sample of questions asked is included in appendix 2. Interviews were either undertaken face-to-face (the majority) or by telephone. Both types were recorded and fully transcribed. Participants were sent a copy of their interview transcription and invited to change, amend or clarify points made. They were also asked to complete a transcription confirmation form which asked whether they a) agreed to have interview extracts attributed to them and be identified by name and/or position and b) agreed to be included in the list of interviewees. All but three participants agreed to the latter and a minority of those listed in appendix 1 preferred to remain anonymous within the text. The interview data were analysed using ATLAS.ti and interpretation focused on exploring the extent to which the interview participants accepted, rejected or renegotiated the discourses identified through the literature. Interview comments are generally paraphrased but direct quotations are also used to illustrate themes and issues. Extracts are often attributed to named individuals except when they chose to remain anonymous. Similarly, direct quotations are identified as coming from a specific interviewee by noting their name in brackets following the quote. Quotes from those preferring to remain anonymous are identified by the suffix (Anon.).

Terminology

A glossary of common acronyms is given in appendix 3. For those unfamiliar with the public library system in the UK, an explanation of terms used frequently is given below.

Local authorities are the governing bodies of officially designated local administrative areas which, in England, can be county councils, unitary authorities, London boroughs or metropolitan districts, in Wales and Scotland are unitary authorities and in Northern Ireland are district councils. Local authorities have a statutory duty to provide public library services except in Northern Ireland where it is the responsibility of the five Education and Library Boards. Local authorities are often referred to as *local councils* and collectively as *local government*. Those elected by local people to represent their interests within the local authority are *local councillors* or *members*. The staff of the local authority, charged with putting into action the policies decided upon by the local councillors, are *council officers*, led by a *Chief Executive*.

The term *public library service* or *services* denotes the services provided by the local authority's public libraries for the people of the community. It can also mean the organizational division within the local authority that provides those services. *The public library service* is also used to refer to the idea of a national, single institution. Although many would argue that there is actually no such thing, and in the strictest sense are correct, the term is often used by people to mean, collectively, the organizations that provide public library services, for example, 'the public library service in the UK is in terminal decline'. *Library authority* also refers to the library service of the local authority as local authorities are designated as library authorities under the 1964 Public Libraries and Museums Act in England and Wales.

Following the lead of MLA, the term *sector* is used to mean the activities, institutions and services relating to culture defined by the DCMS as being the responsibility of MLA, i.e. museums, libraries and archives, so giving us the *cultural sector*. Within the cultural sector, there are the three separate *domains* of museums, libraries and archives and within each domain there are *sub-domains* representing different sections of the domain, e.g. the public library sub-domain, the university library sub-domain, the health library sub-domain. In some cases, interviewees may have used the term public library *sector* (instead of *sub-domain*), as this is a commonly accepted way of referring to public library services collectively. I have not altered their words but have used *sub-domain* myself where relevant.

Various organizations have changed their names over the years. Cilip (the Chartered Institute of Library and Information Professionals) was formed following the unification of the Library Association (LA) and the Institute of Information Scientists (IIS) in April 2002. MLA was Resource until February 2004. Resource was launched in 2000 bringing together the Museums and Galleries Commission (MGC) and the Library and Information Commission (LIC) and adding archives to its portfolio.

Structure

Part 1, The Environment, explores the context within which public libraries are operating and evaluates how they have adapted to new forms of governance and cooperation. It also analyses how they have responded to new approaches to the delivery of public services and changing local and national priorities. Key developments related to the user community and staff are also reviewed here.

The second section of the book, Service Development, focuses on a number of key services provided by public libraries and assesses how they reflect the changes in the environment and ideologies of public libraries as discussed in Part 1. Public libraries in the UK have responded to political, social and technological developments by developing a broad range of initiatives aimed at sections of their user and non-user communities. Rather than give a superficial overview of all the services provided by the public library service in the UK today, this section will concentrate on those areas where development is considered to have been most far-reaching and significant. Discussion of examples of good practice will illustrate how the public library service is responding to the demands now made of it in imaginative and innovative ways. At the beginning of each chapter, the national policy context of each area is outlined before a consideration of how public libraries are responding to the Government's agenda and wider social developments and the challenges they face in positioning themselves as central to local and national policy aspirations. The book ends with a chapter drawing on interview data as well as the chapters preceding it to present a summary of how the public library is viewed by, and what it means to, a range of key stakeholders and how the discourses around public library role and purpose have impacted on services and ideas about future development.

Notes

1 That is the Houses of Parliament in England, the Welsh Assembly, the Scottish Parliament and the Northern Ireland Assembly. The position of the last of these is complicated, however, as in 2002 the Northern Ireland Assembly was suspended following the stalling of the peace process.
2 The MLA website is at URL: http://www.mla.gov.uk/ [18.07.2005].
3 The CyMAL website is at URL: http://www.cymal.wales.gov.uk/ [18.07.2005].
4 Information about SLIC can be found at URL: http://www.slainte.org.uk/slic/ [18.07.2005].
5 Information about LISC(NI) can be found at URL: http://www.liscni.co.uk/ [18.07.2005].

Chapter 2

The Local Authority Context

A Local Service for Local People[1]

The public library service in the United Kingdom is a service managed and run locally. The 1964 Public Libraries and Museums Act, still the legislation governing public libraries today in England and Wales, makes it clear that decisions on the provision of a public library service should be made at local authority level while preserving an overseeing role for the relevant Secretary of State or Minister of the national governing body.[2] Similarly, in Scotland *The Local Government (Scotland) Act 1973, places* on local authorities a statutory duty 'to secure the provision of adequate library facilities for all persons resident in their care' and in Northern Ireland *The Education and Libraries (Northern Ireland) Order 1972* gives the five Education and Library Boards the responsibility of providing a public library service. In all four home countries of the United Kingdom, therefore, public libraries are a statutory service that local authorities (or Education and Library Boards in the case of Northern Ireland) are legally obliged to provide. The 1964 Act for England and Wales charges local authorities to, 'provide a comprehensive and efficient library service for all persons desiring to make use thereof' and makes it the duty of the Secretary of State to, 'superintend and promote the improvement of the public library service provided by local authorities and to secure the proper discharge by local authorities of the functions in relation to libraries'. Following devolution in 1997, this power was devolved to the Minister for Culture, Sport and the Welsh Language in the Welsh Assembly and the Minister for Tourism, Culture and Sport in Scotland. In Ireland, The Department of Culture, Arts and Leisure has responsibility although the Northern Ireland Assembly is suspended at the time of writing. Operation and management are therefore decided and controlled by local authorities although it is the role of the relevant government department to ensure that levels of service are acceptable. There is an inconsistency here as Black (1996) points out because although the public library service is conceptualized and managed at a local rather a national level, it can also be regarded as part of the welfare state, which has a national perspective. Recent discussions of the local nature of public library services and their relationship with central government can be characterized as a tension between the discourses of 'centralized-decentralization' on the one hand and 'new localism' on the other.

There is widespread acceptance that the public library service in the UK is best delivered through local authorities. The DCMS, for example, has stated that it values the devolved nature of the decision making process in library authorities and would not intervene unless a service was failing in its statutory duty (Culture, Media and Sport Committee, 2000). Local authority control confers a range of advantages including cross-departmental working ensuring that local priorities are addressed by agencies with a range of relevant expertise. It is also felt that local decision making leads to services tailored to local communities, responding to local needs and strengthening local distinctiveness and identity. Different service delivery options may be needed in different areas to address similar needs and, from this, innovation and good practice can emerge which can be spread to other authorities. The nature of the local authority, the way it is run and the decisions it makes therefore have a significant impact on the way in which public library services are organized, managed and delivered. Recently, though, there have been indications that the Government is becoming frustrated at the variability of public library service provision around the country, suggesting that there may be a postcode lottery in the public's experience of the public library service. The 2005 Select Committee report commends the 'pockets of excellence' (Culture, Media and Sport Committee, 2005, p. 3) to be found but also cites evidence from the Audit Commission stating that half of the library services in England and Wales are unsatisfactory.

Study participants also commented upon the uneven nature of the quality of library services, many describing it as 'patchy'. In his written response, Lord Andrew McIntosh conceded that the word 'fragmentation' ran throughout *Framework for the Future* and was one of the biggest challenges that the DCMS had to address. Although he said that he thought that most library authorities 'do at least some things well', he also acknowledged that others 'are less effective than they might be'. John Pateman agreed that there was a 'postcode lottery – the quality of the library service you get depends on where you live and who's in control' while another interview participant said that the situation was so uneven that 'a member of the public going into a library won't be able to predict what level of service they'll receive even within one authority very often' (Anon). Bill Macnaught felt that *Framework for the Future* and its action plan would help overcome a perceived inconsistency between services:

> We've got 149 institutions who've got a vague idea of the core business but are going off in all sorts of different directions, the Ideas Stores and so on, and I think one of the benefits of the *Framework* action plan is that we will try to pull it together so that there is a much stronger perception of us being an institution. (Bill Macnaught)

This variability in the standard of library services around the country has led many in the public library community to advocate the development of national offers.

National Offers

As Lord Andrew McIntosh stated, *Framework for the Future* decries the 'fragmentation' of the English public library system run by 149 local authorities,[3] stating that this is a key constraint inhibiting innovation, development and recognition of the role that public libraries can play in local authorities' corporate strategies (Department for Culture Media and Sport, 2003). The document's authors argue that national programmes (or 'offers') will raise the profile of the public library service and that national agreement on the key services that all services should provide will give public libraries a shared sense of purpose. *Framework* is careful to retain a sense of the importance of local authority control, insisting that there is great strength in the local connections that public library services enjoy, but the DCMS is clearly keen on pushing a national agenda. A degree of uniformity is therefore championed in *Framework for the Future* and in *Overdue*, a report written by one of the Demos researchers on whose work *Framework* is based, which warns of the dangers of parochialism as a result of public libraries' strong local roots (Leadbeater, 2003). It could be argued that although the nature and character of library services in different authorities may vary depending on the priorities of the local council, public libraries in different authorities have always shared a number of goals and have offered similar services. While accepting this, the DCMS seems to be arguing that these need a clearer focus, or 'branding', to ensure that public libraries make an impact both locally and nationally. *Framework* advocates that all English library services should focus on the same priorities and that national programmes should be offered in every library, tailored to local circumstances.

A clear steer on what the three key priorities for English public libraries should be (reading and learning; digital citizenship; and social exclusion) is therefore given in *Framework* and, despite the fact that the public library service in the UK has been called 'a genuinely successful decentralized cultural institution' (Greenhalgh and Worpole, 1995, p. 44), there is some indication that what is perceived as a centralizing tendency of the New Labour Government will have an impact on how the public library service is managed. A report by consultants PKF (2005) into public library efficiency, for example, recommends the development of a national procurement model for books and other resources in England and, while careful to underline their belief in the value of locally delivered library services, a joint statement from DCMS and MLA also supports the notion of streamlining processes which might be more efficiently managed nationally rather than locally (Department for Culture Media and Sport and MLA, 2005).

Centralized-decentralization

The DCMS is keen to stress that the national agenda should be given a local flavour, guided by local priorities and needs but it still believes that nationally shared priorities and a sense of purpose will lead to sharing of best practice and resources and thus to innovation and improvement. While accepting that local autonomy enables innovation and different ways of delivering services for different communities, Baroness Blackstone in the Lords debate on the public library service stressed the benefits of shared aspirations and uniform standards across authorities (Hansard, 2004). This is in contrast to a widely held view that centralization often leads to the stifling of initiative 'driving out inclusivity, innovation, diversity [and] organizational learning' (Rouse, 2001, p. 34). The Government's approach to public libraries as set out in *Framework* seems to be in line with its approach to public services in general and in particular its approach to performance management, discussed in relation to public libraries in the section on Best Value below and in Chapter 3. This 'post-ideological approach' (Rouse, 2001, p. 2) to public service management relies on specifying the outcomes desired while allowing public services to be flexible about how they are achieved but there are indications of tensions within *Framework* and the approach of the DCMS which, while stressing local flexibility, emphasizes explicit national quality standards and abhors variation in standards. For those who believe that local people, councillors and staff are the best judges of local need, national direction is intrusive and unwelcome.

An IFLA study found that English civil servants found the tension between locally driven public library services and a national push for performance improvement difficult to manage, especially when local and central governments 'are not in tune' (Usherwood and Pearce, 2003, p. 85). Demands for uniformity, like those expressed in *Framework*, can challenge the diversity of local authority provision and the freedom of local authorities to provide the public library services which suit local needs and character and can become restrictive, dictating not just what is provided but also how. Rouse believes that this denies local government its role as 'the government of difference' and, instead of geographical variations being viewed as a cause for celebration and an indication that local authorities are successfully responding to local communities, they are increasingly viewed as 'problems to be eradicated' (Rouse, 2001, p. 28).

Recently, however, there have been suggestions that central government is starting to loosen its hold over local authorities and is signing up to the concept of 'new localism'. The 2002 local government bill, for example, gave a new range of financial freedoms to local councils, reflecting the new localist view that change must be locally owned and that local choice best meets the specific needs of each area and community. New localism should allow local public service managers discretion to meet users' needs, with goals set by local rather than central government. For public libraries in England and Wales, standards for public library services and the need to produce annual plans or position statements mean that central government has retained quite a hold over local services, an approach referred to as 'steering centralism' or 'steering localism' where 'the thrust has moved towards the local, but the centre still has a large hand hovering above the tiller' (Corry and Stoker, no date, p. 19). This seems to be the line taken by the Government for public libraries as expressed in *Framework for the Future*; a nationally agreed set of priorities with freedom to prioritize at local level according to the needs and circumstances of the community as long as the relevant performance and accountability measures are met. Ranged against the new localists are those who believe that centralism has much to recommend it including the intolerance of variation in standards and inequality in provision (Walker, 2002).

There are issues to be tackled, therefore, of central direction versus sensitivity to local conditions and tradition, of national standards versus the discretion of local service managers and of local political decision making versus the national government's agenda. The extent to which the DCMS will continue to allow local managers the freedom to decide how they deliver services within the parameters of the national agenda as laid out in *Framework* is as yet unknown. According to Andrew McIntosh in his written response, English public librarians welcomed the steer from central government provided by *Framework for the Future*. He added, 'they thought (and I agree) that it was a sense of direction from Whitehall that was the missing part of the equation previously'. Several interview participants agreed that the attention from central government was welcome rather than intrusive. Bob McKee said:

> I think what this Government is doing is trying to create a framework and create some guidance and create some strategic direction and in that sense is giving more attention to libraries and is giving more steer to libraries than previous governments. (Bob McKee)

Another interview participant concurred that the change of Administration in 1997 had been accompanied by a change of approach with regard to public libraries which he felt had been of benefit to public libraries:

> I think when the New Labour Government came in they took a completely different approach to their responsibilities… Certainly under the Conservative Government it was very much the approach to let local authorities get on with it with no sort of central government interference. (Anon)

Framework for the Future was viewed by many interview participants as Government recognition of the importance of public libraries and appreciation of the role they could play in achieving a range of political priorities, one saying 'it was the first time the Government said, here's what we think is important about libraries and we think it's important enough to have produced a document about it' (Sarah Wilkie). Other participants were more sceptical of the value of *Framework,* both its content and its value as a symbol of Government commitment, one noting:

> I think if we're going to have a vision for the future of libraries we want a bit more vision and a bit less average practice and I think we want a bit more apparent government commitment. I did compare it, at the Public Library conference, to the interdepartmental childcare review which came out at roughly the same time and whereas it was Tessa Blackstone (then Minister for DCMS) writing the introduction to *Framework for the Future*, it was the Prime Minister writing the introduction for the other one. And that did strike me as a message. (Cllr Bob Janes)

Other participants were much more receptive of *Framework* and, as Andrew McIntosh suggested, welcomed the steer from central government:

> It is a very genuine attempt by government to send a signal of support for the future of public libraries and it's also trying to set out three clear strands of activity that constitute what public libraries are about and I think that's very welcome... [O]ne of the complaints we've had in public libraries for a long time is that there has been no central vision from government about what public libraries could and should be and so I think I'm absolutely clear that it's welcome. I don't think it's as clear as it could be,… I'm not sure that it's good enough in terms of the clarity of the vision and the roles but the attempt at

leadership is welcome… [A]t the very least it demonstrated that the Government was taking the trouble to set out its thoughts about a positive future for public libraries which has not always been the case. (Bill Macnaught)

Another interview participant suggested that a clear, articulated view from government on what libraries should be doing was helpful in raising the service's profile locally and demonstrating how libraries could contribute to other key agendas within the local authority. One interview participant, though, rejected the whole notion of a central government agenda for public libraries, saying:

[I]t's a little bit prescriptive because the belief here … is that local people have voted in a certain way and they very much believe they're the best people to know what is needed in [the borough]. (Anon)

John Dolan similarly felt that public library services had to be geared, first and foremost to local need:

Part of the difficulty, I think, with having a national drive for the public library [is] that it is very much a locally-based service. If you want to increase the number of people in the construction industry, then the kind of plumbing course you run around the country is going to be very much the same in one part of the country than another. If you want to offer the cultural experience of reading combined with an undercurrent of upping literacy levels, that's going to vary according to the kind of community you're delivering to… I think the real opportunity is that libraries aren't standardized. (John Dolan)

Others felt there was no tension between national prescription and local choice, however, and that national offers can be framed in such a way that they can be used everywhere without damaging local initiative and local choice. According to Martin Molloy, local decision making and local flexibility are retained so that what is developing is a 'national service, locally delivered' and that, in his opinion, was acceptable to many. Lord Andrew McIntosh similarly noted that there was considerable scope for local experimentation:

I don't think the stifling of innovation is an issue. We are not setting down any templates. If Tower Hamlets want to call their libraries *Ideastores* and Hampshire call theirs *Discovery Centres*, that is fine by me. What is most important is that authorities are giving their customers what they want and need. Providing they have thought the thing through properly, I will always uphold a library authority's right to try something new in an effort to improve its service. (Lord Andrew McIntosh)

Sue Wilkinson agreed that the *Framework* approach to national offers would not prevent local services developing their own approaches, saying:

I think it's something that has come out of the concerns of the people who work in the public library field anyway and I think the whole steer of *Framework* is the national offer but then how it's delivered is determined regionally and locally and I think that is generally recognized. Nobody is saying that it has to be done in the same way, what they're saying is that there's much greater strength in terms of advocacy for all of us if we

> can have some common messages and common themes and show that we're working to common agendas. (Sue Wilkinson)

The preceding discussion has given a flavour of the extent to which public libraries have felt the effects of New Labour's 'modernizing' agenda for local government services. The 1998 Government White Paper, *Modern Local Government: In Touch With The People* (Department of the Environment, Transport and the Regions, 1998) set out an extensive reform programme announcing a variety of initiatives with far-reaching implications for local authorities and, therefore, their public library services. Best Value, community planning, e-government, new political management structures and strategic partnerships have all being implemented and have changed the ways in which public library services are planned and managed. One development initiated by the last Conservative administration and completed under the first New Labour government was the Local Government Review (LGR), the recommendations of which were implemented between 1995 and 1998. This major shake-up of local government had far-reaching implications for the delivery of public library services.

Local Government Reorganization

The organization of local government in the UK went through a number of transformations during the twentieth century. Many remember the local government reorganization of 1974, which, in general terms resulted in the formation of large county council authorities making the expansion and development of public library services possible through a larger resource base and enhanced economies of scale. The review of the 1990s aimed to reverse many of the decisions taken in the 1974 reorganization and overcome what were considered some of the inefficiencies of a system which had many layers of local government serving the same area. This, it was argued, would make decision making more responsive and bring it closer to grass roots level, combating what was perceived as remoteness in local government. Local government reorganization was initiated under the last Conservative government and was implemented over the period 1995-1998. The most significant result of the reorganization was the abolition and breaking up of a large number of county councils and the creation of unitary authorities, each of which automatically became a library authority. In Wales, for example, 22 new unitary authorities replaced the previous 13 county and district councils. Outside London in England, there is now a mixture of county councils, metropolitan boroughs and unitary authorities. In the East Midlands, for example, three authorities now govern the area covered by the pre-reorganization Leicestershire County Council. Leicestershire County Council still exists but is smaller and no longer includes the City of Leicester unitary authority or Rutland County Council that were both created in 1997. Similarly, Nottinghamshire was reorganized into a smaller Nottinghamshire County Council and a new unitary authority covering Nottingham City and Derbyshire was split into Derbyshire

County Council and Derby City. Each of these local authorities is responsible for its own library service.

Before reorganization, the likely effects of the changes on public libraries were the cause of considerable speculation in the professional library press, much of it focused on issues of size and efficiency. The omens were not good and many commentators expressed the opinion that this would be a retrograde move that would cause uncertainty, ineffectiveness and inefficiencies. Concern was expressed that small authorities could not provide modern standards of library service without levying charges or co-operating with others. Advocates of the 'small is beautiful' school, on the other hand, argued that size does not guarantee performance and that smaller authorities could facilitate more effective democracy, closer customer relations and better locally-based decision making. The discussion within the library profession was thus focused on issues associated with stock levels, special collections, computer systems, use of specialized staff and access to libraries with fears that the break-up of large countywide services would lead to inefficiency and a decline in the number and quality of services offered to public library users.

The reorganization of the 1990s has now had some years to 'bed down' and although some authorities have encountered difficulties as a result of the changes, others have taken advantage of new opportunities the reorganization has presented and have developed innovative methods of service delivery. In Wales, the creation of a large number of small authorities, many of which are not economically viable, has reportedly had a negative effect on public libraries, exacerbating years of under-funding and reinforcing their low status (Ede, 2003). This was confirmed by Welsh interview participants, one saying:

> We've got 22 unitary authorities. It is my understanding that according to the Audit Commission definitions, only Cardiff is large enough to be considered financially viable as a local authority… There are significant challenges for local authorities in Wales because of the small size of services. (Anon)

Alan Watkin agreed that the size of the authorities and the resources they commanded could cause capacity and image problems. Talking about developing new areas of service and comparing the current situation with that before reorganization when Wrexham was part of the county of Clwyd, he said:

> If we wanted to look at a new area of particular initiative or a project etc., you had 50 to 60 professional staff across the county, no more generously spread in relation to demand but you had that many bodies with that range of talents so you could usually find somebody who had the right aptitude. Now if we look at Wrexham, I think we have 11 professional staff. By definition, the range of skills is limited, your capacity is limited, your capability is limited because there's always going to be somebody on holiday or some other demand so therefore your ability to cover is harder. And also I think there's a detrimental effect in terms of how the Welsh authorities are viewed from the outside, particularly from professional colleagues when you're trying to recruit new staff etc. at professional level. We've all had to re-establish reputations, if we can, for our services. (Alan Watkin)

On a more positive note, The LOGOPLUS project investigated the impact of the changes of staff and users at the end of the 1990s and concluded that, for them, the transition to new authorities has been a largely seamless process with fears of loss of economies of scale much exaggerated (Parker, et al., 1998). Service managers have found that their capacity to target specific communities have been enhanced so that in Leicestershire, for example, the delivery of services to rurally isolated communities has become a central theme of the county council and the library service has been able to tap into sources of funding to improve access to a whole range of local authority, as well as simply library, services (Thomas & Cooke, 2004). Similarly, in Derbyshire LGR has, according to Bob Janes, enabled the local authority to concentrate more on the shire issues and services to former mining villages that he argued were very different from those required in deprived inner cities. For other interview participants, LGR had positive outcomes. In Stockton on Tees, for example, Andrea Barker declared, 'LGR made our library service; it's flourished' while interview participants working in smaller authorities in other parts of the country reported closer working relationships and more direct access to some of the key parts of the council as positive advantages resulting from the reorganization.

Joint Arrangements

Managers have still had to meet a variety of strategic and logistical challenges, however. Co-operation or joint arrangements with other library authorities, for example, is now not just advantageous but often a necessity, especially when communities have been split across a number of authorities. Neighbouring authorities, usually previously the constituent parts of a single pre-reorganization authority, entered into a number of formal or more casual arrangements relating to the provision of many library services principally to ensure a smooth transition to the new arrangements for users and to retain economies of scale (Hawkins and Malley, 1999). Thus, for example, following reorganization Library Services for Education, the schools library service for the old Leicestershire County Council, still covered the new Leicestershire County Council, Leicester City Council and Rutland County Council although Rutland later withdrew from this arrangement. Similar joint arrangements were made covering a whole host of different library services but were most common in the areas of school library services, common catalogues, user access to specialist reference and local collections, borrowing rights, bibliographic services and library circulation systems. For smaller authorities, these joint arrangements can be essential, as one interview participant explained:

> The main areas of joint arrangements are for the ICT services, so we use the same library management system that [the county] does which is something we couldn't manage without because we only have a stock of about 50,000 titles and there's no way we could service the needs of our population on our own so we use the same system… The other main area of co-operation is bibliographical services, so there's joint arrangements for all

> of the purchasing of books which, again, is very beneficial for [us]. Because we've got the buying power of [the county] alongside us, we command much bigger discounts than we would otherwise. (Anon)

Joint arrangements have not always been easy to arrange or maintain, however, and many arrangements, both formal and informal, have collapsed. Initially, some of the smaller authorities were confident of their ability to operate alone and quite fiercely independent, especially as the Department of the Environment at the time discouraged extensive use of joint arrangements believing it undermined the whole concept of unitary status. What is the point of creating a new authority if it cannot operate alone? Even less formal co-operative arrangements can be difficult under these circumstances as Alan Watkin explained:

> More difficult has been maintaining co-operation across authorities because in each of the authorities, the political level is very conscious of its own boundaries. And so you do some co-operative effort but quite quietly and nothing major and so in Wrexham, for example, it's quite clear at the political level it is to be Wrexham doing things because the political statement would be, you wouldn't expect Cardiff or Swansea or Newport to be in somebody else's pocket would you? So we're not. That's the political reality. Other than schools library service, we have no continuing joint delivery. (Alan Watkin)

Hawkins and Malley (1999) found that, for preference, library authorities would not enter into joint arrangements but did so out of necessity and were content to let them continue as long as the benefits outweighed the disadvantages. The economics of joint arrangements have not always proved as attractive as first imagined especially if few of an authority's users make use of the joint service. Even when joint arrangements have proved economically viable and socially desirable, the cost effectiveness and efficiencies of scale of joint arrangements have not always been considered sufficient compensation for the loss of local control and accountability. It is also acknowledged that this is often an unwieldy and difficult way to work and provide services, especially if the party political profiles of the various authorities differ. As time has elapsed, some authorities have withdrawn from the joint arrangements established at the time of LGR with both financial and political benefits, as one head of service in a unitary authority created in 1996 explained:

> We were brave enough to come out of a joint arrangement because I didn't think it was working for us; that was the joint reference service… We just weren't getting what we wanted so we were brave enough to reinvest that £60,000 into our reference service and the elected members really enjoyed that fact that we could come out and not be bullied. Even though the DCMS were asking why the decision had been made, we stuck to our guns and reinvested in our own staff and in our reference service and that's just flourished. I came away knowing there were a lot of joint arrangements I helped put together … but some of them…, you can't just put another authority's money into something that ain't working for you. (Andrea Barker)

Many of the joint arrangements entered into initially are therefore no longer still in place as they were merely expedient arrangements arranged because of a lack of time and resources on the part of new authorities and were often a method of buying time while they considered their options in relation to their library services. As they found their feet and defined their own priorities, some authorities withdrew from joint arrangements, eager to react to the special needs of the area they were now serving and keen to exercise more direct management of services that reflected their own aspirations. Some smaller authorities also found that they could manage well without the resources and services of some of their partners, as an interview participant explained:

> The joint arrangements used to include [the city council]. Mostly those have been terminated. I think there's a few areas of co-operation still and we do still have agreements about joint lending but that doesn't operate quite as easily as it used to. We thought that was going to be a big problem for us because of the central reference library and the facilities they've got there. It hasn't turned out that way, we almost haven't noticed at all. The only area of expertise that we still call on that they are very good on supplying for us is for music. The music library does still provide a very good service to anybody who asks for it so they do provide expertise in that area. (Anon)

The larger authorities, generally the pre-reorganization county councils, were also realistic about the future of joint arrangements. Initially they had been concerned about the fragmentation of collections and specialist expertise and often pushed for joint arrangements to preserve these but they could also see that they could become restrictive as their user profiles would invariably change to become more rurally focused as the large cities were removed from their control. Country wide reorganization was invariably followed by internal reorganizations of the local authority structure that often placed responsibility for the library service into a different directorate to those in neighbouring authorities with which joint arrangements had been organized. The old Leicestershire County Council, for example, was reorganized so that two new authorities, Leicester City and Rutland, emerged alongside a re-formed Leicestershire. In Leicestershire, the public library service is part of the Leisure and Tourism directorate, in Leicester City it is under the Education and Learning directorate while in Rutland libraries come under Leisure and Culture. The nature of the library service and what the authority wants it to achieve locally can vary between partners in a joint arrangement, therefore, and may be incompatible.

In some authorities, though, the continuing squeeze on local authority finances and favourable experiences with the joint arrangements arising out of local government reorganization has meant that their number has, in fact, increased. Although many of the arrangements were made for expedience, others, especially the more costly, have a longer-term future. In addition, Fry et al. (2000) found that although many of the old co-operative arrangements had broken down as a result of reorganization, leading to a reduction in public access to material and a decline in specialist expertise, ICTs were leading to the formation of new types of regional and national collaboration. Local joint arrangements between library services that had once been part of the same authority have, therefore, declined in number although the desire to retain access and availability in a recognizable geographic area means that they are unlikely to disappear entirely.

The local government reorganization of the 1990s demonstrates the capacity of public library services to adapt to and respond positively to change and there has been considerable change within local government driven by the Government's 'modernization' agenda.

Modern Local Government and the Local Authority Structure

One of the New Labour Government's key objectives in relation to local government has been to overhaul what it perceived as outdated and cumbersome political management arrangements, structures and ways of working.[4] The White Paper, *Modern Local Government: in Touch with the People*, (Department of the Environment, Transport and the Regions, 1998) introduced the option of Cabinet-style government which separated the executive and backbench roles of councillors. Much as in Whitehall, the executive (usually a mayor or leader with a small cabinet of key councillors responsible for an area of policy) proposes the policy framework and sets the strategy for the authority. The rest of the councillors (or backbenchers) represent their constituents and argue for changes or make suggestions for improvements to the executive's plans. They also sit on other cabinets which report to the main executive cabinet and which deal with specific areas of policy such as education, heritage or leisure. As an alternative to the cabinet-style government, a directly elected mayor with a council manager was also proposed in the White Paper. The changes proposed were not welcomed by all local politicians, concerned about the accountability and scrutiny of decisions taken by a small group of local councillors or even just one person in the shape of a mayor. Although welcoming most of the modernization agenda, one head of service had reservations about this aspect:

> Where it has a downside, I think, is the abolition of committee structures which has probably disenfranchised back benchers who were heavily involved in the old committees. I think they feel less well informed and the opportunities to actually engage them are fewer than they were in the past. Committee processes have their critics but the information flows were pretty good so we have to find other ways of keeping back benchers in the loop. We can do that very easily when it's development and activities on their patch, but getting the strategic picture to them is more difficult. (Anon)

The new arrangements have also affected local government officials; the professionals and experts who translate the council's decisions into action. Having become used to wielding considerable authority under the old committee system, they may find their relationship with more powerful councillors more difficult to manage although many authorities have streamlined their decision making processes and make extensive use of delegation, allowing council officers like the Chief Librarian to take many decisions relating to their service areas without consulting the relevant cabinet responsible for libraries. The status of the Chief Librarian within the local authority structure is now of interest and can be a significant indicator of how importantly the service is regarded and the extent to which it is considered to have a role to play in corporate strategic policy. Some interview participants expressed concern about the position of the Chief Librarian, one Scottish head of service saying:

> I think there's a bigger issue there and that's the downgrading of the status of the Chief Librarian. I have a Director, I report to the Director, a Head of Community and Cultural Services reports to me and the Chief Librarian reports to him so she's fourth down the hierarchy. (Alan Hasson)

Although Bob McKee commented that 'whinging' about the position of the Chief Librarian was counterproductive and that those working in public libraries had to live with the reality that Chief Librarians were no longer around the Chief Officers' table, others felt that a better case could be made for public libraries if the Chief Librarian was closer to the important decision makers:

> I have noticed that in many authorities now the librarian, city librarian or the county librarians have almost been demoted, they are yet another level away from the people making the decisions. (Margaret Watson)

One head of service blamed a lack of lobbying and influencing skills among public librarians for this trend:

> The reason why we're in a situation in some authorities where the post of Chief Librarian … is slipping down the hierarchy, I think, is because those particular skills are not there, they haven't got the profile and I think that's vitally important. It's a lot of hard work but I think it's essential because it does smooth the way so that the politicians, the members are aware when you go to do things and you want to do things; the groundwork is already done. (Anon)

While accepting that financial pressures to save money often led the local authority to fill the post at a lower grade, he added that this 'had a lot to do with the way that individuals conduct themselves within a local authority' (Anon).

The move toward cabinet-style government has also expedited service integration discussed in more detail below and, in many cases, the head of the library service is no longer a chief officer but a deputy, assistant or senior officer reporting on behalf of the library service via their parent cabinet or committee. A declining status for the Chief Librarian within the local authority structure has been the trend since the local government reorganization of 1974 and is causing concern as it can mean that he or she has less direct access to the executive so finding it more difficult to lobby on behalf of the library service to influence authority decision making and planning. Similarly, if there is nobody in the powerful executive cabinet with an interest in public libraries, strong political support for libraries could be lacking. The new political management structures could prove to be of benefit, though, as they are said to allow for quicker decision making and there is more informal contact between elected members and officers. This has certainly been found to be the case in some unitary authorities where the smaller size of the council has resulted in better relationships with councillors, as one participant commented, 'I think in [this authority] the Cabinet does work better than in a lot of other authorities simply because of the smallness of the authority' (Anon).

The Library Service Within the Local Authority Structure

The new political arrangements, which emphasize council priorities cutting across departmental boundaries, and the fact that many of the new authorities are much smaller means that the responsibility for libraries has often been subsumed into larger directorates of Leisure, Education, Lifelong Learning, Arts, Culture, Heritage etc. The days of the 'Libraries' department were over long before the local government reorganization of the 1990s but it undoubtedly consolidated the move towards multi-disciplinary departments or services as does the cabinet-style political management structure with many authorities adopting systems of panels or working groups which span a number of different work areas. There have been fears that libraries will always be a minor player in any multi-service departmental arrangement, that their purpose is misunderstood and that their potential contribution to major policy initiatives often goes unrecognized. Moreover, as chief librarians are 'down-graded', so there is a danger that there is nobody at a high enough level within the authority to take on a championing or advocacy role for public libraries. As the Libraries department was incorporated into a larger directorate, so the Library Committee, made up of specialists who provided advice to the council on library-related policy and strategy, also generally perished. Sub-committees might not be expected to have the influence or interest of full committees and yet in the 1990s Chief Librarians reported that incorporation into more powerful Leisure Committees, for example, was often beneficial as the Library Committee had been of very low status anyway (Kinnell Evans, 1991). Others, though, feel the loss of the Library Committee means that Councillors no longer have the depth and breadth of understanding nor the appreciation of public library policy and services as previously and, consequently, informed debate about library issues is now lacking.

The changing place of the public library service within the local authority framework has also been a matter for discussion in the profession, focusing on the impact of its integration with other services and fuelling debate about which arrangements best complement the public library's purpose and roles although it has been suggested that as public libraries are a minor service in the grand scheme of things, little attention is paid to their location by local authority decision makers (Lomer and Rogers, 1983). As mentioned previously, public libraries are now in directorates with a large range of other services or 'buried within larger leisure or education departments' according to Leadbeater (2003, p. 11). These 'mega-directorates' vary considerably in their focus and remit and it might be expected that a public library service within a Leisure directorate will have a quite different mission to that within an Education or Culture directorate. Following the 1974 local government reorganization, there were fewer and fewer 'Libraries' departments and, in the 1980s and 1990s, the rise of large Leisure departments prompted considerable professional discussion about the most appropriate 'home' for library services within the local authority structure. Education, Leisure or some combination of Arts/Culture/Heritage were then considered the main options all of which are seen to have advantages and disadvantages as a home for library services.[5] While libraries could take advantage of the influence and budget of the powerful Education department (although since the 1988 Education Reform Act this power has weakened significantly), its values and ethos may cause them to ignore potentially fruitful alliances with other corporate partners involved in more informal types of learning. Another danger is that bookstocks would be biased in favour of supporting the National Curriculum rather than for providing for the needs of the whole community. There is also a perception that Education departments marginalize non-school services. Bob Janes, for example, was of the opinion that, 'I think it's so easy for libraries to be swamped by Education because Education thinks it's the tail and the dog'. He also commented on the high profile of the library service within the authority, asserting 'I think the key to library profile in Derbyshire was when it got out from under Education' (Cllr Bob Janes). In Northern Ireland, the public library service has been delivered by the Education and Library Boards since 1973 and it is felt that libraries often lose out in the allocation of resources as formal, classroom-based education is given priority (Department of Culture, Arts and Leisure, 2002). One participant from Northern Ireland confirmed this perception, saying:

> The minuses are that we're always at the tail because there is such a focus on schools and in the classroom. So Board members are always having to be reminded that there's another whole aspect of service provision that happens outside of the classroom and that is actually interfacing with a huge proportion of the Board's population. (Anon)

She felt, though, that possible alternatives such as the development of a Northern Ireland Library Agency or a transfer of responsibilities to district councils would also cause concerns given the probable limited bargaining powers of the former and the small size of the latter. Others were more positive about being in a directorate with Education. In Stockton-on-Tees, libraries is part of the Education, Leisure and Culture directorate and the head of service felt that an assertive attitude is needed to ensure libraries are not overlooked:

> You have to have a will and an attitude that says you are not going to be subsumed. You have to have a service that's good enough to stand the test of not being subsumed. But you've also got to be open and flexible enough that you want to work with them and it's amazing how it does take time. Everything that's worthwhile takes a lot of effort and I think our attitude is we'll just keep plugging away. (Andrea Barker)

Leisure directorates, like libraries, are concerned with quality of life issues but libraries may suffer from being a small fish in a large pond which contains other services with which libraries have little in common and which politicians hold as a higher priority for resources. Bob Janes certainly felt that libraries and leisure have little in common:

> There isn't really a huge overlap between leisure services and libraries. I think that's a mistaken view quite honestly. I can see that there is a continuum that says libraries, heritage, arts, leisure but there is a huge distance between libraries and leisure the way that local government operates it. (Cllr Bob Janes)

The ethos of the Leisure directorate may also cause problems for libraries, one head of service commenting:

> We are within Culture, Leisure and Sport. We came in within an existing Leisure Department. Leisure is very dependent on income and libraries never can be because try as we might, we will never be huge income generators. (Susan Law)

Other participants felt there were other practical disadvantages to being in Leisure department, one saying that she felt putting libraries into Leisure and Recreation was 'a bit of a disaster', explaining:

> Because Leisure has been seen as an even easier target for budgetary cuts, certainly in our authority, than other areas of work so when you've got sport and leisure and arts and libraries together, they're having to take a share of that budgetary cut that they might be able to escape from if they were in with another composition of departments. (Anon)

In the 1980s and early 1990s, the move towards the incorporation of libraries within Leisure seemed inexorable and a noticeable shift in the culture of libraries was the result but the local government review of the 1990s and changes in national government priorities and structure has changed the picture once again. Although the local authority shapes the reasoning behind the location of services within particular directorates first and foremost and local priorities will undoubtedly be of the utmost importance, the impact of the national agenda and priorities can also be significant. At the time of the inception of the Department for Culture Media and Sport as a government department in 1997, quite a few local authority public library services were incorporated into a Culture directorate, seeing benefits for aligning the management of local provision with national organization. More recently, the Government's emphasis on lifelong learning and its commitment to delivering learning opportunities through ICT via the People's Network and the National Grid for Learning have led to the formation of Lifelong Learning directorates with libraries playing a prominent role.

With libraries having such a wide remit, the danger of pigeonholing them into any one directorate is that their contribution to key policy priorities cutting across the whole range of local authority services may be ignored. Others have argued that the debate about the most appropriate home for public libraries is a red herring and that the important issue is the delivery of a good public library to the public, not where it is located (Culture, Media and Sport Committee, 2000). This is ignoring the potential of public libraries to contribute to the wider council vision, however, which a close alliance with one, single directorate may jeopardize. The current situation with regard to the place of public libraries within the local authority structure has become quite fluid with few discernable trends and with libraries moving directorate on a regular basis. Smaller unitary authorities, in particular, seem to be moving away from the old function type directorates (e.g. Education, Social Services etc) and towards cross-cutting departments concerned with policy areas such as social exclusion or widening access and participation, no doubt in at attempt to try to generate the 'joined-up thinking' that central government has been advocating. These may provide the key to increasing the influence and profile of libraries within the local authority. In Derbyshire, the library service is part of the Community Services directorate that has real advantages according to Bob Janes:

> I think Community Services is at the heart of the social inclusion agenda and I think libraries are at the heart of the social inclusion agenda so I think that's really where it lies. I also think Community Services is at the heart of partnership agendas and I think libraries are at the heart of partnership agenda and they therefore are a significant sized player in that field whereas were they with Education, they'd be an insignificant sized player. (Cllr Bob Janes)

Whichever directorate libraries are placed within, their incorporation into large multidisciplinary departments, function or policy-based, is irreversible and has both supporters and detractors. Some fear that libraries will lose political influence and financial resources in large, multi-disciplinary directorates while others believe that libraries have the opportunity to demonstrate to others how libraries can contribute to a whole host of policy initiatives and harness the resources of the larger parent department. For some services, being a minor player in a large, bureaucratic department gives them little opportunity to influence the political agenda or demonstrate how they can contribute to many of the major themes of governance. Despite the fears of those anxious that public libraries lose power and resources within large, multi-disciplinary directorates, heads of service like Andrea Barker argue that integration with other services has served local people well, providing them with flexible, responsive and innovative services. This has no doubt been aided by the recent emphasis on partnership working. In fact, it could be argued that local arrangements have little significance given the increase in local strategic partnerships within local government, discussed more fully in Chapter 8. During the interviews there was a lot of talk of getting away from the 'silo mentality', internal organizational barriers that prevent efficient working across the authority to improve services to local people and communities that according to one interview participant could be a real problem:

> The big challenge in this area, not just public libraries but throughout the local authority, is the silo mentality where there's just no conception of what other departments are doing. (Anon)

Many interview participants stressed the importance of breaking down those barriers, one saying:

> The other thing that we're concerned with most of all is to place libraries into the bigger picture of corporate priorities and contributions to other things and part of this bigger picture of local government development. Because the library service can't just go on in a sort of silo. (Anon)

According to another interviewee, this necessitated a clear conception of how and where the library service could contribute to the local authority's agenda:

> [You need] an understanding of where information fits into your council's aspirations. And information and knowledge fits very much into the council's aspirations; it fits into the economic agenda, in the economic development agenda, it fits into the learning agenda, the council's learning agenda and it fits into the community safety agenda, citizenship, all those kinds of things, it fits into all kinds of agendas. And that doesn't come easily and it's about, not lobbying exactly, but its about getting involved on a corporate level and being willing to deliver things. (Jan Holden)

It seems that there is a huge job to do in convincing some local politicians of the role that libraries can play in the achievement of many cross-cutting corporate aims and objectives, however. *Framework for the Future* (Department for Culture, Media and Sport, 2003) argues that innovative authorities recognize that library services can play a valuable role at the heart of the local authority while others are undervalued and ignored. As discussed above, this could be due partly to the declining status and therefore influence of the Chief Librarians, many of whom are not now Chief Officers as mentioned. The political skills of the Chief Librarian has a large part to play in how visible the public library service is within the local authority as does the receptiveness of the local authority. Another factor could be a lack of national and local advocacy, stressing the potential of public libraries for contributing to cross cutting strategic agendas on a whole host of issues from lifelong learning to urban regeneration although this has become a priority for MLA in England, determined to demonstrate how libraries contribute to the shared priorities of local and central government.

At the local level, interview participants often stressed the importance of having a strong portfolio holder (Councillors sitting in the Cabinet who are responsible for particular service areas) who was able to make the case for libraries at the highest level in the local authority. One interviewee, talking about the variability in the quality of services around the country, said:

> I think it's local politics and local interest. You might have a very good and energetic portfolio holder in an authority that really pushes the libraries' agenda forward. That sort of enthusiasm may not be replicated in other authorities so to some extent it does start at local level; we're trying to push from the centre but unless there's that spark at local level, unless somebody actually drives the thing forward from their end, it probably isn't going to happen in truth. (Anon)

The heads of service interviewed often confirmed the importance of having an interested and knowledgeable portfolio holder:

> We are fortunate in that libraries are part of a Culture portfolio and it just happens that the Cabinet member for Culture used to be the Committee Chair for Leisure which had responsibility for libraries. So we have a Cabinet member at the table who is personally strongly committed to public libraries, he uses them; that's one of the acid tests isn't it? He is informed about the library agenda and he is a key member of Cabinet. (Anon)

Another head of service underscored the significance of this:

> You've got to have that face around the table at everything where these sorts of things are being talked about to make sure that the service at least is treated fairly, not that it's protected or is treated differently but at least it's treated in the same way as all the rest of the council services. (Anon)

The importance of having that face at the table was stressed by a number of participants especially if, as suggested above, the Chief Librarian was becoming further removed from those making the decisions. Margaret Watson felt that, in these circumstances,

> … the role of the advocate is even more important and getting a champion in the senior management to take your case on and speak up for you because you are not there at the table. I think a lot more needs to be done on that side. (Margaret Watson)

Bob Janes also believed that more could be done to promote public libraries locally:

> In some authorities there's almost a fear of rocking the library boat which I find very strange. And I know libraries were an easy target for local government finance cutbacks in all sorts of authorities but they've got a very important living role to play and I think that it's a great pity that those who actually believe in them don't stand up and make more noise and get themselves better organized. (Cllr Bob Janes)

Others, though, seemed to be fighting a losing battle in trying to raise the profile of public libraries:

> In all honesty, in [this authority] the politicians are only interested in libraries, as far as I can see, if it keeps the kids of the street and the old ladies happy and it doesn't cost them more than it was before. They're not up on what the national agenda is, only what we tell them. Politicians here are definitely very local people and they don't keep abreast of things. For example, nobody's come back to me and said, 'What's all this Tim Coates report?' Not a soul has mentioned that to me and I'm not going to raise it, would you? There's just no point if they haven't picked it up and either they're not reading the national press or they don't listen to Radio 4. We tell them that they have a very good library service, which they have, and they're quite happy with that. (Anon)

Some would argue, though, that it is the job of the Chief Librarian to make the politicians interested, as Lord Graham Tope suggested:

> One of the things I did talking to gatherings of librarians was ask them how many of them had actually asked any of their councillors to come along [to libraries] and the vast majority hadn't even asked; it may well be that their councillors wouldn't come but if you don't ask them you'll never know. And I often ponder about why libraries don't have a very high political standing until you try and close them … and it puzzles me really because, generally speaking, as demonstrated when you do try and close them, they are popular, they are a good thing so why don't politicians pay more attention? (Cllr Graham Tope)

Generating interest and attention is not always easy, though, as suggested by the head of service above and, as another said, takes considerable effort and skills which perhaps not all Chief Librarians possess, as we will see in Chapter 5.

Performance Management in Local Government

The final part of the Government's modernizing programme for local authorities considered in this chapter is the performance management regimes of Best Value and Comprehensive Performance Assessment. Under Best Value, introduced as the replacement for compulsory competitive tendering, local authorities must demonstrate that they have applied the so-called '4 Cs' of Best Value to their services to try to ensure continuous improvement. Councils must *challenge* the way that services are provided to analyse whether there are more efficient and effective ways of providing those services or, indeed, whether they should be providing some services at all. Secondly, authorities have to show they have *consulted* key stakeholders, including the recipients of services, about what is needed from those services and they must also monitor user satisfaction. The third 'C' is *compare* and councils have to gather data on a range of national performance indicators and benchmark the services they provide with other similar providers as well as track their own performance over time. Finally, authorities have to *compete* by demonstrating that their way of providing services is the most cost effective and that the private sector could not provide the same service as efficiently. Local authorities have a duty to undertake internal Best Value reviews, fundamental evaluations of specific services as well as reviews relating to cross-cutting government priorities, to evaluate how successfully they are applying the regime. These are generally published on Council websites.[6] On a national level, Best Value is administered by the Audit Commission (or Audit Scotland, Wales Audit Office, Northern Ireland Audit Office) which undertakes regular inspections of different local authority services and grades them on a star-rating system from no stars for poor performance to three stars for those councils judged to provide an excellent service. The Audit Commission then publishes a report of the inspection which is available on their website as well as the inspected Council's own website.[7,8]

In addition to Best Value, Comprehensive Performance Assessment (CPA) was introduced in December 2002. This is a new performance management framework for local government which assesses the performance of local councils against clearly defined priorities and through the assessment of performance indicators for key services.[9] In an attempt to give a 'lighter touch' to local government performance management, top performing councils will be freed from central government controls and restrictions, and poorer councils will be given more, and better focused, support for improvement. This is in line with the New Labour Government's performance management philosophy for local government which is intolerant of low standards and rewards success through 'earned autonomy' for the more proficient (Rouse, 2001). CPA is the first step in this process, that of making an overall judgment of where each council stands. For public libraries within the CPA regime, Cilip reacted angrily to what it perceived as a slight by the Audit Commission in proposing to give the efficiency scores for libraries and other cultural services (the Cultural Block) half of the weighting given to those of other local authority services, effectively down-playing the contribution of the sector and stating that libraries were not a national priority (Cilip, 2002). This is potentially very serious for public library services as the Audit Commission stated that 'councils that choose to provide a lower level of service should not be penalised for this in the CPA', suggesting that cuts to library service budgets will not impact on authorities' CPA scores (Cilip, 2002, para. 9b). Unsurprisingly, the professional association registered its disappointment especially as the proposals seemed to contradict the many positive statements emanating from Government regarding the vital role that libraries play in relation to education, access, social inclusion and modernizing local government. Concerns about the impact the lower CPA weighting will have on library services have also been voiced in parliament where, in a Commons debate on the Libri *Who's in Charge* report, M.P. Linda Perham expressed her worries that the reduced weighting of libraries would 'enfeeble their status and high quality service' (Perham, 2004) and some interview participants also voiced their dismay, one saying:

> The Cultural Block still has a slightly lower ranking. I think it's a shame. If the ranking had been equal, that would have helped the authorities who perhaps weren't performing as well or not getting the score because I think it would have had that political attention but at the moment, all it's encouraging [councils] to do is focus on education, social services, housing and environment; it's not actually saying that some of the other services are as important. (Anon)

Another head of service agreed, stressing the important role of inspection for local government:

> The down grading of public libraries' assessment in terms of its importance to the overall CPA assessment is not helpful because it means that we are not looked on as favourably, and that's a reality. The thing that drives a local authority it seems to me … [is that] they respond to inspection. (Diana Edmonds)

Best Value in Library Services

Best Value and CPA have undoubtedly had a significant impact on the management of local authorities including their public library services. Complying with the 4 'Cs' of Best Value called for a different approach to managing and planning library services.[10] Challenging why and how a service is being provided involves questioning whether the local authority should be providing a public library service and, if so, why; what does the service contribute to the authority's strategic objectives? Library authorities also need to consider the kinds of services they should be providing, methods of service delivery and to whom they should be providing those services. Although libraries are a statutory service, the legislation is quite vague and there is considerable scope for individual library authorities to shape their provision and ask fundamental questions about what the service should be doing and how. Innovative ways of delivering services to rural populations, for example, may be considered so that co-location with other community services and a higher reliance on ICT may prove a more effective and efficient option than the traditional small, part-time community library. The consult part of Best Value should not pose too much of a problem for library services as user surveys have a long history in public libraries. Many authorities are signed up to the Cipfa Public Library User Survey,[11] for example, and also regularly carry out other surveys of specific services or service points. Reaching non-users in the community has always been a thorny problem for library authorities, however, and they also need to consider how to involve not just users but also other stakeholders including staff, local politicians, partners within the local authority and in the wider community and community groups.

The competition element of Best Value is the aspect most closely aligned to that of the last Conservative Government's policy of compulsory competitive tendering. Having considered whether they should be providing a public library service under the 'challenge' aspect, local authorities then need to analyse who should be providing that service and they may decide to outsource a variety of operations from book supply to ICT facilities management. Although, as we will see below, a very limited number of authorities have outsourced or externalized the whole library service this is very rare as explained by an interview participant:

> Under Best Value… what local authorities have to ask themselves is could anybody else provide this system, having justified that they needed to provide the service. Broadly speaking, there is nobody else who can provide it as has been demonstrated by various studies. I recall in the early days of Best Value Westminster, in particular, did some sort of market testing and came up with the conclusion, much to the disappointment I think of their own council that there was nobody else out there, there was nobody else to do it. There are people that can do bits of the operation like principally the bibliographic side of things and quite a lot of that is now contracted out, but on the broader sort of operation, no. (Anon)

Another interviewee felt that this left the process incomplete for library services:

> The bit missing for public libraries is probably the alternative provider. At best, it is tinkering at the edges. We have outsourced quite a lot but they are bits and pieces and they are not the whole service. We didn't find anyone who had a serious interest in the whole facility management approach including service delivery; there's no money to be made out of that I suspect. (Anon)

The fourth element of the Best Value regime is comparison through benchmarking and measuring performance against a range of performance indicators. The comparison should be internal, trend analysis over time, and with others in the sector. The aim is that services should work towards matching the performance of the top 25 per cent of best performers in their domain. Again, public libraries have well developed mechanisms for analysing the performance of a single authority over time and for comparing the performance of different library authorities on a range of indicators. Cipfa public library statistics gather data relating to resources and usage while the Annual Library Plans (now abandoned) and Public Library Standards have required public library authorities to gather other indicators of quality and compare themselves with other like authorities, although there is debate about the usefulness of some of the performance indicators for measuring impact (see Chapter 3). Best Value indicators have also been developed and for libraries, specifically, these are:

- the percentage of library users who found the book or information they wanted and were satisfied with the outcome;
- the number of physical visits per 1,000 population to public library premises.

In many ways, Best Value can be considered a powerful instrument for change, giving services a structured framework within which progress can be clearly monitored and measured. One interview participant stated that it enabled authorities to identify weaknesses in their library services and therefore address them and another agreed, saying:

> I think there's a benefit in that it opens you up to scrutiny and that is good… I think if you open yourself up to scrutiny, done properly and embraced properly, it should be beneficial. I think the danger is if it's used for the wrong purpose. The Derbyshire use for Best Value is just that, to scrutinize what we're doing against reasonable criteria and to raise performance. It would be possible, I suppose, to use the Best Value regime to look for significant saving, say, as opposed to significant efficiencies, and I think there's a real difference between them. But I think as long as it's not used for that purpose and it's understood, embraced, discussed. (Cllr Bob Janes)

One head of service felt that it had helped his service clarify its agenda:

> I think Best Value has been probably a useful discipline. We, as a library service, had a service review using Best Value principles in year zero, before Best Value was formally introduced. That, I think, was really good in terms of clarifying what we wanted politically and community-wise from the library service. It established the priorities we are working to. It provided a clear base to the priorities we'd set but it also changed some processes quite fundamentally in terms of the comparisons we drew, the challenges we set. (Anon)

It is also said to make services more responsive to the people they serve through consultation processes. Cost savings and enhanced partnership working have been reported as other benefits for public libraries. With a move towards cross-cutting, rather than single service, Best Value reviews and inspections the hope is that the contribution of public libraries to the local authority's corporate objectives can be emphasized, facilitating a more holistic approach to service delivery. Echoing Diana Edmonds' comments above, one respondent valued the role of inspections for raising the profile of library services:

> I can say to you that library services would be perfectly happy to be inspected. I know that sounds a very daft thing but in a recent meeting that we had … one of the key things that comes out is that local authorities only pay any attention to a service that's being inspected. (Anon)

A head of service agreed that both CPA and Best Value had focused attention on library services:

> There are very positive benefits from the CPA and the BV to libraries. It particularly pushes us much further up the corporate agenda and, certainly, when the council is looking at how it can improve its scores on the CPA, they do come to us and say, 'How are we going to improve the performance of libraries? What do we need to do?' So it's a mechanism where we can push our agenda with politicians and actually say, 'Well these are the things that central government are looking for. This is what we need to focus our activities on. (Anon)

Another head of service also felt that Best Value had had significant benefits for her library service:

> The library service, through the Best Value review process in 2000/2001, was shown to be lean, mean, efficient and innovative and the review was the key driver for change. It actually helped us to get further modernization and innovation programmes under way because, for the first time in many years, the council challenged what we do and this has sparked off cross-party debate about the value and relevance of the library service and that was an enormous step change for us. (Anon)

For others, though, Best Value is just another burden, restricting managers' freedom to direct the service in the way they consider appropriate. Indeed, the lack of regard for professional expertise has been a major criticism of Best Value with concern expressed that the 'consult' element of the regime may give a vocal minority and vociferous interest groups the power to distort service priorities to their preferences and a belief that the public are generally unaware of the context within which public libraries are now operating. It may also lead to unrealistic expectations and thus to dissatisfaction (Rouse, 2001). The system could be viewed as essentially top-down with little ownership invested in either the local authority or local people. The number of resources being devoted to Best Value has also been an issue with a suggestion that the amount of staff time spent on the process would be better applied to developing innovative and responsive services. There is a danger that the Best Value process, rather than the quality of service provided, becomes the main driving force. The demand for continuous improvement and efficiency savings in an era of static core funding can also be demoralizing for managers and staff. There is also a question over whether the Best Value indicators for public libraries measure appropriate and measure relevant elements of public library services. There have been criticisms, for example, that they focus too heavily on outputs rather than outcomes and that these are often short-term. Pressure to deliver improvements in one area can have adverse effects elsewhere. There is also concern that the cross-sectoral and partnership working, now such a central part of local authority services as stressed above, has not been acknowledged sufficiently although a move towards cross-cutting Best Value reviews should address this concern.

These kinds of negative views of Best Value and CPA were not apparent in the interviews conducted, however. Although many were unhappy with the current CPA system that has 'downgraded' the Cultural Block, the system of planning, assessment and inspection was generally welcomed. A few felt the system could be improved, however, one participant saying:

> It's been an argument of Chief Librarians even since this process kicked in that the library service shouldn't be part of the leisure service inspection, it should be inspected separately because it's a statutory service, it's meeting a lot of the corporate objectives that leisure and sports and arts don't meet. (Anon)

As discussed above, the 'compete' element is probably the least satisfactory element of the Best Value process for library services because the common view is that there is no natural market for whole service delivery. Nevertheless, some authorities have experimented with contracting out or externalizing all or parts of their library services.

Outsourcing

Although compulsory competitive tendering requirements were repealed when Best Value came into force, services still have to analyse whether any elements of their service could be more efficiently provided by external contractors under the competition element of Best Value. Some would go as far as to suggest that Best Value and other accountability regimes are being used to bring about privatization (Rikowski, 2003). With the mantra 'what counts is what works', the Government has stated that it is unconcerned about how services are provided and who provides them as long as they are effective and efficient. As mentioned above, many library authorities have experimented with contracting out a variety of functions and operations, including bibliographic services and systems development and maintenance. In the 1990s the then Department of National Heritage of the last Conservative administration experimented with several pilot projects to test the viability of contracting out in public libraries. Evaluated by consultants KPMG and Capital Planning Information, their report concluded that, 'there are some considerable question marks over the desirability of contracting-out for the public library service: primarily these revolve around the lack of concrete evidence that the benefits delivered in other service areas which have been subject to contracting regimes could be achieved in the library sector' and also that 'there is no natural market for alternative sources of service provision' (KPMG and CPI, 1995, p. ii). The report thus threw doubt on the desirability of contracting out public library services and also questioned its validity in a sector without a real market. Nearly ten years later, however, the externalization of many operations and services suggest that either the report's authors were mistaken or that the environment has changed so dramatically that outsourcing is now considered both advantageous and practicable.

The later 1990s and early years of the 21st century certainly witnessed an increasing trend towards the externalization of certain library operations driven by the more rigorous accountability processes in local government and a climate of competition. Diana Edmonds certainly felt that the accountability culture including 'the increased desire for efficiency and for good value, Best Value' (Diana Edmonds) had driven more services to consider outsourcing. While the contracting out of operations like IT systems management is relatively uncontroversial, the outsourcing of functions which lie at the core of the public library service's mission, such as stock selection for example, still provokes a strong reaction from library staff. Supporters of outsourcing assert that in-house provision should not be supported for the sake of it when an external supplier may be able to provide a service which is more appropriate to the needs of users and which could add value to their library experience. For some specialized services, valuable expertise may lie outside the library service and could save library staff time, enabling them to devote more attention to service development and innovation. Moreover, while the KPMG report questioned the validity of contracting out public library services, it did comment that the process of drawing up specifications and service level agreements were of value in themselves, leading to a clearer focus on objectives setting and service improvement and enhanced management skills for librarians. Bertram's Library Services suggest that outsourcing 'will enable libraries to make a significant saving on current expenditure' (Bertram Library Services, 2005, p. 8) and explains how Bertram's is undertaking all major elements of the acquisition process (apart from selection) for Brighton Libraries including sourcing, purchasing, cataloguing, receiving and processing stock, invoicing and despatching items to individual library locations.

Opponents of outsourcing feel that the contribution of professional librarians is undermined by the externalization of these core functions, however, and that the local control of services is undermined. This, it is felt, could damage the neutral and safe image of the library within the community. A lot of concern focuses on the role of the professional librarian with some fearing that contractors' drive to cut costs will reduce professional input and could lead to a loss of professional skills and ethos within the public library service. More generally, externalization is also felt to damage systems of public accountability and reduce user involvement in service development.

In the 1990s, the British National Bibliography Research Fund commissioned Capital Planning Information to investigate the potential of outsourcing one of the core operations underpinning public library services; the professional control of selecting stock (Capital Planning Information, 1999). It was suggested that personnel working for library suppliers had access to a fuller range and depth of information than library staff selecting stock and that the information that library staff based their selections upon was provided by library suppliers anyway. This led to the proposition that library suppliers, using information about the library service and the community it served, could select stock instead of the librarians of the service, releasing them for other high priority work such as reader development. Two library authorities acted as pilot sites to test the feasibility and desirability of supplier selection and a full account of their and others' experiences with, and opinions of, supplier selection is given in Chapter 10 but for the purposes of this discussion on outsourcing, it is important to note that while some staff accepted that it might be another valid method of purchasing stock, others felt that their professional role was being threatened and were concerned that the local character of the stock would be lost.

Despite the growing trend toward outsourcing a range of operations and services, it has often been argued that many of the key library procedures involving front-line services to the public will never be undertaken by external agencies because there is no alternative, commercial market for them. Two English public library authorities have experimented with forms of contracting out for the whole of their public library service, however, testing the notion that there is no market in this area. In Hounslow in West London, the borough's Cultural and Community Services portfolio, which includes libraries, has been run by an external contractor, Community Initiative Partnerships (CIP), since 1998 on a trust basis. The organization, a non-profit distributing limited company or trust, manages a range of cultural and leisure services for Hounslow London borough, including its public library service.[12] Handing over the running of a public library service to a not-for-profit trust organization might be more acceptable for many in the profession than leaving it in the hands of a strictly private firm. As noted above, the DNH study in the 1990s concluded that there was no market but in 2001 the information and library services consultancy firm Instant Library was contracted to manage Haringey public library service in North East London following a very negative Best Value report in the borough.

The relationship between Instant Library and Haringey has now finished although the ex-Managing Director and founder of Instant Library, Diana Edmonds, is now Chief Librarian in the borough. She feels that the model in Haringey, where a team of specialist managers were brought in to run the service, had a range of benefits that were immediately noticeable to those working in the libraries:

> The key things that the staff identified were the immediacy of it, the directness, the cutting through the bureaucracy and what they particularly went on about was the fact that they would ask for a piece of furniture one day and it would be delivered the next. They also felt that we controlled contractors highly effectively. We have done refurbishments in all of the libraries at very low cost, very good value and they felt that we had particular control there. (Diana Edmonds)

As well as internal service improvements, outsourcing can also have an impact on the service's profile within the council according to Linda Simpson, Director of Culture and Leisure for CIP:

> Our experience has been that it's raised the profile of the service internally to the council. We've been invited onto working groups and working parties that we wouldn't have been if we'd still been a council department and I think it is something to do with being outside of the authority and a valuable partner… I think, strangely enough, CIP got such a lot of publicity within the authority that people began to realise what really was in Leisure and so CIP managers were invited on to things that, in the past, Council officers would never have dreamed of having you on. (Linda Simpson)

The real litmus test of the success of outsourcing is whether the library service provided to users has improved, of course. Experiences in both Hounslow and Haringey appear to be positive with reports that visits in Haringey have risen by 93 per cent and issues by 42 per cent. Similarly Linda Simpson reported that:

> Obviously the service has improved because a) we have had additional subsidy funding and b) we've had no budget cuts whatsoever since 1998 and that is significant because we went through the whole of the 90s having budget cuts year on year. (Linda Simpson)

Critics of outsourcing would argue that the bottom line is that private enterprises have to make a profit, unlike the local authority, and there is a danger that a private company will not place the needs of the people in the local community above the profit imperative. CIP, though, is a non-profit distributing company with an ethos grounded in the voluntary, community and public, rather than commercial, sector and that, according to Linda Simpson, makes some people more comfortable with the concept. Cross-subsidy between the services managed by CIP are also possible and in fact cross-subsidy from the more profitable leisure centres to the library service have been made (Allan, 2001). Linda Simpson reported that the library service had received £300,000 extra to extend opening hours and support the revenue costs of the People's Network. She explained that the money:

> …was literally taken out of the leisure centre subsidy because the leisure centres were making money which they hadn't under the CCT regime. The money could never have been taken from them within the CCT regime so that's worked greatly to our benefit. (Linda Simpson)

New models of public library service management are emerging, therefore, and new relationships with local authority partners are being forged. It is a matter of waiting to see how these systems develop and mature and the impact they have on users and other stakeholders.

Conclusion

The evidence presented above suggests that discourses of local control and accountability are still strong within the public library community in the UK. Local managers want the flexibility to consult local people and decide the nature, scope and emphasis of the public library service within local communities. Alongside this, especially in England with the publication of *Framework for the Future* (Department for Culture, Media and Sport, 2003), there is a widespread acceptance that a national steer is both necessary and welcome to overcome the 'fragmentation' and 'patchy' nature of the quality of services and to raise the profile of public libraries within the local authority. The fact that the government is taking an interest in public libraries by publishing strategies and plans and, as we will see in the next chapter, by demanding greater accountability, enables those working in public libraries to highlight the work that they do within the authority. Interview participants generally rejected the notion that central government was becoming too controlling, centralizing or interventionist. Rather, the view often expressed was that the Government, through the DCMS in England, was guiding, supportive and active although some questioned the effectiveness of some of its actions and, as discussed in Chapter 3, many were looking for stronger leadership.

It seems that many of the gloomy predictions about life following local government reorganization have proved to be groundless. Many of those from reorganized authorities felt that the transition to the new arrangements had been pretty seamless and while those in new authorities had experienced some initial teething troubles, they were now confident of their future. The small size of some of the authorities in Wales did seem to be causing difficulties, however, and so questions about the optimum size and efficiency of public library authorities remain. The influence that a small public library service can wield within a small authority was questioned, as was the amount of finance available to it. It was suggested that, in a small authority, the 'big hitters' of Education and Social Services seem to command even more of the budget that they would in a larger one, with little left for other services. Their influence and profile is not necessarily diminished, though, and there was a feeling that the close relationships formed in smaller authorities were of real value for the public library service.

Another discourse emerging strongly above is that around ensuring that the library service is on the official corporate agenda and that its profile is high enough to command attention from local decision makers. In this regard, respondents often talked of the importance of a strong Chief Librarian with effective political skills as well as the necessity of having an effective local champion in the guise of a Cabinet portfolio holder with the knowledge, understanding and skill to ensure that public libraries are considered in relation to a whole host of cross-cutting agendas. Best Value, it seems, had often worked in libraries favour in this respect, articulating a clarity of purpose and demonstrating their value and contribution to a range of council priorities.

Notes

1 With apologies to the BBC's *A League of Gentlemen*.

2 Since devolution in 1990, this has been the Department for Culture, Media and Sport (DCMS) in England and the Minister for Culture, Sport and the Welsh Language in Wales.

3 208 in the UK (32 in Scotland; 22 in Wales; 5 Education and Library Boards in Northern Ireland).

4 The other key element of the Government's modernization agenda for local government is e-government which is considered in more detail in Chapter 6.

5 See White, J. (1993), *Frogs or Chameleons: the Public Library Service and the Public Librarian*, Library Association, London for a discussion of how the location of the public library service within the local authority may impact on provision and librarians' management prospects.

6 See, for example, Hertfordshire County Council's Best Value Review of its library services at URL: http://www.hertsdirect.org/infobase/docs/pdfstore/bvrlibsreport.pdf [17.07.2005].

7 See URL: http://www.auditcommission.gov.uk> [accessed 17th July 2005] or see, for example, Worcestershire County Council's Best Value report on its Libraries and Information Services at URL: http://www.worcestershire.gov.uk/home/lib-index-bv-report.pdf [17.07.2005].

8 For more information on the Best Value regime see: Audit Commission, *Seeing is Believing*, London: Audit Commission, 2000. URL: http://www.audit-commission.gov.uk/reports/……. [17.07.2005].

9 CPA results can be viewed on the Audit Commission's website URL: http://www.audit-commission.gov.uk/cpa/ [17.07.2005].

10 The Library Association produced guidance on Best Value for library authorities in England: Angela Watson, *Best Returns. Best Value guidance for library authorities in England.* July 2001. URL: http://www.la-hq.org.uk/directory/prof_issues/br.html [17.07.2005].

11 For details of Public Library User Surveys see URL: http://www.ipf.co.uk/plus/about.htm [17.07.2005].

12 For more information about CIP, visit the website at URL: http://www.cip.com/ [17.07.2005].

Chapter 3

National Agendas

Introduction: State Involvement

Chapter 2 demonstrated that operating within a local authority context has significant implications for public library services but, as outlined in the Introduction, since 1997 national politicians have also taken a growing interest in public libraries, acknowledging that they have 'an enormous amount to contribute to the achievement of central government's key social and educational objectives' (Department for Culture, Media and Sport, 2003, p. 43). Alongside this government recognition that public libraries are at the heart of communities, efficiency and value for money are still priorities for Whitehall and as well as initiatives like Best Value covering all local authority services, the New Labour Government has also introduced a variety of schemes specifically targeting public libraries. These generally focus on accountability and impact and are concerned with raising standards and continuous improvement. Public libraries have not escaped the audit culture, therefore, and as with other public services, the Government is concerned that they provide value for money. According to *Framework for the Future* (Department for Culture, Media and Sport, 2003), English local authorities spend £780 million per annum on public libraries (this has risen to £844 million according to the latest Cipfa (2004) statistics for 2002/3 and over £1 billion for the UK as a whole) and the Government wants to ensure that there are mechanisms in place to monitor that this is being used effectively and efficiently. Despite the encouraging noises emanating from Whitehall about the role that public libraries can play in delivering a whole raft of their policy objectives, substantial new core funding has not been forthcoming, though. Instead, public libraries now find themselves in a competitive bidding environment in which additional funds are sought to supplement statutory funding through a variety of one-off schemes and initiatives.

As noted in Chapter 1, central responsibility for public libraries in the UK is devolved to the governing bodies of the four home nations although the situation in Northern Ireland is complicated because of the current suspension of the Northern Ireland Assembly. This chapter will outline the national contexts within which public libraries are operating and explore recent developments which have impacted on their organization and services. It will explore stakeholders' views of the central administration of public libraries and the role this plays in clarifying and leading public library strategy. The regional and devolution agendas will also be investigated alongside co-operation within both the library sub-domain and the wide cultural sector. The planning and accountability mechanisms now in place for public libraries are discussed before the chapter ends with an exploration of the impact on public libraries of increasing dependence on external funding.

National Leadership

The Role of Government

As the government department responsible for public libraries, the Department for Culture Media and Support (DCMS) is the body in England tasked with representing their interests within government and projecting a national vision of what they aim to do and why they matter. In Scotland, responsibility lies with the Scottish Executive's Cultural Policy Division, in Wales the Department of Culture, Sport and Welsh Language and in Northern Ireland the Department of Culture, Arts and Leisure. As stressed in Chapter 2, in the UK the Government (or Executive or Assembly) department encompassing public libraries has always had an executive role. Public libraries are viewed as, essentially, a local service responding to local conditions. The role of the Government or Assembly minister responsible has been supervision and, rarely, inspection when local authorities are considered not to be fulfilling their statutory duties with regard to public libraries. As discussed in the previous chapter, however, under the New Labour Government, the DCMS in England has been much more active in relation to public libraries than its equivalent under previous administrations, commissioning and publishing a variety of reports and supporting a range of initiatives setting out its vision of what public libraries should be doing and how they should be contributing to the national economy and society as well as their local communities. Similarly, the Government's drive to raise standards throughout the public sector, exemplified by the Best Value regime, has been directed in public libraries in England by the DCMS which has administered a number of initiatives designed to make public libraries more accountable, cost-effective and responsive to the communities they serve. According to *Framework for the Future*, the role of central government in relation to public libraries in England is to clarify how public libraries can contribute to national and local policy priorities, identify a range of services which all public libraries should be offering and administer the performance management regime for public libraries.

Framework is the first attempt by national government to formulate a long-term strategic vision for public library services in England since *Reading the Future* in 1997 (Department of National Heritage, 1997) and its publication could be seen to answer the criticisms of those who claim that the public library service has suffered from a lack of national strategic thinking. There is doubt, though, about whether the DCMS is, in practice, as interventionist and involved in public library leadership as it appears to be on the surface. Although in evidence to the 2000 House of Commons Select Committee on Public Libraries the then Minister for Arts Alan Howarth insisted that it was the duty of the DCMS 'to remind local authorities ... of the very great importance of the public library service which they are under a statutory obligation to maintain as a comprehensive and efficient service' (Culture, Media and Sport Committee, 2000, para. 155), some English public library services have found that calling on the DCMS to support them in the face of cuts within the local authority has had little impact, with the Department refusing to get involved despite library service assertions that the local authority's action will make it impossible for the service to attain the vision set out by Whitehall. The DCMS maintains that public libraries are a local service and it is not their role to influence the budgetary processes of the local authority. There seems to be a contradiction here. Although laying down a clear agenda for the public library service in *Framework*, the Department will not become involved in the local decisions, which will decide whether public libraries will be able to deliver that agenda satisfactorily. For that reason, *Framework* has been criticized as deregulatory rather than interventionist and revolutionary. It has also been said that *Framework* is not aspirational enough and that the better library authorities are already fulfilling the vision as laid out in the document.

As suggested in Chapter 2, these criticisms were articulated by some of those participating in the interviews for this study who had been ultimately disappointed with the final document, as one explained:

> I have to say my first reaction was that it wasn't a very powerful document, both in content and also in style. The printed version with its bits of clip art and so on would shame most other government departments. That was a shame because I think the selling of it, as a government strategy, needed to be much stronger. (John Dolan)

The principal criticism often aired was that the document was not visionary enough, one participant saying:

> It's based in the current, it's not futuristic, it's not a vision… It is not where we're going to be or ought to be in ten years, it's set in yesterday. (Frances Hendrix)

Another interviewee said that, in her opinion, *Framework* was 'more of a descriptive document that it is a visionary document', a view echoed by one head of service:

> Sadly, I am in the camp that I felt the end product was less than it might have been, largely because the document, to me, didn't make up its mind about what it wanted to be… It talked about a vision for libraries for the next ten years but in some ways, that's the element that's lacking… It just feels like a document that probably didn't quite get where it wanted to go. (Anon)

Following on from this was the view that the publication described good practice in public library service as it already was in a great many places, rather than how it should be. As one interview participant said, 'a lot of librarians said, "Yes, well what's new about that? We're doing all that already"' (Anon). Indeed, one head of service said just that in interview:

> I think for us it was a disappointment because it was almost at a stage where we were… Without appearing to be too big-headed, I think we would have said we do 95 per cent of

> that. There's a little bit here that we can do but it was more for other people I think. I think there was a bit of disappointment in that. (Anon)

Another respondent was more scathing:

> It struck me as being a pretty feeble document, actually. One of the reasons it was feeble is that it didn't offer anybody any money but the other reason it was feeble is that it really described things as they were in a great many places rather than as they might be. And I think some of what you might call the strong suggestions there, the added social dimension to libraries, begged more questions than it answered. So we were very disappointed and I'm not impressed with *Framework for the Future* and I don't think it's rocket science and it's not terribly new. (Cllr Bob Janes)

Because of this, one head of service wondered whether *Framework* would stand the test of time:

> What I'll find very interesting, like a lot of so-called major reports we've had in the past, is what it's impact is going to be in 2 or 3 years time. And I know a lot of time, effort and, I would have to say, an awful lot of money is going into the delivery of this *Framework* and I just hope for everyone's sake that something tangible comes out of it; I have reservations. (Anon)

As discussed in Chapter 1, the *Framework* Action Plan is well under way now and has produced some substantial outcomes so perhaps this head of service is now less uncertain of its value.

The other common criticism of *Framework*, as suggested by Bob Janes above, was the lack of detail on funding. Margaret Watson observed:

> My instinctive reaction on reading *Framework for the Future* was, actually, couldn't disagree with anything, I thought it was fine. But, of course, the big thing that it lacked was where the money was going to come from. (Margaret Watson)

A head of service agreed that this was unsatisfactory:

> It didn't say anything about resourcing which has subsequently been rationalized to 'there is enough money to do whatever we want to do, it's just that we're spending it on the wrong things'. That's a convenient political solution but it leaves managers and even some politicians within local authorities with quite a challenge to deliver some of that. (Anon)

By no means all interview participants were critical of *Framework*, however. As suggested in Chapter 2, the vast majority of those participating in the study applauded the very fact that the DCMS had issued a document setting out its priorities for libraries. As John Patemen said:

> I think *Framework for the Future* is the best we have had. It does say we should be doing three things and we are going to be measuring you, and all the rest of it, on three things. (John Pateman)

Even those who found things to criticize could see commendable elements in *Framework*:

> I don't think it had much to do with the future, it was more like a framework for last year but I did like the start to define our core because it put reading and access to learning and digitization and social inclusion and citizenship in at the core and I was very pleased with that. And I just hope that the work that's going on as a response will actually grapple with that. (John Vincent)

Other were more positively supportive and disagreed that is was a weak vision statement:

> *Framework*, although it was perceived to be a bland document, the way that Baroness Blackstone intended it and indeed I think the way that Andrew McIntosh sees it, it's actually quite a revolutionary document for libraries and calls for a great deal of change… Whether it's for ten years, that's hugely optimistic but for now it's quite a good way forward. (Martin Molloy)

Another participant also felt that meeting the vision would be a challenge for most library authorities:

> To some extent it probably does steer down the middle but if you look at the vision it's setting out, then most library authorities would really think of it as pretty tough. If you look at what it's saying about libraries' roles within communities, the advocacy and positioning of services, how they can deliver those big national or local agendas; no-one can say they're doing all that or that they're doing it all very well. (Anon)

The guidance and steer for English public libraries contained in *Framework* as a statement of intent from the Government had been generally welcomed, therefore, and this is because a lack of leadership from the centre has frequently been the cause of considerable criticism.

National Leadership

The reason for the perceived lack of national leadership could lie in the fact that many different bodies have some responsibility for public libraries. In fact, it could be argued that, for public libraries, the Government does not practice at national level what it preaches at local level; joined-up government. While the DCMS is responsible for the strategic direction of English public libraries, they depend on the Office of the Deputy Prime Minister (ODPM) for the bulk of their funding and also have links with the Department for Education and Skills (DfES), the Department of Trade and Industry (DTI) and the National Lottery. It has been suggested that the roles of the different departments and bodies in relation to public libraries have been insufficiently coordinated and that this has resulted in something akin to paralysis in national public library leadership as those responsible for setting the agenda and defining the priorities of public libraries do not have the power to back up their vision with hard funding to carry out their strategy (Leadbeater, 2003) and those with the funding (the ODPM) see the responsibility for libraries lying with the DCMS and therefore take little interest. Many have pointed out that there seems to be no mechanism in Government for different departments to work together, with a tendency to rely on good personal relationships between ministers to drive cooperation (see, for example, Raven, 2001). The 2005 Select Committee report suggests that there is an element of confusion with the public library community about the division of responsibilities and a perception that it has inhibited development (Culture, Media and Sport Committee, 2005). The resulting passivity has been blamed for public libraries suffering from a lack of visibility in the policy arena meaning that have been on the receiving end of developments caused by legislation which they were not consulted about but which have had far-reaching impacts on their services such as the Education Reform Act of the late 1980s or, more recently, policies relating to asylum seekers.

Another reason for the lack of political leadership is that public librarians have, in the past, been careful to retain a neutral stance, remaining above party politics at a local level. While many view this as a positive quality, others see it as a negative one as John Pateman explained:

> Lots of library staff, Chief Librarians, see themselves as safe. The words they use are safe, non-political and neutral and they regard those as strengths; I don't regard any of those as strengths. (John Pateman)

Greenhalgh and Worpole similarly observe that while neutrality can be admirable at local government level and has served public libraries well over the years, at national level, where hard lobbying is part and parcel of securing resources, it is potentially disastrous (Greenhalgh and Worpole, 1995). The emphasis on joined-up government has meant that public librarians' political skills are more important than ever if they are to carve out a role for themselves in the many cross-cutting policy areas with which the current government is concerned. A lack of leadership and advocacy skills within the profession was a concern identified by the 2005 Select Committee report on public libraries (Culture, Media and Sport Committee, 2005). This deficiency is blamed for a lack of understanding and appreciation for public library services within some local authorities, which, in turn, leads to a negative impact on the funding they are prepared to invest in them. As one participant observed when talking about the variability in library services around the country:

> It's certainly nothing as simple as funding problems. It doesn't help if you've got a poorly funded library service but you have to ask yourself why it's poorly funded and it's probably because the Chief Librarian or the portfolio holder hasn't taken much interest. (Anon)

Mirroring the situation at the local authority level, librarians and those in Whitehall working on behalf of libraries must convince politicians and those who hold the purse strings of the role that public libraries can play in a range of Government strategic objectives if they are to secure adequate resources. The question is, then, who is lobbying for public libraries in the smoke filled rooms of Whitehall and why have they not been more successful? There are concerns within the public library community that the DCMS is not the most effective in this regard. The Society of Chief Librarians (SCL) in its evidence to the 2005 Select Committee on public libraries suggested that the Government had:

> ...hidden away its support [of public libraries] in the bowels of the Department of Culture, Media and Sport and it often feels as if [libraries] have dropped off the Government's radar. The influence they can bring to bear on both larger government departments and the ODPM appears to be ineffectual and poorly supported. (Culture, Media and Sport Committee, 2005. pp. 22-23)

Cilip, in its evidence to the Committee, similarly suggested that the DCMS carries insufficient weight and does not have a high enough profile within government to lobby effectively for public libraries. This was also the view of some of the interview participants:

> It can't ever be particularly good because the DCMS itself is too small. It doesn't have the strongest civil servants and when it gets down the library level it's pretty poor. (Frances Hendrix)

A head of service had a similar opinion:

> DCMS have worked harder at making the connections with the big boys or girls: DfES, Office of the Deputy Prime Minister and so on, but you sense, though, that they are seen sometimes as lightweight in that lobbying so they are sort of given a hearing but actions don't always follow. So they don't punch very hard in my view or at least they punch less hard in terms of the library agenda since Chris Smith went as Secretary of State. (Anon)

One interview respondent disagreed that library related matters were not considered sufficiently in the DCMS saying:

> Libraries have assumed a fairly high profile with the Department's pecking order. Put them into ODPM, they'd be lost. (Anon)

This leads on to the related question of whether the DCMS is the appropriate home for public library services. Lord Andrew McIntosh, unsurprisingly, felt that the DCMS was the natural home for public libraries, stating:

> I think you could make cases for putting Libraries in any one of several Government Departments. As well as DfES there are obvious links to the ODPM (because it is a local authority service and because of the link to neighbourhood renewal) or even the Home Office or the DTI [Department of Trade and Industry] (because of the social inclusion and e-government agendas respectively). However, public libraries sit at the cusp of learning, culture and recreation so I think DCMS is the best place for them. There are also some

> synergies emerging with the museums and archives sectors so I think the splitting off of libraries would be a retrograde step. (Lord Andrew McIntosh)

One head of service suggested, though, that the synergies promoted by the DCMS at national level did not always coincide with those of public library services at local level. He explained:

> It is very hard because it's not necessarily the same agenda and what we're trying to do at local level. They're [DCMS] all saying it's about cross working within [the cultural sector] and we're saying well, no, at a local level is isn't about that at all. At a local level it's all about working with colleagues in Education, Children's Services and Social Services, with the Youth Service, that's where it is; it isn't about theatres and all the things that DCMS are. (Anon)

The SCL and others have argued that public libraries should be a part of the ODPM, at the heart of local government. The 2005 Select Committee report suggested, however, that such a move might work against the public library service which would become a small fish in a very large pond and some interview participants agreed, one saying:

> I guess in an ideal world we'd be part of ODPM because that's the Department that's mainly responsible for local government so it would make sense to be under that one umbrella. But it doesn't strike me as being especially relevant because I think even if that were the case, in such a massive department we'd still have the problem of trying to fight our corner and I'm not sure that really it makes much difference whether we're here or there; it's machinery of government. (Anon)

The emphasis on lifelong learning through the People's Network may mean that public libraries fit more comfortably within the remit of the Department for Education and Skills (DfES), especially as it is responsible for Higher and Further Education libraries and could therefore facilitate closer co-operation between the different library sub-domains. The size of the DfES means that public libraries could be overshadowed, however, just as in local authority Education departments as discussed in Chapter 2. Some interview participants suggested that moving libraries from one department to another was not the answer but rather that existing departments had to work more closely together. Unfortunately this did not always happen to the frustration of many, including Martin Molloy:

> DCMS is not a strong department of state and you know that all the money comes from the Office of the Deputy Prime Minister, a lot of the activity comes from the area of the DfES and I must say the DTI which is often left out of this. And it's not been pulled together well and I think the Civil Service has the interest in making sure it's not knitted together well either. So it's not only politicians' fault that it doesn't work but there are too many vested interests in why this is not pulled together and I think it would take something radical to make a change. (Martin Molloy)

Bob McKee agreed that more coordinated working was the key to a recognition of the value of public libraries in many areas of public policy:

> It might not be about changing the separate roles the DCMS, DfES and ODPM have, it's just a matter of getting them to work more closely together so joining up. (Bob McKee)

Lord Andrew McIntosh in his written response suggested that this was happening:

> In the past, Whitehall Departments have suffered from a silo mentality. However, there has been a concerted effort to change the way that Departments cooperate and, for example, my officials are in regular contact with those of the DfES and the ODPM on public library matters. (Lord Andrew McIntosh)

The 2005 Select Committee enquiry concluded that the DCMS was, on balance, the best government department to hold responsibility for public libraries although it called upon the department to 'raise its game and act more effectively as a champion and advocate for libraries across Government' (Culture, Media and Sport Committee, 2005, p. 24).

Advocacy

The strategy set out for English public libraries in *Framework for the Future* is to be driven into action by the Museums, Libraries and Archives Council (MLA).[1] In 1995, Greenhalgh and Worpole lamented the lack of a national policy body to campaign and lobby centrally for the support and development of the public library service, in contrast to, for example, the arts, sports and even museums domains (Greenhalgh and Worpole, 1995). In England, MLA (the Museums, Libraries and Archives Council, originally called Resource) was established to fill this gap on behalf of the cultural sector, including public libraries, by providing leadership, vision and advice to government to ensure that libraries, museums and archives are at the heart of government thinking when considering culture, education, economic prosperity and social justice. Leadbeater, however, is scathing about the role and value of MLA, accusing it of being too pre-occupied with internal structures and organization to focus on taking a leading role in the sector and dismissing the body (or 'quango' in his words) as having little credibility among librarians and a low visibility with both local and national policy makers (Leadbeater, 2003). The 2000 House of Commons Select Committee on Public Libraries referred to it as 'shadowy' (Culture, Media and Sport Committee, 2000, para. 13) and the Wilip consultation exercise reported some critical comments about Resource's effectiveness and relevance to date including its lack of success in acting as an advocate for the library domain with government (Ede, 2003).

Some interview participants agreed with these criticisms. Bob McKee, for example, felt that its role in relation to advocacy was not clear:

> There's a question: what's MLA's role in terms of advocacy? Because it's actually part of government, it's a non-departmental public body but it's sponsored by government so it's not an independent voice. So I think if you're looking for advocacy, then you don't look to MLA; they're on the inside of government. (Bob McKee)

Martin Molloy disagreed, believing that MLA must take a lead on advocacy. He also felt, though, that they had not made a particularly strong impression:

> We must work with MLA and try to get it to be good but I think there is a lot of work for MLA to do to gain confidence and make a mark because I think in both areas of leadership and advocacy things are a lot quieter than they ought to be and nature abhors a vacuum and that's where other bodies try and move in and other alliances are made. (Martin Molloy)

Others were more positive that MLA was having an impact and successfully lobbying for public libraries:

> MLA, I think they themselves would admit, had a difficult first few years. I sense, though, that they are now finding their feet. They've got a new Chairman and Chief Executive firmly in place now and I anticipate that they will find a stronger voice in the next year or two than they perhaps have had over the last two or three years. (Chris Smith, MP)

Unsurprisingly, perhaps, a representative from MLA agreed:

> I think if you look at the existence of MLA, we're now three years on, we've got a rising profile, much stronger profile in government and therefore able to be much stronger advocates for museums and archives and libraries. (Sue Wilkinson)

Nevertheless, ensuring that the cultural sector is at the forefront of regional and national decision-makers' minds is still considered a challenge by many in the sector and its domains.

Others have commented that while MLA has been effective at representing the museums and archives domains, it has lacked a clear focus in relation to its role *vis-à-vis* the DCMS as far as public libraries are concerned. Another criticism often levelled at the Council is that it has failed to build strong links with the DfES which has a stake in public libraries. To overcome these perceived difficulties, Leadbeater suggested the creation of a National Libraries Development Agency (NDLA), which would bring together the functions of the Treasury, the DCMS the ODPM and the DfES. He asserts that this would unite strategic and funding responsibilities and would thus be more effective as a political body as well as driving through improved performance and innovation (Leadbeater, 2003). The PKF (2005) report on public library procurement also recommended that the case for a national agency is re-examined although it notes that wide consultation within the public library community was necessary to establish the terms of reference of any such agency and whether it should, for example, just focus on purchasing or whether it should have a wider remit.

In the past, calls for a national coordinating body have been perceived as a threat to the cherished ideals of local control and the suggestion that such a body should identify the core services of public libraries throughout the nation is viewed with alarm by those fearing for the future of all those services not deemed at core (Black, 1996). Interview participants did not express these fears although there was disagreement about the need for a national agency or body for public libraries. One head of service supported the establishment of a national public library service:

> Personally, I would favour a national library service because the different politics and priorities of every authority across the country can be a barrier to progress and improvement. In London, for example, we have the politics of the individual boroughs to consider alongside those of the GLA [Greater London Authority] and they may conflict. (Anon)

Other participants felt that a national agency would give a clarity to public library advocacy efforts, which, in their opinion, was currently missing. Talking about Leadbeater's suggestion for a National Library Development Agency, Frances Hendrix said:

> I think it would have been the best thing since sliced bread. You say would it have been feasible? Anything can be made to be feasible. It was felt not to be politically appropriate because it would have required a change and how would it have been funded? It could all have been sorted out and I think it could have made a huge difference. The trouble, I think, with the MLA is its lumpiness with museums and archives and, quite frankly, I don't think there's much commonality. (Frances Hendrix)

Bob McKee felt, though, that the establishment of a new body was not the solution to the problem of public libraries' low political profile:

> The answer isn't the creation of a new agency. Charlie Leadbeater in *Overdue* has this thing about a National Library Development Agency and that's just not the answer. Why create another bit of bureaucracy? No, the answer is for government to get its act together. It talks a lot about joined-up government so what we're looking for is a whole government approach… So I think it's not about a new agency; it's about getting the messages right and getting the connections right between the existing departments. (Bob McKee)

Others were more practical:

> I see no signs that the Government intends to create a kind of department/agency so I don't see a lot of point of going down that road… Yes, a development agency is a nice idea and it could perhaps work but it's not where the Government wants to go so it's not my job to go around leading a kind of subversive attack on government policy; they want MLA, we must work with MLA. (Martin Molloy)

Margaret Watson similarly felt that a national agency was not currently on the Government's agenda and that actions to date suggested that it was unlikely to be for some considerable time:

> I'm not sure where [a national agency] would take us. At the moment the Government has set up MLA; we're talking about cross-domain working, we are talking about all the issues MLA is responsible for. We've got the Wilip report … which is about joined-up

thinking in the library bit … and we are working with museums, archives etc., and it seems to me that it would be quite difficult to claw back just the libraries bit. I can't see that really happening unless there is a change of government and they rethink MLA. (Margaret Watson).

It seems, then, that a national agency is not on the cards and so the public library community must use other means to push the public library case. Many interview participants agreed with Bob McKee's view that, 'we have to work a bit harder to make the value we add more visible' (Bob McKee). A variety of bodies including MLA, DCMS, Cilip, the Society of Chief Librarians (SCL) in England, Wales and Northern Ireland, the Scottish Library and Information Council (SLIC) and LISC (Northern Ireland) is involved in public library advocacy but opinions were divided on how successful they had been. One Scottish participant felt that, although Cilip Scotland and SLIC had been reasonably successful in lobbying and raising the profile of libraries,

I think a lot still needs to be done. I think politically there's still a real lack of understanding of the power of libraries… there's still a lack of appreciation of just how many people libraries reach. (Anon)

A head of service picked up on this political invisibility:

You've got the political element of where we don't seem to engage. We get our own ministers saying nice things about services but then they're not going to be that critical of the service. (Anon)

Some participants blamed a lack of leadership within the profession for the poor political profile of public libraries:

My view is that whilst Rome burns around us, the Chief Librarians, the leaders of the profession, really are fiddling. Their annual conference this year is called 'A crisis of identity' and it is all about the stuff around the edges. I think that is irrelevant about what is happening in the real world. (John Pateman)

The relevant influencing and advocacy skills which would help the public library community make its case for public libraries and provide clear leadership were felt to be lacking from the profession, as mentioned in the previous chapter. Frances Hendrix said:

You know, when you write to the press or when you get somebody in a corner to lobby them, you don't drone on, you've got to be quick, sharp, funny and sexy to put your point across. We're not trained to do it and we're not very good and doing it and we're terribly defensive when the criticism comes. (Frances Hendrix)

Martin Molloy felt, though, that the library profession was no better or worse than any other in this regard:

> You do need good advocates, you do need good leadership and I think that there are, as in most things – in most public sector services and private sector services, there are excellent leaders in the library sector and there are some pretty poor ones. There are some good communicators, good advocates and there are some awful communicators and awful advocates and that needs addressing but it's by no means unique to public libraries. (Martin Molloy)

Some participants questioned the value of the professional lobby anyway because, as Bob McKee suggested, 'the most valuable advocates for the value of the public library service are not librarians because we would say that wouldn't we?' (Bob McKee). Similarly, one head of service questioned the value of some of the current lobbying efforts:

> What we don't seem to do well is go beyond that professional lobby. I think SCL and Cilip are very active in representing the public library bit of the profession but I don't think civil servants and ministers are that interested in professional bodies lobbying. (Anon)

The need for people from outside the profession to advocate on behalf of public libraries was emphasized by many interviewees including Bob McKee:

> When we're looking for advocacy and championship, what we need to look to is people outwith our own community… If part of the advocacy argument is that we make a contribution to the learning agenda, the economic agenda, the social inclusion agenda and so on, we need people from those stakeholder groups and they're the most powerful advocates we have. So, yes, we need to do a bit more to get our own advocacy act in order but actually, it's really about identifying those other champions in other fields and helping them to find a voice; that's the key. (Bob McKee)

Some participants doubted that this would be an easy task, however:

> If you look at, say, the sports world or the museums world, the people who are active in the sector have a much stronger voice publicly; they're either famous or knighted or something and they also seem to have more clout within the public domain and that gives the DCMS the wherewithal to make other approaches to the Treasury or to the DfES or ODPM. Libraries, I fear, don't have that so we count that much more on the DCMS itself to develop that strength and I think they've still got a long way to go. (John Dolan)

Other participants felt that it was right and proper that a lead should come directly from government. Martin Molloy, for example, felt that 'leadership from the top' was needed but that this was not consistently forthcoming:

> The problem is when you change Ministers. I'm not complaining about Andrew McIntosh because in my experience this happens every time you get a ministerial change; that Minister has a different view about what they've inherited and, in a way, they're signed up to it because it's happening but they're not necessarily signed up to it in the way the person who thought this was a good idea at the beginning and was driving it through was. (Martin Molloy)

Another participant agreed that the personality of the DCMS Minister with responsibility for public libraries was important and felt that libraries had been served well in recent times:

> I think [leadership] often comes down to individual ministers and actually, certainly at the Junior Minister level, the last three, Alan Howarth, Baroness Blackstone and now Lord McIntosh[1] have all had a particular interest in libraries and that helps a lot in pushing that particular portfolio to the front of the Department's agenda. There is a growing awareness that libraries do have this wider role than that which they were once perceived to have and, in some ways, with central government trying to get its act together and work together rather than having a silo mentality, actually saying to the likes of ODPM and DfES, 'Actually, public libraries can contribute a lot to your agenda'... There is this sort of burgeoning of realization of the things libraries can do. (Anon)

This more positive view of the increasing effectiveness of public library lobbying efforts was shared by Bob McKee who felt that the message was starting to get across, as did Chris Smith:

> Politicians generally are beginning to wake up to the degree of support that public libraries have in local areas and you have only to look at what happens when somebody suggests that a library should close; suddenly the entire community gets galvanized about it and that happens in place after place. The message is, I think, gradually getting through to politicians of all political colours that libraries are well used, they're well supported and people feel very strongly that they need to be protected and defended. (Chris Smith, MP)

The views expressed above are mostly based on experiences in England and, as indicated in the Introduction, devolution may have changed professional and political relationships in the other three home nations of Scotland, Wales and Northern Ireland.

Devolution

As explained in Chapter 1, government offices for Scotland and Northern Ireland had responsibility for public library matters even before devolution and so the experience of the transference of duty for cultural matters to the new devolved administrations has had different impacts in Scotland, Northern Ireland and Wales. In Scotland, some interview participants felt that devolution had not made much difference to the way that public library affairs were conducted, one saying, for example:

> My perception is that the civil servants based in Edinburgh prior to devolution worked closely with SLIC and what was the Scottish Library Association at that time and I really think that that relationship to some extent has just carried on. (Anon)

Alan Hasson agreed:

> The change from a Scottish Office direction to a Scottish Executive direction has not really manifested itself in anything particularly hugely practical at the moment… Nothing fundamental that I can see has originated from the Executive. (Alan Hasson)

Other Scottish respondents felt that the impact was beginning to tell, however. One said that although he did not think services had been affected greatly, relationships and structures were changing and that this was not always beneficial:

> It's had an impact on the Scottish Library and Information Council [SLIC] and its role. It's been given a stronger policy role with the Executive. I think it's changed that. In some ways it's not always been helpful in that there's more of a divide, more of a tension between what MLA are now doing and what's happening here. I think we are not as fully aligned with some of the UK issues as we might be... I know colleagues here think we are not as engaged with things happening south of the border as we might be… Some of the People's Network stuff, some of the things around disability, there's more content development, more funding streams and support streams available than is the case here. (Anon)

Another Scottish interviewee agreed that structures were changing but felt that this was having a positive impact on services:

> [Devolution has] focused library services on delivering strategic priorities… Prior to that I don't think we'd have had that focus. We have been able to marshal the troops so we are making arguments at Executive level and what we then have is our membership delivering that at a local level. Now, like in everything, there are degrees of success in doing that but there is an expectation in government that libraries have a role to play, for instance, community planning, community learning and all that. So I think it's given a more local focus to delivering strategic things and also there's an interest; it's an agenda of interest. We've had debate in the Parliament about libraries in November to celebrate 150 years of public libraries in Scotland so it has given us a focus. (Anon)

Interestingly though, she felt that the support and interest from the central administration was not always followed by local action:

> The support that we get at strategic level from the Executive is, ironically, not always matched by the delivery by the local government. That's not to say we have bad library services but at times what you get is this strategic support… but the age old argument with local government is that you've got to give us money to do it. Now, what we actually know is that it's not always about money, it's about configuring and delivering your services differently. (Anon)

In Northern Ireland, the situation with regard to devolution is difficult because of the suspension of the Good Friday agreement and the Northern Ireland Assembly. Here, according to one participant, devolution had complicated structural and financial issues. As in England, public library matters are the responsibility of one body although their funding comes from another:

> Now the public library funding stream is coming from the Department of Culture, Arts and Leisure which is the smallest of the Northern Ireland government departments with very, very little scope for flexibility within the budget. This is a kind of double whammy for us. We're still within the [Education] Boards as a kind of minor player and our funding comes from another minor player. So that has definitely posed problems for us, particularly since devolution. (Anon)

In Scotland and Northern Ireland, then, there have been some developments and even difficulties posed by devolution but perhaps not the significant changes experienced by public library services in Wales which, prior, to devolution, were managed centrally from England. As suggested in Chapter 2, the initial impact of devolution, accompanied by local government reorganization, was probably a detrimental one as the old county council public library services were broken up into unitary authorities leading to considerable budgetary and logistical difficulties. Devolution had also, though, had its positive benefits as Alan Watkin explained:

> Since the Assembly has been created… although the pot is smaller it's far more accessible. If the Culture Minister walked in here now, we'd say 'Hello Alan', 'Hello Alun' quite genuinely because we'd recognize each other by first names. Now I've met the Minister for Libraries and the Minister for the Arts in England but she wouldn't know me from Adam. So there's that much closer links and a closer working relationship. This will be reinforced though the foundation of CyMAL. (Alan Watkin)

He also felt that the approach to public library services in Wales was diverging from that in England, for him in a positive direction:

> For me, the most important impact the Assembly's made is bringing in public library standards in Wales. And I've had the opportunity to talk privately and publicly on a platform with the Minister of Culture where basically he's committing to carrying on these whereas in England they're up in the air. (Alan Watkin)

The establishment of CyMAL (Museums, Archives and Libraries Wales) is also one very concrete and practical outcome of devolution in Wales. Again, the approach to the establishment of a body to coordinate services and activities across the cultural sector is different in Wales where CyMAL is a policy division of the National Assembly unlike its counterpart, MLA in England which is an agency separate from government, as one participant explained:

> If you take the MLA body, public libraries go to MLA, MLA then goes to DCMS, DCMS then goes to Cabinet. That's short cut in Wales in that public libraries come to CyMAL, CyMAL goes to Ministers. (Anon)

This has its advantages according to the same participant:

> There is a much shorter and clearer communication path for policy ideas or concerns than there would be if we were a separate agency and I think that's an advantage for public libraries that I hope they'll exploit. Strong communication is going to be a very important

part of CyMAL's initial responsibility; communication with the Assembly's strategic agenda, which is *Wales: a Better Country*, and communication to the Minister of what the issues are plus, of course, some informed advice for him. (Anon)

Devolution does seem to be beginning to have an impact on services development and strategic planning for public library services in the other three home countries, therefore. In England, too, decentralization through the regions is increasingly advocated as an effective and efficient way forward for services.

Libraries and the Regional Agenda

Local partnerships and relationships have become vital for public library services and library authorities are playing an influential role in many local alliances designed to promote community well-being as we will see in Chapter 8. The wider regional perspective has also been given a higher priority by the Government in recent years with the publication in 1997 of *Building Partnerships for Prosperity*, setting out its agenda for the English regions and committing itself to devolving responsibility for political and policy decisions on social, economic and cultural issues to regional bodies (Department for the Environment, Transport and the Regions, 1997). The regional focus will continue and is set to become increasingly important, particularly as European strategies and funding are increasingly directed at a regional level.

Regional cooperation is nothing new for public library authorities; networks of cooperative arrangements involving library and information services from all sub-domains have a long history, primarily through the Regional Library Systems first established in 1931 (Circle of Officers of National and Regional Library Systems (CONARLS), 2003). Recently, however, the focus has widened with library services joining regional consortia, which include not just library and information organizations but also other agencies. The emphasis on the regions as key drivers of economic and social regeneration has led to the formation of a number of new bodies including Regional Assemblies, Regional Development Agencies and Regional Cultural Consortiums. Similarly, the role of existing regional agents such as the government regional offices and their representatives in various departments including the DCMS, have been reinvigorated. Single regional agencies funded by the MLA for museums, libraries and archives (The North East Museums, Libraries and Archives Council, or NEMLAC[2], for example) have also been created with the aim of contributing to more effective and efficient co-ordinated strategy between a region's different cultural bodies. These developments are having a significant impact on the ways in which local authorities and individual local services operate and challenge established ways of working. *Renaissance in the Regions*, a Resource report on how museums should respond to the regional agenda, listed the implications of regionalism, all of which could apply equally well to public libraries (Resource, 2001a). The challenges the report identified included the development of a regional voice; the ability to think regionally; issues of integration; and, the ability to see new regional structures as an opportunity to bridge local and national policy making.

Supporters of the regional agenda believe that cross-sectoral arrangements will lead to more creative and effective service delivery and give fresh impetus to policy and strategy resulting in decentralized innovative capacity. The *Carpe Diem* report on regional cooperation involving libraries asserted that the benefits of cooperation include a strategic rationale; a means to develop and improve services; cost-effectiveness and better access to external funding opportunities; networking which improves communication and leads to better co-ordination; and a higher profile (Circle of Officers of National and Regional Library Systems (CONARLS), 2003). Regional involvement is considered to provide the scope to produce coherent strategies, co-ordinate service and development needs and voice regional concerns related to a range of policies. Collaboration can also promote efficiency and economies of scale, according to Cilip Chief Executive Bob McKee, who suggested that public library services' ICT procurement, stock management and staff training would all benefit from regional cooperation (Cilip News, 2004).

These benefits were recognized by many interview participants although the regional agenda was more important for some that for others. An interviewee from Northern Ireland, for example, explained that regional cooperation across the public library sector and beyond was essential for public libraries there:

> In a small place like Northern Ireland, it is very important and ELFNI [Electronic Libraries for Northern Ireland] again is the biggest manifestation of it. But equally it makes sense in terms of our relationships with archives and museums. (Anon)

Advocates of regionalism also warn of the dangers of not being involved in regional activities, missing out on funding and of being the target of change initiated at a regional level rather than influencing it. Moreover, despite their increasing involvement in local partnerships, it is argued that if public libraries do not engage with the regional bodies being established, they will miss the opportunity to convince policy makers of the contribution that public libraries can make to a whole host of policy initiatives and fail to exploit increasingly important funding streams.

Detractors of regionalism, on the other hand, question the extent to which co-operation on a regional basis has added value to public library services and activities and have reservations about how far public libraries should go down the regional route when their strength has always lain in providing local services to local communities. While local government reorganization and the resulting smaller administrative units discussed in the previous chapter have often been celebrated for bringing services closer to the communities they serve, regional engagement can pull in the opposite direction, making strategy inaccessible, remote and resulting in a loss of ownership. This was certainly the view of some interview participants, one of whom said:

> I think you've got to start with what you've got in your local area. If that's against the national agenda or the regional agenda then tough, they have to come after. (Anon)

Bob Janes concurred, saying:

> Derbyshire is not very committed to regional agendas if we're honest. If you said 'regional government' to our leader he's probably throw you out of his first-floor window so I think it's fair to understand that; we are not pro-regional government. We deal with regional offices when and if we have to and try to build our relationships with them for the benefit of the county rather than the benefit of the region to be honest. (Cllr Bob Janes)

Andrea Barker explained that although the library service tried to work regionally, that was not really where the priorities of the council lay:

> I think elected members really do enjoy a set of officers who are able to work sub-regionally, regionally and nationally but, at the end of the day, they're minded of the people that the service is for and that's the Borough of Stockton and the surrounding environment… It's got to be a service for our people, to those who want us, who work, live and study within the Borough of Stockton. (Andrea Barker)

The impetus towards a regional agenda seems unstoppable, however, and public libraries need to engage or be left out in the cold. Although the Regional Library Systems and other regionally-based library domain bodies have a long history of bringing together the resources of different library authorities and different types of libraries, it has been suggested that these focused essentially on operational issues such as inter-lending etc., rather than cross-cutting strategic themes which the Government is encouraging (Doughty, 1999). The DCMS consultation paper published in 1999, *Libraries and the Regions*, recognized that some Regional Library Systems were taking a developmental role and working with others across their regions on a range of cross-cutting projects and initiatives (Department for Culture, Media and Sport, 1999). The regional activities of others, though, were still essentially based on the core function on facilitating inter-library loans. Since the publication of this paper, however, the regional agenda has strengthened and in response there have been significant developments in public library regional activity. Public libraries are now involved across the regions with:

1 other library and information service providers to facilitate access to the area's information, cultural and learning resources, greatly enhanced by the development of digital resources and facilities;
2 other local cultural agencies such as museums, archives and arts organizations to ensure advocacy and development for the cultural sector
3 partners from across the public, private and voluntary sectors to reinforce their contribution to the region's strategic vision including educational, social, economic and cultural goals.

Each of these is considered in turn below. Although the benefits of cooperation across the sector are stressed by many key stakeholders, there are fears that alliances across the LIS (library and information services) domain can be too inward looking and concerned with operational rather than strategic issues and that strong alliances across the cultural sector can work against other important cross-sectoral collaboration.

Regional Co-operation Across the Library and Information Domain

Co-operation through Regional Library Systems and other organizations and initiatives across the LIS domain in the regions is well established and ICT is enhancing the range of services and initiatives involving library and information services from across the public, academic, school and corporate domains. The Wilip (Wider Libraries Programme) report commented on regional collaboration and found that participants in its consultation process believed strongly in the concept of seamless information provision on a regional basis (Ede, 2003). Similarly, the CONARLS report *Carpe Diem* also reported that while stakeholders believed the different library sub-domains should retain their own channels of communication, a domain-wide approach had significant benefits at regional and national levels (Circle of Officers of National and Regional Library Systems (CONARLS), 2003). *Carpe Diem* also suggested that because local government reorganization has resulted in the creation of smaller public library authorities in some areas, regional cooperation was important to ensure users had access to appropriate resources and expertise and to capitalize upon the economies of scale that larger units generally enjoy. This was certainly true for one small unitary authority established under the local government reorganization of the 1990s although it had its difficulties, as one interviewee explained:

> We've put a lot of effort into the regional working and the regional bidding. We've got quite a bit of money through the [regional library system] programme for reader development and that's really the only way, apart from those big national projects, to bid for funding. We have to work cooperatively which is good because we obviously build relationships but at the same time, it's a huge resource problem for us because we don't have bundles of staff waiting around to go and do projects with people. (Anon)

Cooperation across the public library sector, in particular, seems to be very strong despite the difficulties arising from local government reorganization mentioned in Chapter 2. Kath Owen, for example, said:

> We are working much more closely together as a region than I can remember ever doing before. There's a very strong East Midlands Public Libraries training group…, we've got a regional reader development conference coming up, we did regional NOF work. (Kath Owen)

Some would like the cooperation between public library services to go even further although there is recognition that getting agreement from local councils would be difficult:

> I always said at local government reorganization that there was an opportunity actually being missed there to start making some regional library systems because if you could

> knock out a bit of the local politics, there's no reason why you couldn't have one IT system and one database; it's technically quite possible but there's lots of other things that get in the way of that. (Anon)

Ayub Khan was also in favour of regional library systems:

> I think I'm coming to the conclusion that we'd be better having regional library systems as opposed to really local ones so that you can create an impact or have economies of scale. (Ayub Khan)

Another participant was opposed to this idea:

> I think it would be too big and I think what you'd end up with is the lowest common denominator and when I think of this region, some of the [library services], I'm just not happy with that. I don't think you'd end with the same service that we have and [two neighbouring authorities] have; you'd end up with a lower level of service. (Anon)

One of the more successful examples of collaborative working across the library and information services domain was that of the West Midlands' Libraries Partnership which was highly successful on a regional level, receiving project grants from local, national and European funders. This network brought together the 14 public library services in the area and its 11 Higher Education Institutions. As well as providing strategic representation and advocacy, it also led development projects and linked with other cultural agencies in the West Midlands area including museums and archives. These relationships became more formalized in 2003 when the Libraries' Partnership merged with the West Midlands Regional Museums Council and the West Midlands Regional Archives Council to form a new organization called MLA West Midlands: the regional council for museums, libraries and archives.[3] On a slightly smaller scale, local agreements between different types of library and information services are becoming more common. In Wrexham, Alan Watkin explained the workings of GaLW (Gateway to Libraries in Wrexham), which included the public library services and local further and higher education institutions. Users registered at any of the cooperating libraries can use the services of the others. As well as extending user services, these cooperative arrangements can bring other benefits such as joint training and development. In fact, cooperative training seems to be the area where there has been the most action across the library sub-domains as one interview participant explained:

> We have struggled, I have to say, to find other areas that people will buy into. We've looked at various areas, like a book purchasing cooperative, but they've all just withered on the vine. Although everybody's said, 'Oh that's a good idea', they've not actually been willing to take it forward. (Anon)

She blamed the lack of progress primarily on problems related to the interoperability of systems.

Successful initiatives and activities across the library domain can enable public libraries to carve out a strong position within the emerging regional cultural and economic structures. Regional collaboration between different types of libraries is not always simple, however, and according to Wilip barriers remain including different funding channels, lack of commitment by the parent institution, a residual competition culture between the Further and Higher Education sub-domains, a lack of capacity to drive collaboration forward and incompatible systems (Ede, 2003). *Carpe Diem* also warned that attachment to sub-domain networks and communication channels can send 'fragmented, contradictory and unco-ordinated messages to policymakers'(Circle of Officers of National and Regional Library Systems (CONARLS), 2003, p. 28). Divisions within a domain can also inhibit partnerships outside it as *Renaissance in the Regions* reported in relation to museums (Resource, 2001a) although the establishment of regional museums, libraries and archives councils is encouraging ever closer cross-domain working.

Regional Co-operation Across the Cultural Industries

Within the cultural sector, Regional Cultural Consortiums and single regional agencies (museums, libraries and archives councils) like MLA West Midlands bring together a range of organizations and bodies concerned with the arts and culture and have had some success with securing funding from bodies such as the European Union, the New Opportunities Fund and the Research Support Libraries Programme. The aim of the single regional agency is to ensure that the interests of the libraries, museums and archives sector are represented in Regional Assemblies, Regional Development Agencies and Regional Cultural Consortiums and they can have a number of valuable outcomes including better links between organizations in the cultural sector which should encourage the sharing of information, a clearer strategic focus, the development of collaborative projects and the exploration of innovative methods of service delivery. Good examples of co-operative working across the domain were provided by the 'Get it Together' programme in 2002 through which museums, galleries, libraries and archives were invited to work together and put forward proposals for small grants for stimulating and inspirational projects. Under the programme, for example, Buxton Museum and Art Gallery worked with Derbyshire Libraries and Heritage/Literature Development on 'Lifelines', a multi-media arts project initiated by the County Literature Development Officer in partnership with Learning Through Arts, an arts group based in Winksworth, which explored and celebrated the lives and cultural backgrounds of Derbyshire residents. As the evaluation report notes of the 41 projects, 'Most of them were new collaborations between museums/galleries and libraries/archives and proved to be an interesting learning experience for organizers and participants alike' (Clive, 2003, p. 3). Many digitization projects also bring together resources from a range of cultural institutions. Noah (Norfolk Online Access to Heritage) is a good example of a cross-domain digitization project within one local authority which allows users to search across the collection records of archives, libraries and museums and 'opens the door to the combined on-line collections of Cultural Services at Norfolk County Council'.[4] On a wider regional scale, a local studies website 'Tomorrow's History' has been developed by archives, record offices, libraries, museums, archaeology services, universities and commercial organizations in North East England. The site is managed by the North East Museums Libraries and Archives Council and funded by the Heritage Lottery Fund.[5]

Despite these examples of successful collaborations across the cultural institutions of a region, Margaret Watson felt that the regional MLAs had experienced teething problems which had left some sceptical of their benefits. Increasingly, though, she thought that they were beginning to have an impact:

> There has been such a lot invested in making MLA work and I think it has taken a while and I think it's still a bit iffy around the country because the regional MLAs have been set up at different times and taken longer. But certainly I can say in the North East things are really beginning to happen. The first year I don't think we found the benefit at all, the first two years. But now, I really think we are beginning to see some joined-up thinking and some of the collaborations and some of the training are working really well. And people are beginning to think of the museums, libraries, art galleries. (Margaret Watson)

Alan Watkin agreed that co-operative working across the cultural sector had its benefits:

> We do get joint initiatives, colleagues from the different domains talking to each other to some extent. The biggest example I've got is I've taken the local studies library out of the library and it's gone into the archives which sits in the middle of the museum… What it's meant is our archive service is now more popular that the two well established ones in Flintshire and Denbighshire, we get more visitors. So there's an obvious synergy of bringing all the historical material together. (Alan Watkin)

Advocates of cross-domain regional cooperation suggest that libraries, museums and archives together will have a higher profile than any of the single cultural domains working alone and that by collaborating they are more likely to ensure that the potential contribution of the cultural sector to a range of regional policy objectives is properly represented. It is argued that, under-resourced and under-represented on an individual basis, by combining together libraries, museums and archives can have an impact that could confirm them as key players on the regional stage (Circle of Officers of National and Regional Library Systems (CONARLS), 2003). One participant felt that cooperation across the cultural sector had many potential benefits for the individual domains:

> I think public libraries have got a lot to learn from museums on learning. Public libraries and local authority museums in particular have enormous synergy. So perhaps public library services can learn from the way museums are interfacing with learners, the way that people use the museum experience as a way of learning… Museums have probably got a lot to learn from libraries on how to organize resources, particularly with the development of the electronic side. (Anon)

Some in the LIS domain are reportedly lukewarm abut cooperation with other cultural agencies, however, preferring to focus on collaboration between the different types of library services (Ede, 2003) and feeling that libraries should not be shoehorned into collaborating with museums and archives for the sake of it. This seemed to be the view of one participant who said:

> I think obviously there's a lot of commonality in museums and archives but I don't think it should be the over-riding consideration. (Anon)

A Welsh participant agreed that the different domains could not be forced to work together:

> You can't force a marriage. This is an arranged marriage, this is not one that the three domains came together and said, 'Well, yes, we've looked at this, this is what we want to do'. It is, in my view, a sensible thing to do as the three domains in Wales are far too small to have any identity on their own but they have to be in a context within which the three domains want to work together because, ultimately, we can't force them to do anything. (Anon)

A Scottish participant also felt that some of the agendas of the different sub-domains within the cultural sector did not sit easily together:

> I think there's a fallacy that puts libraries, museums and archives together because they don't easily site anywhere else and I think there's a real mistake in trying to put square pegs in round holes and say that library and museums are memory institutions. That's just nonsense... Now there's elements of overlap, I wouldn't disagree with that but stronger partnerships [for libraries] I think are support learning and literacy and that wouldn't necessarily happen through a museum or an archive. (Anon)

Another barrier to regional cooperation between the different cultural domains is that some of the individual bodies representing the various domains have a strong presence and guard their own territory jealously. This can mean that links between some regions' various cultural bodies are weak, hampering collaboration, a serious obstacle to accessing those funding streams which increasingly emphasize cross-domain working. The issue of 'people, personalities, egos and entrenched attitudes' was considered the biggest barrier to regional cooperation by participants in the research for the *Carpe Diem* report (Circle of Officers of National and Regional Library Systems (CONARLS), 2003, p. 78). *Renaissance in the Regions* painted a picture of fragmentation and competition within the museums domain alone and the capacity for in-fighting between the different domains must be even greater. One participant admitted there were some difficulties in forging partnerships and encouraging regional cooperation across cultural institutions and services. Talking about barriers to regional cooperation, he said:

> I think it's not that museums don't work in partnership but I don't think they're used to regional partnership... So I think that within public libraries and within museums there are different experiences; I think museums are behind public libraries in that sense. Where I think there's a common problem is that I think there's a lot of places where the public library service and the museums don't actually want to work together... I think there is still quite a bit of historical rivalry, particularly between the big local authority services. (Anon)

Wider Regional Co-operation

Finally, libraries are trying to make their mark in the wider regional arena through collaboration with a range of public, private and voluntary bodies and organizations. How successful public libraries (or, indeed, the whole LIS domain) have been in convincing other regional players of their potential to contribute to cross-cutting themes and how effectively public libraries engage in regional networks is debatable, however. With regard to lifelong learning, for example, in England the regional agenda is becoming increasingly important with the establishment of the Learning and Skills Councils (LSCs).[6] Public libraries need to ensure that they are fully engaged in these so that their contribution is not overlooked and so that they have a stake in their region's policies, strategies and, importantly, financial support for lifelong learning. The part that public libraries can play in lifelong learning is clear for those within the sub-domain and yet there is still a challenge for recognition outside it of the extent to which they are ideal agencies for promoting lifelong learning at grass roots level because of the links they have and because of their presence within communities. One participant explained the difficulty that public libraries often face in making their mark on the learning:

> I think we'd like to get more engaged with Learning and Skills Councils but it's not proving easy. For a start, they are sub regional and they're very driven by accredited learning; if you're looking at informal lifelong learning, it's not easy to get in. (Anon)

Advocacy at a strategic regional level of the public library role in relation to lifelong learning is still necessary, therefore, even though on an institutional basis there are many examples of good practice and innovative service delivery (see Chapter 9).

If libraries in some areas are still struggling to stake their claim for involvement with the lifelong learning agenda at a regional level, it is even more difficult for them to convince key stakeholders of the contribution they could make to other cross-cutting themes with which they have had less involvement in the past, such as economic regeneration. The Library Association Policy Advisory Group in its review of the impact of devolution and regionalism on the LIS domain suggested that, 'it would be difficult to argue that the LIS sector or profession is recognized as a key player or component in this area' (Library Association Policy Advisory Group, 2001, para. 4.3), although acknowledging that there had been library successes in the citizenship and modernizing government areas. Participants in the Wilip consultation exercise were also realistic about libraries' ability to play a leading role in key regional priorities, suggesting that the domain should focus on asserting their expertise and contribution to those areas which were likely to deliver greatest benefits, namely the Government's agenda on learning and skills, community development and e-government. Many library services have done this successfully as we will see in the chapters in Part 2.

There is work to be done, however, if the domain is to position itself effectively to regional and sub-regional bodies like LSCs and to convey and develop the contribution of public libraries to society with the aim of achieving higher investment. More effective advocacy at both regional and national levels is considered part of the answer and to achieve this local, regional and national bodies and organizations need hard evidence on which to base their claims for public library involvement in cross cutting policy objectives. Many of the participants in the consultation for the Wilip report stressed that evidence of the impact of public libraries was needed along with better data collection and analysis methods although it has been stated the amount of data gathered on public libraries through surveys and monitoring systems is greater than for any other type of library (Ede, 2002). Perhaps the exploitation of the information gathered needs to be considered more carefully so that it illustrates value, impact and the quality of service. There is also a view that the data collected needs to more effectively support current policy initiatives such as lifelong learning and social exclusion. In response to demands for evidence, impact and effectiveness, a number of systems of accountability have been introduced since 1997 that have collected measures of performance and are being used increasingly to demonstrate the value of public library services.

Planning and Accountability

The impact of the culture of evidence-based management has been as far-reaching in the public library world as it has been in other public services. Part of the New Labour Government's 'audit culture', systems such as the Annual Library Plans and Public Library Standards were designed to make services more accountable in their use of public funds and improve the quality of services provided to local people. Performance is now defined in terms of outcomes within the context of clearly specified standards and a transparent reporting and regulatory framework. The approach is a target-driven one, exemplified by the development of the Public Library Service Standards, and the achievement of targets is expressed as performance indicators with the focus on quality outcomes and improvements in terms of efficiency and effectiveness (Rouse, 2001). Explicit national standards are an important feature of the performance management framework for public services, therefore, and comparing and sharing good practice is also considered vital. For public libraries in England, the Government has introduced a variety of planning and reporting mechanisms, many of which have run for a few years before being abandoned or replaced by a different system. The 2005 Select Committee report on public libraries criticized 'the chopping and changing' (Culture, Media and Sport Committee, 2005, p. 10) that has taken place in the regulatory framework for public libraries including changes to planning and reporting processes.

The many changes to the processes have undoubtedly been frustrating for the managers and staff of public library services but interview participants were generally supportive of the introduction of formal planning and accountability measures, often explaining that they were 'an extremely useful political weapon' (Alan Watkin) within the local authority. Bob McKee agreed saying:

> I think the requirement on local authorities to produce Annual Library Plans and to at least assess their achievements against the standards, those two things taken together, done in the political domain, actually has focused attention politically at local level on the resourcing of library services and there's genuine evidence that it's resulted in increased investment in library services. (Bob McKee)

A minority of participants diverged from the overall positive view of the plans and standards that have been introduced since 1997, one saying:

> If you're asking me the extent to which all these central initiatives have impacted, certainly as far as I'm concerned not very greatly other than it's irritating and time consuming for staff having to produce plans and so on. (Cllr Graham Tope)

Another participant, while generally supportive of national plans and standards, felt that local needs should be given more prominence:

> We need national standards to perhaps illustrate what should be a minimum requirements or level of service but it's really the local impact that is more important to the user coming in so it's how we get the balance between the two but I think getting that balance right is what the modern public library service is all about. (Anon)

In general, however, participants were in favour of nationally agreed planning mechanisms and standards although specific criticisms of the processes and their operation were frequently aired.

Plans and Position Statements

Introduced by the New Labour Government in 1998 (although first suggested by the last Conservative administration in *Reading the Future* (Department of National Heritage, 1995)) and dispensed with in 2002, the Annual Library Plans (ALPs) had the aim of raising standards in public libraries by outlining the aims and objectives of every public library authority in England and detailed its performance against a range of local and national indicators.[7] Each authority was given a rating of its plan from 3 ('good') to 0 ('inadequate – resubmit') with 2 meaning 'satisfactory' and 1 'poor'. Although there was initially a view that ALPs may not be successful because they were imposed in a top-down manner on public library services and, therefore, lacked local ownership, the evidence suggests that, for many, they proved to be an effective planning and advocacy tool. Library managers generally welcomed the structured and rigorous approach to reviewing their services and developing action plans for the future. All authorities worked to a common framework that gave a clear overview of how library services were contributing to national as well as local objectives.

The ALP guidelines were initially criticized for being too prescriptive and not giving scope for involving stakeholders but alongside the public library standards it has been suggested that the ALPs had the effect of raising the profile and enhancing the standing of the public library service within the local authority. The contribution of public libraries to the council's cross-cutting objectives were identified in the ALP, for example, leading to more effective partnership working within the authority. Moreover, with a clearly documented strategic framework, supported by hard data in the form of performance indicators measured against other similar local authorities and a clear statement of the strengths and weaknesses of the service, the Annual Library Plan was frequently a powerful weapon in the battle for resources. Being able to justify requests for funding by referring to the plan and the service's strategic objectives often paid dividends in a competitive bidding culture.

After an initially uncertain reception, then, the ALP system was generally appreciated as a way of sharing good practice, identifying the contribution of libraries to partnership working across the local authority and focusing services on meeting the needs of users. Their administration was not without difficulties, though, many of which related to issues surrounding performance management systems in local government generally. For a start, the relationship between ALPs and the other performance management systems including Best Value was not straightforward. The different processes were often administered by different government departments with the Office of the Deputy Prime Minister (ODPM) overseeing Best Value, for example, and the DCMS assessing the ALPs. This complexity and pace of change within the performance management framework caused problems and there was a more general problem of initiative fatigue and information overload on behalf of both library services and their users. Resource suggested that what it called 'this Babel of measures and activity' (Resource, 2001b, p. 2) did not produce significant improvements in services nor provide a clear picture of where main challenges facing public libraries lay. Furthermore, there was (and still is) concern at the resources required to comply with the requirements for performance management data, especially in smaller authorities, with a lack of co-ordination between different bodies and a resulting duplication of evidence. It was also suggested that ALPs encouraged sectoral thinking and constrained joint planning with other local authority partners. In common with performance management systems in other public services, indicators which focus on the success or efficiency of individual services are likely to encourage managers to focus on improving the performance of that specific service, rather than overall authority performance, and discourage more risky, innovative approaches to service delivery. Finally, there was initially concern that the rating of library plans was based more on the quality of the plan than on the quality of the library service provided.

In 2002 partly in response to some of these criticisms and following the publication of *Framework for the Future*, ALPs in England were replaced with Public Library Position Statements (PLPS). The PLPS represented a change in focus to the ALPs with the former being a much more streamlined, succinct document aimed principally at the DCMS; the audience for the ALPS was conceived as being much wider. The ALPs, for example, had to be approved by the local council's executive body thus potentially raising the profile of the library service within the local authority. The PLPS, on the other hand, was essentially an internal planning document. Although it involved less work, therefore, the potential impact of the PLPS was less than that of the ALP. The aim was for a lighter touch, focusing specifically on those library authorities considered to be failing their communities in some aspect of service. The PLPS was also intended to address how the individual library service was responding to the *Framework for the Future* vision and how it was moving towards compliance with any of the public library standards it had not met. In 2004, the PLPS system was also discontinued, with 87 per cent of authorities having been assessed as either 'excellent' or 'good' against the *Framework for the Future* agenda. As the 2005 Select Committee report notes, however, the degree of engagement with *Framework for the Future* is not necessarily a measure of the quality of services and it disputes whether it is 'job done' as the DCMS abandonment of the plans and position statements suggests. In fact, the Audit Commission judges 50 per cent of library services to be 'unsatisfactory' (Culture, Media and Sport Committee, 2005, p. 10).

The 2005 Select Committee on public libraries questioned the wisdom of abandoning the Annual Library Plan process which they felt had been 'an improving product' (Culture, Media and Sport Committee, 2005, p. 9) and some interview respondents similarly regretted the demise of the reporting system and was what perceived as a watering down of the regulatory framework. One participant said of the Annual Library Plans:

> They were valued by the sector themselves as an advocacy tool that they could wave and say, 'We've done this, we need this, here's a document that proves it'. So I think it's certainly a loss at local level but [library services] are still coming up with these planning documents which I suppose they'll no longer be able to say will be seen by DCMS; maybe that's the loss in their eyes. (Anon)

The same participant also commented that the benefit of the Annual Library Plan process continued to be experienced:

> While [Annual Library Plans] are a loss, I think we feel they have at least introduced the culture of planning into library services to a much greater degree and that will carry on so it's not a complete loss. (Anon)

Others were not sorry to see Annual Library Plans disappear, however, as one participant explained:

> We hated doing Annual Library Plans; a complete waste of time and effort and the more they went on, the more angry we got about it because they were expanding into documents of 100, 120 pages and we were thinking, 'This is absolute nonsense. Why are we spending all this time writing about what we're going to do?' (Anon)

The situation with regard to planning and planning documents in the other three home countries of the UK varies. Although, as in England, library managers produce annual reports for their own local authorities or Education Boards in

Northern Ireland, they are not required to report to ministers. In Wales, although there is no requirement to submit a plan to the Welsh Assembly, services do have to report on their achievements as one participant explained:

> What we have are reports against where the library service feels it's actually made progress against the standards. As far as I'm aware, there are no plans to bring in library plans in Wales. If you look at the size of the authorities, really I would rather they were focused on delivering services than producing reports. The standards are important and it's important that they can profile themselves against achieving the standards because I think they benefit from that but I really don't want to take their time away [by] just writing reports about services. (Anon)

Scottish public libraries and those in Northern Ireland have never had to submit plans to the central department responsible for their administration at a national level although a couple of Scottish participants regretted this, as one commented:

> I think if we were to introduce Annual Library Plans where useful comparisons could be made with other authorities then I would really be up for that, I think it could make a difference across the country. (Anon)

Another Scottish participant also expressed the view that Annual Library Plans would be welcome and helpful for providing more drive and focus to services. It is unlikely that they will be introduced, however, or reintroduced into England with the DCMS seeking a lighter regulatory touch and hoping to drive improvement through the Public Library Service Standards instead.

Public Library Standards

The downplaying of the contribution of public libraries in the English CPA system, as outlined in Chapter 2, was felt all the more acutely, given the recognition of the development in public libraries and their remit which was apparent in the foreword to the first public library standards for England introduced in 2001 where libraries were described by Chris Smith (then Secretary of State for Culture Media and Sport) as 'a vital element in the public services of this country' (Department for Culture, Media and Sport, 2001, p. 3). The original standards, drawn up by the Department for Culture, Media and Sport (DCMS) in collaboration with the then Library Association and the Local Government Association, were quite a bold step, defining just what library users could expect and what kinds of services local authorities must provide to comply with the 1964 Act. Before the introduction of the standards, library authorities could largely determine the quality of service provided to users as long as it was judged to be 'a comprehensive and efficient service'. In fact, even following the publication of the standards, local authorities still established their own levels of service because the standards were not statutory, rather, they were designed to provide a clear and common definition of what was expected of 'a comprehensive and efficient service'. The standards were linked to Annual Library Plans and then to the Public Library Position Statements that local authorities submitted to the Department for Culture, Media and Sport.

The profession broadly welcomed the standards in principle although some concerns about individual standards were raised and, like the Best Value indicators, there was criticism that inputs and outputs, rather than outcomes and long term benefits, were the focus.

Nevertheless, many interview participants welcomed the standards as a positive move. Chris Smith, who was the first Secretary of State for Culture, Media and Sport, felt that, alongside the People's Network, the introduction of the standards had been the greatest achievement of the New Labour Government for public libraries. He explained:

> We were always hidebound by the problem that there was a general statutory duty on local authorities to run a comprehensive and efficient service but nowhere was it defined and it would have been pretty difficult for anyone to take a local authority to court and argue that they were not fulfilling their statutory duty. So I was very keen to try and give that some teeth and get an agreement in place about the standards which broadly could be regarded as representing comprehensive and efficient. (Chris Smith, MP)

As well as providing clarity, interview participants also commended the standards for delivering extra resources as Martin Molloy explained:

> The public library standards, the impact of those, has been that there has been real investment in libraries over the last few years and there has been a real development. (Martin Molloy)

Bill Macnaught agreed, saying:

> There is actually a very strong body of evidence to demonstrate that these standards have had a positive effect in public libraries up and down the county… Certainly in some authorities it's had a transformational effect in terms of the resource going into public libraries so in that respect it's a jolly good thing. (Bill Macnaught)

Other participants were slightly more sceptical of some aspects of the standards but still felt they could be used for the benefit of the public library service:

> I've no great confidence that public library standards prove anything other than you can count a row of beans but the very fact they're there does mean it's possible to go to Cabinet to budget review or to Council and say 'We need to spend X on buying books. We need so much floor space' etc. So they have their uses. (Cllr Bob Janes)

In 2004, the original 26 standards were reduced to a list of ten and renamed the Public Library Service.[8] Revised to reflect *Framework for the Future* and the CPA process (Library and Information Update, 2004), some of the original standards were reportedly dropped because they had been achieved (ICT connectivity, for example), others because finding an appropriate target or method of measurement proved too difficult (number of qualified staff or quality of stock, for instance) and others because library authorities were unable to reach the target set (physical visits and opening hours). Whatever the reasons, some in the public library community are worried at what they perceive as a weakening of the standards. John Pateman was one of those disappointed with this development:

> I got a document from the Society of Chief Librarians telling me that the Public Library Standards are being streamlined, which is a euphemism for being reduced, at a time when we need more not less standards. And the rationale for this is to lessen the administrative burden on local authorities. Well what a lousy reason for not having library standards. (John Pateman)

Others were in favour of the reduction, however:

> There are fewer of them [standards] which has got to be welcomed. I'm still not absolutely sure that they are the ones that are measuring an effective public library service, whatever that may be, but at least we haven't got to worry about the 30-odd that we've got at the moment. (Anon)

The ten standards with which library authorities must aim to comply are currently:

1. the proportion of households living with a specified distance of a static library;
2. aggregate scheduled opening hours;
3. the percentage of static libraries providing access to electronic information resources connected to the internet;
4. the number of electronic workstations with access to the internet and the library's catalogue;
5. dealing with requests for books;
6. number of library visits;
7. adults' satisfaction rate;
8. children's satisfaction rates;
9. number of books and other items acquired annually; and
10. time taken to replenish the lending stock.

English local authorities must report on their progress against these standards through Cipfa (the Chartered Institute for Public Finance Accounting). The new standards have been criticized for representing 'rather limited ambitions' (Culture, Media and Sport Committee, 2005, p. 3). Although the DCMS insists that the standards are a 'work in progress', many in the public library community are dismayed that there is no mention of number of loans, the provision of material for disabled people, free access to the Internet and services to combat social exclusion.

As the 2005 Select Committee report notes, though, it is irrelevant what is on the list of standards if local authorities do not take them seriously (Culture, Media and Sport Committee, 2005). And local authorities will not pay them much regard if the Government does not. Little if any action is taken against authorities performing poorly against the library standards. As John Pateman commented:

> To be quite frank, some Chief Librarians and councils would laugh at the standards because they will say, 'We don't meet them; so what? What is going to happen? Is

> DCMS going to come down? We are so scared of DCMS'. DCMS don't even fund the library services so what's the point? (John Pateman)

Although in theory the 'scores' resulting from a library service's performance against the standards are fed into the local authority's CPA evaluation, in practice it seems that the weighting given to the library standards score is insignificant. The DCMS similarly 'appears not to react to them at all' (Culture, Media and Sport Committee, 2005, p. 26). Critical voices have, therefore, questioned the purpose of the standards. If they are not compulsory and backed by inspection, what is their point? The standards are meant to 'encourage improvement in the performance and penetration of library services' (Department for Culture, Media and Sport, 2004, p. 2) but failure to meet them does not incur any penalties or sanctions. Unless they are supported by statutory powers there will be little urgency to try to comply.

The 2005 Select Committee report warns that 'performance information is weak at present' recommending the collection of more useful data and more appropriate performance measures (Culture, Media and Sport Committee, 2005, p. 27). One interview participant insisted though that despite fears about the watering down of the standards system and the loss of the planning regime, library services were still subject to rigorous evaluation and review:

> It's not that libraries are left without any sort of monitoring because the monitoring takes place through the new Comprehensive Performance Assessment system. They're part of that bigger system and if they're not doing stuff properly at local level, like they still don't have plans, they're going to get caught out by the Audit Commission who are policing the whole thing. To put it in a crude way, one of the first things that an inspector is going to say if he arrives in a library authority is 'Give me your planning documents'. (Anon)

The four home countries have different approaches to library standards. In Wales, standards similar to those in England were also introduced in 2001. Analysis of library authorities' performance against the standards and their plans for meeting those on which they fall short are required in reports as described above. Differences in the standards and in the monitoring arrangements in England and Wales reflect the recognition that library services must focus on local needs, priorities and circumstances. As well as standards relating to provision of material in the Welsh language, the rural nature of much of Wales is also acknowledged in the standard for accessibility which matches that of English County Councils, that is, 85 per cent of the population should live within two miles of a static library point. The Welsh standards also put more emphasis on the role of ICT, noting that all static library service points should have *free* Internet access in comparison with the English Standards which just state that each is expected to provide access without mention of charges. One Welsh participant explained the purpose and perceived value of the standards in Wales:

> The standards in Wales are operated separately. They are not predicated on the same thing as in England where it's much more light touch. One of the reasons in Wales that

> they are more prescriptive is to address this issue of moving libraries forward. We haven't evaluated them yet, they've only been going two years, but the anecdotal evidence I'm getting from librarians is that they have been very useful and successful in levering more money from local authorities because even though they're not statutory, the fact that they exist and the fact that the Assembly is monitoring the progress of local authorities has been very helpful. (Anon)

In Scotland, the Convention of Scottish Local Authorities (COSLA) published recommended standards in 1986 which were updated in 1995 (COSLA, 1995). As stated in Chapter 1, the Scottish Executive has asked SLIC to review the planning and regulatory framework. Currently, the COSLA standards are only recommendations of an advisory status, however, and there is no central reporting processes although individual library authorities in Scotland make reference to them when presenting reports to local council meetings. The lack of teeth of the Scottish standards is illustrated by the fact that councils consistently fail to meet some of them (Library and Information Update, 2004) and yet no sanctions are imposed, highlighting the fears of many in England that standards without rigorous measures and penalties for non-compliance are taken for granted. Alan Hasson felt that the standards nevertheless have their uses:

> The biggest influence I think of the COSLA standards is really two-fold and that is it's a reasonably concise document you can give to politicians and, secondly, it's formed the basis for the performance indicators that Audit Scotland ask us to do and some of them are very useful. (Alan Hasson)

He conceded, though, that they lacked force and this gave authorities the excuse to limit the resources provided to public libraries:

> In all the authorities I've worked in, both before and after devolution, the council has approved the COSLA standards and said that they will go towards them but there's always been a lovely wee phrase, 'as and when resources permit' which, as I'm sure everybody else has said to you, is when the moon is green. (Alan Hasson)

Other Scottish participants agreed that the COSLA standards were 'almost a wish list' (Anon) and that they had 'very little impact on council policy; they don't drive resources or anything like that' (Anon). One participant felt, though, that the standard of public library services would have suffered without them:

> While library services are sometimes seen as a Cinderella service and sometimes treated as a Cinderella service, if we hadn't had those broadly agreed standards…, there's no doubt we would have been worse off here. We wouldn't have been able to do the things we've done, for example with the People's Network on a national basis if we'd not had those standards in place. (Anon)

She also explained the approach being taken to the development of the standards for the Scottish Executive:

We're trying to develop the standards and look at the whole areas of readership and ICT and learning and digitization and embed them in the standards so we can say there should be, for instance, a core set of electronic resources for every citizen in Scotland… and then how you measure that… We'll try to do them as neutrally as possible so we're not tying ourselves to something that, if the cultural landscape changes this time next year, that those things are not deliverable. (Anon)

The development process, she explained, was also predicated on an outcomes-based self-evaluation model:

…so that people can actually see as they're developing their own services if they're meeting their agreed targets before you put in some kind of system of peer review attached to it. (Anon)

In Northern Ireland there are currently no agreed standards for public libraries. The Library and Information Services Council (NI) recently produced draft Standards for Public Libraries in Northern Ireland, based on the standards that existed for England and Wales, and has presented them to the Department of Culture, Arts and Leisure (DCAL) for consideration. At the time of writing, they are still in draft and have not yet been adopted by DCAL and will probably be adjusted in the light of the revision to the standards in England. Again, the issue of sanctions for non-compliance was not resolved and was causing particular problems in Northern Ireland, although it has resonances for the English standards too, as one participant explained:

The very big sticking point here of course [is that] normally the people imposing, setting the standards are not the same people who have to fund the provision which is why DCAL a) can't be seen to be promoting standards which are lower than elsewhere but b) they know they can't possibly afford to implement the draft standards. Whereas elsewhere it could be used as a stick to beat someone else, here they've only got themselves to beat. (Anon)

Although library managers in England generally considered the standards to be an important and positive development, the emphasis on counting the countable, rather than trying to measure value, has led to concern that pressure to meet concrete targets for crude measures such as issue or visitor figures could have an adverse impact on other less easily measured but perhaps more socially rewarding services such as services to adult learners or people with disabilities. John Dolan certainly felt that the standards were measuring the wrong things:

[The standards] are looking at measuring the number of hits where we ought to be looking at standards of provision. [The standards are] standards of provision rather than standards of take up. The service has failed because not many people use it as opposed to the service has failed because they haven't provided the right kind of service. And I think that depends where you want to put the onus and if the onus is being put on avoiding increasing expenditure then the standard will reflect that by saying here's a standard about how many people use it, how many visits, how many site hits or whatever. (John Dolan)

Sue Wilkinson agreed that the standards were 'still being driven by outputs and processes and not by outcomes' (Sue Wilkinson). Another participant questioned the use of the term 'standards' and suggested that the various planning, policy and accountability measures for public libraries did not combine well:

> They are not standards, they are targets. What I would prefer to see would be standards or targets underpinning the strands of policy priority. Because now I think we have got a weird animal. We have got *Framework for the Future* which has got activity-based priorities but doesn't suggest any measures. We have got a bundle of PIs [performance indicators] based on the national standards targets which are going to be tweaked… I don't think the strands tie up. (Anon)

The standards have also been criticized for not taking the different nature of library services into account sufficiently. The differences in service needs and delivery issues between, for example, a large rural county council and an inner-city London borough can be substantial but one set of standards was designed to suit all although some standards do have varying targets depending on the type of authority.

Despite the fanfare and goodwill with which the English standards were introduced, their role was downplayed in *Framework for the Future*. Many regard this as a retrogressive move because they have forced local councillors to pay attention to whether their public library service is providing a 'comprehensive and efficient' service as defined by the DCMS. The lack of clarity about the future role of the public library standards is causing disquiet as there is evidence, as suggested above, that their implementation has resulted in extra resources being made available to public library services to help services comply. It is feared that a downgrading of the importance of the standards, alongside the abandonment of Annual Library Plans, will allow councils to reduce their commitment to public libraries and diminish their profile. In Wales, the rigorous application of the standards developed there is considered to have protected resources and the light touch now adopted in England is seen as a threat (Ede, 2003). One study participant said:

> The standards have definitely increased our profile within the authority and we're not terribly happy about some of the moves that are being mooted for the new standards… We feel that's really going to push them down the political landscape and they're just going to be something that people brush aside. (Anon)

Alongside the Public Library Service Standards, MLA has launched a number of other initiatives for English public libraries related to impact and accountability. Designed to complement the standards, a new set of impact measures has been developed which will attempt to demonstrate just how public libraries contribute to five of the seven shared priorities agreed between national and local government: raising standards across schools; improving the quality of life for children, young, people, families at risk and older people; promoting healthier communities; creating safer and stronger communities; promoting the economic vitality of localities. These measures are intended to demonstrate the impact that public libraries have on people and communities and measure library activity in six core areas considered to contribute to the five shared priorities identified.[9] This is no easy task as one participant suggested:

> [We're] trying to come up with some impact measures which actually go to the heart of what libraries actually contribute to local communities. Assessing the impact of libraries is a bar of soap we've been trying to grasp for, I suppose, 15 years. Well now we're engaging with that and trying to turn the concept into something meaningful. (Anon)

The publication of the MLA impact measures occurred after the interviews for this book took place but many interview participants indicated that they would be well received and welcomed a more qualitative approach to the measurement of the impact of public library services:

> If you look at all the people who've achieved anything, they all have a story to tell about how the public library helped them and brought them on and that ought to be alerting the nation to the fact that here is an institution that is important. So I would like a qualitative assessment of libraries, I've argued that with library standards for a long time, rather than just a quantitative measuring up. (Martin Molloy)

Establishing methods of measuring impact was urgent, according to Andrea Barker:

> What I fear at the moment is that there isn't enough about the impact of what we do. There's some great stories and great case stories… but we need to know how to measure. (Andrea Barker)

According to one participant, libraries had a long way to go towards collecting the kind of data that would help them prove their impact on the local community:

> What libraries have not been very good at, because they've not recorded it, is the outcome of what they do. If somebody comes in and reads their way through the library, we don't know they've done that, well we do because the system would tell us, but we don't query it and we don't know what they got out of it. And until we start collecting that sort of data, which to me is very intrusive, we're not going to know. Like we don't know the racial make up of our borrowers, our registered borrowers; you don't need that to issue a book to them so why collect it? We never have collected that, we've only recently managed to get dates of birth. (Anon)

Jan Holden made some similar points and was also worried about the intrusive nature of some of the data that might need to be collected to assess impact:

> I think that's one of the problems with libraries; you can't actually quantify what you've done. You can quantify how many people have come through the door, you can quantify how many books you've got and how many people have borrowed books and how many people have logged on to a computer but you can't actually say, 'This person came here, they did this and they progressed to that'. And when you're talking with colleagues in Education, it is all about tracking and monitoring and progression. In a library we don't

> have that and I think that's a good thing because it means there's no pressure on people, there's no pressure on them to prove they've done X, Y, Z. (Jan Holden)

John Pateman was worried, though, that the impact measures developed would be quite weak:

> We are promised new impact measures which will be more locally focused and will aim to highlight the contribution that libraries make to wider corporate agendas which is promising but is it going to be consulted on? And you can guess who they are going to ask; the safe, risk free Chief Librarians who have got their heads in the sand. I think what will happen is whatever starts off as quite interesting will be diluted and made safe. And they're not going to be introduced until 2005 and 2006 so there is a gap. (John Pateman)

In addition to the impact measures, a peer review process has been developed. The Improvement and Development Agency (I&DeA), a local government body, is trying to identify the factors that contribute to successful public services. A self analysis diagnostic tool has been developed for public libraries which will be used in peer reviews undertaken by accredited senior personnel (chief librarians, chief executives and other senior managers) from other library authorities who will then produce a 'challenging' assessment, leading to a six month improvement plan for the service under review (Stevens and Wilkie, 2004). The improvement programme will be focused on those services considered to be performing poorly and it is hoped that it will facilitate the spread of best practice and continuous improvement. A report on the pilot and actual reviews undertaken to date report that the process needs to be refined but that there have been some positive outcomes including a raised profile for the library service within the local authority and increased interest from councillors and council staff (I&DeA and MLA, 2005).

One issue that has provoked considerable debate within the public library world is that the introduction of the schemes designed to raise standards have not been accompanied by extra core funding. Rather, the improved levels of service and innovative delivery mechanisms are to be funded through efficiency savings with any additional funding coming from bids to a range of external bodies and organizations. For many, this is insufficient for a service suffering from years, if not decades, of underinvestment.

Public Library Funding

New Labour's interest in public libraries has resulted in a higher profile for a service that in the past has been perceived as 'a good thing' but not as particularly dynamic or at the heart of local authority strategy. Accompanying this increased visibility has been a growing expectation that public library services will expand into new areas and attract new audiences. They are now expected to contribute positively to the social policy agenda in areas like lifelong learning, social exclusion and citizenship and develop innovative digital services to assist the progress of the information society. Stagnant budgets, however, mean that public libraries must resource any expansion primarily from additional external sources of funding and although *Framework for the Future* outlines an impressive role for public libraries at the heart of local authority thinking and policy, those setting the long-term strategy for public libraries do not hold the purse strings, as indicated in Chapter 2. Bob McKee felt that this was a serious problem that needed to be addressed. Talking about what, in the past, he has called the 'dysfunctional division' between the DCMS and the ODPM, he said:

> Well it is dysfunctional. The interesting quote is from Tessa Blackstone who recently called it 'an uncomfortable split'. She would never talk about it when she was Minister... She's no longer the Minister but she still has a responsibility for speaking on cultural matters in the Lords and she spoke in a House of Lords debate a few weeks ago and she said, 'There is an uncomfortable split'; that was her phrase. And what she's referring to is that DCMS have the responsibility for superintending the public library service but the funding structures run through the Office of the Deputy Prime Minister [ODPM] because they're funded through the Standard Spending Assessment, the local government settlement. There is no direct passporting of money for libraries, there is no direct link between DCMS and libraries in the way, for example, there is a funding link between DfES and schools and I think there's a problem there. If you look at other statutory services like schools, Charles Clarke [then Education Secretary] has direct leverage; Andrew McIntosh, the present Libraries Minister, has no direct leverage. So whatever he wants to do to try and improve public library services, there's no lever he can pull that has an immediate impact on local authorities, he can only really recommend but, ultimately, the decisions lie with local authorities. So it's actually a three way split between DCMS on the one hand, ODPM on the other, local authorities on the other and you could almost throw DfES in as well because of the incredibly close links between libraries and learning. (Bob McKee)

Lord Tope agreed that the division of responsibilities made funding decisions more problematic:

> DCMS would encourage us to do all sorts of things but, actually, it isn't a funding department, it's part of the local government settlement. It's fine but... we didn't meet the national standard a few years back now on opening hours, not quite. At the time, it would have cost us another £200,000 a year and I think we all felt that if we had £200,000 extra to invest in the library service it wouldn't be for opening for another hour when we didn't really need to... The DCMS might be encouraging this but DoE [Department of the Environment – now ODPM] as it then was wasn't allowing us the money to do it. (Cllr Graham Tope)

Goodwill and warm words at both national and local levels have not been translated consistently into bigger budgets, therefore, although, as we saw above, some heads of service asserted in interview that increased funding has been forthcoming as a result of the public library standards and other accountability measures introduced in England. Public libraries in some part of the UK appear to be faring better than others, however. As mentioned in Chapter 1, the situation in Northern Ireland is particularly dismal at the moment with library closures a real possibility. One participant from Northern Ireland explained:

> The funding situation that we're facing at the moment is dire and we've no feeling that anybody in DCAL but more critically in DFP [Department of Finance and Personnel], which is our equivalent of the Exchequer, has any appreciation of the contribution libraries can make or the hole that they would leave if they weren't there. There's no understanding of anything other than the bottom line, there's no appreciation of qualitative measurement. (Anon)

In England, the 2005 Select Committee report stated that overall spending on the public library service had increased but suggested that this had not had the impact it might have had because of a lack of efficiency in many library services. The report recommended a substantial shift of resources to frontline services (Culture, Media and Sport Committee, 2005), something also emphasized by Tim Coates (2004) who insists that the materials budget, opening hours and refurbishment budgets should be all be increased and can be achieved without increasing public library budgets but through savings made in reducing the number of staff involved in management and in streamlining acquisition processes. John Pateman agreed with Tim Coates' analysis when talking about delivering an inclusive library service:

> Fundamentally it doesn't need money. Tim Coates quite rightly said, 'We have got enough money at the moment but we are not spending it properly.' I fully agree with that; it doesn't need money it needs political and professional will and we are lacking both. (John Pateman)

Other respondents felt, though, that Coates' calculations just did not add up as one head of service explained:

> Although I agree with some of his analysis, half his solutions are just really off the top of his head. We have done the calculations. I don't know what he counts as the 'over paid top-heavy management' but we only have ten posts, in one of the biggest library services in the country, paid at Principal Officer and above. Of those, five have direct operational management responsibility for service delivery and two have responsibility for support service delivery. So that only leaves three of us who are wholly strategic and I don't think that is bad for a business that turns over 12.5 million and employs 600 people. (Anon)

The PKF (2005) study of public library procurement agreed with Coates that processes could be streamlined but found no evidence of over-staffing in management as he suggested. It also noted, though, that staff who were not involved in customer services roles but rather in back-office processes were mainly concerned with book procurement and if their recommendations made about streamlining processes were followed though, these staff members could be released to customer facing roles. The report also questioned whether higher spending always made for a better or more effective library service. The study found a huge variation in the amount that the library services in its sample spent per active borrower per annum, ranging from £66 to £147. It also noted, though, that the libraries were broadly comparable in terms of customer satisfaction, suggesting that high spending per customer does not necessarily translate into a high customer satisfaction score. It was concluded that there was 'no proven correlation between spend and effectiveness' (p. 32).

Public libraries receive funding from a variety of sources, the most important of which by far is the local authority. Overall, for 2003–04 local authorities will spend £69.5 billion on local public services and local taxation based on property values, the 'council tax', will provide a proportion of funding for local services but less than is commonly supposed. In fact, the vast majority of local government funding (52 per cent) comes directly from central government in the form of the Revenue Support Grant and other contributions in recognition of the fact that local taxation cannot support all the services required, especially in less affluent areas where the need is greatest but revenue from council tax is smallest. The council tax makes up 26 per cent of council revenue and non-domestic rates (business rates) 19 per cent (Local Government Association, 2004). The ODPM distributes funding to local authorities through a mechanism known as the Standard Spending Assessment (SSA). This is the Government's assessment of how much each local authority needs to run its services. The ODPM then allocates a block, or unhypothecated, grant to local authorities (the 'local government settlement') without stating how much should be spent on services such as the public library service. Within individual authorities, the largest proportion of the budget is spent on education services which usually take around 42 per cent of budget, then social services which take around 19 per cent (Local Government Association, 2004). That does not leave very much for everything else the local authority has to provide. This can prove particularly difficult when the budgetary situation of the local authority is tight as one head of service explained:

> There has been a change of administration and we now have a Conservative council whereas previously it was a Labour/Lib Dem joint administration. The Conservative administration has had a very difficult time since their election in May 2002 in that the whole financial structure of the council has been under enormous pressure. For the past two years, the council has received a very poor settlement from the Government. That has meant that we have been in severe crisis, in terms of being able to passport sufficient money to education and be able to support community and social care services. Even though libraries support the key priorities of the council, we are not a key priority ourselves. (Anon)

The same head of service added later that inward investment was a real challenge for the library service, commenting:

> The council is under severe financial pressure and appeals to government over funding don't seem to be having any effect. Education and community services are the key drivers and money requirements. It will be a challenge for me to retain over the next few years the budget I've got now, because of a constant pressure to achieve savings together with the challenge of building capacity to continue to deliver and develop the service. Capital funding is severely limited so whatever we try and bid for, there is no guarantee that we will receive an allocation. (Anon)

The public library service is therefore in competition for resources with a range of other essential local services and generally commands just one to two per cent of the local authority budget. This low figure has often prompted commentators and those working in the public library service to call it the 'Cinderella service' of local authorities and some have even demanded that library funding be ring-fenced by central government which would ensure that this statutory service has the resources at its disposal to meet its responsibilities under the 1964 Act. As the 2005 Select Committee report notes, though, this approach would be against government policy now seeking to maintain 'a lighter touch' in relation to libraries (Culture, Media and Sport Committee, 2005). The Secretary of State for the DCMS maintains that it is the responsibility of each local authority to allocate funds as it sees fit although this lack of a steer from Whitehall can be frustrating for Chief Librarians seeking to lobby local councillors for increased resources for public libraries. In fact, few interview participants were in favour of ring-fencing either and Bob McKee felt that it would become increasingly difficult anyway as local authorities focused on, and were increasingly organized along the lines of priorities which cut across different directorates rather than functional departments. He felt that a revision of the performance assessment regime in local government was the key to obtaining more resources for public libraries:

> If you follow my analysis about thematic local government, it's very difficult to ring-fence money to individual service departments… It's not about saying let's ring-fence the money for libraries, it's about saying let's get the CPA structure right so that focuses attention on libraries and let's get the arguments right about what libraries contribute to those big themes and let's take it from there. I think ring-fencing is a bit like saying you must put the words 'Chartered Librarian' in the essential column [of a job description]; it's old-fashioned, defensive, monopolistic and we're not in that game any more, we're in the game of winning the argument, proving value, evidencing our value. (Bob McKee)

Others have similarly suggested that instead of putting their energies into whining about a lack of resources, public librarians should focus on revitalizing their services, making them indispensable to local and national priorities thereby attracting more adequate funding (Leadbeater, 2003). Lord Graham Tope was also not in favour of ring-fencing money for public libraries or any local government services, in fact:

> I'm generally not in favour of ring-fencing; that's a general local government answer rather than a particularly libraries one. I think part of the freedom is the right to be able to make the decisions about how you allocate funding. Alright, you may not agree with the decisions, it's the right to make the wrong decisions sometimes. But I think if you go down the road too far of ring-fencing specific grants, I'm generally not in favour of that although I can understand why those who do less well, are less well perceived, would want to do that. (Cllr Graham Tope)

As discussed above, a lack of detail on the issue of funding is the most common criticism raised of *Framework for the Future*. While there is no mention of additional funding, references to improved marketing and business connections as ways in which resources can be increased are numerous. It is unlikely, however, that better promotion and relationships alone will ever be sufficient to fund the developments envisaged by the Government. There is also the question of how comfortably such increasing commercialism fits with the public library ethos of access to information and literature as a public good. Some have suggested a Standards Fund and performance targets which would reward services that achieve certain levels and quality of service. At the moment, though, new core funding seems to be a distant hope and so library services are increasingly looking to secure additional resources through competitive bidding for funds.

The Bidding Culture

Public libraries cannot charge for their core book lending and reference services but they can raise money from a variety of charges and income generating activities although this generally amounts to less than 10 per cent of their income. Fines for the late return of material and charges for services such as reservations and the borrowing of audio-visual resources (music CDs, DVDs, videos etc) provide valuable income for public libraries. Aalto and Knight (1999) list a range of sources and activities that could provide public libraries with additional income including Friends groups, events, endowments and foundations. They acknowledge, though, that public libraries face a variety of barriers which prevent them embarking on fundraising activities in a major way including staff and public resistance and their traditional neutrality which could make them resistant to accepting income from a private company or concern.

On top of the more conventional income generation activities such as charging for audio-visual resources and book sales, public libraries are also being encouraged to bid for funds from a variety of sources to supplement their core funding in a number of key areas, leading to a perceived bidding culture. It has been suggested that this model of funding has a long history. Robert Fulford, quoted in Aalto and Knight (1999), points out that Andrew Carnegie initiated the system of matched funding in public libraries by agreeing to erect library buildings in exchange for a community's commitment to staff it and stock it. Nevertheless, the scale of the current bidding culture is well beyond what Carnegie could have envisaged with funding from a range of government agencies, departments and charitable bodies increasingly being channeled through competitive tender or the submission of bids for grants and financial support. Thus, the DCMS/Wolfson Challenge Fund has funded ICT provision and reader development work in public libraries successful in their bids while finance from the New Opportunity Fund (NOF) was distributed to every authority on the basis of their plans for ICT provision and staff training (see Chapters 5 and 6 for details). Looking outside the UK, financial assistance for programmes and activities may also be available through the European Commission. For government, this type of funding arrangement is an appealing one as it can channel resources into its policy priorities with the hope and expectation that many of the projects or activities initiated will be 'mainstreamed' and funded on a ongoing basis by the local authority once they have proved their worth.

Although certainly welcome for those successful in bidding, others protest that this one-off funding is no basis on which to run a statutory service and that sustained improvement requires continual, stable investment. Competitive bidding, by definition, has winners and losers and this makes it difficult to predict with any certainty the levels of funding available for development or innovative services and their maintenance. The condition of many public library buildings, for example, has become a grave cause for concern but while other cultural services have been able to apply for Lottery funding for capital projects to build or refurbish buildings, public libraries seem to have fallen through the cracks in relation to this important source of financial support because they are a statutory service and the funding rules state that government-funded activities are ineligible for support. And this does not just apply to buildings, as one head of service explained:

> We were hoping to get into the Full Disclosure programme with plans to retrospectively catalogue collections in the city and county of local history which are not on the catalogue. We took lots of soundings with HLF [Heritage Lottery Fund] locally and we attended the road shows and we listed to the BL [British Library] and in the end we were told our bid was totally inappropriate because it was really a mainstream issue, it was a core activity and the collections weren't at risk and they weren't collections anyway… So we wasted a lot of time, I don't think the Government appreciates how much time is actually diverted and clearly there are the big overheads of the distributing bodies as well. (Anon)

Instead of lottery funding, then, some local authorities are increasingly turning to the Private Finance Initiative (PFI) to fund new ventures, especially library buildings. This scheme, introduced by the last Conservative government in 1996, enables local authorities to buy capital-intensive services from the private sector and brings private sector funding and operational management into the public sector on a risk-taking basis.[10] Bournemouth library, which won the Prime Minster's Award for Better Public Building in 2003, was financed via the Private Finance Initiative, for example, and the new Jubilee Library in Brighton opened in 2005 was also funded under the PFI. Some disquiet has been aired about PFI projects, but it still looks likely that in the future, large capital projects involving public libraries may be funded through public-private partnerships, therefore, although some would argue that such activities should be financed through direct taxation or through a Lottery stream to fund capital projects in public libraries.

A study of the impact of the bidding culture in local government reported that bidding for funds has become an accepted aspect of public library management; 97 per cent of public library respondents to a questionnaire had submitted bids for funding in the previous three years (Parker et al, 2001). The research also identified a range of problems, such as a lack of information about potential sources of income, as major issues facing the public library sector while also acknowledging that successful bidding had yielded real benefits. It is acknowledged by many in public libraries that funds obtained through bids can lead to service developments which might not be affordable from core funding and can lead to innovative, entrepreneurial solutions to service development which often involve working in successful and productive partnerships, but the issue of sustainability is currently taxing public library managers, particularly in relation to the necessity of keeping ICT hardware and software up to date. In fact, the People's Network funding was not distributed on a competitive basis and many in the public library sector speak favourably of this model of funding which required each service to document its ICT needs and plans for provision, the funds being distributed accordingly. Nonetheless, if public libraries are to play the vital role envisaged for them of enabling access to digital resources to promote community activity, creativity and learning, they will need a rolling programme of ICT upgrading and replacement. The NOF programme has equipped public libraries with a range of relevant ICT equipment but it could be argued that the issue of how to sustain development was not addressed adequately. *Framework for the Future*, for example, quite justifiably drew attention to the success of the NOF funded programmes of ICT provision and staff training yet made no mention of further funding to sustain developments. Managers will have to plan carefully to ensure equipment and staff skills are kept up to date and will need to persuade their local authority decision makers that the ICT services they provide in public libraries are value for money and worth on-going investment.

The sustainability issues surrounding the People's Network are discussed in Chapter 6 but it is not just the maintenance and development of ICT services funded by challenge funding that worries library managers. Many interview participants were concerned about how services established through successful bids for funding would continue after the funding finished. Although one head of service said, 'I think anyone that takes the money and doesn't have an exit strategy needs shooting' (Anon), another participant could understand why library services were attracted to this type of funding and felt that they were becoming more responsible in their attitude to it:

> You see a pot of money and it looks attractive. It's short term so you drop everything, you work jolly hard to get it and you have no idea how you're going to sustain it. I think we're getting to the point now where you recognize that unless we know where we're going after we've done that and unless it fits with our priorities, it's probably not worth chasing. (Anon)

The participants in the group discussion at Stockton-on-Tees also felt that library services had to act responsibly in bidding for funds:

Sue Anderson	Whatever you bid for…, there's no point in putting that it, you need to sustain it because if it's successful, you don't want to take that away, do you?
Laurayne Featherstone	That's one of the things we always look at.
Andrea Barker	Otherwise people think you're just getting money to tick boxes and it doesn't matter about the service after that year and it doesn't matter about the poor soul you've employed.

Sue Anderson	But that is what happens in a lot of places with the bidding culture.
Andrea Barker	Yes, because they can't see the bigger picture, Sue. They go for quick wins, and there's nothing wrong with that, but we tend to do a bit of both. A quick win, that's fine, but we have to be careful about the perception of people out there and we're not just going, tick this, tick that and to hell with the consequences.

One participant, though, was more positive about the benefits of this type of funding. Talking about some funding her service had recently obtained for work with early years groups, Glenys Willars said:

> I'm not regarding it as short-term funding. I mean I know it is but the first community outreach worker that we had was in post for three years and that was renewed each year. The contract will now go to March 2006 and I cannot see any reason, unless we make a mess of it or the funding dries up, why it would not continue beyond that. (Glenys Willars)

She added, though:

> There is another side to that in that I think that short term funding is a problem if it's a short term project and you have no way of sustaining that. Sometimes that is clearly the case and there is not going to be any money through the mainstream programme to sustain that and so what you've done is build up a service that you then have to take away. (Glenys Willars)

The bidding culture is considered, in some circumstances, to have led to short-termism, therefore, and although no public library would turn down pump priming funding it does tend to lead to a situation of feast followed by famine and produce funding regimes which are inflexible and could even divert attention away from local need in favour of perceived national agendas. There was concern among participants that challenge funding can distort priorities because of the pressure to obtain external funding, one head of services saying:

> The bidding culture, it does encourage a focus on programmes that are not really priorities simply because the money is there and there is a pressure to lever in external funding. It's big for me in this Department because we have got a Youth Service and the Arts Service, Learning Skills in Employment. Learning Skills in Employment lever in twice the money they get in the base budget. Budgets are compared and if we are not doing very well against others then questions are asked. (Anon)

Another head of service felt that libraries had to be careful about what they bid for:

> When we first started applying for external funding about six years ago, we started off with DCMS Wolfson funding. Applications had been made in the past for various funding initiatives and had never been successful and we couldn't believe it, that we'd actually been successful in this, it was just amazing. That then gave us the confidence to

apply for more money but we quickly realized that we couldn't just be chasing funding, it had to fit in with what we saw the purpose of the library as being… So we learnt that you don't create a group of partners just to access funding that is perhaps peripheral to what you see as the main business; it's taking away resources and staff and management time, and the results might be very good but it might be for a very small group of people, perhaps. (Joyce Little)

According to another participant, this type of bidding can also unbalance book collections:

In some libraries, where they've access to loads of funding because of their geographic location, you can end up with lots of imbalances in stock as well. Some libraries had thousands to spend on teenage books so they've got this huge teenage section and then very small and under-resourced other sections. I think some of these funding opportunities can be very specific on how you can spend the money. (Anon)

This leads on to another criticism of challenge funding; that it favours some areas over others. Although there has been concern that socially excluded areas may be at a disadvantage as any assessment of bids may not consider relative local deprivation, some participants made the point that it was, in fact, the relatively wealthier areas that were losing out under the bidding regime, a point made forcefully by one head of service:

I actually think it's appalling. I object to any government deciding that some people can have more of what is all of the public's money and I've never been able to get over that notion, it's totally wrong. The whole country contributes and then why do eight authorities get it, or whatever it is, and the others don't? Government doesn't have any money, government only has what the people give it. Now, alright, there are more affluent places but I think what's happening is that you're almost getting the reverse of what the argument was and why they needed to redirect resources; the areas that are perceived to be quite well off are actually the ones suffering most in terms of the resources that they have available and the services that they can actually deliver. (Anon)

A participant in another borough said that his service had experienced similar problems:

If there is a government agenda then you've got to jump on board and for some of it, [here], it isn't that easy because we don't have the social exclusion that you have in some areas. If you look at the indices, we're way up at the top, there's very little deprivation, we don't have a very large ethnic minority population so sometimes we've lost out on some of the funding that's been provided to support some of the Government agenda. (Anon)

It has also been suggested that the bidding culture breeds dependence on initiatives and that this can lead to demoralization as there is never enough time to respond satisfactorily to calls or tenders many of which are extremely complex. In 2001, Martin Molloy, head of Derbyshire's public library service, reported that his team had to rewrite a bid for a Public Service Agreement seven times although the reward, £45,000 to fund laptops and mobile phones for the housebound service, was undoubtedly worth the effort (Raven, 2001). Interview participants often felt, though, that the work involved in bidding and, if successful, managing the service or project funded was sometimes out of proportion to the return:

> Sometimes the bidding culture takes so much time and for what benefit? A few pieces here and there. (Andrea Barker)

Asked whether she thought the bidding culture has encouraged development, one head of service replied:

> It has but I do think it constrains development as well because along with the bidding culture you need the capacity to concentrate on the bids, not only identifying the potential of a bid and preparing your bid but, if you get it, being able to deliver it, manage it and sustain it. I do not have enough resource to call upon within my service or across the council to do this properly. (Anon)

Bob McKee was similarly concerned about the effort involved in bidding for funds and managing those funds if successful:

> I'm ambivalent about the bidding culture. Yes, it draws out innovation, it draws out creativity [but] it's a lot of hard work; some people find it massively frustrating. The flip side of the bidding culture is the tick-the-box culture so you bid for something and then you spend half your life ticking boxes to prove you're spending the money correctly… The bureaucracy gets in the way so it's not just the time consumed by the bidding process, it's the time consumed by the bureaucratic process, it's the recurrent frustration of spending a lot of time on bids that fail. (Bob McKee)

This last point was also picked up by another participant:

> The overhead is huge, you have got to take money and people or you have got to employ consultants without any guarantees of success. Some of the lottery distribution bodies are just bizarre. We have had some big schemes, Millennium Commission schemes, which took a good year to get the bid approved and then lots of regulation and monitoring. (Anon)

Smaller authorities may be at a particular disadvantage when bidding for funds because they lack the internal expertise and resources to prepare successful bids and because finding partners for initiatives that require matching funding, especially in rural areas, may be more difficult although European funding tends to target disadvantaged and rural areas specifically as suggested above. Nevertheless, with fewer staff resources and less expertise there is a danger that small library services may lose out on funding to larger, better resourced authorities and, as a consequence, fall behind in terms of service quality. This point was raised by participants from smaller authorities. As one said:

> The ones that do well like [name of authority], they've a funding manager, they've got a marketing manager, they've got this, they've got that and fair play to them. We have to manage with our core team of enthusiastic people. (Andrea Barker)

Her colleague also felt that smaller boroughs lost out because they found it more difficult to find matching funding:

> It can be a wonderful thing but if you can't find that matched funding that can be another problem…, there's always something you've to find to go for that bid and the big boroughs can afford to do it and really, sometimes, it's not the larger boroughs that need that particular service, it's the smaller boroughs who could do with that helping hand. (Sue Anderson)

A participant from another small borough confirmed that it was difficult. Acknowledging that libraries did seem to have a higher profile with government now, he added:

> The trouble is, all the money they're putting through the bidding mechanism and that has been an immense problem for us because we don't have the capacity to bid. (Anon)

Another interviewee agreed, saying:

> In the larger authorities you've got people who are paid to put funding bids in and a percentage of the funding actually pays their salary. We've nobody here like that. So the bidding culture, I think, has been brilliant for your [name of authority] and your usual authorities where they really have raked in a hell of a lot of money but it's been difficult for us. And I think there was a danger where it was almost going to become sort of the norm, that this was going to be the future but I think a lot of people actually said, 'This cannot be the future, there's got to be more mainstream funding, we can't just carry on like this'. (Anon)

In fact, it has been suggested that the variable standards of public library services across the county noted in *Framework for the Future* are partly the result of the development of the bidding culture under which some authorities have been highly successful at securing additional funding for service development and innovation (Cilip News, 2003). There is also a view that success breeds success in this area although many would argue that funding should go to those authorities with greatest need rather than those able to write the most persuasive bid document. Competitive bidding inevitably establishes a win/lose situation and those who are often in the losers' camp can start to feel so demoralized and demotivated at their lack of success and the time and energy they have expended for no return that they cease to be involved in further bidding opportunities. The competitive situation arising from the bidding culture can also lead to resentment among those who fail or those who feel that they do not have the resources to compete, elements of which can be detected in some of the quotes above. This could disadvantage the whole sector according to one participant:

> The bidding culture generally I think is counterproductive… I'm not sure that it is a healthy situation. When there are bidding regimes, the communication process slows down. Librarians generally are very open communicators, we are inclined to share information, it's in the professional ethic and personal psyche. I suddenly noticed at regional meetings of Chief Librarians that we were very circumspect about the bids we were putting in because you realized it was a competition. (Anon)

Few participants had anything positive to say about the bidding culture and its impact on library services. Although some services had undoubtedly benefited from the injection of cash when successful, the process was generally considered too resource intensive and frequently disappointing and frustrating. In Wales, the Welsh Assembly had adopted a different approach as one participant explained:

> The Assembly's way of distributing funding is very transparent but it is a grant culture as opposed to a bidding culture. We're still discussing this with the Minister but I think the approach we're going to take is that libraries need a strategic development programme which, to me, is not about challenge funding. We actually do need to move libraries forward as a step change and we need to move everybody forward. I think the dangers of challenge funding are that some libraries move forward a lot more quickly that others and we're really going at the speed of the slowest camel in this. (Anon)

Bob McKee had some similar suggestions for an alternative method of distributing funds in England:

> Frankly, I would prefer not to have the bidding culture, I would much prefer to have a culture that says, 'We want to achieve these five objectives and here's the money to do it and then we manage performance.' If we have to put some money into something that encourages innovation and rewards performance then I'd rather we did it through things like peer review and performance management rather than creating this artificial bidding culture. The bidding culture was a Thatcherite device to apply the competitive principles of the market to the delivery of public service. It don't work; the present government hasn't had the balls to get rid of it, yet. (Bob McKee)

Conclusion

Despite the strong discourses of local accountability and control identified in Chapter 2, support for national agendas for public libraries was also solid. Many participants expressed the opinion that national governing bodies had been taking more interest in public library services and that they were moving up the political agenda. There were some differences between the different home nations, though. Those interviewed from Northern Ireland, for example, were often unconvinced that there was much understanding of the full role that public libraries could play in the life of the people of the province. In England, although there were some criticisms of *Framework for the Future*, many feeling that it was not visionary enough, there was overwhelming support for the concept of a national guiding document which establishes key areas and themes for public libraries to be working towards and little evidence of conflict between national and local leadership. The positive reception for the concept (if not always the tone or content) of *Framework* suggests that many in the public library community have been searching for a lead from government and discourses around leadership, particularly those focusing on a perceived lack of strong leadership within the profession, were common. Many felt that the problems started at the top and that the DCMS was not sufficiently robust or at the heart of government thinking to have much impact but there was disagreement about the appropriate 'home' department for public libraries in England although there was a general consensus that the present arrangements were unsatisfactory. Leadbeater's suggestion of National Library Development Agency did not find much favour either. Although some thought it was a good idea, few felt it was a practical proposition and believed that efforts would be better spent trying to secure advocates or champions from outside the public library community but admitted that this was no easy task.

The focus on *Framework for the Future* and activities arising from its action plan has led to more attention being paid to English public libraries although some significant changes have taken place within the public library services of the other three home nations since devolution. Gradually, differences between the nations are starting to emerge although a difference in approach, rather than role or purpose, is most obvious. The disparity in the size and scale of the library systems in the different home nations is probably primarily responsible for this so that the smaller systems in Scotland, Wales and Northern Ireland enable a closer working relationship to develop between policy makers and service deliverers and facilitate more of a bottom-up approach than in England. English devolution and regionalism is currently on hold following the rejection of the idea of an elected regional assembly for the North East in 2004. There was little enthusiasm among interview participants for more extensive regional co-operation either. Public libraries have always had co-operative arrangements with other public and academic libraries within their vicinity but few advocated more extensive region-wide ties although some of those from smaller authorities were more in favour than those from larger systems. Local politics was a key issue, though, that often seemed to prevent closer working between different authorities, with local politicians keen to preserve boundaries and maintain a distinct identity. Looking beyond the library domain, there was a feeling that there were some synergies between libraries and other cultural institutions such as museums and archives but also a sense that this was not where public libraries should be focusing their energies primarily. Perhaps as the regional MLAs become more firmly established, regional co-operation across the cultural sector will increase. Outside the cultural sector, public libraries are still, it seems, having difficulty convincing other key partners of the role they can play in local and regional agendas. Although many library services have established successful partnerships with a range of bodies, they still find themselves overlooked too often. This is explored further in Chapter 8.

One of the problems public libraries have faced in engaging with others outside the sector is a difficulty in demonstrating their contribution to key policy priorities. To resolve this, as well as to improve the quality of services, a variety of accountability and performance measures have been introduced by the New Labour

Government. Discourses around the various processes that have been brought in were largely positive and, in fact, many lamented the abandonment of mechanisms like the Annual Library Plans in England which were often viewed as a way of engaging local politicians. What many view as the dilution of the Public Library Standards was similarly criticized as was the fact that, without inspection, they had little teeth although in Wales a more rigorous approach is being taken. In England, a 'lighter touch' is seen as necessary by Whitehall to free public services from excessive bureaucracy but many interview participants seemed to feel that public libraries have, historically, suffered from a light touch and hands-off approach from central government and the demands made on them by Annual Library Plans and standards were welcome evidence of interest and recognition and a signal to local councils that the public library service must be satisfactorily administered and adequately funded.

The interview evidence suggested that the standards, in particular, had been successful in levering more funds for public libraries from local authority coffers although there were fears that the lighter touch described above will have a detrimental effect in this regard. Currently, interest in increasing efficiency is high following the Coates (2004) report and the PKF (2005) study. Opinions were divided on the possibility of efficiency savings, however, and there was more concern over maintaining the share of the local authority budget that the library service currently received in the face of a squeeze on local authority funding generally. Discourses around the bidding culture were generally negative. Even those from services that had been successful in securing funding through bids and grants were sceptical of the strategy of distributing funds through these mechanisms in the long term. Key themes within this discourse included the problems of sustainability, the time and effort involved in bidding, the lack of a level playing field and perceptions of unfair competition. Although any extra funding is welcome when obtained, there was a general perception that a 'few pieces here and there' (Andrea Barker) will not address the real problems that many services are facing in maintaining services and buildings.

Notes

1 David Lammy was appointed Minister for Culture with responsibility for public libraries in May 2005.

2 See NEMLAC website at URL: http://www.nemlac.co.uk/ [16.09.05].

3 See MLA West Midlands website at URL: http://www.mlawestmidlands.org.uk/ [16.09.05].

4 See Noah website at URL: http://www.noah.norfolk.gov.uk/ [16/09/05].

5 See Tomorrow's History website at URL: http://www.tomorrows-history.com/ [16.09.05].

6 Learning and Skills Council Website is at URL: http://www.lsc.gov.uk/National/default.htm [16.09.05].

7 The DCMS Library Position Statements website gives access to English library authorities' plans and statements from 1999–2003 as well as a range of other resources

related to the planning and reporting system. See URL: http://www.libplans.ws/ [16.09.05].

8 The Public Library Service Standards are available at URL: http://www.culture.gov.uk/NR/rdonlyres/2374D642-E0E0-40BF-8BE4-F12047103DBE/0/PUBLICLIBRARYSERVICESTANDARDSFINAL1OCTOBER.pdf [16.09.05].

9 Information about the public library impact measure is available at URL: http://www.mla.gov.uk/action/framework/framework_04a.asp [16.09.05].

10 For more information see URL: http://www.hm-treasury.gov.uk/documents/public_private_partnerships/ppp_index.cfm [16.09.05].

Chapter 4
Public Library Users

New Library, New Users

This chapter will focus on the *raison d'etre* for public libraries: their users. Plenty of statistical information is available on the public library user (e.g. the annual statistics provided by Cipfa (the Chartered Institute of Public Finance Accounting) and by LISU (the Library and Information Statistics Unit) and while this chapter will review some of the key statistics related to public library use, it will focus primarily on whether, and if so how, the public library user community has changed as public libraries have broadened their remit and as government changes to local authority performance management and accountability measures have altered local council tax payers' views of public services. Citizen engagement and user-focused services are increasingly being promoted as key public service policy philosophies. The 1999 government White Paper on modernizing government stressed the need to ensure that users are at the heart of all decisions about public services (Cabinet Office, 1999) and, for library services specifically, *Framework for the Future* (Department for Culture, Media and Sport, 2003) was clear that library authorities must use their resources to provide the services that people want.

Facts and Figures of Public Library Use in the United Kingdom

Much is made of the popularity of public libraries in the UK. Their membership (over half the population are registered members of public libraries) is often compared favourably to the number who go to cinemas or attend football matches (Department for Culture, Media and Sport, 2003), both of which attract considerably more public attention. The inference is that this popular and well-used institution punches below its weight in terms of recognition of the role it plays in the everyday life of the British public. The LibEcon database shows that the UK has the highest percentage of registered users among the countries it covers (56 per cent of the population according to its data), comparing favourably with the statistics of public library registration in Germany (10 per cent), the United States, Canada, Australia and New Zealand (all at 21 per cent), Sweden (27 per cent) and Denmark (35 per cent). Only Iceland and Finland (41 per cent and 46 per cent respectively) come close to matching the extent of public library membership in the UK.[1]

As noted in Chapter 3, public libraries are the most measured of all library and information services and the gathering and analysis of data relating to their user profile and activity is extensive in the UK. From just one of the many surveys and data collection exercises which take place in public libraries we learn that the largest proportion of public library users (28 per cent) visit the library about once a week; that the age groups who visit the library the most are those in the 65-74 age range and those aged 35-44 (each represents around 17 per cent of users); that more females than males visit the library (59 per cent compared with 41 per cent); that the mean distance that users live from the library is about 2.5 kilometres; and that the largest proportion of those using the public library are retired (37 per cent) followed by people in full-time employment (24 per cent). Over 90 per cent of public library users are white and of those who are not, the largest proportion (around 4.5 per cent) are of Asian or Asian-British origin (Cipfa, no date). There is a perception that public library users are middle class, middle aged people and yet the statistics do not seem to bear out this assumption. Although it is true that the higher social classes (AB – professional and managerial)[2] use libraries in excess of their proportion in the population as a whole, the data show that all social classes use public libraries and that use is reasonably proportionate (see Table 4.1).

Table 4.1 Library use by socio-economic grouping

Class	Presence in UK population %	Library users %
AB	18	22
C1	25	28
C2	27	25
D	15	12
E	15	13
Total	100	100

Source: Adapted from: Hawkins, M. et al., 2001.

The services that people make use of in the library does vary by class, however, with those in the higher social classes making more use of the non-fiction facilities provided (Book Marketing Ltd, 2000), for example, and they also vary by age although, again, overall use by different age groups is more evenly distributed than often thought. One research project devised a categorization scheme of users by age and their public library activities the researchers called 'the seven ages of library use' (Hawkins et al., 2001, p. 260). At the 'nursery' stage, less than 50 per cent of pre-school children are library members and are usually taken by their carers to branch or community libraries to borrow picture books. It should be noted, however, that this research was undertaken in 1999 and the successful Bookstart scheme (discussed in more detail in Chapter 9) may well have had an impact on the library membership of this group. The second stage is 'primary school' when use increases steadily both for school work and reading for pleasure. Because these children generally still need to be accompanied to the library, they are still more likely to use their local branch library. Use of the public library for children at the 'secondary school' (those over 11 years old) declines as other activities begin to take up their time but 'young adults' (15 – 19 year olds) in full-time education use public library services more, especially in town centre libraries. Although they may not borrow books, they use the facilities to study and to access resources not available in their school libraries. '19-35 year olds' do not use public library services heavily and their use tends to be born from necessity rather than pleasure. It is difficult to generalize about the library use of 'mature adults' in the 35-60 year old age range as use is often dependent upon their circumstances as well as their inclination. Finally, 'elderly people' use the public library primarily for pleasure, especially for their fiction-reading needs and, as they are less likely to own their own transport, they are heavy users of local community libraries.

For many, though, the official, rather positive figures from Cipfa and others, seized on by politicians and officials keen to prove the wide use of the service, mask some real problems relating to the public library user community. As Alistair Black points out, nearly half of the population does not hold a library ticket, a poor showing for what is a free service (Black, 2000) and, according to Terry Turner, the regular, active, core usage of public libraries is actually around 30 per cent, made up of predominantly white, middle class people (Turner, 2001). John Pateman agrees that only around 30 per cent of the population are active public library users, adding that the 'much touted figure of 60 per cent is a myth' and that those who do use the library regularly are homogenous in terms of race, class, age and gender (Pateman, 2004, p. 34). Expanding on this in his interview, he commented:

> Libraries are actively used by 30 per cent of the population. So, OK, 60 per cent of the population may own a library ticket, but so what? Only half of them actively use it, go in week in week out. So let's knock that 60 per cent myth on the head. As far as I am concerned it is a myth and I know Cilip use it as an advocacy tool but it belies our starting point really. If you look at that 30 per cent who actively use us, 2 out of 3 of those are middle class by what ever definition you want to apply to class these days, whether it is a political definition or an economic definition. That 30 per cent are very homogenous in their make up, they are predominately white, they are predominately middle class, predominately elderly and predominately female. (John Pateman)

Pateman argued that libraries need to reach out to the other 70 per cent of lapsed and non-users and encourage them to use public libraries and that their needs should be the basis of programmes and services. Public library user surveys, however, focus on active users and their needs therefore become paramount, reinforcing the status quo. Further discussion of the nature of the public library user community and how some libraries are trying to encourage a wider diversity of users to use their facilities is included in Chapters 7 and 8.

There seems to be a lot of popular mythology around the nature of the public library user community. Although those like Pateman and Turner insist that only around 30 per cent of the population are active library users and, of those, two out of three are middle class, others insist that 'the middle class myth of libraries is dead' (Culture, Media and Sport Committee, 2000, para. 44), basing this assertion on research evidence showing the high value that excluded communities place on library use. In interview, John Vincent acknowledged that the profile of the service depended very much on what the library does but still felt that:

> There are certainly [library services] which I'm very well aware of which fall into that stereotype absolutely, where the users are middle class, middle aged, mostly white and, from my training work, quite a lot a lot of library services that I've worked with say that, regrettably, that's the case. (John Vincent)

Martin Molloy, on the other hand, insisted that the image of a middle-class user profile was a stereotype, at least for his service, and explained why, for some, it was a very convenient one:

> Every time local politicians want to cut the service or close it down, it's very convenient for them to say, 'This is only being provided for the middle classes'. So if you're to the left of the [political] spectrum, what you're saying is, 'Why are we wasting money providing services for people who can go out and buy?' and all the rest of it. And if you're to the right of the spectrum, the same answer holds true really because you're saying, 'We've so improved society, people can afford to pay for all this, so we're going to let them pay for it, we don't need this service'... So until we can break out of that by having proper marketing, communications structures, until people see reasons why libraries are delivering things that are really worth having in political terms and there's commitment to back them up, there's always going to be a danger that this old hag-ridden tale of the middle class service is going to keep on reappearing. (Martin Molloy)

There were some interesting discussions about 'traditional' users, supposedly in contrast to the 'new' users brought in to the library by, primarily, the ICT facilities and services now provided. Frances Hendrix supported Tim Coates' (2004) view that many of those who were once stalwarts of the public library were losing interest because they felt the library had little to offer them:

> [The library's] traditional users are dying out; it's traditional users, white, middle class, want a good read. They're increasingly buying their own books. (Frances Hendrix)

One participant was unconcerned about this, feeling that public libraries should target those who need the most help. Asked for his vision of the future of the public library, he said:

> The vision would be a library service which redefines the term library in a much broader kind of way, accepting the fact that this is a society divided by class. And certain classes, because of the resources they control, have their own means of satisfying their needs so refocusing the role and purpose of the library in a classed society and openly coming out and saying that the public library service is not open to all, well it is open to all, but it will be a needs-based service meeting the needs of people who cannot afford a library .... and be up front about it, not putting resources to meeting the needs of people who have other ways of satisfying their needs. (Shirz Durrani)

Few other participants expressed similar views but many acknowledged the need to reach out to those beyond their 'traditional' user base:

> It's a slightly flippant comment but I think it's quite interesting... Somebody said in the context of the *Who's in Charge* report [which said that] the public library will be dead in 15 years, that actually, we'll be dead in 15 years if we focus all our energies on retaining our traditional users because they're the ones who'll be dead in 15 years, the sort of 65 plus. (Sarah Wilkie)

John Pateman seemed to agree:

> [Libraries'] core users are dying, literally, or finding alternative uses for their time and money. Issues are in free fall, visits have plateaued and libraries are not reaching out to new and different people. (John Pateman)

Alyson Harbour was also concerned to attract new users:

> I think from the point of view of the traditional users, users who have left over the last 20 years have left because they're too busy, there's an alternative provision and so on. I think we're very unlikely to lose the rest of our traditional users except, as I said earlier half jokingly, when they die. But what we have to do is recognize that they are going to die and what we have to do is get the library customers coming in at an earlier age and then staying. Libraries are very good at serving people up to the age of about 11 and then from 65 onwards but what we have to do is keep them after the age of 11 and not wait until they're 25 and have got their own kids because then they're only coming in for their kids. (Alyson Harbour)

One participant, though, felt that these 'traditional' users were the bedrock of the service and it was important to retain their goodwill and custom:

> We have to keep our traditional users happy, they're the people who are here, you alienate them at your peril. They're an easy target and if you upset them and they go away then the whole thing will go down even faster. And it's easier to encourage them to take more than to get new people in. They're the quick win. (Anon)

Perhaps part of the problem and confusion about new and 'traditional' users and the user profile of public libraries lies in the lack of reliable and in-depth information about users and especially non-users. Many in the public library field agree that better management information is needed to ensure that the library is meeting the needs of the community and targeting resources most effectively. Pateman (2004) complains that little is known about regular users, let alone non-users, with most library authorities and staff reluctant to ask for 'personal' data on ethnicity, occupation, age etc. as suggested in Chapter 3. Alyson Harbour felt that although this kind of information could be invaluable for marketing and targeting purposes, libraries were very poor at collecting it:

> A lot of the tools that libraries have been using for years are just inadequate. The average library management system in this country is telling libraries nothing about our customers. It tells you everything about where the books are going but it doesn't tell you who they're going to or what kind of people they are or anything. Think about the trouble supermarkets go to to get loyalty cards to track their customers so they can find out what they're doing. We've got a membership scheme, we've got a national membership scheme, we could know everything about customers of libraries across this country and yet all we measure on is active users, one use a year. (Alyson Harbour)

John Pateman agreed that the current information collected was inadequate for planning purposes:

> I think visitors' numbers are the best indicators of library use, better than issues for example because people coming through the door use us for all kinds of things, they don't even have to join and have a ticket. If we count them, that is a better indicator than people borrowing books. But having said that, we also need to know who the visitors are. We don't know their age, race, gender, their class, we don't know why they're visiting us. We also need to know why people have stopped visiting us and have never visited us. We haven't got the answers to any of those questions. (John Pateman)

As noted in Chapter 3, some participants felt that asking for this type of information was intrusive but not all are so sensitive about asking for personal details. In Poole, for example, the library service now asks new members for data relating to age, ethnicity etc. and is even rejoining all existing users to ensure the service has full and accurate information about the people who use it.[3]

Users and Usage

Trend analyses of statistics relating to public library users have been undertaken and over the 1990s showed a picture of decline for many traditional library services. Although membership remained relatively stable, visitor numbers fell from 6.9 visits per capita in 1992 to 5.4 visits in 2001 (Creaser et al., 2003). Membership is one thing, therefore, but use is quite another although the most recent Cipfa figures released in June 2004 showed an increase in usage by 1.5 per cent across the UK with some authorities reporting more substantial increases (Cipfa, 2004). In Liverpool, for example, visits have risen by 25 per cent over the last two years. Many interviewees also pointed out that these figures are for 2002-3, before the People's Network really began to have an impact on the footfall in public libraries. The most worrying statistic for public libraries is the fall in book borrowing discussed in more detail in Chapter 10 although, again, individual library authorities have bucked the trend. In Shropshire, for example, the proportion of the budget devoted to stock has risen to 18 per cent and loans have risen by 4 per cent (children's loans by 15 per cent) (Library and Information Update, 2004). Nevertheless, there is still concern that people's use of the public library for certain core activities is in decline and although the latest statistics from Cipfa are encouraging, over the 1990s the use of many services considered central to the public library mission was, and in some cases still is, falling. In 2001, 70.3

per cent of users visiting the library borrowed, returned or renewed books, 33.9 per cent browsed and 23.3 per cent sought information or tried to find something out (Cipfa, no date). This compares with figures of 77.6 per cent, 27.4 per cent and 22.2 per cent for the same activities in 1997 (Creaser et al., 2003). The book lending activities of public library users have clearly declined, therefore, although their use of the library to seek information has increased slightly as has their tendency to look through the material held by the library. The use of the library as a place to study has also increased from 6.9 per cent in 1997 to 9.1 per cent in 2001. This increase could be partly due to the increase in IT connectivity of public libraries brought about by the installation of the People's Network (see Chapter 6). 6.2 per cent of public library visitors used a computer in the library in 2001 and 6.1 per cent used the Internet (Cipfa, no date). This is the first time that Cipfa has gathered data relating to ICT use in public libraries and so no comparative data from previous years are available.

Many interview participants were positive about an upturn in visitor numbers. Martin Molloy said that people were coming back to libraries for all sorts of reasons:

> We're getting genuine new people, we're getting people who gave up on libraries a while ago but it's part of the mix, reader development and reader groups and so on are also bringing both new people and people that had used libraries but no longer are, they're bringing them back into the equation. (Martin Molloy)

Joyce Little explained that the award of Beacon Status to Liverpool Libraries had recognized the increase in use the service had enjoyed. This had involved some hard work but had addressed some fundamental issues:

> We demonstrated that we had undertaken a period of change that had revitalized the public library service, that had brought people back into library and increased performance and we'd done that through extending opening hours, through re-investing in our book fund, our materials fund because we buy more books, and through our People's Network Centres. (Joyce Little)

The People's Network was credited by many for attracting more people to public libraries, as one participant suggested:

> The uptake [of the People's Network] has been magnificent. I've recorded an increase in visits of up to four per cent in 2002/3 and over five per cent in 2003/4 and that can be attributed mostly to the People's Network. (Anon)

Another participant agreed that the People's Network and the related online facilities and services it has generated has had a huge impact on visitor numbers but these were not always apparent nor counted:

> The thing that nobody takes account of is electronic access to libraries. I printed out [some figures about] electronic renewals, nearly 120,000 book renewals online either by the Web or the message hotline. People don't actually come because they're doing it

remotely. People can join the library as well, 600-odd have joined online. I think that sort of electronic use is not part of the public library standards. (Anon)

The increase in visitors number reported by Cipfa was confirmed by those participating in the study, therefore, and, as we will see below, while this was very welcome, it was raising some management issues.

User Satisfaction

Overall user numbers may be in decline but those members who are still using public libraries seem relatively satisfied with the service provided; 90 per cent of visitors rated the overall library service as 'good' or 'very good' in 2001 (Creaser et al., 2003). Some individual items showed a rise in satisfaction over the same period including staff helpfulness, staff knowledge and expertise and time spent waiting for services. Cipfa, on whose statistics the LISU analysis is based, changed some of the items on their user questionnaire for 2001 so many of the items are not comparable although it is interesting in the light of the fall in book issues that in 2001 73.4 per cent of visitors rated the 'books and other materials' available in the library as 'good' or 'very good' compared with just 68.8 per cent of visitors who rated the 'range of materials' as 'good' or 'very good' in 1997. Other services have shown a decline in satisfaction as judged by users, however, including services for children (1 per cent fewer visitors rated these 'good' or 'very good' in 2001 than in 1997) and hours of opening (71.1 per cent in 2001 compared with 77.5 per cent in 1997). Apart from this last figure, none of the statistics on satisfaction shows a lot of movement. All the satisfaction ratings are above 50 per cent, the lowest being that for the provision of seating and tables which 69.1 per cent of visitors rated as 'good' or 'very good'. The overall picture is of a service that is satisfying the needs of its users.

It has been said, though, that high satisfaction rates disguise low expectations on the part of users. The groundbreaking Hillingdon project on public library effectiveness in the 1970s was one of the first to suggest that public library users have low expectations of provision and are, therefore, easily satisfied with the service they receive (Totterdell et al., 1976). Asked whether he thought public expectations had risen, John Pateman said:

I don't think expectations have risen, I think they have always been low but I think they have been disguised. For example, the Public Library Users Survey which we all rely on, which is only a user survey once again, consistently gives library good satisfaction ratings, very high – 80 per cent and 90 per cent, even though we know the service is poor and getting worse. So what is going on there? I think it is partly the halo effect; people tell us what they think we want to hear.

Bob McKee agreed:

A lot of the problems with the customer satisfaction research into libraries is that all that research is subjective and it's based on expectation. So if you're used to this sort of library service and that's what you think a library services is, you base your expectations

> and satisfactions on that, so you don't see what could be, you only see what is. (Bob McKee)

There is also a perception that users do not complain about public library services for fear of losing them altogether and are inclined to give very positive responses to questions about service quality and their satisfaction with those services. Martin Molloy confirmed this but felt that people were becoming less inclined to tolerate poor service:

> On the one hand, people are grateful for what they get and they put up with a lot on the back of that. On the other hand, people in society have got a lot less willing to put up with bad service and they're a lot more vocal about making their feelings known. (Martin Molloy)

Reinforcing this last point, other participants felt that user expectations had risen primarily because of the level of service they received from commercial operations. Talking about the impact the Internet bookseller Amazon.com had had on the library service, one interviewee said:

> It's changed people's expectations as well, it's shifted them entirely. When I started ten years ago, people were quite happy if you said [a reservation will] come in a fortnight. Today they look at you aghast if it's going to take more than a week, they really can't understand what the problem is. And that's something libraries have got to deal with, really on a national level. (Anon)

Although some participants commented that they thought users' expectations had risen because of commercial ventures like Amazon.com and attractively designed bookshops, others felt that expectations remained low. This can lead to complacency on the part of library services and one issue that public libraries have been accused of not tackling adequately is that of non-use.

Non-users and Lapsed Users

Framework for the Future urges libraries to put more effort into attracting non-users and lapsed users into libraries while continuing to satisfy the needs of current users (Department for Culture, Media and Sport, 2003). Some are concerned that key groups of opinion formers and age groups ('young trend setters and middle-class professionals') have deserted the public libraries and stress that an effort must be made to recapture their interest and custom to ensure a well-informed and articulate advocacy movement on behalf of the service in government and the media (Worpole, 2004, p. 10). Although there are actions that public libraries could take to reach those sections of the community who do not use them currently, there was some resignation among interviewees that there are people who will never use public libraries for a variety of reasons. Bill McNaught wondered if the decline in library usage was partly attributable to a natural process associated with, what he called, 'product lifecycle':

> If it is just one of these things in terms of product lifecycle, you know, in the 60s there were fewer things competing for our leisure time and it's a reflection of a changed society, then we can stop beating ourselves up. But as long as you've got Tim Coates saying 'It's because you've got lousy library managers', we need to come up with the evidence to say what it is we should be doing better to reverse trends. (Bill McNaught)

Martin Molloy agreed that competing demands on people's leisure time meant that visiting the library was no longer the entertainment alternative that it was once and felt that, given this, libraries had done well to maintain the visitor numbers they had:

> If you look at the range of offers that there are for people now in terms of going to the gym, buying books, going to multi-screen cinemas, DVDs, videos in the home, all of that, and if you look at the number of visits to libraries and the size of the issue base, things like that, it's actually tremendously good. If there wasn't this hang-over from the 1950s when, frankly, there wasn't anything else other than the public library in a sense, if there wasn't a hang-over from that in statistical terms, I think people would be talking about what a great job this public service does. (Martin Molloy)

Pateman (2004) has argued against complacency, though, pointing out that high levels of use, across a wider cross-section of the population, has been achieved elsewhere citing the examples of Scandinavia and Cuba. In interview, he argued that to achieve this libraries need to change their focus:

> I think that libraries have always been focused on users not customers, and users have always been the minority … rather that non-users, the majority, so the focus is wrong.

Quoting from his service's Best Value report from 2002 he said:

> 'Whilst there was extensive consultation as part of the Best Value review, we found no evidence of focused, non-user research to help the service identify why it appeals to only a limited number of residents'. This is the big thing I have got about the focus on users; not non-users, not lapsed users. (John Pateman)

Julia Fieldhouse similarly suggested that public libraries have been quite blinkered in the past:

> It's the classic thing that we've been very internally focused, catering to the audience we've always had, concentrating on books because that's the professional thing, as opposed to being outwardly focused on what we could and should be doing and looking at people who are not coming into libraries. (Julia Fieldhouse)

Another participant agreed that consultation had to go beyond surveying users of the service:

> It's fine to ask your users and if you ask your users I'm sure you'll get 99 per cent satisfaction rates because people who use libraries, generally, are very happy with their

use of those libraries. I'm much more interested in the non-users. So certainly I think we've got an obligation to go out there and look for new audiences. (Anon)

Some library authorities have already turned their attention to non-users and lapsed users. Margaret Bellamy explained that Leicestershire library service was trying to find ways to reach lapsed users in particular:

Next year, we're going to do a lot of work with lapsed users. This year we did the PLUS survey and the thing that came out of that was the opening hours. So we did work with that, you know, if we change the opening hours, will more people use us? With lapsed users, it's not just opening hours, it's the whole thing: are the books there? Did they stop using us because their life circumstances changed? And also, a year ago, we started re-registering all our borrowers so in a year's time, we'll look at the database and see who's actually used us in that time. I know one authority, they surveyed their lapsed users and people were very indignant because they weren't lapsed users, they'd just stopped borrowing, they continued to use the library but they just didn't borrow anything. The other thing is our occasional users: why do they use us occasionally? Is there anything we can do to make them more frequent users? (Margaret Bellamy)

John Pateman believed that this kind of research was essential to reach lapsed users which he calculated at 30 per cent of the potential library using community:

Really, we just let them drift away and we haven't bothered. We have often got their names and addresses still on file. They are very easy to reach but we haven't made the effort. (John Pateman)

Other authorities are working hard to contact lapsed users and encourage them back into the library, as Alan Watkin explained, while also noting that just encouraging people back to the library was not enough, there had to be services that they wanted to use as well once they were there:

We do a system here now, if you haven't used your library card in six months, you get a letter saying something nice, 'Do you know we do this now' and actually some people get the letter and think, 'Oh yes, the library, I haven't been there for while'… But if you've got a product, the product should be good enough when somebody comes in to want to come and use and that's something we've learnt from the leisure side. (Alan Watkin)

One respondent seemed to agree with Tim Coates' (2004) assertion that public libraries had been neglecting their core or traditional users by trying to attract those who had not used them in the past:

[I'm] not necessarily saying you ditch all the work with the various socially excluded groups and all the rest of it but these are not going to bring back your numbers, they're just not. (Anon)

Attention to the barriers that prevent or discourage people from using public libraries, therefore, could encourage non-users to try the service and persuade lapsed users to return. As Margaret Bellamy suggested above, one barrier is access and there is a perception that the issue of opening hours is a particularly thorny issue (see, for example, Proctor et al., 1998). Coates (2004) suggests that one of the reasons people have stopped visiting public libraries is because of the short opening hours but Moore (unpub.) reports that there has been considerable improvement in recent years. He details how opening hours are recovering from a low point in the mid 1990s, noting that in 1975–76 over 160 libraries were open for more than 60 hours per week. By 1995–96 this had fallen to just nine but in 2002–03 this had risen to 42. Chapter 7 includes a discussion of how importantly participants view an extension in opening hours for increasing library use and also explores how some authorities are extending or altering library opening hours in response to public demand.

Despite the increase in opening hours that Moore details and interview participants confirmed, the satisfaction figures cited above show quite a marked decline in satisfaction with opening hours supported by anecdotal evidence from a range of sources. A recent discussion about libraries on the BBC Online website suggested that some of those responding were dissatisfied with the opening hours of their local libraries, commenting they were 'useless' for anybody working regular hours (BBC News Online, 2005). Other participants were more supportive of their local public libraries, especially those that had recently extended their hours of operation into the evenings and weekends. Surveys of non-users show that very few of them do not visit the public library because of access, problems such as inconvenient opening hours or location, however (Table 4.2).

Table 4.2 Reasons for not visiting the public library: adults and children, 1998

	All non-visitors %	Adults %	Children %
No need/reason to	39	44	19
Too busy/no time	22	26	5
Buy books/AV instead	17	20	13
Not interested in books/reading	14	17	3
Borrow from friends, family etc.	12	14	5
Not interested in any services	8	9	3
Too young/others borrow on behalf	6	1	30
Use other libraries instead	5	3	14
Get info from elsewhere (e.g. Internet)	5	5	3
Not well/housebound/don't get out	4	5	2
Opening hours inconvenient	4	4	3
No public library convenient to get to	3	3	1
Doesn't have services required	2	2	1
Other	4	3	4
Any reason given	88	90	82

Source: Bohme, S. & Spiller, D. (1999).

Lack of need and lack of interest appear to be the main factors keeping people away from public libraries and policy makers and politicians perhaps need to accept that there is a sizeable proportion of the population who have no desire, interest or need to use their local public libraries. As the Audit Commission concluded, '[i]t needs to be recognised that there is a significant minority of non-users who feel they will never use libraries in the future' (Audit Commission, 2002, p. 14). One survey of lapsed users did suggest that for this group, access issues such as opening hours had been influential in their decision not to use the library in the previous year, however (Bohme & Spiller, 1999). Twenty-four per cent of respondents stated that the reason they did not use the library was because the opening hours were not convenient although personal reasons such as a lack of time and a tendency to buy books were more frequently cited reasons for no longer using the public library.

Social changes also have an impact on who does and does not use public libraries and why. The Audit Commission noted, '[t]he principal reasons why non-users do not use libraries are to do with lifestyle issues – not interested/not got time – and these will be difficult to address' (Audit Commission, 2002, p. 14). The long work hours culture in the UK means that many people are now time poor although often more conventionally affluent. Alyson Harbour felt that this was at the root of much of the decline in library use:

> The problem is the world has changed and the library service hasn't really noticed. In *Framework for the Future*, there is a lot of allusion to the fact that the loss of trade to libraries and the increase of book sales in the commercial sector are directly related. My gut feeling is that they're not. My gut feeling is that the loss of trade in libraries is directly related to most families having two working parents, or a much higher percentage of families having the need for two working parents, and just social change. (Alyson Harbour)

She later added that this was having an impact on some of the core users of libraries:

> I was brought up going to the library, my mum took us every week, swapped our books over. Well that just doesn't happen these days for most people. (Alyson Harbour)

Britons work an average of 43.6 hours per week, the highest of the European countries with one in six working over 60 hours a week in 2002 compared to just one in eight in 2000 (Department of Trade and Industry, 2002). The leisure time people do have is precious to them, therefore, and although one of the things they may enjoy doing with their increasingly scarce resource of spare time is reading or researching a topic of interest to them, their relative affluence and time pressured lives means that they are more likely to send for a book or CD through Amazon.com or spend time surfing the Internet at home rather than visit the public library. That leaves the public library to cater for those who have plenty of time on their hands and/or those with less disposable income unless they can find ways of meeting the needs of the others. Frances Hendrix believed, though, that public libraries were missing out on a chance to cater for those at the other end of the economic spectrum who she characterized as:

> …the busy people who are working but would pay, like they do for a gym, like they do for a trainer, like they do increasingly for somebody to help with their shopping, like they do with buying off the Internet. You know, busy people want it delivered when they want it to their door. You could develop, if you were allowed, services at that end. (Frances Hendrix)

There is also a perception that local people often do not realize or understand the extent of the services on offer in public libraries, especially large town centre libraries, and that better promotion is needed. Marketing, outreach work and consultation are advocated as ways in which the public library service can find out more about users' needs, involve them in service planning and development and explain and publicize the services offered. There is concern that people's image of the public library is still rooted in the reading room of the 1950s and that many do not appreciate the changes that have taken place in public libraries with the installation of networks and ICT and the provision of leisure, information and learning resources in many different formats. John Pateman explained:

> Non-users don't use libraries and lapsed users may not have used them for some time so they don't know what to expect, that's the problem, they don't expect that libraries will meet their needs because non-users believe libraries are not for them. (John Pateman)

Changing Uses

Many interview participants agreed that the increasingly sophisticated level of ICT now available in public libraries, particularly the Internet, has encouraged a different type of user into the library and persuaded people to view the library in a new light:

> The stories keep coming back from the services about the change in demographics of the users so new young men, which have always been a problem, at last getting into the library, suddenly it's a cool thing to do because of the stuff they can do with IT. So, yes, it has changed the image. (Anon)

Sue Wilkinson agreed that the People's Network had succeeded at reaching out to non-users and that libraries had been successful at capitalizing upon this:

> I think the People's Network has been very important for bringing in a new audience and I think libraries have been very responsive, just in terms of their stock selection and periodicals and their approaches. (Sue Wilkinson)

Another participant felt that it was critical that libraries could sustain the interest generated by the People's Network:

> [The People's Network has] got such spin-offs in terms of getting new users and heightening the profile of the public library service and I think if librarians can respond to that, as lots of them are, then I think that will put public libraries back on the agenda. (Anne Ollier)

It could be argued that all new services attract new users. The introduction of lending services for videos, then CDs, then DVDs probably had the same effect but it is likely that the expectations of those attracted by the People's Network is slightly different to those entering the library to borrow resources, in whatever format. The evaluations of the People's Network carried out under the auspices of MLA indicate that new users have been attracted to public libraries by the installation of networked PCs and that around 40 per cent of these have subsequently become members (Brophy, 2003). Similarly, social inclusion policies and strategies have attempted to open up library services to excluded groups through targeted initiatives employing community development, partnerships and other proactive ways of working. The aim of these activities is to increase library use by under-represented and socially excluded groups and to broaden the base of public library users. If successful, such programmes will also have the effect of changing the profile of the user community. These changes, whilst welcome to managers eager to prove the inclusivity of their services and the impact of their activities on the local community, may have brought different groups into conflict with each other.

New users attracted by Internet facilities, for example, may have a very different attitude to the public library and a different perception both of other users and of the staff than more long-standing users. This has resulted in a variety of behavioural issues which public libraries have not had to confront before including noise management and the difficulty of finding a balance between encouraging new elements into the library while not driving away existing users as Kath Owen explained:

> The People's Network has brought more people in, different types of people, different types of users which is good and we welcome that and that's another aspect of social inclusion, of course. But for some people it's a warm place where they can come and mess around, cause problems, be abusive to customers and staff… The anti-social minority is an unfortunate by-product, so to speak, but it is one that we have to be prepared to deal with. (Kath Owen)

Alan Watkin agreed that some users could be difficult but they often came from the sections of the non-using library population that libraries were trying to attract:

> If you talk to [a colleague in another authority] he would say his biggest problem in areas of deprivation is the fear staff have and the actual physical assaults they suffer. And how do you get around that? We've had members of staff resign. But nevertheless, some of those groups are the very groups we need to get inside to genuinely achieve the library's mission. (Alan Watkin)

Bryson et al. (2003) found that many public library services are taking a new approach to user behaviour which includes a more relaxed attitude to refreshments, noise and more active behaviours. How well the old and the new interact is another matter, though; 'the quiet of the reference library and reading areas competing with the clatter of keyboards' (Seered, 2003, online resource). Bryson et al. (2003) noted that the provision of ICT and the library's growing role as provider of lifelong learning opportunities has had an impact on the use made of library space. In some cases, the more traditional library services have had to be compromised to meet new demands. Although library managers try to balance the needs of established users with those of the new, their efforts have had mixed success as one participant explained:

> All our users have their own agenda and if you don't handle it carefully you can upset some of them and I think that's perhaps what has happened in a lot of libraries. (Anon)

The spotlight has been on the impact that ICT has had on the use made of public library space and the atmosphere inside the library but it is not just technology that has had the effect of bringing new users into public libraries. As libraries have sought to embed themselves within the community, they have often become a focus for many diverse community activities. Again, some have questioned the impact this may have on their more traditional users although Martin Molloy, responding to author Anne Fine's address at IFLA 2002 which criticized the impact of technology on the public library world (Fine, 2002), takes issue with the view which seems to suggest that some library users (those avidly reading books) are more worthy recipients of public library membership than others (Molloy, 2003). Jan Holden agreed that some users, as well as librarians, need to change their views of what libraries were for:

> To this day, people who are traditional library users want a reference library, a lending library that's got traditional books in it and a library that doesn't have that many people in it, particularly not young people of different classes or different racial backgrounds. (Jan Holden)

Service developments have undoubtedly had an impact on the range of people entering the library and the use made of the public library space and service managers need to consider how to manage this. Bryson et al. (2003) discuss how some of the new public library buildings they studied risked alienating older users because of the emphasis placed on attracting youngsters. One Head of Service commented to the research team that, '…it is difficult to serve two groups in very close proximity to each other because of the different expectations…' (p. 68). The challenges related to integrating old and new users attracted by ICT facilities in the same space are discussed further in Chapter 6 but public libraries do need to confront these issues to ensure that neither are disadvantaged, as one participant explained:

> There is an issue for a frontline manager of staff about balancing all these different user groups because they do seem to be becoming more polarized as we offer different services. The things like People's Network, the young men coming in and there is a perception, in the Tim Coates' image of a traditional user type, that that use of the library is not appropriate, sitting at a computer maybe playing a game, maybe nattering to your friends while you do it. And there is an issue for library staff of balancing a broader range of needs and expectations than we had 20 years ago. (Sarah Wilkie)

This broader range of needs and expectations also includes attention to the changing attitudes towards public services held by both existing and new users.

The Public Library Consumer

As well as new users being attracted to the public library, it is also possible that the attitudes and activities of existing users have changed, demanding a response from public library managers. The accountability, efficiency and openness measures discussed in Chapter 3 are considered by many working in public libraries to have made users more aware of issues of service standards and perhaps raised their expectations. When those expectations are not met, the user will be dissatisfied. Even the change in nomenclature from reader or user to customer or client suggests a different relationship between the library service and its target community and is a reflection of changes taking place between user and provider in the public sector generally. Previous Conservative administrations and this New Labour Government have been keen to introduce the principles of consumerism into local government including the introduction of market mechanisms enabling citizens to exercise choice and to receive redress when things go wrong (Docherty et al., 2001). *The Citizen's Charter* and *Charter Mark* scheme introduced by Conservative Prime Minister John Major in the 1990s has been continued by New Labour's *Service First: The New Charter Programme* which retains the focus on responding to customers' needs and expectations and delivering satisfaction. The *Charter Mark* quality award is conferred on those public services which have met its six criteria.[4] This approach is advocated as shifting power from the professionals, bureaucrats and decision makers running public services to the customer who ultimately judges the quality of the service provided, meaning that members of the public are now active consumers of services rather than passive recipients and that services have to be adaptive and responsive.

The focus on responsiveness to the users of public services is paramount for the Government who would argue that, in the past, services have been designed around the problems and perspectives of those who run the services rather than those who use them. With explicit statements of service levels, users now know what to expect from public services, have clear standards against which they can judge performance and mechanisms through which they can complain if the service is found wanting. To overcome a perceived public sector weakness on the needs and concerns of users, service user involvement is championed through consultation and communication with the aims of improving service delivery and enhancing the democratic legitimacy of local government (Audit Commission, 2003).

Citizen-consumerism

There are concerns, however, that the attempt to import consumer values into public sector provision can have negative consequences for services and for the communities which they serve. According to one commentator, '[c]onsumerism is a model that prioritizes the individual over the community, encourages passivity, downgrades public spaces, weakens accountability and privatizes citizenship' (Needham, 2003, p. 33). It is argued that public services have constraints which limit their ability to replicate the consumer choice provided by private sector companies and that the Government's drive for 'citizen-consumerism', with its focus on the maximization of customer satisfaction, individual choice and complaint, could be damaging for public services because of its individualistic and self-regarding nature which ignores what might be best for others or for the whole community. Within this philosophy, people have little incentive to become involved in civic and community life outside their need to use a variety of public services. Thus, the citizen-consumer makes choices, and complains, based on his/her own preferences and this can distort services in favour of narrow, sectional interests rather than the common good, especially as it has been shown that some groups use complaints procedures more than others and that young people and vulnerable adults, in particular, are reluctant to complain because of a fear of victimization, a concern that they will alienate staff who will view them as fussy and demanding and a fear that complaints will have a negative effect on the service and service provider (Preston-Shoot, 2001).

Some participants expressed concern about the introduction of the philosophy of consumerism into public services. Talking about the shift to a customer focus, John Pateman said:

> To me, a customer-library relationship is transactional, it's commercial, it's consumerist and it's market driven whereas a citizen-library relationship is democratic, accountable, community driven, fundamentally different. And in that relationship, citizens literally own and pay for the service; it's their service through their council tax and they have a direct say in how it's managed through local councillors. Whereas customers, to me, pay for what they can get or what they can afford. So I think that's been an unhelpful shift. (John Pateman)

For public libraries, there is a danger that a lack of engagement and interest from the local community encourages users to take the services they provide for granted until something goes wrong and then they will complain. In fact, it has been suggested that the one way in which the public service user community does resemble consumers is in the willingness of some of its sections to complain (Bagehot, 2003). Vogt (2004) argues that complaints offer public libraries the opportunity to understand weaknesses better and to react to them quickly although acknowledging that a low number of complaints do not necessarily give an accurate picture of user satisfaction as only about 5 per cent of dissatisfied customers even make a complaint. Martin Molloy felt that this was changing, however, with an increasing number now willing to voice their concerns about aspects of the service:

> When I started here, having adverse comments about the service was a rarity. [Now], the complaints and comments scheme, they're not always complains but comments, constructive comments from people, helpful stuff about how we can improve the service as well as times when people have felt it's not worked the way that it should, but those are regular, they're incoming all the time. (Martin Molloy)

He went on to explain why he thought there had been an increase in this type of feedback:

> I guess if 20-odd years ago we'd put these forms in libraries and asked people to fill them in [they'd have said], 'I don't fill forms in, I don't do things like that'. But you know yourself now if you're walking on the streets people are always coming up to you with a questionnaire… and people get used to it and they start thinking, 'Well if that hasn't worked, I'm going to fill that in and I'm going to do something'. (Martin Molloy)

Although the satisfaction of customer needs and attention to their complaints must be the guiding principle for public library services, some feel that the language of performance measurement and accountability has confused and undermined the value of professional values and citizen rights. Instead of customer needs being the highest priority, customer wants now reign supreme, 'in particular, the "wants" of those customers who are most strident, powerful, and audible in their demands' (Roach and Morrison, 1998, p. 19). Some participants felt that the rise of customer choice in public services had had an impact on how people approached the library and the services it provided. John Vincent explained the changes in people's attitude to the public library and its staff that he had witnessed over the years:

> I worked on the front line in public libraries until about 1974, and '74 to '96 I was either a subject specialist or a manager and I didn't work with the public direct. And then in 1997 I went to work in a London borough really partly to earn some money and partly to get my feet back on the ground about what real library life was like. And the one thing that had significantly changed was … that people came in with booklists, for example, students, quite often mature students and they made no effort and wanted to make no effort to find anything for themselves because their view was that they paid their rates and it was our job to plough around the library finding these books for them… I've found that's one of the most significant changes in that period, that it is about, 'I know my rights and I pay my council tax and therefore if I bellow enough you'll have to do what I want'. (John Vincent)

Consultation

The consultation processes which are seen as an important aspect of improving customer choice have also been criticized as emphazising market research and quantitative measure of customer satisfaction rather than more participatory methods which would involve public service users in real discussion (Needham, 2003). Some of the standards set by services in pursuit of quality awards like the *Charter Mark* can be criticized as arbitrary and for not measuring real satisfaction. Many public library services have developed user charters which detail the services that users can expect, including specific response times for waiting to borrow a book, to answer an information query or to answer the telephone, for example. Speed of response is important for users, especially those with busy, time-pressured lifestyles, but perhaps more important for many is a courteous and friendly service and one which is able to provide an accurate and complete response to any query. These are more difficult to measure, however. Furthermore, regarding the user as a consumer or customer and emphasizing the nature of choice can raise user expectations to an unattainable level; inability to satisfy those expectations could lead to resentment and perennial dissatisfaction with services. Also lacking from the discourse of customer satisfaction is a notion of what services like public libraries contribute to society as a whole rather than to the satisfaction of individual consumers. Techniques like opinion polls, feedback forms and satisfaction surveys encourage respondents to report their experiences as individual service users rather than consider wider issues of community need and service priorities.

The need to provide quantifiable measures of satisfaction for Best Value can encourage services to neglect the more imaginative, discursive forms of consultation for quantitative surveys. The former are also more time-consuming and resource intensive. Nevertheless, the interviews for this study suggested that many library authorities were trying to find ways of engaging local communities in service development. One participant explained:

> We have customer focus groups for every area of service delivered: adult, children's, local studies, reference, ethnic services and customer focus groups for every branch library and they are quite active. (Anon)

It is possible that the charge about only consulting users could be made here but the participant insisted that these groups did identify needs that perhaps might not have been identified otherwise:

> The customers wanted things like the prayer room, we call it meditation space. Now that came out directly as a result of customer consultation, and a crèche. I think we are really relevant for our communities. (Anon)

Others were making efforts to reach those who were perhaps not regular library users as another participant explained:

> We have now, I think it's two youth juries where we bring the kids in, we talk to them about the services that are being provided, what do they want to see, they help with a little bit of the selection of the stock, the magazines, things like that. We also engage with specific groups within the community. We have a very strong link, for example, with [the Borough's] Dyslexia Association and, again, we have a lot of feedback and

> work with them very closely in making sure that the provision is right and the young kids there have actually been involved in buying collections which have proved very popular in all libraries. (Anon)

User and non-user consultation was an item high up the agenda of many interview participants, therefore, although John Pateman felt that current initiatives to engage communities in the planning and delivery of services usually did not go far enough:

> Users have no control really about how library services are delivered, even though they have the biggest say and biggest stake. They still have no real control about what goes on the shelves, opening hours, stock selection, they're not involved in selecting performance indicators or success criteria or impact or outcome measures. They don't even know what they are, they're not even reported on. They are passive recipients of an archaic service, is how I will sum it up. (John Pateman)

Competition and Choice

Finally in this discussion of the consumer-citizen, the notions of competition and choice for public services have also been challenged. People may pay for services they do not use, need services that cannot be provided because of lack of resources or not even know what kind of services they really need (Needham, 2003). In relation to public library services, the local user has little or no choice and the service is free. In fact there is a net outflow of resources to that user (Hood, 1986). For public libraries, then, the idea of competition and choice is of limited practical value and it could be argued that service users do not necessarily want choice anyway, just good services which do their job. Vogt (2004) would disagree, arguing, like some of the interview participants above, that people now have a range of leisure, education and leisure options demanding their time and that the public library must retain its ground and present itself as an attractive and viable alternative to all the other competing alternatives. She insists that customer satisfaction is essential for public libraries to attract new users and retain existing ones. Garcia et al (2001) agree, suggesting that public libraries are competing for market attention in the areas of information provision and recreation/entertainment. So while a public library may not necessarily be in direct competition with another public library (although this is possible especially in London or those areas which have many public library authorities in close proximity to one another), it does need to compete for its share of the users' time and attention. As Garcia et al. (2001) enquire, do people want to read or will they go to see a film? Will they come and meet friends at the library or will they go to a shopping centre? Would they rather sit on a sofa in a book shop or sit and read in their local public library? One interview participant agreed with this analysis, suggesting that libraries increasingly need to focus on their unique selling points because, 'the leisure side of libraries, people have a lot of choices, there are choices available for leisure users' (Anon).

As commercial services and retail organizations have become more sophisticated in their efforts to attract customers, so users have become more demanding in what they expect from service providers. Together with the modernization of local government and the emphasis on value for money of the public sector, moves to increase user engagement have made the public more aware of services provided by the local authority and that they should be responsive, accountable and effective. Whilst, there has always been an element of the 'I pay my rates' mentality, with some users complaining about the level of service, the recent emphasis on performance indicators and standards, as well as higher expectations on the part of the user, have undoubtedly had an impact on the relationship between user and provider as John Vincent above suggested and expanded upon later in his interview:

> There isn't really a debate about the terrible adage that the customer's always right. I've been to libraries and observed where people are just being treated like doormats. And I'm not encouraging the staff to be stroppy and rude and so on but I do think there's a line at which you shouldn't actually have somebody treating you the way that some of the public does. And it's really interesting to kind of open up all of that and I'm not sure that debate's happening either at the moment. (John Vincent)

While public libraries must be committed to user orientation, satisfying as many people as possible by using resources optimally (Vogt, 2004), it could be argued that an individualistic consumer orientation does not fit well with the Government's other emphasis on community and its mission to regenerate local community feeling and pride, discussed in detail in Chapter 8. Vogt (2004) acknowledges that individual customer demands do not always fit well with the library's mission and a balance needs to be found between satisfying individual users and the public service role.

Conclusion

The discussion above suggests that there are conflicting discourses surrounding the profile of the public library user, with some commentators and interview participants suggesting that public libraries are now visited by a wider range of people of different ages, classes and origins than ever previously. On the other hand, there are those who maintain that the public library continues to serve a narrow section of the British public. On both sides of the argument, representatives characterize the other's evidence as 'mythology'; either the mythology of the dominant middle class user or the mythology of an inclusive, well-used service. In fact, as some interview participants highlighted and despite user surveys and increasingly sophisticated library management systems, surprisingly little is known about the make-up of the public library-using community. There does appear to be some reluctance to gather and analyse data relating to users' backgrounds. Whether this is because services are worried about what they will find or whether it is due to a reluctance to pry too far into people's private lives is a matter for debate but this kind of data would help authorities target non-users more effectively and assist them in their marketing efforts because until services are able to identify which sections of the community are not using public libraries, they cannot speculate why and try to address any barriers or problems with the service discouraging use.

There is widespread recognition, though, that public libraries need to tackle the issue of non-use and although there are those like Pateman who suggest that many public library services are too complacent about their user profile and are happy catering for the needs of the few rather than the many, the interviews suggested that those participating recognized the need to engage users in consultation and act on the information gathered in order to engage their interest in the service. There was a general acceptance that public libraries had been too user-focused in the past and although this seems like an odd criticism to make in these days of customer-facing services, the argument is that by attending to the needs of those who use the library most, those who do not have been neglected and have either drifted away from public libraries or have never entered them in the first place. Tim Coates (2004), supported by some interview participants, has suggested almost the opposite, that is, that those users who have been the bedrock and majority of the library using public have abandoned services as their needs, primarily for quality books and information resources, have been ignored in favour of trying to meet the needs of non-users. This argument perhaps skates over the fact that the public library service is part of the local authority and, as such, has an obligation to try to attend to the needs of all those who live in the community, including those who have no interest in the book-related services provided by the library. Nevertheless, even those who found much to criticize in Coates' analysis still felt that 'traditional' users should not be neglected in favour of the pursuit of 'new' users.

This possible conflict of interest between the provision of services for 'traditional' and 'new users' was another prominent discourse of the interviews, in particular. Traditional users were characterized as those who wanted access to a wide range of quality fiction and non-fiction to borrow on a regular basis and who wanted to use the library as a quiet, contemplative space in which to read and study. New users, on the other hand, were typified as those usually attracted to the library by the free ICT available through the People's Network and who did not necessarily understand the library's rules, written or unwritten, about acceptable behaviour and 'library etiquette'. These new users' attitudes towards fellow users and staff were often considered difficult although some participants felt that the public's stance towards public services and their staff had altered irrevocably anyway due to the importation of consumerist language and policies from the private sector. Changes in people's social habits and lifestyles, as well as their attitudes, were also a prominent theme of the interviews and were often proposed as a reason for a drop in use of public libraries. Many participants used similar if not identical words to one head of libraries, explaining that public libraries can no longer rely on supplying its conventional services to its core users, however well it may do that: 'The world has changed and we have to change too'. (Anon)

Notes

1 Data for 2001 at URL: http://www.libecon.org/ [02.11.05].
2 For an explanation of the NRS social grade categories in the UK see URL: http://www.businessballs.com/demographicsclassifications.htm [02.11.05].
3 For information see URL: http://www.seapn.org.uk/resources/libraryjoining.html [02.11.05].
4 For more information about the Charter Mark scheme see URL: http://www.chartermark.gov.uk/index.htm [02.11.05].

Chapter 5

Public Library Staff

A Public Library Staffing Crisis

Concern about the quality and nature of the public library workforce has been voiced increasingly loudly over the past decade. It is said that the workforce is stagnating, that new graduates are not attracted to the sector and that turnover is slow, limiting the introduction of new blood even further. The Chief Executive of Cilip, Bob McKee, has summed this up as 'a greying of the profession' (Culture, Media and Sport Committee, 2005, p. 39). It is not just at entry level that public libraries are facing staffing problems; difficulty in filling senior specialist positions has also been reported in some areas and a crisis in leadership is predicted by many (for example, Usherwood et al., 2001). Others suggest that the lack of diversity within the UK public library workforce means that it has become institutionally racist with negative consequences for both use by the community and the recruitment of staff (Durrani, 2002). This image of a rather stale, moribund staffing establishment does not fit comfortably with the image of the modern, dynamic, proactive institution that the Government seeks to promote. Staff training is one way of addressing this and although the New Opportunities Fund ICT training programme has meant that staff development activities for public library staff in the UK have been at an unprecedented level, there is concern that, aside from this, investment in continuous development is limited (Department for Culture, Media and Sport, 2003). Training and development are key to maintaining relevant and responsive services and to retaining high quality staff (Usherwood et al., 2001) but interest in ensuring that the best use is made of public library staffing resources is also partly motivated by the amount spent on them; staff costs constitute 55 per cent of public library gross expenditure (Maynard, 2003). Effectiveness and efficiency requirements, then, are focusing attention on the public library staff establishment, its supply and the use made of it, with growing calls for a radical approach to its management.

The Staffing Establishment

In 2001–2002, there were 26,861.9 staff employed in public libraries, the decimal number the result of the part-time nature of much public library work, discussed further below. Within this figure, 6,523.8 were professional staff and 20,338.1 were all other manual and non-manual staff including library assistants of various levels. The total number of staff employed fell by 494.5 or 1.8 per cent over the period

1996–97 to 2001–02, the professional staff establishment bearing the brunt of reductions – down 4.4 per cent compared with 0.9 per cent for other staff (Cipfa, 2003). Moore (unpub.) reported a more satisfactory picture for England for 2002–03, however. The number of staff employed in English public libraries increased by eight per cent, meaning that the overall staffing level is slightly better than that recommended by the 1962 Bourdillon standards (Ministry of Education, 1962). Moore notes, though, that there is a real problem concerning the number of professionally qualified staff, their numbers falling steadily since 1975–76 from nearly 7,500 to just over 5,000 so that they now represent just 24 per cent of the staffing establishment. The Bourdillon standards recommended that 40 per cent of staff should be professionally qualified. As Moore, suggests, '[t]his makes it difficult to provide a high quality service' (Moore, unpub., p. 2).

As staff numbers contract, library services need to make the best use of their workforce because although the staff establishment has decreased, workload could be said to have increased as public libraries diversify the services they offer. This is certainly the view of staff, according to a number of studies of the public library workforce. Goulding (1996), for example, found that support staff often felt overburdened by the amount of work they had to do and by the rate at which they were expected to perform their duties. Staffing levels were also identified as a concern in some authorities' final Public Library Position Statements in 2003.[1] Only one per cent of respondents to the workforce study by Usherwood et al. (2001) cited overwork as a factor causing staff to leave the public library service, however.

Whatever the perceptions of staff of their workload, various developments have meant that certain activities might actually have decreased, thus justifying the decline in staff numbers. It could be argued, for example, that IT has made many tasks, including bibliographic services, circulation desk duties and even stock selection activities, less labour-intensive so that fewer staff can now undertake the work. Similarly, the contracting out or outsourcing of some operations has also had the effect of reducing the main staff establishment while increasing the number of those working in or for the library service but not on its payroll. This can be viewed as a good illustration of Charles Handy's model of core and peripheral workers. Using the idea of the shamrock, the Irish national emblem, Handy argues that today's organization is made up of three different groups. The first leaf represents core workers made up of qualified professionals, managers and technicians. They are essential to the organization, well paid and therefore expensive. To save on costs, the numbers of such workers are often reduced, downsized or restructured and their work is contracted out to second leaf workers, '[a]ll non-essential work, work which could be done by someone else, is therefore sensibly contracted out to people who make a speciality of it and who should, in theory, be able to do it better for less cost' (Handy, 1991, p. 73). The third leaf represents the flexible labour force; part time and temporary workers. While often cost-efficient for the library service, this type of workforce raises a whole host of management issues discussed more fully below.

One participant felt that despite these changes, other developments meant that the workload of library staff had increased:

> Although we've automated a lot of things, the customer interaction of working with things like computers is quite a load and it's completely different and is actually more time consuming than the old load of issuing and discharging books was because the customers need more attention, need more personal one-to-one whereas issuing and discharging books was a fairly speedy process, that you dealt with someone in a couple of minutes and you moved on. Customer enquiries on computers are often much longer than that and takes someone away from the counter completely which means that overall you're needing that higher level of numbers of people there to keep working with them and answering enquiries. (Anon)

For England and Wales, it was hoped to develop a public library standard relating to numbers of staff with appropriate qualifications in information management and ICT although not overall staff numbers. Both the original English and Welsh standards stated that 'appropriate levels of qualified staff' must be provided and that target numbers of qualified staff per 1,000 population would be proposed following research commissioned by Cilip. As noted in Chapter 3, this standard has now been dropped in the new English Service Public Library Standards which went out for consultation in June 2004 because it has proved too difficult to classify 'professional staff' and to standardize across authorities. The Welsh standards still state, though, that at least 29 per cent of the total staff should have appropriate library or information qualifications but the Assembly was also awaiting the results of the Cilip study to set targets for qualified staff per 1,000 population.

The 2003 Library Position Statements all generally commended the commitment and experience of staff but many expressed concern about the quality and quantity of supply, stressing that services are undergoing extreme organizational and cultural change and need staff who are able to respond positively and flexibly. There was often an acknowledgement that traditional roles need to change to deliver a modern service and, for some, recruiting younger staff and those from communities not currently using the service were priorities to transform the culture. This is supported by research undertaken by Roach and Morrison (1998) who found that people from ethnic minorities are under-represented within the public library workforce and that this presents a barrier to service effectiveness in ethnically diverse contexts. There is, therefore, a whole host of recruitment and retention issues with which public library services throughout the UK are grappling.

Recruitment and Retention

Study participants often spoke of the recruitment problems their services were facing and although many said that they did not have difficulties retaining staff, this sometimes caused problems in itself as Jan Holden explained:

> In this county, we don't have very much of staff turnover because it's quite a long way from anywhere… Turnover is a big issue [because] sometimes you might have people in a job whose skills actually are not best suited to what you want them to do. (Jan Holden)

Another participant agreed that a lack of new blood and exposure to different systems and ways of working can be an issue. Agreeing with Bob's McKee's analysis that the profession was greying, she said:

> Certainly we've got an ageing staff, a third of my staff would be over 50. Recruitment – our difficulties aren't huge at present because we have low staff turnover… We're fortunate to have quite a large number of staff who are doing distance learning and whilst it's not great to have all the new qualified staff coming up through the same course, the same route and their experience just being based [here], it's filling the gaps as and when we have vacancies. (Anon)

Other services were experiencing recruitment difficulties, however, and the problems seemed to be that adverts for vacant positions were not attracting large numbers of applicants and that those who did apply were often not of the quality expected and needed. The problems of attracting appropriate, high calibre recruits to the sector, identified by Usherwood et al. (2001) in the *Public Library Workforce Study*, persist, then, and are part of a wider problem of public sector staffing. An Audit Commission report on recruitment and retention in the public sector found that six main factors encouraged staff to leave their jobs: bureaucracy and paperwork; insufficient resources; a lack of autonomy; feeling undervalued; unfair pay and the modernization agenda (Audit Commission, 2003).

Analysing the factors that discourage graduates from taking up public library positions or cause them to leave, Greenhalgh and Worpole (1995) point out that the publishing and book selling industries are able to both attract and retain a high calibre graduate staff, unlike public libraries, even though wages are often lower. They suggest that personal discretion and freedom in day-to-day decision making, contrasted with the rather bureaucratic nature of public library work, make these professions more attractive than librarianship although the changes to public library services' organizational structures discussed below may have overcome some of these problems. *The Public Library Workforce Study* found that there were three sets of factors deterring would-be recruits from applying to public libraries: negative perceptions of the job; poor career prospects; and negative assessments of terms of contract. Individual items were organized within each of the three categories and the results, reproduced in Table 5.1, show that perceptions of poor career prospects were most likely to discourage potential candidates although the most cited single deterrent was low pay. These results suggest that perceptions of internal organizational and job-related factors are limiting recruitment to public libraries although external developments can heighten their impact.

Table 5.1 Factors deterring potential recruits to the public library service

Factor	Frequency cited	% of citations
Perception of job		
Negative image/expectations	88	17.0
Low status	19	4.0
Lack of IT infrastructure	10	2.0
Mundane/routine work	5	1.0
Decline of public service ethos	4	0.5
Difficult clients	3	0.5
Badly organized service	2	0.5
Stressful job	2	0.5
Total	*133*	*26.0*
Career prospects		
Limited opportunities for progression	78	15.0
Pressure on resources	45	9.0
Negative perception of local government	37	7.0
Uncertain future	21	4.0
Lack of opportunity to develop skills & specialisms	7	2.0
Inability to provide training and development	2	1.0
Total	*190*	*38.0*
Contractual considerations		
Poor salary levels	129	26.0
Poor conditions of service	24	5.0
Temporary/part time nature of some contracts	5	1.0
Total	*158*	*31.0*
Other		
Lack of recruitment opportunities	8	1.0
Difficult local area	6	1.0
High entry requirements	4	1.0
Fear of change	4	1.0
DLIS* deterring potential recruits	1	1.0
Total	*23*	*5.0*
Total citations	*504*	*100.0*

* Departments of Library and Information Studies

Source: Usherwood et al., 2001.

The burden of debt most graduates accumulate because of the abolition of student grants and the introduction of university fees, for example, has surely had an impact on attitudes towards public library wages and, consequently, supply at entry level. Graduates emerging from their first degree owing an average of £12,069 (according to the latest Barclay's Bank student survey) will be understandably reluctant to accrue further debt by embarking on an expensive Masters programme (fees are generally about £3,000 per year and grants or scholarships are scarce).

The comparatively poor pay in the sector was identified by study participants as a reason for the recruitment problems that many public library services were facing. Kath Owen explained:

> There's definitely more money to be found in other areas and if you look at the Gazette [Cilip's appointments bulletin], the vacancies in there, and just look at the numbers of vacancies in special libraries, particularly law ones, most of whom are paying considerably more than we are in public libraries. (Kath Owen)

Margaret Watson agreed that pay was a factor deterring potential recruits to public library work:

> I am very concerned [about recruitment] because, wearing another hat as a library school educator, trying to actually convince students to go for jobs in the public library sector is not easy… On our undergraduate programme nobody at all, except one person one year [expressed an interest in public library work] and that was because she had done her work experience in a [public] library and she thought she would enjoy it. But until she said she was interested nobody had expressed any interest because most of them were picking up jobs that were far better paid in the private sector. (Margaret Watson)

She later added:

> Talking to colleagues in the public library sector, they are quite concerned, they just can't get the right calibre people. It's usually, 'Why doesn't the library schools produce them?' The thing is the library schools are producing them but they are choosing not to go into the public library sector and I think it's about money, I don't think it's the job. (Margaret Watson)

Other participants disagreed with this, however, feeling that it was the job, or at least the image of the job and the public library environment, that discouraged new graduates from applying for work in public libraries, as one explained:

> Talking to colleagues who are also having problems recruiting, the best students in library schools don't want to go into public libraries; they want academic, professional and they see public libraries as very much the poor relation. (Margaret Bellamy)

Frances Hendrix felt that work in local authorities, in general, was not attractive for new graduates. Talking about the necessity of recruiting people with business skills she said:

> I don't think that we probably attract that sort of person into local authorities because who in their right mind would want to work there? We certainly don't necessarily attract them

> to library schools and library schools are very proud of the fact that many of the library and information studies students go to do other things. I mean, you boast about it – publishing, book selling, advertising, PR; they certainly don't go into public libraries. (Frances Hendrix)

One participant felt that public libraries could do a better job of marketing themselves to potential recruits:

> I think there is also a link to the marketing work and the advocacy thing. It's about trying to use that to maybe improve the image of the work, the profession, which again is one of the ways where the recruitment thing could be tackled so that it is actually seen as an interesting field to go and work in so people don't think they're going to work in a gloomy, dusty building with a load of books that they'll just be putting stamps in. (Sarah Wilkie)

Another interviewee agreed that more information about the kind of work that public libraries are now involved in would help them attract more and better quality recruits:

> If we can generate some excitement about what public libraries are doing and where they're heading and how they're transforming and changing, that will start attracting the right sort of people… It's not that hard, Martin's [Molloy] done it in Derbyshire to a very large degree. It just needs a few people to be a bit imaginative and present themselves well. (Anon)

Martin Molloy himself suggested in interview that there were reasons to be optimistic about recruitment:

> One of the most encouraging things for me is the attitude of young people now. For a long time Thatcher's legacy of 'private good, public bad' overwhelmed us and it was very difficult to encourage young people to come into our area of work. Now I think there are generations coming through who do actually believe in society and do believe in putting something back and they do see that social inclusion is relevant and they suddenly see that perhaps public libraries are again somewhere where they could make a difference. (Martin Molloy)

A lack of knowledge or understanding of the public library field and what it can offer as a career can be a deterrent for potential recruits, however. Although university libraries in the UK continue to offer graduate trainee positions for those needing to gain library experience before applying to study for a Masters course in Librarianship or Information Science, comparable posts in public libraries are now few and far between. As Margaret Watson suggested, those who gain some work experience in a public library setting usually enjoy the variety of the work and appreciate working with and for a wide range of people. This kind of experience is difficult to obtain, however. Nottinghamshire public library service still runs a trainee programme in conjunction with the Nottingham City service and Kath Owen explained the importance of this for both the individual trainee and the service:

> We still have trainee posts in Nottinghamshire, only two of them now, and there are two in the City still and I wouldn't want to lose that. I know that colleagues ... certainly feel that they benefit hugely from having a trainee. And our trainees generally seem to be pretty successful in moving on and some of them come back to us although there's no guarantee of that, they have to apply with everyone else... I just think that more authorities ought to be prepared to designate a post and have those posts because there are benefits there, definitely. (Kath Owen)

Margaret Watson felt that some of the blame for a lack of applicants for public library positions lay at the door of library services themselves which, she felt, often demanded too much of new recruits in terms of work experience and that this caused difficulties, given the lack of availability of placement and trainee positions:

> Some of them [new graduates] can't even get a professional post in the public library sector because they won't take on someone unless they have got some experience. I think they've got to be more flexible. (Margaret Watson)

Those committed to public library work as a career do not always have the chance to explore the type of work undertaken nor the organizational climate and culture of public libraries, therefore, although Usherwood et al., (2001) found that work experience in public libraries was sometimes a soul-destroying experience which could actually deter potential recruits to the profession. Similarly, courses or modules devoted to public librarianship on Masters or undergraduate level Library and Information Studies programmes are increasingly rare and although general modules may include an introduction to public libraries and their work, focused study is more uncommon. Here there is an issue of supply and demand, though. British universities often have limits on minimum numbers of students which make modules viable. Modules which do not attract sufficient numbers are not able to be offered or run and options focusing on public libraries are not always the most popular. Dissertation and project work still gives those with an interest the opportunity to research the area in some depth, however.

Some participants blamed a lack of interest by the 'library schools' in teaching public library topics and although this might be the case, in my experience few public library services, with some honourable exceptions, show a great deal of interest in the library schools, have little contact with them and are probably, therefore, quite unaware of what is taught and how. It is also not true that graduates do not enter public library work. Loughborough University' first destination data for the postgraduate 'librarianship' programme (MA in Information and Library Studies) for the year ending 2003 (the latest full data available) showed that nine of the 29 who responded (31 per cent) entered work in a public library service. Considering the range of career opportunities within librarianship and the difficulties often mentioned in recruiting people, that seems a reasonable figure. The rest, by the way, did not enter publishing or PR as Frances Hendrix suggested. In fact, all but three had the word 'librarian' somewhere in their job title and those who did not were clearly working in an information-intensive job.

Although many participants were quite gloomy about the future prospects of the profession, Kath Owen was more positive. Acknowledging that the wage paid to new recruits was a significant deterrent, she nevertheless felt that because of this, those who did apply to work in public libraries were very committed to the work and the ideals of public library service:

> People have to really want to work in public libraries, I think, but then perhaps the net result of that is that you actually get the people who do really want to work there. And, certainly, in terms of vacancies, we're not getting the same field that we used to get but we are still getting some really good people. (Kath Owen)

As she later added, you only need one good applicant for each vacant position.

Skills Gaps

The Demos report on workforce development for the cultural sector identified eight skills gaps: leadership, management, advocacy, awareness of the 'new agendas' of learning, access and inclusion, customer care, technology and technical expertise, new ways of working and commercial skills (Demos, 2003). The report commented that many employers feel that newly qualified entrants are not well equipped to join the workforce and do not have the right mix of skills. Similarly, the public library employers responding to the *Public Library Workforce Study* (Usherwood et al., 2001) said that they often had difficulties recruiting entry level librarians with suitable experience, skills and personal qualities. Employers in the study attached most importance to personal skills, such as communication and people skills, when selecting new staff to work in their organizations. A study focusing specifically on the personal qualities required by new entrants to the profession revealed uncertainty about whether graduates had high reserves of the personal qualities needed to be good public librarians, however (Goulding et al., 1999). The research, which asked public library employers to identify the qualities they felt were most essential for work in the area and also those they considered missing in graduate entrants, found that the ability to accept pressure was highly desirable but often sadly lacking in recruits as were flexibility, energy, commitment to organizational goals and well developed written communication skills, all considered essential for success (see Tables 5.2 and 5.3). Some of the other qualities in the 'lacking' list also give cause for concern. That employers judged new entrants to be unfriendly is a serious issue in a people-oriented profession. Similarly, the amount of team work now required within public library staffing structures means that those not able to work successfully with and for a range of colleagues are in danger of undermining the effectiveness of the system.

Table 5.2 Essential personal qualities of new recruits to public libraries

Rank	Essential qualities
1	Able to accept pressure*
2	Reflective
3	Able to deal with a range of users
4	Dedicated
5	Written communication skills*
6	Inquisitive
7	Flexible*
8	Committed to organizational goals*
9	Leadership qualities
10	Energetic*

*Also in top ten most lacking list

Source: Goulding et al., 1999

Table 5.3 Personal qualities lacking in new recruits to public libraries

Rank	Lacking qualities
1	Committed to organizational goals*
2	Friendly
3	Reliable
4	Flexible*
5	Able to accept pressure*
6	Energetic*
7	Written communication skills*
8	Able to work with and for a range of colleagues
9	Thorough
10	Open minded

*Also in top ten most essential list

Source: Goulding et al., 1999

Study participants identified a range of skills needs and skills gaps within the current staffing resource although one participant felt that public libraries had not yet really established the kind of skills and qualities they needed to take services forward:

> I suspect the workforce problem is vast. I suspect we need to be much more clear about what we need in that workforce by way of skills, expertise to deliver the modern library service, going back to what is a modern library service at this stage; that's still being worked through. Once we've got that I think we can then see what workforce we need

> and then at that point you can start doing some matching of people, where they are and what we need. And that becomes a more manageable task. (Anon)

Another participant agreed that services needed to think hard about what staff were now expected to do and whether those skills were being laid out clearly in job application documentation:

> The issues are very definitely about whether we have the right skills sets in public libraries to meet modern libraries' [needs] because I don't think many people have stopped to think about that. Are we thinking about that in our recruitment? Somebody said to me the other day, 'Do job descriptions really reflect what we actually want people to do?', especially around front line staff. A lot of people have not even thought about that, I think, and the skills they want. (Sarah Wilkie)

Dissatisfaction with the quality of applicants for first professional posts is a common theme in the research and literature on this topic but the evidence suggests that library authorities are having staffing difficulties at just about all stages of the hierarchy. Before they were discontinued, the Public Library Position Statements had to address the staffing issues that services were facing and outline the actions being taken to improve leadership, staff capacity and skills. In response, many of the 2003 statements discussed critical staff vacancies and the difficulty of recruiting staff with specialisms in key service areas such as children's work and reader development. Services often had to re-advertise posts when they did not attract the calibre of applicant they are seeking and many were worried that their capacity to deliver quality services were, or would be shortly, limited. This is exacerbated by low turn-over in many authorities and, as indicated above, there is talk of stagnating staff establishments caused by a lack of new blood and resulting in a shortage of fresh ideas. Kath Owen felt this was causing difficulties at management level:

> You've got less people moving up to middle management and then onto senior management and, yes, I think that at sort of middle management we've definitely seen a reduction in numbers of applicants. (Kath Owen)

The problem of recruiting staff from across the different cultural communities of an area has already been mentioned and this is another obstacle which may prevent public libraries delivering new services which meet the needs of a large proportion of the population. If staff with different backgrounds cannot be recruited, cultural sensitivity and respect must be shown by all staff who may need training to interact appropriately in a culturally diverse community (Larsen et al., 2004). Larsen et al. (2004) assert that no public library system anywhere in the world (except, perhaps, with the exception of that in Singapore) has staff adequately and proportionately reflecting the cultural and linguistic structure of its community. This is certainly true of the UK where, despite positive action initiatives, the public library workforce remains stubbornly homogenous. Only 286 out of 20,000 members of the Library Association are Black; and only 3 of the 286 earn more than £27,000 p.a, suggesting that Black people are not making it into positions of influence.

Study participants often identified this as an important issue that must be addressed. According to John Pateman:

> Staff either don't reflect the population or they reflect the majority, the dominant members of that community. (John Pateman)

John Vincent agreed, suggesting that the stereotypical image of the librarian often had more than a grain of truth attached to it:

> It's really interesting, through all the training we do, the one thing we keep coming back to time and time again is our image. And our image is exactly that – we're white, middle class, posh, very clever, still go 'shush' all the time and, depending on where we are, we're either terribly, terribly smart, you know the twin set and pearls image, or we're terribly scruffy. But I think that although that's a horrible stereotype, there is some truth in that. Very few library services are able to, or are perhaps making the effort but are not able to, reflect the community in their staffing... So you go to library services where there are very few, if any, Black staff, very few young staff (which is an increasing problem), very few men. (John Vincent)

Another participant also felt that the image of libraries and library work needed to change because, currently, her service was not attracting staff with the necessary commitment to the work and service development. Presenting quite a damning picture of staff, she said:

> The staff you attract, because of the image, are the mirror-image of all the other staff. So in this town you will get white women, because women have a higher employment level than men. So you're getting white women and they're nice women, of course, because it's a nice job and they can work part time etc. And a lot of them have that level of commitment and that level of commitment is not enough. Obviously, staff have different levels of commitment to their jobs but there are certainly some, and staff who have been here for a long time, who come for a chat. (Anon)

Although the recruitment pool may be limited, it could be argued that, once recruited, it is the job of the library service to instil a positive working culture and appropriate ethos in staff through training and development.

Martin Molloy, like John Vincent, identified the lack of young men coming into the profession as a challenge but when talking of staff diversity, most participants focused on ethnic or cultural diversity. In interview, Ayub Khan discussed the proposed new library at Birmingham (where he was then employed) and felt that a design incorporating a lot of glass could play an important part in encouraging use by showing the public that there are 'people like us in there'. He explained:

> It's not just the library building but it's the staff that's in there, the profile of people who are there which is to do with age, it's to do with cultural background. (Ayub Khan)

He also felt that the lack of diversity within the profession was one challenge that prevented public libraries changing to accommodate new users and new uses as quickly as they otherwise might:

> If you look at the library staff population, it doesn't really reflect the society out there… When you look at its profile and how it's managed in terms of senior management, there's very few people from Black and minority ethnic communities. It's not really reflecting the dramatic changes. Birmingham is poised to be one of the first Black cities in the UK with a majority minority population but I'm not sure whether that's really being reflected in the population we see in the library staff and I think there's a big area of work that needs to be done there. (Ayub Khan)

Leadership

The need to draw leaders from a wide range of backgrounds is also stressed by Durrani (2002). He laments the lack of initiatives to widen the public library leadership base to include more black people and suggests that giving a more diverse group of leaders the opportunity to influence policies will result in fairer and more dynamic services. In response, Resource and then the MLA funded the Quality Leaders Project designed to address the dual challenges of providing services which meet the needs of all communities and equal employment opportunities for library workers from Black and minority ethnic groups.[2] Through leading a development project aimed at improving services to the Black community, the Quality Leader, a Black library or information worker identified as having leadership potential, was mentored through the organization and management of the project. Those taking part in the project reported that, through the scheme, they developed a wide range of knowledge, skills and attitudes essential to a leadership role (Durrani, 2002).

In interview, though, Shiraz Durrani acknowledged that there had been some problems recruiting sufficient participants:

> I think we were a bit idealistic developing a programme like that which was funded from outside which will give new skills to Black managers and we thought perhaps we could come to a situation where we were perhaps developing a new generation of heads of libraries from that. It didn't do that because we found it difficult to even recruit Black people to even come to those courses, the people who headed libraries didn't think it was necessary to develop their Black staff and they kept saying, 'Oh, we can't release them' and they were sort of quite low level so we shifted our balance slightly. (Shiraz Durrani)

Many authorities are worried more generally about leadership potential and succession planning with fears that the whole public library field, as well as individual services, will be left rudderless at a time when strong advocacy on behalf of public libraries is more important than ever. In recognition that the whole cultural sector is concerned about the quality of its leadership, the Clore Leadership Programme was established to develop leadership abilities and skills.[3] In 2004, Ciara Eastell, Principal Assistant County Librarian for Somerset County Council, was selected as the only librarian among the 27 Fellows from across the arts sector to participate in the initiative. The report of the Clore Duffield Foundation task force, established to consider leadership training within the sector, identified a number of barriers to training effective leaders for the sector including a lack of time, money, organizational ability and clear career structures (Clore Leadership Programme Task Force, 2002). The report also commented that there was strong professional 'anti-managerial' resistance to leadership training within the sector, arising from the perception that good leaders are born not trained. The model of leadership appropriate to the cultural sector was considered different in many important respects to the conventional business model of leadership. Lacking a simple 'bottom line', cultural leaders instead have to satisfy a diversity of interests and constituencies and although business leaders may need to serve multiple stakeholders, they do not have to align their strategies with the latest requirements of social policy, as in the cultural sector. Conditions of law and governance are also different in the cultural sector and making long-term strategic plans as well as ensuring constant innovation in conditions of scarce resources are required of cultural leaders.

For public libraries specifically, the *Public Library Workforce Study* gave dire warnings that public libraries will face serious leadership problems unless action is taken to address issues such as rewards and career ladders (Usherwood et al., 2001). Whilst some library authorities have flattened the career ladder so that those beginning their career can see an achievable path to the top, they are still struggling to appoint at managerial levels. Good leaders have a clear vision for their service and are able to enthuse and motivate others to work towards that vision but Usherwood et al., (2001) found a general consensus that there was a lack of leadership in the public library profession and no clear understanding of how the next generation of leaders could be fostered. Leadbeater (2003) agreed that public libraries have neglected management development resulting in a shortage of management talent at the very time that strong leadership is most critical. Perhaps the extent and intensity of the pressures and frustrations directed at senior managers from both above and below for a rather modest wage make these positions unattractive although Martin Molloy felt that this was often exaggerated and was more hopeful of the future:

> I firmly believe that for bright young people there will be fast tracking because all over the country the middle manager in the mid 50s [age] range will all be disappearing and there will be opportunities. And when we talk about poorly paid posts and so on, I sometimes think that's over-egged. There are poorly paid posts around, there are also some pretty well paid posts as well. (Martin Molloy)

Nevertheless, many interview participants agreed with one head of service's opinion that there were 'very real recruitment issues at a senior level' (Anon). Martin Molloy, who felt that some of the initiatives described below had been successful and, as indicated above, that the profession had reasons to be optimistic about the future leadership of the profession, acknowledged that the current situation was not good:

> I've got to say at the moment that probably the present leadership tranche is part of the problem, not part of the solution but they are part of the solution in terms of being able to

see where the problems are and trying to ensure that we've got new people coming through. (Martin Molloy)

Alan Watkin suggested that part of the leadership crisis public libraries were facing was related to the fact that library staff were too inward looking and were unable or unwilling to work on a wider corporate basis:

I suppose there's reluctance or a lack of drive by library-based colleagues to position themselves so that they can compete across the portfolio. I don't know too many taking management qualifications. When I got this job, I recognized that the fact I'd been OK as a librarian didn't count for anything; the guy who came from the sports side was OK on the sports side. So what? And I think that is a factor and that may be actually about the difficulty having access to opportunities. (Alan Watkin)

Concern about a potential leadership crisis has led to a range of initiatives and activities designed to nurture future leaders for the profession. The Society of Chief Librarians has held leadership masterclass weekends, the Laser Foundation has organized 'Think Tank' weekends of young managers (known as the Bright Young Things or BYTs) identified by their authorities as future leaders and MLA is developing a leadership programme as a result of *Framework for the Future*. Despite these national initiatives, the alarm often voiced in the professional press and at conferences about future leaders for the profession is not always accompanied by action on the ground. Frances Hendrix commented in interview that the Laser Foundation's call for nominations for the BYT initiative had had an underwhelming response; just three authorities sent nominations. Similarly, all heads of library services in England were contacted by mail and email for participation in the *Framework for the Future* leadership programme. Again, only seven nominations were originally received and the consultancy firm, FPM, had to telephone all authorities that had not responded. Even then, only 56 per cent of authorities nominated individuals to participate in the programme. In spite of the hand wringing and predictions of crisis, it seems that not all services are willing to commit staff time when the opportunities present themselves.

Nevertheless, one participant was optimistic about the *Framework* initiative and explained what it was setting out to achieve:

Where we're starting is the basis that there are big, big problems with workforce in libraries. We only have limited resources, we only have a limited period of time to get things started and we have to start somewhere. For that reason, we're saying start with leadership where you can actually do a lot of work intensively with a small group of people that will start to have an effect across the whole organization. We're implementing a new leadership development programme. At the core of it, two things really, one is developing a common shared vision so that understanding of what libraries are all about, where they're going, what they're for and how to get that across; that starts stressing of lot of these other advocacy issues. And the second part is about skills and it's based on good practice models that are already out there. It's not inventing anything new, nothing fancy but it's tailored to where libraries are and the kinds of needs that their leaders of today and tomorrow are facing. It's about getting 450 people … with potential. (Anon)

Many other participants recognized that the skills set necessary to lead a public library service was changing and, as suggested in Chapter 2, that lobbying, influencing and political skills were increasingly important but not always abundant within the profession:

> I think public librarians have been far too keen not to engage politically which I think is idiotic. If you don't engage politically you're marginalized immediately. So that's a big mistake that we've made and we've far too long stood on our professional dignity and [council] members and other officers find that ridiculous. (Martin Molloy)

Frances Hendrix felt that these kinds of skills were not just hidden but lacking. Talking of new recruits to the librarianship profession she said:

> The people that [want to enter public library work] I think have this very strong public ethos of wanting to help people; very laudable. However, you don't seem to get people that have that and have a business brain as well, who want to do things at a lower costs, who want to publicize things better, who want to be innovative. There aren't so many of them. (Frances Hendrix)

The need for chief librarians to understand and even enjoy the cut and thrust of political manoeuvring was emphasized by Garcia and Sutherland (1999) who asserted that awareness of the feelings, perceptions, agendas and actions of key stakeholders including politicians and users is essential if chiefs are to successfully fulfil their responsibilities. They outlined the seven attributes needed to develop skill in the political arena. Firstly chief librarians must know the structure and reporting relationships within local government inside out. They also need to influence the perception of the public library service, as stressed in Chapter 2, to ensure it is considered an important institution within the community. Thirdly they should act ethically but also understand that compromise is an important part of the political process. Fourthly, appropriate communication that respects confidentiality and engenders trust in both staff and elected officials is necessary. Their fifth attribute is planning which is considered an integral part of library operations but which should also be responsive to capitalize on opportunities as they arise. Fiscal management is the sixth dimension of political skill and is often the most politically charged process with perhaps the most immediate and direct impact on library services. Chiefs have to acquire sufficient funds and then use them effectively and responsibly. Finally, chiefs need to develop services which meet the needs of the community and the aspirations of councillors.

The solutions proposed by Usherwood et al. (2001) to overcome the problems of recruitment, retention and leadership potential facing public libraries included better marketing of the attractions of public library work to potential recruits, better co-operation between Departments of Library and Information Studies and public libraries, strengthened work experience and trainee programmes and increased commitment to continuous professional development. Many authorities' 2003 Public Library Position Statements echoed these suggestions and emphasized mentoring, training and appraisal to retain good staff and encourage their career progression and leadership potential. Some also commented that, with the widening of skills needed for public library work, services should look beyond the traditional recruitment pool, which so many consider limited, and recruit people who bring valued new kinds of skills into the service. Sommerlad et al (2004b) have also questioned whether professional qualifications should be a requirement or whether, in fact, they act as barriers, deterring the best people from applying.

There has always been resistance to the appointment of staff without professional qualifications to professional and senior positions from certain quarters, though, and this would, in fact, seem to go against research findings which indicate that public library experience and understanding of the public library environment are essential qualities sought by employers (Usherwood et al., 2001). The new *Framework of Qualifications* proposed by Cilip also stresses the importance of knowledge of information management theory and practice for Chartered status and while acknowledging that there is a range of routes by which staff could gain that knowledge, still insists that those applying for Chartership acquire it through a course or some other route (Cilip, 2003).

Study participants were divided on this issue, some feeling that the only way to acquire some of the skills lacking from the profession was to recruit from outside, as Alan Watkin reluctantly conceded:

> I can see a real danger, not very far away, within a decade, [when] maybe we've got the resource, maybe we know what we're doing but we ain't got the right people to deliver it. And I hate to say this because I first came into the job when it just became a graduate profession [but] maybe that isn't the right answer. (Alan Watkin)

Picking up the issue of the difficulty of recruiting appropriate professionally qualified staff, Margaret Bellamy suggested that the calibre of staff from other professional backgrounds was often higher. She explained:

> We went to recruit [for a librarian position] and had four applications and two of them didn't have the qualifications. At the same time, we'd recruited some Early Years people and some ICT development people and they'd come in and they were absolutely brilliant. So have we got lucky here or have we got unlucky there [with the librarian position]? But we recruited again for non-librarians for a project and the quality was above what we'd get for librarians. (Margaret Bellamy)

This had led her service to look more favourably on the recruitment of staff without professional qualifications and train them in library routines:

> We had trouble recruiting librarians. We had trouble recruiting for basic librarians but we also had trouble recruiting at middle level as well; the standard was not particularly good. We'd also had posts funded from things like Early Years, LSC, non-librarian posts and we had a much better standard for that and people came in and they seemed to be able to pick up the library side of things quite well. (Margaret Bellamy)

Shiraz Durrani felt that this strategy, recruiting people from outside the profession and training them in library work, was the correct strategy for many of the positions now available in public libraries. Talking about his service's recruitment of a youth worker he said:

> She has no library experience and we wanted it like that. I don't think libraries have the youth skills and we can give her library experience and so on but we can't do it the other way around. (Shiraz Durrani)

Others regretted the fact that a professional qualification was no longer considered necessary, especially at a higher level where multi-disciplinary working was having an impact as one head of service explained:

> I am a professional librarian responsible for a very wide range of services. There is no guarantee that when I leave or retire that my successor will also be a librarian and I think this may well not be the case. (Anon)

She added that her experience as professional librarian had given her advantages which she felt that those from other professional backgrounds would lack:

> [My background] has given me a huge wealth of experience of actually working on the front line and dealing directly with local communities at first hand and getting to know your client base. I have been a professional librarian for 24 years and I have worked in every area of public librarianship. I received an excellent professional training through my degree course and work placement… My experience of working in public libraries helps me to manage the interface with the public. I am fortunate that in [this area] we have an excellent professional network and we do work in partnership with each other and share experience. I don't think you get that kind of synergy in many other areas of work. (Anon)

Kath Owen agreed that her background of service in public libraries had been of benefit but also felt that her current job had little to do with librarianship:

> I used to have long arguments with my husband, who's nothing to do with libraries, who used to tell me that I did not need to be a librarian to do my job and actually I have to agree that he's absolutely right. The fact that I've got experience of being both a library assistant and a librarian helps me enormously and has stood me in extremely good stead but in order to do the job that I do today – my job is in management, managing people, training and developing people because I have a strategic role across the whole county for that and that's actually where my areas of expertise need to be. So from that point of view, yes, why can't you bring somebody in who hasn't actually got the library experience but has the appropriate other experience? (Kath Owen)

Although some of the quotes from Margaret Bellamy above suggest that she was happy to recruit from outside the profession, she still felt that qualified librarians had specific, desirable skills. Explaining some of the changes to Leicestershire public libraries' staffing structures discussed further below, she outlined the requirements for some of the posts which were advertised internally:

> We said [candidates had to be] Chartered or actively working towards Charter because we didn't want to exclude librarians straight away, in their first jobs, but it is quite clear that they have to be working towards Charter; they have got time but if they don't get Chartered, that's the end of their contract. Because I do feel strongly that there are certain things that librarians are quite good at and you do need librarians to do those. (Margaret Bellamy)

A quick flick through Cilip's appointments pages suggests that public library authorities still require professional qualifications for librarian positions but many final Position Statements suggested that many were considering advertising strategies and changes to job descriptions that would attract applicants without a formal librarianship degree. The debate at the Cilip's Public Library Group Spring Conference in 2004 focused on precisely this issue with those in favour of appointing managers from outside the profession stressing that the issue of leadership training and succession planning had been neglected by public library authorities and that services needed people with strategic planning skills, able to attract external funding and persuade councils to put public libraries at the heart of their policies and plans. These were few and far between in public library services today, it was argued. Those against this view agreed that high quality leadership skills were currently lacking but suggested that there was a pool of talented people ready to be mentored and inspired and who had the professional expertise, skills and knowledge necessary to provide a vision for the service.

The future of the public library workforce, its supply and nature, was an issue of concern for study participants, therefore, with many suggesting that a fresh look at staffing policies and plans was needed. Similarly, library service structures are also considered in need of an overhaul by many managers, concerned that staff are organized so that their skills are used both effectively and efficiently.

Organization and Use

As the workforce is the biggest area of expense for public libraries, innovative methods of organizing and using the human resources at their disposal must be a priority. Organizing a smaller workforce to ensure it is meeting its current commitments, as well as being able to take advantage of new opportunities, is a complex business. Very often a long term staffing strategy is neglected by public libraries as managers focus on short term exigencies although there is now a recognition that a long range view must be adopted by individual services and by national policy makers. Public library services appear to be constantly tweaking their staff structures, often in response to budget cuts. As Kinnell (1996) comments, restructuring is often a euphemism for measures taken to cope with the loss of professional posts and the need to spread specialist skills more thinly. In the 1970s and 1980s, team librarianship was adopted by most authorities. This involved a move away from the old hierarchical system characterized by a librarian in every service point assisted by a range of professional and support staff members and strong central control from library headquarters where the specialists (in children's work, for example) were based. Instead, librarians were organized into a kind of matrix structure of both geographic and functional teams with specialists working within communities, taking devolved decisions based on the needs of the area and reporting to a small senior management team at headquarters. Librarians were now generally peripatetic and given responsibility for specific services in a number of services points, leaving the day to day running of libraries in the hands of support staff. At the time, this was quite an upheaval for many staff but was considered necessary to reorient a service which some considered too tied to library buildings at the expense of work in the community. The branch system was also criticized for not using librarians' specialist skills to their best advantage while the team system could deliver specialist services at the local level, giving public libraries a strong community orientation. On the down side, it has been said that those working in a team-based structure get little management experience, especially staff management experience which can be debilitating for a service struggling to find the next generation of leaders.

Organizational Structures

The local government review of the 1990s led to further internal restructuring as the size of many authorities contracted meaning that team librarianship was often no longer viable, especially in unitary authorities where professional staff numbers can be as few as four (LISU, 2003). Flatter structures are the only option for services with a small number of professional staff but, in any case, there seems to be a consensus that flatter structures deliver the flexibility and adaptability that public library systems need to respond to today's fast-moving policy environment. Sommerlad et al. (2004b) reported moves to reduce the middle tier of professional librarians to increase the number of frontline staff, freeing up professional librarians to do more developmental and outreach work. This is echoed by the PKF (2005) report on public library procurement which recommends a review of library service staffing structures to ensure that as many people as possible are 'customer facing' (p. 6). Perhaps more controversially, Tim Coates (2004) also advocated cutting the number of 'backroom staff' and the management establishment to put more staff on what he calls the 'opening rota'.

Kath Owen indicated in interview that staffing patterns were changing in response to changing user demands. She explained that increases in opening hours had led to an increase in the number of staff employed and, in Nottinghamshire, that had taken her back to some basic calculations:

> The way in which our staffing was allocated across the county was based on 25 year old formulae which were totally out of date and it was a very, very complicated formula which, when we tried re-applying it, didn't make any sense whatsoever. So we decided we'd look for a more straightforward way of doing things and actually what we did… was to look at individual buildings and say, 'Now what do we need to staff a building? How many people do we actually need to staff this?' (Kath Owen)

Financial pressures, rising user expectations and the impact of technology have also had an impact on organizational structures, encouraging public libraries to search for paradigms that are more responsive, flexible and user, rather than internally, focused (Boissé, 1996). Technology, in particular, is identified in the literature as the key driving force encouraging organizational change, but customer and community orientation have also been important in moving away from traditional hierarchical structures towards flatter structures based around team working. Hierarchies and bureaucracies are considered too rigid and controlling to be able to react effectively and promptly to changing user needs. Sommerlad et al. (2003) suggested that locally-based teams, involving all levels of library staff, reflect the demands of users and give staff the freedom to develop local initiatives. Flatter structures are said to speed up decision making by shortening the management chain through which decisions have to be approved, promoting a more relaxed, creative and dynamic environment. Although there are concerns that flat, team-based structures can confuse lines of communication and responsibility, the benefits are seen to outweigh the disadvantages with decisions taken closer to the action being more responsive to users' needs.

Flatter structures are also seen as a way of overcoming some of the staffing difficulties outlined above, particularly the worries over leadership and succession. Leadership is now exercised at levels other than just at senior management and the fewer levels of hierarchy means that the gap between middle management team leaders and the senior management team is narrower, enabling leadership potential to be easily spotted and nurtured. Below leadership level, though, one problem associated with flatter structure is career development. Conventional career progression involving a steady rise through the different levels of the hierarchy is just not possible in a flat structure which, by its very definition, has fewer stages through which an individual can ascend. The lack of opportunities for promotion was the factor cited most often as the reason that librarians left the public library service in the *Public Library Workforce Study* (Usherwood et al., 2001). Restructuring and delayering were identified as a factor reducing opportunities for progression and contributing to stagnation and a lack of ambition by middle managers. It might also mean that younger staff do not get the management experience, especially staff management experience, that they need to progress. Kath Owen disagreed that this was the case, however:

> If you're a librarian, the chances are you'll be managing projects and therefore you'll be managing the people involved in those projects. You might be leading a small functional team of some sort. If you're going round to a branch library and doing some work there, the staff there will be referring to you, asking you for support, assistance, advice so you get that experience anyway, even though it's not actually designated as such. (Kath Owen)

In organizations with little opportunity for upward movement, managers are encouraged to move sideways to expand their capabilities by acquiring new skill sets and developing new competencies but this demands a quite different mindset and attitude towards career development than the conventional one acquired through experience of more traditional hierarchical systems. For those with solid career aspirations, rigid tiers of management provide a clear map of progression and promise of better remuneration. In contrast, employees working within flatter structures may struggle to find avenues upwards and this lack of promotion opportunity can result in low motivation and a high turnover of staff. This certainly seems to be the trend within public library services with management respondents to the *Public Library Workforce Study* (Usherwood et al., 2001) voicing fears that organizational restructuring and the cutting of higher management posts was creating a block on upward opportunities and stifling ambition. Services now need to address how to reward and, therefore, retain quality staff within their flat structures.

Although public library organizational structures may be flatter and team-based rather than hierarchical, many are still organized around the traditional core functions of lending and reference services. This may not be the most effective structure for the widening of public library roles as envisaged by the Government and many senior practitioners in the field. Function-based structures like these can cause separation, leading to information blockages around the organization. Some public library services are experimenting with staffing models that they consider will be more flexible and responsive to the needs of their users. Leicestershire public libraries had a major restructure of staffing patterns completed in 2004 and head of service Margaret Bellamy explained in interview that a variety of pressures had encouraged the service to examine how staff were organized including the People's Network, *Framework for the Future* and a perception that their group structure was leading to a lot of duplication of effort and skills. She also felt that specialist posts meant that staff were not responsive enough to user demands:

> We had concerns that we had librarians in specialist positions and people weren't doing things because that was the librarian's job, that was the children's librarian's job and therefore if you went into a library and they weren't there it was, 'Oh I can't do that'… We wanted flexibility for staff, we wanted staff to be able to everything and not be in ghettos. (Margaret Bellamy)

This has led the service into quite a radical new structure which is very centralized and standardized and with library assistants, or library service assistants as they are known in Leicestershire, taking on a lot more responsibility to 're-professionalize' the librarians and leave them to focus on service development and on increasing use by targeting non-users and infrequent users and encouraging their use of the county's libraries.

Flexible Working Patterns

Another issue that public libraries need to address in relation to their staffing structures and patterns is how they accommodate the increasingly diverse set of working patterns and contracts which staff are now working under. Temporary and part-time workers are not new to public libraries but research suggests that their use has increased as has their diversity so that the term 'flexible worker' now also encompasses staff working on job-share, term-time only, casual and annual hours contracts (Goulding and Kerslake, 1996a). Public library managers have traditionally used flexible working patterns as important tools in their labour use strategies and workers such as part-time and temporary staff are considered the solution to various workforce planning problems, enabling services to manage daily and seasonal fluctuations in demand, ensure trained staff are available outside core working hours and recruit and retain staff who do not want to work the conventional 9 to 5 working day. The benefits of part-time work was recognized by one participant who felt that it could be an entry point back into employment while, at the same time, increasing the pool of potential labour for libraries:

> [Part-time work] attracts the people coming back into work. We've just employed two people who've been out of work for 11, 12 years bringing up families and it attracts them back in and gives them a starting point. (Anon)

She also acknowledged, though, that flexible working patterns could cause headaches for the organization:

> I think one of the issues is all the full-time posts going onto job share which huge numbers of them are now doing. I think it has a long-term knock-on implication for why we can't get young staff in [to the profession]. We can't get youngsters in because youngsters need full-time work but now they're only being offered part-time posts and I actually think that is quite a large implication for us and I almost think we've gone too far, bending over to support everybody's need to go job-share, part-time at the cost of the youngsters trying to get into work in the profession. (Anon)

The challenges of managing a workforce with a range of different working patterns and with a range of different needs are increasingly being acknowledged, therefore (Goulding and Kerslake, 1996b), and managerial attachment to flexible working patterns for economy and efficiency reasons could be loosening as they recognize the logistical and organizational strains associated with their management. Some of the 2003 Public Library Position Statements suggested there was a move towards full-time rather than part-time posts although other types of flexible workers, such as supply or casual staff who can be called into work in an emergency, were increasingly in demand but difficult to find in some areas (SEMLAC, 2003).

To overcome the difficulties associated with contracting staff establishments and recruitment freezes, many public libraries have turned to different models of staffing including the use of contract workers. In those authorities which have outsourced operations, staff working in the contracted-out areas will not be employed directly by the local authority but by the company running that aspect of the library's service. Lawes (1995) identifies the lack of organizational commitment as the most intractable problem facing public library managers with a sub-contracted workforce, often caused by a lack of integration with the existing staff. Staff with a strong public sector ethos may object to working for a commercial company with its different cultural norms and mores and could suffer a lack of confidence and identity crisis (Lawes, 1994). They may also feel like second class citizens beside permanent staff, especially if there are differentials in benefits like holiday allowances. Lines of communications can become more difficult in a contracted out service area with staff sometimes unsure who they report to and also experiencing an arms-length relationships with directly employed staff which can inhibit pro-active working across the organization. The Demos study (2003) also reported that current workforce development policies and practices were based upon a conception of the whole organization and that provision for what it called 'the fuzzier parts of the workforce' (p. 23) was weak, an increasingly pressing issue considering the sector's increasing reliance on outsourcing. Despite these difficulties, contract workers are considered a cost efficient method of providing additional staff resources within current budgetary constraints, although they must be managed sensitively to be most effective. Similarly, the use of volunteers in public libraries is gaining in popularity despite professional concern that they should not be used to compensate for the reduction or withdrawal of public library services caused by redundancies or failure to fill vacant posts.

Volunteers

Although volunteers have been used extensively and to good effect in the past by public libraries for outreach services, e.g. services for the housebound, where they can help provide access to professionally run library services, their use for other public library activities has been limited. Recent research into the use of volunteers by English public libraries found that use was increasing in both scale and diversity, however. 85 services outside London were using volunteers for a range of activities including helping users with ICT and running reading groups (Cookman et al., 2000). Volunteers enable work to be done that would otherwise not be undertaken, they draw on a large range of skills, they facilitate lifelong learning and help with social inclusion. Volunteering is also viewed as a good way of making libraries more representative of the communities within which they are based (Institute for Volunteering Research, 2002). The Lending Time project, led by CSV (Community Service Volunteers), has established volunteer programmes in partnership library authorities and, according to the report giving details of the project, has helped diversify and strengthen the workforce mix in participating library services enabling them to reach out into communities and attract users from a wider cross section of society (CSV, 2003). John Pateman in interview agreed that the use of volunteers was one way of making the staff more representative of the community served:

> Obviously we can do that through natural wastage and recruitment but also we can fast track the process through, for example, volunteer programmes, using volunteers from traveller communities to come in and work alongside staff, break down the barriers and they will be the advocates for the traveller community. Because you can't expect the white middle-aged Lincolnshire woman who has never met a traveller in her life, or a black person for that matter, to suddenly understand the culture and the needs and all the rest of it; that's an unreal expectation. (John Pateman)

Studies have found, though, that few library services have well-thought out policies or practices on volunteer use and management, despite acknowledgement that volunteers are not cost free or a cheap option and that they require training, support and expenses (Institute for Volunteering Research, 2002). Questions have also been raised about what volunteers can do that is not already done by library staff. The CSV report lists a range of activities which are nearly all done by permanent staff, raising fears of substitution. There are ways in which volunteers can add value, however, undertaking tasks that library staff would be hard pressed to do given their current responsibilities, helping visually impaired people travel to a reading group, for example. They can also mobilize support for the library among hard-to-reach groups as they often have links within the community. Larsen et al. (2004) note that volunteers can be particularly helpful within refugee communities, helping them make connections with groups of immigrants and assisting with language barriers. Nevertheless, public library services need to be clear about the needs of the organization for volunteer labour and the commitment volunteers require in terms of time for development and support.

Another key issue related to the employment and use of a flexible and/or peripheral workforce is their training and development as there is evidence that they are often either not included in public library services' training plans or there are problems associated with organizing appropriate training opportunities for them (Goulding and Kerslake, 1996c). In fact, it is not just these workers who may be missing out on training in public libraries and there is growing disquiet about the extent and nature of staff development throughout public libraries in the UK.

Staff Development

A unique experiment in public library staff training was launched in the UK in 1999 and yet MLA (then Resource) announced in 2001 that, 'the quality of training that public library staff receive is a matter for serious concern' (Resource, 2001, p. 16). As noted above, it has been suggested that, apart from the People's Network ICT training that has taken place, development activities for staff are lacking. Some study participants disagreed that public libraries were neglecting staff training and development, however. Kath Owen asserted:

> There's masses of training going on particularly in reading development and, increasingly, there's going to be more and more on social inclusion both at local level and at a regional level. (Kath Owen)

Another participant agreed that, in her service at least, training was a priority:

> I think overall our training programmes in this authority are very good. There is plenty of training on offer and there may be areas where we miss strengths but they're certainly not critical areas and I think overall most of the staff get whatever opportunity they want to

> go on training and are encouraged by their line managers that X training would actually be good for them and encouraged to go. (Anon)

She later added:

> I think it would be grossly unfair to say there isn't opportunity for training for staff outside of ICT and I think we've bent over double to maintain other training whilst the ICT training has been going on which has been very hard work at times. (Anon)

Despite these positive testimonies, the literature reports a general dissatisfaction related to public library staff development, often the result of the perception that public library authorities are failing to commit the necessary investment to ensure that their staff can deliver services effectively. The ICT training programme, which was the focus of much of the recent training in public libraries, was funded through an external source, the New Opportunities Fund (NOF), now the Big Lottery Fund, not authorities' own training budgets. NOF, a government body, was established in 1998 to distribute a proportion (28 per cent) of the proceeds of the National Lottery to 'good causes' including education, health and environmental projects throughout the UK.[4] As noted in Chapter 3, although public library services have not been able to apply for lottery funding for capital or operational projects, they have benefited from special programmes designed to improve ICT facilities and services in public libraries. The funding has been distributed under three headings: *infrastructure* to connect all static public library service points to the Internet; *digitization* to digitize important sound and image collections and make them freely available; and *training* to train all public library staff in the use of ICT. £100 million was committed for the hardware, software and telecommunication infrastructure to connect public libraries to the People's Network (the 'brand name' for the Internet in public libraries), £50 million was committed to digitization and £20 million was committed to public library staff training (a parallel programme was established to train teachers and school librarians).

The impact of the People's Network on public libraries and their staff is discussed in depth in Chapter 6 but the investment can be regarded as government recognition of the important role that public libraries can play in enabling community access to ICT and the benefits that result from connectivity including the acquisition of ICT skills and access to lifelong learning opportunities and e-government services. It was also acknowledged, though, that to make the most of the facilities made available through the infrastructure and digitization programmes, users would need support and staff training should be a priority (Library and Information Commission, 1998).

ICT Training

Before the training began, public library staff competence in using ICT, let alone helping others to use it, was patchy to say to the least. Jones et al. (1999) found that staff lacked confidence in their own skills and were particularly uncomfortable with the thought of having to provide advice and guidance to users. The low ICT skills base of public library staff was perceived as a real threat to the success of the People's Network and both *New Library: the People's Network* (Library and Information Commission, 1997) and *Building the New Library Network* (Library and Information Commission, 1998), the two reports which set out the vision and practicalities of making the public library system the focus of citizen and community ICT connectivity, stressed the need for staff training to ensure public libraries could deliver the services required. To clarify the kind of training needed, *Building the New Library Network* (Library and Information Commission, 1998) established eight outcomes which the NOF ICT training programme aimed to address:

1 Competence with ICT
2 Understanding how ICT can support library work
3 Health, safety and legal issues relating to ICT
4 Using ICT to finding information for users (including evaluating information)
5 Using ICT to support reader development
6 Using ICT to support users to ensure effective learning
7 Effective management of ICT resources
8 Knowing how to use ICT to improve efficiency

Library authorities' attention was primarily focused on the first outcome, with many authorities opting to train their staff for the European Computer Driving Licence (ECDL) qualification[5] although the low skill level of some staff meant that they were initially enrolled on CLAIT[6] (Computer Literacy and Information Technology) courses to prepare them for the ECDL (Spacey, 2003). Both the CLAIT and ECDL syllabuses cover the basics of using a computer as well as applications such as word processing, spreadsheets, databases, presentation software, electronic communication and the Internet. A formal evaluation of the success of the NOF ICT training programme has been published (Sommerlad et al., 2004a) and a number of other independent studies have also focused on the training, concluding that staff and management response to the training has been positive overall although some difficulties remain. Spacey (2004), for example, found that all the training methods used throughout the programme, both formal and informal, were rated favourably by staff, indicating a positive attitude to training generally and a desire to get to grips with the technology which is becoming increasingly important to the public library service mission. She reported that both staff and management felt the training had improved the confidence of staff in terms of what they could personally achieve with ICT as well as with helping the public. Dodd et al. (2002) similarly reported that the confidence levels of public library staff were higher after completing the ECDL and this encouraged many to take supplementary training covering the other seven NOF outcomes. Brophy (2003, p. 14) emphasized the importance of a 'sympathetic environment' for users new to ICT and reported user appreciation of the help provided by library staff, assisted no doubt by the training.

Generally, the programme was a success and highly praised by participants for being well managed, flexible, having clear outcomes and deadlines, for the support it offered reluctant learners and for keeping everybody informed and engaged (Demos, 2003). NOF-funded evaluations reported a significant development of public library staff ICT skills from a very low base with many staff using their new skills to extend their roles and offer additional services to users (for example, Sommerlad et al., 2003). The development of a learning infrastructure in public library services was another positive outcome noted (Sommerlad et al., 2004b). One Welsh participant agreed that the training programme had been a huge success and, in fact, was the most significant aspect of the legacy of the People's Network:

> I thought the most important programme of the People's Network was the training, providing ICT training for all Welsh librarians… Local authorities trained 1,740 librarians in Wales and that's a terrific achievement to get them through ECDL… I've talked to librarians who went through ECDL, library assistants who went through ECDL and they are so much more confident now about advising members of the public who come in. (Anon)

That is not to say that everyone's experience of the training was positive, however. Sommerlad et al. (2003) reported that some staff had been disappointed that the training had not been linked more closely to their work roles with many feeling that some of the elements of the ECDL, such as using spreadsheets and databases, were not relevant to their jobs. The final evaluation report of the People's Network suggested that staff attitudes and the outcome of the training was affected by the nature of the training provided, existing skills and also the wider organizational culture, staff moral and training support structures (Sommerlad et al., 2004). Although the programme has been hailed as a success, there is some evidence that there have been casualties along the way with the changes in job remit and skills required too much for some to cope with, resulting in resignations and early retirements (Spacey, 2004). As outlined in Chapter 4, new users introduced to the library by a variety of new services and facilities may have clashed with existing, long time library-goers; they may also have come into conflict with staff. Homework clubs, for example, will attract more school aged children into the library, perhaps also drawn by the ICT facilities available and while the public library has always welcomed children, the influx of a large number of youngsters can sometimes leave staff struggling to cope and feeling that they are now working in a very different place from that to which they were initially recruited. Staff on the ground are often more attached to some of the more traditional aspects of the library service, such as book lending and the provision of information and can be 'very particular about their roles and responsibilities' (Froud and Mackenzie, 2002, p. 25). This can present barriers for managers trying to re-position the public library service within the local authority and peoples' consciousness and also the receptivity of staff to the training provided.

The challenge is to change the image that staff have of themselves as lenders of books only, to also encompass the role of enabler of ICT within the community but with the average age of library workers around 47 years, it is perhaps inevitable that some will leave their jobs rather than have to learn new skills and take on new responsibilities (Froud and Mackenzie, 2002). Not all people over the age of 40 find technology baffling or frightening, of course, and we must be wary of dismissing older staff as unable to adapt to using ICT. The advent of the "silver surfer" proves that there are no age limits on enjoying the benefits of online communication and resources. Nevertheless, research shows that older public library staff have inferior ICT skills and are less likely to see themselves using the Internet (Spacey, 2004). Those public library staff unable to cope in an environment in which ICT takes a more prominent role may not be the only ones to leave as a result of the NOF ICT training programme, though. Dodd et al. (2002) report that staff equipped with good ICT skills are now leaving the public library service for higher paid positions, adding a new worrying dimension to already troubling retention problems.

One of the most significant findings of the evaluation by Sommerlad et al. (2003) was that staff do not only need enhanced ICT skills to operate effectively within the new public library environment; 'soft skills' which enable them to exhibit 'appropriate emotional behaviour' are also needed to deal effectively with the increasing diversity of users now using the public library as a result of the People's Network. For frontline staff, customer service skills are increasingly important. Customer care training was a feature of public library service training programmes in the 1980s and 1990s, primarily in response to the customer charter movement discussed in Chapter 4. Always important in a user-oriented environment, skills including listening, responding appropriately and giving instructions are now being given a renewed emphasis because of the People's Network and its impact on the public library culture and atmosphere. Increasingly, staff need to be able to act assertively both to handle users not used to the public library environment and perhaps behaving unacceptably and also to set limits on the amount of support and assistance users can expect as some, especially novice users, can be very demanding.

This area of learner support skills is a difficult one for staff to tackle as there are no national standards or guidance relating to their roles or limitations. A common understanding of how far library staff should go in assisting library users in their studies or skill acquisition is lacking both between and even within authorities so that while users in one branch library might receive minimal assistance in using the ICT available in the library, those in another library or in another authority may be given more active support with staff taking a more supportive role in guiding users through their learning options. Sommerlad et al. (2004) found, however, that the library staff participating in their study felt that a formal ICT training role was beyond their level of competence and outside their remit. One study participant agreed with this view. Taking exception to the notion that the training had been inadequate she said:

> I think that depends on what it is you perceive public library staff are there to do. If you perceive that they're there to be tutors then, yes, probably, they didn't get that [training]. but I don't see that's their role and I don't think it's right for us to start competing with local colleges whose role that is. I certainly think here we've got a really clear line

> between helping people where we can and referring them to the right places to learn more if that's what they really need to do. (Anon)

Each authority approaches the provision of ICT assistance differently and expectations for staff differ, therefore. In some authorities, staff deliver learning, in others they assess or mark work whilst in others their role is confined to offering information, advice and guidance although the boundaries between all these can be very blurred as Dodd et al. (2002) found. Much depends on staff workload, skill level and their readiness to take on what many consider an extension of their role but even those authorities deciding that they cannot offer in-depth learner support still need to enhance their staff's training and coaching skills as they are invariably called upon to help users access electronic resources. This aspect of the training associated with the People's Network has been neglected to date. Although supporting users' learning is listed as an intended outcome of the training, the scale of the effort needed to bring the majority of staff up to the level of outcome one was underestimated, meaning that the higher level skills have not been given the attention intended.

The programme, and its funding, finished in 2004 and it is doubtful that individual authorities will be able to fund large-scale learner support training from their own budgets, leaving staff unprepared for this role. Although training managers welcomed the input of funding and the activity it supported, Sommerlad et al. (2004) reported concerns that this the level of training was unlikely to be sustained once the funding ceased, an issue also raised by study participants, one saying:

> I think the one [issue] we haven't resolved yet is how we're going to carry on from NOF because, basically, we can't afford to carry on in the way that we were, we haven't got the money to invest in the training. We haven't come up with an answer to that yet; it's certainly on my agenda to think about. (Kath Owen)

Another participant also expressed concern about the size of the training budget, feeling that it was too small to sustain the level of ICT training activity that had been ongoing. She was particularly concerned that new staff entering the service would not have received the same degree of training as existing staff and that this had implications for the service offered. One interviewee also felt that ongoing training was necessary not just for new staff but to maintain the ICT skills of those who had been through the training:

> I think there's a necessity to build in real time training opportunities because for those staff who are not really using technology a lot, if they get stopped by a user in the library, they're not going to know anything. So I think that training plans have to be continuous, have to be relevant to the staff. (Anon)

New Skills

The People's Network has been the most high profile development which has had a significant impact on staff roles and, consequently, the type of skills and training they require but other activities have also highlighted skills gaps and training and development needs. Sommerlad et al. (2004b), engaging in some future gazing, suggested possible future scenarios for public library services, taking advantage of their increased ICT capabilities. They asserted that staff will need a range of capabilities, dispositions and skills to be effective in the scenarios of the future public library they describe. Past and current service developments are also requiring different skills and competencies. Reader development work and social inclusion policies have highlighted the need for practical skills but also cultural and attitudinal issues which need to be addressed though equality awareness training. As Glenys Willars suggested, 'I'm expecting staff to be able to do things that perhaps they've never done before or not wanted to do before' (Glenys Willars).

For professional staff and those involved in service development, working in partnership and the local government environment of accountability and bidding culture demand a range of political, collaboration and advocacy skills, many of which were outlined in Chapter 2 and highlighted above in the discussion of leadership. Partnership working, for example, involves a change in attitude. It could be argued that the library service used to be quite isolationist and even fiercely independent, worried that when cooperating with others in the local authority libraries would always be the minor partner and in danger of being overlooked or swallowed up. As we have seen, partnership is now considered the way forward for a dynamic service and libraries see themselves as part of the bigger picture but this involves a change in outlook and also the development of political skills to ensure the public library service takes advantage of the opportunities that arise.

Some participants doubted that many staff had the skills necessary to form beneficial partnerships for the library service, however. One interviewee said:

> A lot of libraries have really struggled to change their pattern of thinking and working and relate to [partnership working] and make the case, being much more pro-active to make that partnership work. They just sit quietly in a room and in that context you will wither and die and that's crudely what's happening to some library services and that's why others are really good, because they're excellent at it. (Anon)

Alan Watkin agreed that working collaboratively across the local authority or even the same directorate did not come easily to all staff:

> It's quite difficult, I'm finding and I'll admit this, to get the guys and girls on the front line to do that; they're amazingly reticent to actually work together and contact each other on a day to day basis. For example, in one particular site in a village where the library is all of 50 metres from the leisure centre there was no cooperation or contact. In the end I resorted to walking between the two and taking their respective brochures. I can't get them to talk to each other. (Alan Watkin)

Resourcing Training

The skills now needed to succeed at all levels in the public library service are not necessarily those closely associated with librarianship, therefore, but, as discussed, there is growing concern that the people with the skills necessary to succeed in this environment are not attracted to public library work. Because of this, many authorities in their 2003 Public Library Position Statements referred to the need to either 'grow their own' or bring in those with the essential qualities, but without formal library or information management qualifications, and give them the necessary background and experience to succeed through training and development, as discussed above. Both seem reasonable solutions to the perceived management and leadership crisis, although the second meets some opposition from within the profession as Jan Holden explained:

> We have found it very difficult to recruit qualified librarians into posts here because we're miles away from anywhere and it's quite an expensive place to live and all that kind of stuff. So we've been looking at ways of developing our own library qualification and employing people who've got the people skills and the outreach skills and the vision skills. And all the technical stuff that you may or may not need in that role can come later. But it's about getting the right people to do those jobs in the first place and that is causing friction between the more traditionally qualified people. (Jan Holden)

According to many commentators, library authorities have proved themselves generally incapable of devoting the resources necessary to make a real difference to the skills levels of staff. The training budgets of public libraries generally stand at two to three per cent of expenditure. Here, public library managers are faced with a dilemma, though. Resources for training usually come from the staffing budget and so managers wanting to increase the amount spent on training will need to make savings in some other aspect of staffing. A lack of resources underpins many of the difficulties public libraries face when trying to increase the skill levels of staff. As well as a lack of money to send staff on expensive external courses or programmes, a tight financial regime means that public libraries cannot employ additional or casual staff to cover for those attending training so opportunities to participate in training on a regular basis are limited. Similarly, staff wanting to practice and maintain the skills they have learnt through the NOF ICT programme, for example, find it very difficult to leave their normal duties because of the minimal staffing levels. The nature of local authority salary grades limit library services' freedom to promote workers who gain additional skills but the lack of financial reward for undertaking training can make some staff reluctant to participate.

Some of these problems are easier to overcome than others but initiatives which try to address them have been developed. Cooperative training involving more than one library service which has the benefits of economies of scale and shared resourcing has worked well in some areas and should be made easier with the support of the regional museums, libraries and archives councils. Training in reader and literature development is already organized on a regional basis through *Branching Out*, a collaborative training activity between library authorities and Regional Arts Boards. More extensive use of in-house and cascade training which can be tailored to the specific circumstances of the individual library service can also help raise skills levels and has the added benefit of developing coaching skills in the staff member delivering the training. Dodd et al (2002) found that staff appreciated being trained by somebody from within the service as it made them less worried about asking for help and so boosted their confidence and Kath Owen agreed that this was an economic and effective method of training:

> Our training budget is minute. We've just sort of found our way round it. A lot of training anyway is not going away on a course, a lot of training, particularly for library assistants, is on the job and in fact a lot of them don't want to go off anywhere else so there's a lot of things that go on internally, that is home grown for a better way of putting it. (Kath Owen)

Organizing the training at a convenient time is still an issue, though, and some authorities are committed to opening an hour later on one day a week so that this time can be devoted to training. While welcome as an indication of a commitment to training, an hour a week is unlikely to have much impact on filling the skills gap that many authorities say they are facing, however.

Conclusion

The discourses identified from both the literature and research interviews which related to the public library staffing establishment were generally negative or at least troubled. There was concern about the number of new entrants to the public library profession and their calibre. Interview participants were not generally worried by high staff losses or turnover rates but in some ways this was a problem in itself, causing concern that the number of full-time positions for new entrants was restricted thus limiting the injection of new blood. The fact that public library services were not attracting good recruits in sufficient numbers was highlighted as a grave matter of concern, then, and a variety of reasons was offered to explain this. The image of the profession and of the work undertaken by public librarians was felt to be a stumbling block as was the wage, considered low compared with other types of work within librarianship. That few potential recruits had the opportunity to experience work in a public library setting was considered to be partly to blame for the poor image of the profession and the work. It was felt that if those committed to a career in librarianship had the opportunity to become familiar with the public library environment, they might be more inclined to consider public librarianship as a serious career option. The issue was raised of whether public library services expect too much of applicants.

Many job adverts for public library work note that experience in a public library setting is desirable if not essential and yet if public libraries are not offering placements and work experience opportunities, it is difficult for potential recruits to meet the criteria. A couple of participants felt that public libraries were not very sure about the skills that they wanted their staff to possess and that this was because of a lack of clarity about what the service was setting out to achieve. By clarifying the mission of public library services, a more definite picture of the ideal person to deliver services should emerge. This also holds true of leadership positions. Here, the impression gained was that poor leadership in the profession is an urgent issue that must be tackled and a variety of initiatives is underway to do just that although commitment from library services themselves often seems to be lacking.

Discourses around training were more positive from study participants although the literature found much to criticize in public library training activities. Generally, the People's Network training was judged a success but there were concerns about sustaining that training and ensuring that other developmental activities were not neglected at the expense of ICT training. The literature and participants highlighted a number of important skills gaps which need to be addressed to ensure that public libraries continue to develop and remain relevant for the whole of the community. Some participants advocated the recruitment of people from outside the librarianship profession and although this has always happened to some extent to fill specialist positions, it is now being supported more generally to fill the skills gaps that public libraries see are developing as they widen their remit and develop activities that take them away from the core library-based services towards engagement with a wide range of political and social agendas which they hope will highlight their continued relevance and thus guarantee their survival.

Notes

1 See the Position Statements at URL: http://www.libplans.ws/ [04.11.05].
2 Quality Leaders Project website URL: http://www.seapn.org.uk/qlp.html [04.11.05].
3 Clore Leadership Programme Website URL: http://www.cloreleadership.org [04.11.05].
4 New Opportunities Fund Website URL: http://www.nof.org.uk/ [04.11.05].
5 For more information see URL: http://www.ecdl.com/main/index.php [04.11.05].
6 For more information see URL: http://www.clait-training.com/ [04.11.05].

PART 2
SERVICE DEVELOPMENT

Chapter 6

The People's Network

The Policy Context: UK Online

The New Labour Government's determination that the UK would climb aboard the 'information superhighway' was first articulated in print in *Our Information Age,* a policy document detailing how it intended to harness the potential of ICTs to ensure they benefited the economy and, more generally, British society as a whole (Central Office of Information, 1998). ICTs, it was argued, could improve educational effectiveness, combat social exclusion, improve individuals' economic position and facilitate the smooth running of democracy through e-government services. Access to and exploitation of ICTs have thus become a central plank of government policy which emphasizes that technology has the potential to radically change people's work and leisure time and provide social and economic benefits.

To transform Britain into one of the leading knowledge economies, the Government appointed an e-Envoy to drive forward 'UK Online' a programme of activities which aimed to increase ICT use by the general public and ensure it was spread equitably, improve conditions for e-commerce and enhance the electronic delivery of public services. For public libraries, the Government's policy to extend access to the Internet to all who wanted it was the policy that initially had most impact, followed closely by the development of e-government services. Public libraries have featured large in government initiatives to extend Internet access beyond those connected at home or through work. In response to concerns about the digital divide, which can leave some people lacking the information resources available to others and exacerbate existing social divisions, the UK government took steps to try to ensure that access to ICTs, and the Internet in particular, was available at low or no cost in various publicly accessible community locations. As a result, in England over £400 million was invested in a national network of 'UK Online Centres', around half of which are located in public libraries. The Government is committed, therefore, to ensuring that by 2005 everyone who wants to has the opportunity to access the Internet and although motivational barriers continue to discourage some from Internet use, the 2003 UK Online Annual Report showed that the Government was near to reaching its target (UK Online, 2004). Physical access was no longer the key issue it used to be, according to the report which stated that the Internet was available to all through home, work or in the community and that 96 per cent of the population was aware of a place where they could readily access it. Furthermore, over three million people reported that they had recently accessed the Internet in a library, suggesting that these public access points can provide a valuable safety net for those who cannot afford home connection.

Despite this positive picture, some challenges remain including persuading reluctant users, particularly the socially excluded and elderly, that there are benefits to the technology and more generally extending its use for e-government, the other area in which public libraries have a large contribution to make. The Government wants more people to interact with government through the Internet, believing this is a productive use of the technology which can improve the efficiency, convenience and quality of public services. According to the UK Online Annual Report, all local authorities now have websites and two-thirds of central government services have been e-enabled (UK Online, 2004). The report gives examples of the kinds of services now available online including health information through NHS Direct Online,[1] jobs and careers information,[2] advice and application forms for higher education,[3] childcare information[4] and town and county planning guidance and application forms[5]. In addition, local authority websites give information on all aspects of the services they provide directly as well as agendas and minutes of council meetings and contact details for local councillors. Information once available only in paper format is now widely and freely accessible online and although the structure and presentation of some local and central government sites could be better, the ease of accessing government information has generally improved through the implementation of online services.

Public libraries were among the first local authority services to take advantage of Internet technology to publicize their services and offer online access to facilities such as their catalogues and enquiry services. The UK Public Libraries Page run by Sheila and Robert Harden lists the URL of every British public library website and awards commendation marks for those considered to be making the best use of the Internet, not just for publicizing their services but also adding value through the implementation of new web-based services and facilities.[6] Some public libraries are making innovative use of Internet technology, therefore, and, as *Framework for the Future* reports, public libraries are playing a vital role in breaching the digital divide and providing access to government services through the People's Network (Department for Culture, Media and Sport, 2003).

The People's Network Project

The potential for public libraries to play a key role in fulfilling the Government's vision of a network of community-based, accessible ICT centres was set out in two key reports published by the Library and Information Commission (LIC), a predecessor body of MLA: *New Library the People's Network* (Library and Information Commission, 1997) and *Building the New Library Network* (Library and Information Commission, 1998). The first of these set out how ICT could enhance many of the services provided by public libraries including education and learning, community history and identity and citizenship information while the second detailed how the People's Network, as it was now known, could be established, making a number of recommendations to the Government on achieving the vision. The basis of the LIC's proposals was that public libraries should be the vehicle for a national digital network which would connect communities, enable the development of ICT skills within the general population and provide access to a range of cultural and educational materials and services (Culture, Media and Sport Committee, 2000).

The Government accepted the recommendations of the LIC and, as a consequence, public libraries have benefited from ICT funding from the New Opportunities Fund (NOF).[7] Special NOF programmes were established to improve ICT facilities and services in public libraries, as detailed in Chapter 5, with the result that all public library authorities in the UK now provide Internet access in their public libraries. There is no doubt that this aspect of the programme has been a success. As the formal evaluation of the programme states:

> This universality of physical access and consistency in standards represents both a remarkable technical achievement as well as an organisational feat in implementing such a large scale infrastructure initiative within the scheduled timescale and budget. (Sommerlad et al., 2004, p. 28)

There are now People's Network terminals in every public library in the UK and the number of public access terminals increased from 9,000 to over 30,000 over the period October 2001 to July 2003 (Sommerlad et al., 2003). Over 4,000 public libraries provide broadband access to the Internet and other online services, representing an increase in connectivity from just one per cent in 1995 to almost 100 per cent in less than a decade (Sommerlad et al., 2004). In England, 3,000 public libraries are designated UK Online Centres, places where people with limited or no access to ICT can use the Internet free or at low cost and get support in developing the skills to use the technology and throughout the UK there are now more than 4,000 public library learning centres which offer access to equipment and online resources such as the Internet and email facilities, community information, government services, learning materials and a range of office software applications. Provision is one thing, of course, use is quite another but the final evaluation of the People's Network project suggested that, 'level of usage of the PN terminals in public libraries…. reveal a consistent picture of significant demand for public access' (Sommerlad et al., 2004, p. 75).

The roll out of the People's Network, like its sister programme of ICT training for public library staff discussed in the previous chapter, has been judged a success. It has been completed on time and within budget and, according to official evaluations (Sommerlad et al., 2003 and 2004; Brophy, 2002 and 2004; MLA, 2004) has had a positive impact on the image and culture of the public library service. Brophy (2003, p. 1) goes as far as to call the People's Network 'a turning point for public libraries', suggesting that it is changing how both users and politicians view public libraries. He reports significant benefits for users, particularly those from disadvantaged groups, and the provision of additional funding from local authorities impressed by the achievements of the People's Network to date and its ability to deliver services which meet many of the Government's social objectives. Sommerlad et al. (2003) report how the more advanced public library services are moving beyond merely providing public access to ICT to develop services which exploit its opportunities to deliver key local and central government policies. They comment that the People's Network is identified as raising the profile of the public library service within the local authority, significantly enhancing its attractiveness as a partner especially with regard to the lifelong learning and social inclusion agendas of local and central government.

Study participants were also often enthusiastic about how the People's Network had enabled public library services to engage at a strategic level within the local authority. Talking about the ELFNI programme in Northern Ireland, one participant said:

> It's a PFI contract that seems to work so there's kudos there but also now we have a single network, you know, 1200 PCs in 126 libraries. We can talk strategically to all sorts of players…, we can talk a lot more coherently at a strategic level. (Anon)

Another interviewee suggested that this has encouraged local politicians and potential partners to understand the potential of libraries as 'part of networks, and not just IT networks but policy and community networks' (Anon). As a result, services that would benefit the user were being developed as John Pateman explained:

> The other benefits I should have mentioned of People's Network is it does facilitate joined-up working. It enables the library service to work with the heritage service or adult education and youth, for example. A virtual environment joins services up that are more difficult to join up initially in the real world because you have got a youth centre, a library, adult education facilities. Our aim is to merge all those together and have a one-stop shop, if you like. We wouldn't call it any one of those three, we would call it an Idea Store but until we can get there, we can do joined-up working through the People's Network, through the Internet. So those People's Network terminals are portal entry points into all kinds of new opportunities. (John Pateman)

The increased visibility for the public service within the local authority and beyond afforded by the People's Network was confirmed by another interview participant who stressed that this could have beneficial financial outcomes:

> We had an event where I did a presentation and there was a question on cultural change and I actually asked everyone in the audience (it was a public library audience), I asked them to raise their hand if they felt the People's Network had raised the profile of libraries and they all put their hands up and, you know, that is a real shift in attitudes. A good example of what I'm talking about is in the West Midlands where because of the investment in the People's Network infrastructure across the region, libraries across the country, they've levered half a million quid from the local regional development agencies. And there are stories like that from all over, you know, it's been fabulous. (Anon)

According to the staff surveyed by Sommerlad et al. (2004), the People's Network has also had a noticeable impact on users' view of the service, reinvigorating its role as a key resource at the heart of the community and, in fact, the People's Network has also benefited staff, helping them connect to the changing identity of the public library service. Overall, Sommerlad et al. (2004) reported that the People's Network has 'created a reservoir of credibility and good will towards the library service' (p. 117). The environment of the public library seems to attract many who have never before had the opportunity to use the Internet or online services, perhaps drawn by its community location, neutral and trustworthy public image and the availability of encouraging help on hand when needed. Sommerlad et al. (2004) reported that users were overwhelmingly positive about the provision of ICT in libraries, especially free access to the Internet, the speed of the connection, the range of software on offer and the up-to-date equipment.

Study participants agreed that the People's Network programme had had a positive impact on library usage, one stating:

> The uptake has been magnificent. I've recorded an increase in visits of up to four per cent in 2002/3 and over five per cent in 2003/4 and that can be attributed mostly to the People's Network. (Anon)

Another felt that the public's opinion of public libraries had improved because of the programme:

> Looking across the audiences, I think it is a service that can make a high impact and can certainly deliver on its agenda though projects like the BBC's Big Read and that kind of thing, it's shown that public libraries can do something that's as high profile as that. (Anon)

One interviewee felt that the People's Network, in conjunction with other changes, had changed people's awareness of their local public library:

> We've had an opening and both Members [of the Council] and members of the public were saying at that how much has changed, how modern they are, how bright. We've tried to link the PN [People's Network] to library refurbishment where possible so we've done a facelift, mostly internal – the outside sometimes leaves something to be desired – but we've done internal facelifts and lighting and other things so what they're getting isn't just a few PCs stuck in, it's a better overall library experience as part of it. So I think it has changed the perception. (Anon)

Martin Molloy felt that this was particularly the case among young people:

> Young people tended to like libraries but they found them terribly old fashioned, they weren't up to date in terms of new technology and so on. Well, you don't get that kind of reaction from young people today when you talk to them and that's all about the investment in the People's Network. (Martin Molloy)

And Alan Watkin agreed that that the People's Network had enabled public libraries to reach out to new audiences:

> [The People's Network] has given us the opportunity to reposition the library service in terms of its marketing sell and we have libraries… where the kids make an orderly queue. (Alan Watkin)

Other participants similarly felt that new users had been brought into public libraries by the availability of ICT facilities:

> The impact [of the People's Network] has been about increasing the range of people that come through the doors of the library, that's basically the biggest impact. So it's about offering a free service and offering an opportunity for people to find out and it's enabled us to welcome a huge range of different kind of people into the library. (Jan Holden)

John Pateman was more sceptical, however:

> The question is, does it attract new users or do existing users just do different things? I think it's a bit of both. I think fundamentally we don't have the evidence to answer the question, that's the problem with the library service again, we don't systematically collect quantitative or qualitative evidence to prove what we're doing. (John Pateman)

The official evaluations and study participants suggest that the public has generally welcomed the provision of online services in the public library, although some dissenting voices have been raised. Within the profession, too, reaction has been mostly positive, centring around discourses of the hybrid public library which propose that ICT services have given public libraries a new lease of life, raising their image with its key stakeholders and enabling them to deliver new services high on the Government's agenda while still fulfilling their traditional objectives albeit in more effective and creative ways. Again, though, there is a conflicting discourse which questions whether public libraries should rush to embrace the technology quite as wholeheartedly as they appear to be, raising questions about the impact of ICT on the library environment, public library priorities and the viability of their long-term future. Currently, the former, more positive discourse is dominant as public libraries explore how ICT can be integrated alongside their traditional resources to support existing services and provide them in new, inventive ways.

The Hybrid Public Library

Most commentators and practitioners agree, then, that far from spelling the end of libraries as often predicted, technology has reinvigorated them. This is despite repeated warnings that the Internet is in competition with public libraries in a number of ways; as a supplier of consumer, job or school-related information, for example, or in the provision of leisure reading material in the form of newspapers and magazines and even readers' advisory services through formal and informal online book reviews (D'Elia et al., 2002). D'Elia et al. (2002) suggest that there are three possible scenarios for public libraries in relation to the impact of the Internet on user behaviour. Obsolescence is the most extreme outcome where the

Internet does away with the need for public libraries, paralleling the supremacy of the car over horse-drawn vehicles. The second scenario envisages the public library changing to offer services which complement but do not duplicate those provided by the Internet, corresponding most closely to the impact that the invention of television had on radio which had to radically revise its programming and schedules to survive. The final scenario sees the maintenance of the status quo, with the Internet and public libraries continuing to offer similar services but to different user groups, much as the cinema and home video industry both continue to thrive although offering the same product. In the UK at the moment, it seems that most librarians and commentators adhere to this final scenario, still anticipating an information role for the public library and predicting that its mixture of print and electronic information provision will remain the dominant model and continue to meet users' needs for some time to come. One study participant felt that technology was enabling public libraries to reinforce and strengthen their position as key learning and information providers:

> I think [the People's Network has] given us an opportunity to reinvent what we're about and to, in some ways, restate what we've always been about. We've always been about information, we've always been about books and we've always been about supporting learning and it's just given us more modern tools to say, 'That's what we're still doing and we can do it as equally now as 150 years ago'. (Anon)

Bill Macnaught agreed that the People's Network was enabling public libraries to use 'the latest technology to continue what we have seen as our historic role of making information available' (Bill Macnaught).

In the United States, D'Elia et al. (2002) found that 40 per cent of respondents to their survey used both the public library and the Internet, suggesting there is a strong association between library use and Internet use and that use of one does not preclude use of the other. Their research also supported the status quo scenario outlined above, with users suggesting that, at the moment, the library has advantages relating to the accuracy of the information it provides, privacy and as a place to go with children. Their respondents, although positive about the role of public libraries as information providers, also suggested the middle change scenario was not far away, however, and that libraries will need to start thinking about how and where to position themselves within the complex information and leisure marketplace. While a continuing role was envisaged for public libraries, respondents felt that they needed to change their mix of services and more clearly differentiate what they offer in comparison with other information providers.

In the UK, the 2000 House of Commons Select Committee on Public Libraries was clear that the tendency to stress the competition between the book and the Internet was unhelpful and a false antithesis in many ways (Culture, Media and Sport Committee, 2000). The Committee asserted that ICT would supplement, not supplant, books and printed resources although warning that technological development in public libraries must not take place at the expense of the more traditional resources. Its attitude to charging for the Internet, recommending that no charges be levied for networked and multimedia services, also underlined its view that the technology was now part of the core service provided by public libraries, sitting comfortably alongside its print-based resources. The Library Association (now Cilip) in its evidence to the Committee similarly commented that the mixture of media and resources lay at the heart of the attraction of the public library and other witnesses also stressed that investment was needed in both ICT and printed material as the public library will be providing both in the future in response to public demand.

In fact, more than one witness to the 2000 Select Committee enquiry suggested that ICT had stimulated demand for book-related services and that, in the 'mixed' or 'hybrid' economy within which public libraries now operated, the rolling out of electronic services encouraged use of existing, more traditional resources. One study participant offered some anecdotal evidence of this phenomenon:

> We do have some evidence of the People's Network bringing new users into the library and moving on to other services, particularly minority ethnic groups. We have a number here in [this town] of Latvians working in the meat factory. They came in to email home, they're now using language courses etc. So there is some, I don't have quantities, but there is some evidence there. (Anon)

John Pateman felt that this was wishful thinking, though:

> Our experience is that when the People's Network does attract new users, they come in and use the People's Network and go out again. They don't come in and use it as a part of a broad range of services that we have on offer. They use it, send their emails or whatever, and go. (John Pateman)

Whenever an innovative service has been introduced into public libraries (cassettes, videos, CDs, DVDs etc.) claims have been made that those coming to the library to borrow the new resources will naturally also turn to what are perhaps considered the other more worthy resources available. In the United States, the Gates Foundation reported that around half of rural and small town libraries recorded an increase in circulation since public access computers had been installed (Gates Foundation, 2004). There is little hard evidence, however, to confirm that this kind of cross use happens and there is also an undercurrent of elitism in these discussions. Nevertheless, it is possible that the availability of public library catalogues online, for example, has brought new book borrowers into the library who are now able to establish from their own homes whether an item is in stock and whether it is available. This relatively straightforward use of technology enables public libraries to carry on doing what they have always been doing although perhaps more effectively. The potential of Internet is far greater than that, though, and many library services are exploring ways or enhancing, extending and introducing new services through the use of technology.

Enhancing Services with the People's Network

In the UK, generally, ICT is not considered to have changed the mission of the public library service. Rather, it has enabled public libraries to fulfil their obligations in more effective, innovative and creative ways. There is a sense, though, that although the fundamental role of the public library has not been changed by technology, its image and significance has been, or will be, transformed. Commentators write of how ICT has the potential to revolutionize the public library service in the eyes of the public and policy makers, raising its value as it plays an increasingly important role in supporting a range of social policies. The Government wants the People's Network to enhance education and lifelong learning, facilitate access to information and knowledge, promote social inclusion and provide a user-friendly entry point to government services, all fundamental elements in its social programme. Public libraries have responded by developing a range of services and activities in these key policy areas.

Lifelong Learning

As outlined above, discourses around public libraries and ICT in the United Kingdom focus on how technology is assisting in the provision of services considered core to the library's mission. Supporting education, always an important role for the public library service as discussed in Chapter 9, has been given renewed emphasis by this Government and the DCMS is keen for public libraries to develop new learning services to be delivered through the People's Network (Department for Culture, Media and Sport, 2003). As well as participating in the UK Online Centres initiative, many public libraries are also part of the *learndirect* programme which offers adults access to lifelong learning opportunities, often online. The UK Online Centres are seen as providing an entrée to learning ICT skills while *learndirect* focuses on developing broader skills, often using ICT to provide learning opportunities in a wide range of subjects.[8] Government funding has been devoted to providing the infrastructure and resources through which public libraries can become places that people go to learn new skills, therefore, and the Bill and Melinda Gates Foundation gift of $4 million has also been allocated to public libraries to support ICT learning centres in socially excluded neighbourhoods by enabling them to purchase local ICT hardware (terminals and printers). This has led to a further 1,903 Internet terminals being implemented in 413 libraries across the UK, in recognition of the fact that people need access to ICT facilities and resources before they can develop skills in using them.

Much of the learning agenda in public libraries has focused initially on enhancing people's basic ICT skills in recognition of the fact that they need to be able to use technology competently before they can access the other benefits that it brings. Users have to be comfortable with Internet technology before they can search for leisure, consumer or job-related information, for example, or before they can access central and local government websites to find information about welfare rights and other public services. Similarly, they need to be able to set up and use an email account before they can communicate with friends, relatives, officials or those with similar interests to them at a distance. They also need to be at ease with using a range of electronic resources including online and CD-Rom multi-media learning packages to take full advantage of the other learning opportunities available. The other main reason that the lifelong learning agenda in public libraries has focused on ICT skills training is that the Government is concerned about ICT skills shortages. According to figures from the British Computer Society (BCS), 98 per cent of staff need IT skills as part of their everyday jobs and yet nine in every ten British companies believe they have computer skills gaps (BCS, 2002).

Public libraries offer an accessible and informal environment in which people can gain basic ICT skills which can enhance their employability and give them the confidence to develop more advanced skills, perhaps at college. As we will see in Chapter 9, a common view among study participants was that libraries play an important role in leading people back to learning, as Kath Owen explained:

> I think [the People's Network has] done a huge amount of good. It has brought a different interest, a new interest to a lot of people who don't want to go to a college but are quite happy to give something a try in a library. (Kath Owen)

This might be because library users are used to asking librarians questions and with asking them for help and it seems that they are also comfortable requesting support to use the ICT facilities available in the library. Sommerlad et al. (2003) reported that an increasing number of public library users view it as a place to find out what the Internet is all about and services have responded by offering a range of different types of support and training courses. The final evaluation report on the People's Network project confirmed that ICT training and support was the most prominent People's Network activity in library services, suggesting that the case study libraries investigated had helped many thousands of users to become confident and competent in handling ICT and exploiting its uses (Sommerlad et al., 2004). In interview, Alan Hasson confirmed that this is a role that public libraries and their staff are playing:

> What you've got is people who've invested in all this kit and who are coming in and saying to the staff, 'I can't use this, show me what to do'. I think it may be because this area has the highest age profile, certainly in Scotland and it maybe in the UK, and a lot of these people are grandparents or whatever who've basically bought it to keep in touch with their family and they just can't. (Alan Hasson)

Certainly it seems that just about all public library services have provided training to increase the confidence and competence of users in using ICT. 'Web Taster' sessions and 'Internet for the Terrified' courses are now commonplace in public libraries and often focus on groups which have had less opportunity than others to use technology. By targeting specific groups, not only are public libraries fulfilling social exclusion objectives but the trainers can also ensure that they are tailoring the courses to participants' specific interests. In trying to reach out to socially excluded groups, library authorities have developed beginner-level Internet courses for, among others, older users, Asian women, those with disabilities, women returners and adult basic skills learners, at times and in locations that are convenient for them. Similarly, libraries are also organizing courses based around people's interests through which they can gain familiarity with ICT. Family and local history are very popular, for example, and the wealth of online resources in this area means that trainers can introduce users to a range of ICT applications while holding their interest through the content they are accessing. This 'situated', 'themed' or 'context based' approach to ICT skills is recommended by Sommerlad et al. (2004, p. 44) in their formal evaluation of the People's Network project. They reported, though, that the approach was rare and that resources to support such an approach were also lacking in public libraries.

In many cases, library staff provide the training but it is also delivered by representatives from partner organizations or agencies such as UK Online or local adult education providers, especially for the more advanced skills because, as we saw in Chapter 5, public library staff can be reluctant to become engaged in user training. Underconfident of their own skills and with some novice users requiring considerable support, staff with other demands on their time can be reluctant to provide extensive advice and guidance to users. John Vincent felt that staff were sometimes ambivalent about providing help to users:

> There's a real divide, I think, between people who have embraced the People's Network and think it's wonderful and they're thrilled that it's bringing in the teenagers and people to use email to email abroad and so on, and those who think that it's really nothing to do with us and we're not paid to be technicians. (John Vincent)

Although some staff are eager to take on the role of ICT facilitator, others shy from the increased responsibility this involves especially as it is rarely accompanied by extra remuneration. Spacey (2004) found that time and work pressures can negatively affect staff attitudes about helping the public use the Internet, a potentially serious issue as the Government envisages public library staff playing a vital role in assisting users overcome any anxieties they may have about using ICT, thus enabling them to use the facilities provided effectively and enhancing information literacy skills within society. Despite some negativity, though, staff are reported to be generally positive about helping the public use ICT, many welcoming the wider accessibility of the Internet in public libraries which can help raise the profile of the public library within the wider community and provides a valuable service to those who cannot afford Internet connection at home. The MLA evaluation of the People's Network (MLA, 2004) emphasized that, because of the People's Network training and familiarity with the hardware and software, staff were increasingly better able to support users in accessing services.

Nevertheless, lack of motivation or reason to use ICT may still leave some unconvinced of the benefits of the technology. One user in the People's Network evaluation by Sommerlad et al. (2003), for example, was competent in using ICT including sending email but said that there was nobody that she could communicate with electronically. The report concluded that public libraries now needed to make the transition from showing people how to use basic ICT and supporting their use of it to demonstrating its potential in day-to-day situations and how it can be relevant to their everyday lives including how it can support their other lifelong learning activities because as well as helping users obtain basic ICT competence, public libraries are also expected to play an important role in helping learners along a 'learning pathway', 'developing and building on their basic level ICT skills to take advantage of the full range of learning opportunities on offer' (Sommerlad et al., 2004, p. 34).

As we will see in Chapter 9, public libraries have many advantages as centres for informal learning and are one of the most popular places for people to undertake learning outside the formal education system. The Government is keen for them to consolidate their learning role by supporting lifelong learners through the use of ICT facilities and resources. *The Learning Age* (Department for Education and Employment, 1998), the government green paper setting out the Government's vision of how learning throughout life can build human capital, emphasized the role of the public library in providing access to a wealth of information and educational resources and commented that this would be enhanced by the development of ICT facilities. As Sommerlad et al. (2003) suggested, though, one of the challenges for public libraries in this policy area is how to encourage users to progress from learning basic ICT skills onto further learning opportunities. Here, the partnerships that libraries have developed with other agencies within and outside the local authority can be invaluable and there are many models of good practice in this area which are explored in Chapter 9.

Digitization and Content Management

There is also a requirement for public libraries to provide access to, and to package effectively, a variety of good quality, relevant and attractive learning content for use within new IST-based learning environments. The National Grid for Learning[9] provides access to a wide range of high quality materials for both formal education providers and lifelong learners which can be accessed through the People's Network machines in public libraries and public libraries have also been taking a prominent role in the NOF-digitize programme and other initiatives which are financing the digitization of local and national collections of documents, maps, photographs, and sound and image archives. The EnrichUK[10] web site enables users to search 150 digital collections funded by NOF and demonstrates the creative use being made of the cultural and historic resources held by libraries, museums and archives around the UK and their potential to support both the formal school curriculum and the less formal learning and studying that takes place in public libraries. With so much good digitization work underway, public libraries now need to ensure that users are encouraged and supported to make the most of it, exploiting the sources available.

Information has long been recognized as a key right and as an important facilitator of citizenship and public libraries have a long and reliable tradition of providing free and open access to it. As more and more information is available online, it seems natural that public libraries should continue to fulfil their mission by providing access to resources through ICT. In fact, it could be argued that public libraries have a responsibility to provide the equipment and facilities through which users can access digital information and help overcome the disparity in the resources available to the information rich on the one hand and information poor on the other. Providing access and support may not be enough to close that gap, however, because although there is a wealth of information available on the web, accessing quality, relevant resources can often be frustrating. There is a role here again for public librarians as content managers. As already highlighted, people are likely to be more committed to learning how to use ICT if they can be shown that it gives them access to information and resources they find useful and interesting and many library services are trying to encourage use by identifying and signposting websites considered to provide quality assured, reliable, accurate information relevant to the needs of users. The resources are selected and organized by library staff, based on the needs of the community and experience of frequent requests for information on specific topics and themes.

Those who predicted that the Internet would spell the end of libraries said that end-user searching would do away with the need for librarians to answer reference of information enquiries and although there is no doubt that disintermediation has occurred to some extent as users become familiar with systems and software, there is still a need for public libraries to manage and organize the resources now available and for staff to be on hand when help is needed. In many respects, the Internet has made the information-related tasks of library staff more, not less, demanding. While many users can now find information and resources on the Internet by using search engines, there is a perception among library staff that the enquiries they are still receiving are becoming more complex as users have not been able to find the answer to their query themselves and still need mediation for their more involved needs. In fact, Sommerlad et al. (2003) reported a low use of public library ICT facilities for information seeking, suggesting that those using the library to find information still prefer to either consult print resources or the staff who are now using more sophisticated search engines and techniques to find the answers to more in-depth queries. The Internet has also extended the range of information resources available to public libraries. For smaller libraries and authorities, in particular, the Internet has enhanced access to a wealth of information resources which the library could not afford to buy or which it did not have the space to stock. It has also made co-operative purchasing more attractive and feasible. In Wales, for example, the 22 public library authorities have made a co-operative purchase of Oxford Reference Online, enabling users to search over 100 standard reference works via council websites at no cost.

Social Inclusion

The digitization initiatives underway around the UK have a role to play in other important aspects of government policy, including those of social inclusion and neighbourhood regeneration. The digitization of local collections which previously have not been easily and universally accessible can lead to deeper knowledge of an area, engender a strong sense of place and even a sense of pride in the area's history and traditions. In turn, this can promote civic identity and encourage community involvement. The evaluation of the People's Network project reported that the exploration of community history and identity was an activity that many public libraries were involved in, often in partnership with other local cultural organizations, through the building of digital collections (Sommerlad et al., 2004). Activities and services around family and local history resources available online were also common. Local people can also be encouraged to become involved in the creation of content which can expand their skills, encourage neighbourhood activity and produce resources which are both useful and a source of pride both to those responsible for them and the whole community. In Wales, for example, the Powys Digital History Project covers the local history of six communities in Powys. The website was created by Powys archives, museums and libraries staff with the help of local people.[11] Similarly, Staffordshire Past Track, funded by a NOF-Digitize grant, is making resources available on the Internet 'that represent the cultural identity and community history of Staffordshire'. Project contributors include museums, libraries, local history groups, community groups, businesses and local people.[12] The official evaluation of the People's Network, though, reports that few digitization and content creation projects or initiatives involve local people, especially those from socially excluded groups (Sommerlad et al., 2004). Opportunities to create local ownership and build community identity are therefore being missed.

Generally, public libraries are using ICT to overcome social exclusion in somewhat simpler ways, often focusing on overcoming the digital divide. Overall, public libraries have been successful at extending ICT use to those groups identified by the UK Online Annual Report as being left behind by the ICT revolution (UK Online, 2004). As the Gates Foundation report on Internet use in public libraries in the United States found, public access computing available through public libraries is benefiting socio-economic groups with the greatest need, especially the children and young people within these disadvantaged groups (Gates Foundation, 2004). Similarly both Brophy (2002) and Sommerlad et al. (2003) report that the ICT access available in public libraries in the UK has attracted people from socially excluded groups into libraries. Despite falling hardware, software and ISP (Internet service provider) costs, there will always be a proportion of the population who cannot afford home connection and for whom the public library will continue to be a key site to use and learn to use the Internet.

The formal evaluations all suggest that the People's Network has been successful in bridging the digital divide, reaching out to those from socially excluded groups and communities and attracting people who had had little or no previous contact with computers. In interview, Jan Holden agreed:

> [The People's Network is] just enabling us to be more inclusive, it's enabling our staff to become much more tooled up, if that's the word to use, in using technology and in teaching others to use technology and it's just made our service a much broader service. (Jan Holden)

For those living in socially excluded communities, access to ICT and skills in its exploitation can help them overcome many of the obstacles hindering their full participation in the economy and society. The Government's Social Exclusion Unit outlined the benefits of ICT access and use for those living in disadvantaged areas in a report published in 1998 (Social Exclusion Unit, 1998). For children, access to ICT can help them achieve at school while computer literate adults will find it easier to enter the labour market, especially when there are key skills shortages in this area as discussed above. ICT can also build individuals' pride and self-respect, encouraging them to express themselves and communicate with others (Policy Action Team 15, 2000). This enhanced contact through communication networks can improve the range of information resources available to the whole community, making it easier to access services and mobilize action for the benefit of the neighbourhood. Local access to web-based information, resources and opportunities to participate in online communities can thus empower socially excluded individuals and communities.

For a variety of reasons, though, people living in disadvantaged areas are less likely to have access to ICTs and socio-economic status lies at the heart of the digital divide. In socially excluded areas, ownership of computers is less than the national average and, according to a recent report, '[j]ust 12 per cent of those in the lowest income decile have home internet use, compared with 85 per cent of those in the highest income decile' (Office of the Deputy Prime Minister, 2004, p. 23). Furthermore, unemployment is higher within socially excluded groups and access through work is therefore lower, those who had poor experiences of the school education system can be reluctant to undertake formal training especially in an educational institution and many socially excluded neighbourhoods have high proportions of black and ethnic minorities for whom English is not their first language and who need special language support. Public access to, and readily available support in using, ICT is particularly important for these areas, therefore, and public libraries are playing a prominent role in extending access and skills to the socially excluded although this often needs special consideration. In 2001, the five Education and Library Boards in Northern Ireland carried out an equality impact assessment into the ELFNI (Electronic Libraries for Northern Ireland) project which is delivering public access to the Internet throughout the country (EFLNI, 2001). The assessment aimed to discover whether there was evidence of differences in uptake between different groups and whether they had particular needs, experiences or issues that need to be addressed in relation to accessing the Internet and using it effectively. The results suggested that some groups, including those from minority ethnic groups, older people and people with disabilities, may need special consideration and additional support if they are to make full use of Internet provision in public libraries.

The final evaluation of the People's Network project suggests that these groups do not always receive appropriate support from public libraries, however (Sommerlad et al., 2004). The report noted the 'uneven activity' (p. 72), stating that only a minority of services had made special efforts to reach out to socially excluded people with services tailored to their specific needs. In interview, John Pateman agreed and said that this was because of, 'a reluctance, uncomfortableness about saying we are going to offer this service proactively to one group in the community and not another' (John Pateman). Shiraz Durrani agreed that public libraries had to think more creatively about how to use the People's Network to combat social exclusion. Talking about a project to reach out to older people within the community, he said:

> One of the ideas that has come is to buy laptops for older people and to connect them because how many of them can and do come to libraries? And if they don't, does this mean that they are permanently excluded from this technology as a tool? So if you're talking about social exclusion, it's age connected, it's gender connected, it's race connected and unless there's some creative thinking about what the issues are and how one connects.... We can't just put computers in and hope we've got rid of exclusion. (Shirz Durrani)

Some public library services are finding imaginative ways to reach out to these groups which do not readily have access to the Internet and who may have special needs which prevent them using ICT in other venues. The evaluation report acknowledged that there had been successes in reaching out to socially and digitally excluded groups and reported that many services had strategies aimed at drawing these groups into the library and encouraging their use of the ICT facilities provided although this was very resource intensive. Joyce Little explained how the ICT facilities available in public libraries had enabled Liverpool public libraries to reach out to socially excluded groups:

> We've noticed with the influx of asylum seekers and refugees into the city, where they were initially housed in the city, usage of that local library which is an inner city, very poorly used library, usage just rocketed and they were queuing for the computers so they could access websites in their languages, email home. So we put in additional tutor support and so on. (Joyce Little)

People living in areas of social deprivation are more likely to suffer from long term illness and disability and access to online information and relevant discussion groups can reduce exclusion. Public library services around the UK are trying to open up ICT facilities to those excluded because of disability. Assistive technology for users with disabilities can be prohibitively expensive for an individual to buy and public libraries are playing a valuable role in opening up access for those who cannot use standard ICT equipment. Tracker balls are provided for those with arthritis and other physical disabilities who cannot use a mouse easily. Video conferencing is available from some public libraries and is a valuable way of including people with hearing impairments in meetings and of enabling them to contact other service providers. Screen magnification and text-to-speech output are important for people with visual impairments. In 2002, Brophy reported the percentage of library authorities who provided assistive technology (Table 6.1). Services are providing adapted technology, therefore, although the need to keep this up-to-date and to involve people with disabilities in its selection and testing was stressed in the ELFNI report (ELFNI, 2001). The necessity of keeping abreast of new developments and legislation in relation to disability was also stressed by one interview participant:

> Obviously, the implementation of the DDA is another thing that public libraries will have to face, probably again it might be more at local authority level but certainly, if they're going to link into all sorts of sites which don't necessarily comply, there are policy issues, management issues around those. (Anon)

Table 6.1 Library authorities providing assistive technology

Accessibility facility	Availability (% of library authorities)
Screen magnification	72
Text-to-speech output	64
Alternatives to standard mouse	60
Alternatives to standard keyboard	59

Source: Adapted from: Brophy, P., 2002.

The needs of housebound people and those in residential or nursing homes are also being addressed in some authorities through the lending out of laptops with Internet connections. In Essex, for example, Essex Library Service has been running *Readers Without Walls* since 1999 to include housebound people in reader development activities. Housebound readers have access to laptops to use the library catalogue and Internet book pages from their homes. North Lanarkshire Council also offers the loan of laptop computers with Internet access to people with special needs, including housebound readers.

The Gates Foundation Report found that the impact of ICT access through public libraries was particularly pronounced in rural areas in the United States, dramatically enhancing the quantity and quality of information available to users (Gates Foundation, 2004). Wireless links on mobile libraries were being used to provide supported access to isolated and disadvantaged rural communities, for example. Similarly, MLA, in cooperation with the Department of Trade and Industry (DTI) and the Countryside Agency, are trialling WiFi hotspots in 10 public libraries across England to extend broadband connectivity to rural communities. The advantages of the public access Internet facilities provided by public libraries in these communities are particularly strong. Users unable to reach medical services readily can access NHSDirect Online to obtain health information, for example. Children and young people who live miles from their school libraries or central public libraries can access resources to support their studies through the National Grid for Learning and other subject-based portals. Those with limited transport options can interact with local government and other agencies through e-government services, and rural businesses will be able to connect to the Internet via broadband.

The impact of the People's Network in combating the digital divide has been substantial according to official reports, one noting that 25,000 people have completed a course or gained a qualification online, 50,000 have used the computers in projects designed to help their local communities and 8,000 have found new jobs through use of the People's Network (Brophy, 2004). Some still feel that more could be done, however, with a NOF report warning that much of the work around social inclusion is ad hoc and lacks strategic direction (Sommerlad et al., 2003). Pateman (2004) also warns that around ten per cent of library authorities now charge for use of the People's Network and in Buckinghamshire use fell by over 30 per cent when a charge of £1 for 30 minutes was introduced. The 2005 Select Committee report on public libraries 'names and shames' the library authorities now charging for Internet use and condemns the practice strongly, insisting that the provision of Internet access should now be considered part of the statutory service and that charging 'contravenes at least the spirit of the 1964 Act' (Culture, Media and Sport Committee, 2005, p. 36).

Pateman (2004) suggests that Brophy's claim that the People's Network has been particularly successful at reaching out to the more disadvantaged sections of society is an overstatement, a suggestion reinforced by the findings of a Joseph Rowntree-funded study which found that use of the Internet at public access sites by those perceived as excluded is generally low (Loader and Keeble, 2004). The authors suggest that despite the claims made for community-based ICT initiatives in challenging the digital divide, evidence of their success is lacking. Of particular concern for public libraries is their conclusion that:

> The location of many public access sites in libraries, schools, further education colleges and the like may be a significant barrier for those who do not consider such institutions as 'a part of their lives' (p. 42).

Public library services need to adopt approaches which encourage the excluded to see libraries as places where they feel comfortable and able to ask for assistance, reinforcing the comments made below about the need to strategically manage the ICT provided through the People's Network programme so that it achieves the inclusive vision set out in *New Library*. This was critical for John Pateman:

> I think that the People's Network is regarded in some quarters as a panacea, a magic wand that, you know, if you put computers in a library then you have cracked this access issue; it doesn't work like that. Put it in libraries, new and different people will use the library; it won't happen in my view, it needs to be managed, it needs to be marketed and it needs to be promoted and targeted and it needs to be a means to an end and not an end in itself. It's a sort of worship of technology. (John Pateman)

Public Libraries and E-Government

Buckley (2003, online resource) notes that the '[p]rovision of services and/or information through the Internet is an explicit objective in most developed countries'. The Internet is viewed as having enormous potential to improve public services by guiding users through the complex mass of information and advice available and by conducting routine operations and interactions over the Internet, thus reducing the time users have to spend waiting for an appointment and also perhaps the strain on overworked specialists. By providing services electronically, governments around the world hope that they can tackle two main issues representing, according to Buckley (2003), the two sides of citizenship: rights and responsibilities. Firstly, as stressed above, the provision of information is essential if people are to find their way through the maze of regulations, rules and procedures governing rights such as access to services and welfare benefits. Secondly, by giving people the opportunity to email officials, politicians and local activists as well as access government policy and strategy documents readily and comment electronically on them, it is hoped that citizens will become more engaged with the political process, overcoming a perceived apathy and lack of interest in mainstream politics and government at both local and national levels. In addition, the new technologies can be used to strengthen the civic agenda through the creation of information and knowledge sharing groups and communities of practice (Sommerlad et al., 2004). E-government thus encompasses simple information provision, communications, interactions such as online applications and the transaction of complete services (Wimmer, 2002) as well as consultation and participation in the democratic process (Whyte and Macintosh, 2003) although administratively-oriented processes have taken precedence over participatory approaches in most governments' plans and strategies to date (Chadwick and May, 2003).

In the UK, which is described by Accenture (2002, p. 5) as a 'visionary follower' (compared to the more mature 'innovative leaders'), the Government has set a target of 2005 for all public services to deliver 100 per cent of services, which are capable of being delivered that way, electronically. National government departments and agencies are urged to deliver services and information online and there is a national government portal – Directgov[13] – through which citizens can access information from a range of government departments and agencies arranged under thematic and audience headings such as 'employment', 'learning', 'parents' or 'disabled people and carers'. The 2003 UK Online Annual Report stated that there had been good progress in the provision of services electronically (UK Online, 2004). All local authorities now have websites and the number of sites through which the public can make transactions, rather than merely access information, is growing. Two-thirds of central government services are also e-enabled with the UKOnline (now Directgov) portal the fastest growing government website in 2002–2003.

Encouraging public bodies and services to provide e-government services is just one measure of success, however, and surely the most important indicator is the extent to which e-government is used and accepted by the public. Mellor and Parr (2002) report that despite high levels of government investment, use of e-services in the UK is well below average, well behind uptake in Ireland, for example where 30 per cent of adults use e-government services compared with just 18 per cent in the UK (TNS, 2003). According to UK Online, 50 per cent of the internet population (29 per cent of the adult population) had visited a website in the previous 12 months (UK Online, 2004). This compares with 75 per cent for New Zealand, 68 per cent for the USA and 64 per cent for Australia (TNS, 2003). Similarly, while some services had shown high levels of use (university applications and driving theory test bookings, for example) the level of e-government transactions remains low with only eight per cent of Internet users saying they had used government transaction services online (UK Online, 2004). The reluctance and/or inability of some to engage with Internet technology has already been discussed although the Government hopes to have overcome the bulk of the resistance through its investment in public access points and skills training, much of it through public libraries. Worries about the security of online transactions may also deter some from using e-government services and, at the moment, it appears that other delivery channels such as the telephone, kiosks and face-to-face discussions are considered more trustworthy and to have clear benefits over the Internet. In fact, kiosks allowing users to a menu-driven set of information pages are becoming increasingly popular once again (Froud and Mackenzie, 2002). Once hosting PRESTEL services allowing users to access menu-driven community information pages, kiosks are now linked to the Internet to provide easily updated information on a range of council services. In Sutton, kiosks called *i+points* providing council and public service information were introduced in 2001. The nine kiosks also provide free email. In 2003, the kiosks were accessed 117,000 times, excluding email, compared with 95,000 visits in 2002. Other authorities including Islington, Southwark, Kensington & Chelsea, Westminster, Lambeth, Bromley, Knowsley and Bristol have also introduced similar systems.

To encourage greater use of e-government services, the Government is now investigating the use of intermediaries. As public libraries are prime sites for the use of the Internet outside the home, it is likely that they will be required to fulfil this role although the extent to which staff are willing and prepared to provide practical support to people accessing and using e-government services remains to be seen. In Tameside, for example, the local authority's 'Customer First' e-government project through which members of the public can request services and pay bills via the Internet has been extended into public libraries. Similarly, in Derbyshire the provision of ICT facilities in rural public libraries and on mobile services is seen by the council as an important way of providing access to a range of e-government information and services, especially to those in socially excluded communities. In both cases, users may need help, and support from library staff will be important to encourage use and engagement.

Public library services are considered to have an important and multi-faceted role to play in the delivery of e-government services in the UK, therefore. Firstly, the public library can provide many of its services electronically and, in fact, was one of the 20 target services identified by the European Commission for e-delivery alongside others such as income tax returns, car registration, careers services and enrolment in higher education (Europa, 2003). Secondly, public library services have considerable expertise in the collection, organization and dissemination of information and can therefore play an important part in the establishment and maintenance of local authority e-government services. Thirdly, and as we have already seen, public libraries can overcome the digital divide by providing public access to ICT and delivering training activities which ensure that people have the facilities and skills to take advantage of e-government services. These different but overlapping responsibilities mean that public libraries have a strong claim to be key players in the e-government agenda, according to Froud and Mackenzie (2002) and the evaluation of the People's Network project found that the People's Network grade of service provided clear benefits to those seeking e-government information (Sommerlad et al., 2004).

Public libraries therefore need to consider how they can deliver their own services electronically and also how they can assist their local authorities develop its e-government capacity while encouraging people to develop the skills and confidence to use e-services and perhaps assist them to undertake online activities which link communities and build local networks. The MLA-funded evaluation of the People's Network concluded, however, that, 'there was little evidence of initiatives around e-Government and the local economic development agenda' (MLA, 2004, p. 7) in public libraries which are also, it seems, doing little to support 'civic literacy' (Sommerlad et al., 2004, p. 47). The emphasis in public library e-government activities seems to be largely focused on providing access to local government information and transactional activity, the evaluation reported, with little use of the technology neither for strengthening citizen rights and entitlements nor as a tool for empowering citizens and fostering democratic dialogue and participation. Nor were public libraries doing a great deal to address gaps in provision for socially excluded groups with special needs, such as those with low literacy levels or minority language needs.

Nevertheless, many of the local digitization projects of the type described above have been successful in engaging communities through ICTs and encouraging them to cooperate via the technology. Froud and Mackenzie (2002) state that libraries are the ideal vehicle for fostering this kind of community engagement. With their excellent track record of providing access to digital resources and facilities and leading projects that encourage online participation, public libraries can help ensure the Internet is used for democratic purposes by promoting e-democracy projects and encouraging community involvement. At a somewhat simpler level, many library services offer users the facility to undertake transactions online. They can check their borrowing records, renew materials, make reservations and check the catalogue via the Internet. Electronic service provision is reality in public library services throughout the UK as Jan Holden explained:

> [The People's Network is] enabling us to remodel our service into much more of a virtual service and improve contact with customers so that we can email more people now and they can interact with their library, order stuff online and what have you. (Jan Holden)

Some library authorities have also been successful in playing a leading role in the design and maintenance of the local council's website. Froud and Mackenzie (2002) give the example of Leeds public library services which is responsible for running the council's website and developing it for e-government services. In other areas, too, the public library service is often at the top table when e-government decisions are taken. Sommerlad et al. (2003) report that the library service is often seen as a key pilot site and contributor to the e-government agenda within local authorities. Public libraries have a long tradition of providing reliable and accurate citizenship information and so facilitating online access to council services and resources might be expected to come naturally to them. Although they may not control the corporate e-government agenda, this role more likely to be invested in the information systems department of the authority, they can be key players with a responsibility to provide quality content which meets the needs of the community. Librarians' understanding of how people ask questions and their information handling and management skills means that they should take a leading role in both designing the customer interface of council websites and ensuring the logical organization of the information and resources provided. Working effectively in partnership is, once again, vital to consolidating public libraries' role in the authority's e-government agenda and ensuring they are recognized as having a major part to play in the delivery of e-services. This was happening in some places according to Helen Connelly:

> [The People's Network has] also helped some library services to position themselves at the heart of implementing e-government. It's meant it's kind of changed their position and their voice within local authorities generally, and given them an enhanced role in things they should be involved with. (Helen Connelly)

Doubts about the People's Network

The largely positive picture of ICT provision and activity in public libraries presented above cannot disguise the fact that the People's Network also has its critics. Despite the House of Commons Select Committee's dismissal of tension between the book lending and ICT provision functions of the public library in 2000, anxiety about the impact of ICT on public libraries have been raised as already outlined in Chapter 4. In their evidence to the 2000 Select Committee, the Library Campaign and Libraries for Life for Londoners (pressure groups campaigning to protect public libraries against cuts) expressed concern that development in ICT was taking place at the expense of more traditional services. User groups are worried about the impact that ICT facilities may have on the quality of others services, convinced that book collections and the stock of printed resources will suffer as a result of the drive to increase ICT provision in public libraries. Although the installation of the People's Network infrastructure was funded by NOF and not from library service budgets, some are concerned that the ongoing costs associated with maintaining the network will divert funds from other parts of the service, a fear shared by Margaret Watson:

> The investment is incredible and to keep the People's Network dynamic and alive, they are going to have to invest more money and I am worried that some of the more

> traditional services, which are what the community say they need, are actually falling behind. (Margaret Watson)

Similarly, ICT makes staffing, security and space demands which are a concern for some library user groups, worried that traditional services will suffer (Culture, Media and Sport Committee, 2000). While not completely Luddite in attitude, believing that there is an important role for ICT within public libraries, the more sceptical commentators believe that ICT has been seized upon as the saviour of the public library service without due consideration of its full implications including the on-going up-grading and maintenance of equipment and the floor, shelf and study space given over to ICT, especially in smaller libraries. The higher profile that the People's Network has given public libraries, discussed above, can also be a double-edged sword, according to Alan Hasson:

> I find this fascinating because, yes, it has changed the image amongst politicians and we can now make a bit more play for things like one-stop shops and active citizenship and all the rest of it. But you've also got politicians who it creates a lot of hostility with because what they're saying to us is, 'Spend the money on books'. And we're saying, 'That's great, you give us the money and we'll spend it on books; this is National Lottery funding'. (Alan Hasson)

One participant felt, though, that many of those who object initially eventually come to accept the People's Network facilities:

> Many of our residents at first really didn't like the idea of the People's Network and posed questions along the lines of, 'Are you going to take away book shelves for computers?' We have shown to them that this is not the case and now all of the PCs on the net are booked solidly. So we have shown that you can have traditional and new sitting side by side. (Anon)

The importance of managing far-reaching service changes, such as the installation of People's Network PCs sensitively, cannot be over-emphasized. One head of service interviewed commented that users have their own agendas which need to be handled carefully and she felt that libraries had not helped themselves by, 'throwing in IT without thought, and throwing in the People's Network without thought of putting that across to those traditional users' (Anon).

Even critics of the People's Network acknowledge, though, that public libraries must move with the times and that the Internet has a wealth of resources and applications which enhance library services while, at the same time, attracting many previously reluctant users of public libraries. Evaluations by both Brophy (2003) and Sommerlad et al. (2003) report that new users are being attracted to the public library by the People's Network and although a growth in library membership and use is always to be welcomed, the new visitors can cause difficulties for staff and long-standing users as we have seen. Young people, for example, are drawn by ICT but they also need desk space for their studies and quiet areas for individual, concentrated study and reading. Anne Fine gives the example of a young boy reading with his hands over his ears, trying to block out the noise of the computers and their users (Fine, 2002). Elderly users can also find it difficult to adjust to the increase in noise levels which these new users often bring with them and disapprove of the young people's social behaviour and occasional unruliness (Sommerlad et al., 2004).

The domination of public library space by particular groups can lead to conflicts over use and 'ownership' of that space. The conflict that may arise between various user groups over the social ownership of recreational spaces can be acute with tensions between adults and young people particularly common (Tucker and Matthews, 2001; Crane, 2000). As we have seen in Chapter 4, the People's Network was considered by interview participants to have brought new users into the library with an influx of young people coming in to use the ICT facilities for both recreational and learning purposes. This can have its drawbacks, however, as Glenys Willars explained:

> [The People's Network has] meant that we've had an awful lot more young people come and use libraries which is good but it's also brought a downside because we also have a lot more disruptive youngsters in our libraries, silly boys just out to wind up library staff. (Glenys Willars)

Encouraging young men to use public library services has been something of a holy grail for British public libraries in recent years (King and Tilley, 2001; Sloan and McKay, 2000) and so the interest in public library use generated by the People's Network within this group is gratifying for service managers and staff but managing and balancing the needs and expectations of different groups has now become an urgent priority. One interview participant was concerned that long-standing users can feel annoyed and inconvenienced by the introduction of more ICT facilities and the users they attract:

> The traditional users are perhaps resentful of the onslaught of computers, especially if it's meant that it's wiped out a couple of bays of books and they're attracting a rag-tag population of teenagers or whatever. (Anon)

Conflicts between users wanting to use the same ICT facilities can also cause resentment, especially if some of those wanting to use them are not residents, as Alan Hasson explained:

> I know that there have been specific points made about 'hogging' of the kit in various places… The one that stands out is …Peebles, you may know Peebles Hydro. Well, what we've got there is we get queues of South Africans and New Zealanders to use the free access to the Internet and they're doing it because they're basically young folk, kids, who are working at the Hydro for a pittance on their break year and, of course, it's a way they can keep in contact with their parents. (Alan Hasson)

According to Alyson Harbour, this can also be a problem in Bath where tourists, using the free Internet access in the central public library, could lead residents to ask, 'well why are all those foreigners using it because I want to use it and I pay taxes' (Alyson Harbour).

Staff can also be unsure whether the public library is the appropriate place for some of the services facilitated by the Internet (Spacey, 2004). Although supportive of the provision of online learning and electronic information resources, they can be ambivalent about the use of free email facilities, for example, which bring quite a different user into the library and one participant felt that this could cause staff resentment:

> There are some staff who fear the library is changing or is going to change and they don't want to see it change. So there's still quite an unsettled feeling, I think, about what this all means. (Anon)

Sommerlad et al (2004) reported that email use was central to the use of the People's Network in public libraries while, in contrast, learning, perhaps the key impetus behind the People's Network project, was not a strong feature. Picking up on this uncertainty about the value of some of the services now provided in public libraries, a cartoon in *Community Librarian* in 2003 shows one librarian extolling the socially inclusive nature of free Internet access, his colleague responding that, 'Yes, au pairs can email their boyfriends, businessmen can check their investments, spotty boys can look up porn' (Community Librarian, 2003, p. 14). Some staff resent the library being turned into 'a glorified Internet café' or an 'an amusement arcade' (Spacey, 2004, p. 108), clearly indicating a degree of discomfort with the direction in which public libraries seem to be moving.

Issues like these can impact on how staff feel about helping others use the technology available and how valuable they feel the technology is within the public library setting. Public library staff participating in Rachel Spacey's (2004) doctoral research were asked to respond to a number of statements regarding the usefulness of the Internet within the public library setting. Ratings were made on a five point Likert type scale ranging from '1 - strongly disagree' to '5 - strongly agree' (Figure 6.1). Consideration of the mean Likert scores revealed that responses ranged between three, 'neither agree nor disagree' and four, 'agree'. This suggests that while the Internet was considered generally useful, in some cases its usefulness was less apparent, especially, it seems, when network problems impacted negatively on its use. Although staff did make positive comments about the Internet which were often related to the access to the wider range and greater quantity of information now available, network and connection time problems often negatively affected staff perceptions of the usefulness of the Internet. Frustration with the system crashing or going down and slow response times exacerbated by firewalls, filters and password protocols could make enquiries and assisting the public a stressful experience and sometimes meant that accessing printed material was faster. Staff views of ICT and the Internet are mixed, therefore. Although a large majority of staff is comfortable with the technology and enthusiastic about its use, a minority is negative for a variety of reasons including a general fear of change, a perceived conflict between ICT and the more traditional library services accompanied by a fear that existing skills could be undermined, technical difficulties and problems related to public access to the Internet such as users viewing inappropriate content.

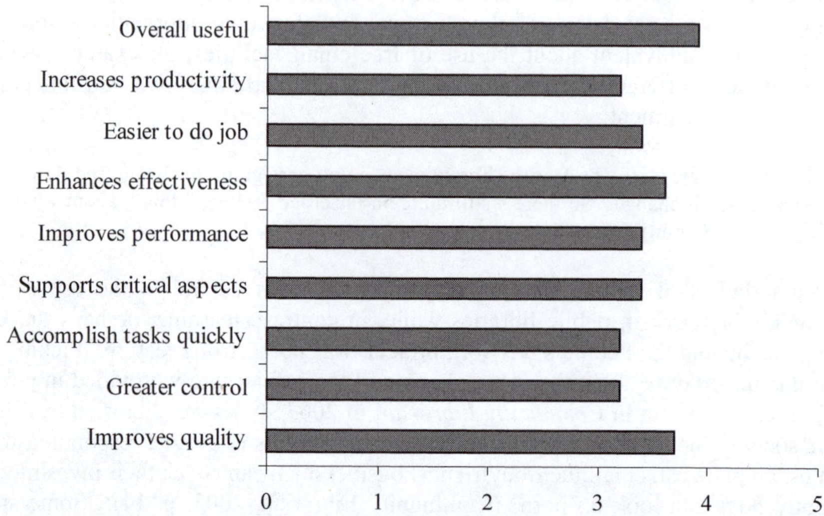

Figure 6.1 Staff perceptions of the usefulness of the Internet
Source: Spacey, R. E., 2004.

Public library staff with negative views about the People's Network are in the minority, therefore, but can still be a problem in a service trying to convince both the public and policy makers that the public library service is an ideal vehicle for breaking down the digital divide and spreading ICT skills within the community. Staff holding negative attitudes might influence both colleagues and the public and could affect the service given to library users. Sommerlad et al. (2004) also reported some continuing staff anxiety about the People's Network with staff worried about the continuing increase in user expectation, the rapid advancement of technology, the management of new types of users and being accountable to provide a professional ICT-based service.

Another reason that staff, and some users, may not be entirely happy with the presence of ICT facilities in public libraries is that the cost of hardware, software and connection have all been steadily decreasing so that accessing the Internet is cheaper and more readily available from home. In 2002, over half of UK households had a home computer according to the Office of National Statistics General Household Survey.[14] Because of the rise in home ownership, one staff member participating in the *Tomorrow's Library* project in Northern Ireland questioned whether public libraries need to provide public access, considering the falling cost of home connectivity (Department of Culture, Arts and Leisure, 2002). A similar argument could apply to books, though, especially following the demise of the Net Book Agreement which has been followed by large discounts on books available from a range of different outlets. Besides, practitioners and policy makers argue that Internet access is still too expensive for individuals and families on low incomes. Sommerlad et al. (2004) reported that a majority of users in their study stated that it would be difficult or impossible to access the Internet if it was not provided by the public library. They should not be excluded from profiting from the benefits of the information society and, as illustrated above, public libraries are playing an important role as gatekeepers and facilitators of access to the world of digital resources for disadvantaged groups in society. Martin Molloy emphasized this point in interview:

> People talk about [home ownership of computers and say] the average is high and we won't need public libraries. Well the average may be but actually home ownership is incredibly low and if we were not providing access through public libraries, lots and lots of people here would not have knowledge of computer services or any access to them. Internet access and so on would be a dream. (Martin Molloy)

Managing the People's Network

The final evaluation of the People's Network project noted that library managers expressed a range of concerns about the impact of the ICT facilities, the new services and activities associated with these and their management (Sommerlad et al., 2004). It also reported, though, that the People's Network itself had had a positive effect on internal library operations and management, requiring new strategies and processes for managing the services and facilities provided which often resulted in the streamlining of operations. ICT is now embedded in many processes and there is a more receptive climate for further technological change. The report also made the point, however, that library services are at different stages of adoption and development, depending primarily on leadership and organizational capacity which was often reliant on an understanding and vision at the top of the organization. The evaluation report concluded that there was uneven development between and within library services and that some services were more advanced than others in the uptake and development of services based around the People's Network. The report categorized services as 'progressive', 'on the move', getting started' or 'stuck' depending on their progress (Sommerlad et al., 2004, p. 124). Within individual library services, the evaluation reported that some services and uses of the People's Network were more advanced than others so that while, for example, considerable effort had been spent on supporting ICT-related lifelong learning services, those around e-government had been relatively neglected. Development, the report suggests, reflected local priorities, staff capabilities or interests and available funding.

Funding to maintain the network is vital, of course, and how to sustain the momentum of the People's Network is an issue exercising public library managers. The challenges involved in continuing to provide free public Internet access and maintaining the development of innovative ICT services are recognized by policy makers and practitioners both at home and abroad. In the US, the Gates

Foundation report identified five key areas requiring ongoing financial investment and support: hardware and software upgrades; Internet connectivity; technical support to keep systems running; staff training and keeping libraries open (Gates Foundation, 2004). In the UK, equipment upgrades and continuing expenditure on staff training have been noted as creating a continuing drain on library services' core funding with few signs that this will be met by the provision of additional resources (Moore, 2004). The Gates Foundation Report (2004) commented that users who were the most reliant on public access computing, such as those from socially excluded and rural areas, were also the most likely to be affected by any cuts made to the provision of Internet services in public libraries as the libraries they use have less reliable funding, older staff who are perhaps less comfortable with technology and difficulties accessing technical support. Furthermore, the report noted that finding support for public access computing is increasingly problematic in an environment in which bridging the digital divide is no longer given the priority it once was.

In the plans that local authorities submitted to receive NOF funding for People's Network infrastructure, they were required to account for how they would sustain the hardware and software after the NOF programme had ended. Mainstreaming network services was essential to maintain services and some authorities had worked hard to ensure upgrading would continue. One participant was scathing about those library services that had not planned for future upgrading and maintenance:

> I think that anyone that takes the money and doesn't have an exit strategy needs shooting. There are too many library authorities around... who have failed to address sustainability issues. Now some authorities are going backwards, introducing charging… Some authorities have not taken on board the long-term cost implications. I suppose we couldn't have refused the money, which is why some people have got themselves in a mess. (Anon)

Another agreed but said that some services had been successful in establishing sustainable funding models:

> Many services have been successful in doing deals with corporate IT, you know, we do this for you, you give us some money, integrate the networks, somebody else shares the cost with you. There's all sorts of models like that. (Anon)

In Northern Ireland, the ELFNI project is a collaborative programme involving all of the Education and Library Boards in the province, establishing, among other services, a single computerized library management system and the implementation of the People's Network.[15] The nature of the programme means that heads of service in Northern Ireland have few worries about sustainability as one explained:

> Sustainability of the People's Network isn't an issue. We've got a ten year PFI contact, that's the glory of ELFNI, and the funding is there in the recurrent budget to support that. And because it's PFI, the feeling is that the Government won't leave us high and dry with

> it. So, certainly, sustainability longer term might just be an issue but we're talking ten years hence. (Anon)

Many English and Welsh participants expressed considerable concern about short-term sustainability, however, although one head of service suggested that public library services perhaps ought to accept that they will have to mainstream People's Network facilities even though this might mean a lower level of service which, in turn, could mean less emphasis being placed on this aspect of service:

> I think we've got our penny-worth out of the People's Network. Of course, what we don't know is where the next two penny-worth is going to come from to keep it. And it may be that it's one of these things that we say, well, that's had its day, it's now part and parcel. Of course, we'll provide but we're not going to make this big thing about it any more. People can still come in [to use the Internet] but as more and more people have their own access to it, perhaps that's not the plank we need any more, to sort of say, 'Oh, the only way we're going to get people back is to put more and more technology in'. (Anon)

Other study participants suggested, however, that funding the maintenance and upgrading of People's Network equipment was an urgent problem:

> There is a huge issue out there [with sustainability]. If you talk to the library authorities, seven out of eight, probably more of them, would tell you it's a real worry to them, that they have invested money and they don't know whether they have the revenue funding to maintain it, where the replacement money is going to come from and they don't know how they're going to develop that infrastructure and make it better and update it. (Anon)

Many agreed, one saying:

> Implementing The People's Network has been the most ambitious and challenging externally funded initiative we have ever encountered and it required a huge level of effort and commitment from the staff. To their credit, we implemented the whole scheme on time and to budget but we are now facing the challenge of sustaining and developing all of the infrastructure. I feel great frustration with central government over this. The amount of funding we all require to refresh the People's Network is modest compared to other areas of expenditure but we are constantly faced with the prospect of bidding for funding and the prospect of an uncertain future if funding is not available. (Anon)

Another interviewee indicated that this could have a knock-on effect on other library services, suggesting that some of the fears of the users of the more conventional services expressed above had some foundation:

> A whole bunch of money has been given to ICT and then suddenly it's gone and the local authority is expected to pick up the slack. And in the meantime, it may have to slash some of the book budget to make up that slack and then they get slapped around the head by something like *Who's in Charge* for not buying enough books, not enough selection, that kind of thing. (Anon)

Some participants expressed the view that, given the benefits shown to flow from the People's Network services and facilities as demonstrated by the various evaluation reports, the Government should be prepared to grant library services additional resource to sustain it:

> It wouldn't do [the Government] any harm to put a relatively small sum of money into maintaining [the People's Network] for a fantastic return. (Anon)

The fact that the People's Network has been such a success has caused problems in itself. Sommerlad et al. (2004) suggest that libraries and their staff were initially taken by surprise at the demand for the facilities provided although, towards the end of the evaluation period, the project team had the impression that demand had peaked and was slackening off. Nevertheless, the heavy demand was reported as a persistent source of dissatisfaction which was sometimes directed at non-UK residents such as asylum seekers who are heavy users of the facilities to maintain contact with friends and family at home. To prevent this type of negativity, the flow of users needs to be managed and this has resulted in library services adopting a range of strategies to try to ensure equitable use. The systems introduced to help manage the People's Network can be cumbersome, though, and staff often feel that although user expectations are high, the extra responsibilities connected with managing the Internet including making bookings, troubleshooting and guidance had not resulted in the deployment of more staff and so users were often disappointed at the level of support and service they received.

Some authorities have been experimenting with new ways of managing some of these issues and Sommerlad et al. (2003) list some examples including the use of volunteers to provide individual ICT support to novice users, express terminals with a maximum 15 minute time slot, encouraging older users to visit when it is quiet, and scheduling training courses outside peak hours. Other services have prohibited certain activities such as games and chat rooms, suggesting again that there are some uses of ICT that are not considered appropriate in the public library setting. Some services have a more liberal attitude, however, feeling that the less serious aspects of PC use can encourage wider use:

> [The People's Network PCs] can be used for anything providing it's legal. So if a kid wants to come in and play games on them, they can… A very large part of our ethos is that we want to get people coming into the library because if you don't get people through the door, they're not going to see what's there. (Joyce Little)

A related issue of PC location was one raised by participants in the official evaluation of the People's Network (Sommerlad et al., 2004). Acknowledging that ICT facilities can create quite noisy spaces, one library manager participating in the study suggested that scattering terminals throughout the library is perhaps the best strategy 'so that people perceived terminals as just another service among the book stacks… PCs should be seen as part of and integrated into other activities and services' (Sommerlad et al., 2004, p. 33). Space is at a premium in many public library service points, especially the smaller ones, and often they simply do not have the space to accommodate PCs comfortably. Similarly, many of the older buildings are just not suitable for convenient installation of network, cabling and equipment. To manage potential conflict between users, some services have dedicated times that different types of users can use the ICT facilities and others have special areas for teenagers away from 'serious' adult users (Sommerlad et al., 2004, p. 86). One participant said:

> We just have to manage it. There are ways. If you look at the way a lot of new libraries are being zoned and designed it's not that difficult to do. We can find ways of helping manage that but libraries are used by different people, that's the beauty of it. (Anon)

Improper use of the facilities is another issue that troubles library staff. They can resent policing the services and find the various password protocols, firewalls and filters sometimes slow the system to an unacceptable level. Approximately 75 per cent of public library services in the UK use filters (Brophy, 2003) and although library staff are worried about users accessing inappropriate material, Spacey (2004) found that the filters and firewalls installed to prevent this created their own aggravations. As well as slowing the system, staff also had to deal with annoyed users who could not access legitimate material which had been stopped by a filter. On the other hand, they did not want to confront users angry about the pornography they or their children had accessed.

Study participants were often concerned about the policing of acceptable use of the facilities, one feeling that public libraries had not thought through the issues sufficiently:

> I don't think there has been a debate on filtering in this country, compared to the knock-down, dragged-out fights you had in the US between the ALA and government. There's not any degree of negotiating what the implications of that are. But there are other things, like downloading things onto floppy disks and all sorts of procedural issues that libraries do have to take on board. (Anon)

Another participant, echoing the points made by Joyce Little above, suggested that heavy-handed, restrictive policies would limit use:

> We took a decision that the only thing we would block would be porn. We thought, OK, people want different access, need to access political sites or whatever, young people use chat and if you block that, you're getting less use... We'd be reluctant to go over the policy that we have but our schools, for instance, have a much, much more rigorous, more structured policy which we originally decided not to go down. We've got AUPs [Acceptable Use Policies], we've got guidance up, we've done the staff training and all the rest of it but I think we're having to re-evaluate that at the moment and see. (Anon)

It seems, then, that many study participants took a liberal attitude in relation to the use of People's Network facilities although some were having to revisit their AUPs in the light of experience. Generally, though, they were in favour of as wide a use of the facilities as possible, as one participant explained:

> There's no point having an Internet terminal where people can't use email and chat, especially if you've got people doing genealogy kind of work. A lot of that can happen around bulletin boards and chat. (Anon)

Network problems and system support are other difficult issues for services to confront. As suggested above, network crashes and technical problems cause problems for staff and users. This can be the result of the piecemeal introduction of equipment into some public library services but whatever the cause, staff on the ground often have to deal with the consequences which can be frustrating and stressful. Sommerlad et al. (2003) noted that staff had not been trained in trouble-shooting although many had developed skills, knowledge and understanding of the network and applications. The final evaluation of the People's Network project (Sommerlad et al., 2004) found that although many of the initial 'hiccoughs' related to rolling out and bedding down the infrastructure had been resolved, some technical and logistical problems remained including the operation of peripherals such as printers, virus software, systems failures, delays in software installation, firewalls and filtering, securing adequate bandwidth and automated booking systems.

These practical issues need to be thought through and different library authorities will perhaps find different solutions depending on resources and circumstance. On a more strategic level, the question of how best to manage the People's Network so that it delivers the benefits envisaged in *New Library* and *Building the New Library Network* (Library and Information Commission, 1997 and 1998) is concerning many in the sector. As Loader and Keeble (2004, p. 208) comment, '[s]imply showering communities with technology will not address the digital divide'. There are also concerns that the technology is just a 'bolt on' facility which has added to the services provided by the public library service but has not really been integrated into existing, mainstream services, although there is some evidence of integration with reader development activities. This means that established ways of thinking and acting are not being challenged and the potential of the technology is not being fully realized, leading to 'strategic paralysis' (Sommerlad et al., 2004, p. 130).

Some participants agreed that public library service use and development of the People's Network demonstrated a lack of vision. John Pateman, for example, was less interested in the micro-management issues of funding and sustainability and more concerned about how library services were using the People's Network to meet social objectives:

> We have been given a gift. And what interests me, we crow loud and hard about how well we managed the project – we put it in on time and on budget – but we don't talk about how we are using it or how we are managing it. The reason is because we aren't. (John Pateman)

He explained why he was so concerned about what he felt was a neglect of strategic objectives for the People's Network:

> My big beef with the People's Network is that it is not being managed to meet the objectives it was established to achieve. My view [is that] it was established…, very simply, to bridge the digital divide and it's not being managed in that fashion. For example, ten per cent of library authorities, one in ten, are charging for People's Network, so that isn't managing the People's Network to achieve that objective. Very few library authorities, in my experience, are targeting the People's Network to meet the needs of those who would benefit from using it the most, that's those without access anywhere else; people who haven't got it in their house, can't afford it, they haven't got it in school, constrained resources, not a computer per person and if they're not working or haven't got one at work. (John Pateman)

John Dolan agreed that some of the original aims of the People's Network had become lost:

> I also personally think… that the report on the People's Network, the original report [*New Library: the People's Network*], really set out a vision that we perhaps forgot to exploit. We turned it into the basis for the installation of equipment and the staff training and so on but I think implicit in that document was a strong vision as well. (John Dolan)

Another head of service agreed that libraries had to take advantage now of the interest in public libraries generated by the People's Network and that they could not afford to be complacent:

> It will be a crying shame if we didn't build on that [interest]. I think we've a window of opportunity with that but that level of visits won't necessarily be sustained if access becomes easier and we need to be thinking about other ways to exploit the network that isn't necessarily dependent on physical visits. (Anon)

Frances Hendrix also felt that public libraries needed to explore other uses of the technology beyond access:

> I think technology could have been a much greater driver for change than it has been. The library profession should have taken the Internet when we were calling it the superhighway and made it their own. I think the People's Network… has not done for me as much as it could. We should have been into content much, much earlier, much quicker and we're still not really there… What libraries should be doing now is looking at the next few generations of technology. (Frances Hendrix)

John Dolan agreed that public libraries now had to move beyond merely providing access and giving people the skills to use the hardware and software available, although that had been an important first step. He felt that, having achieved that, public libraries should now be looking to give people 'access to real opportunities' (John Dolan) by:

> …mov[ing] into the other kinds of content that were originally envisaged around citizenship, around e-learning, not e-learning about e-skills, but e-learning about whatever. And giving people access to exchange and dialogue. (John Dolan)

The evaluation of the People's Network acknowledged that these were challenges that library services needed to address (Sommerlad et al., 2004). In particular, the evaluation report advised that library services should explore opportunities to develop group and community-based learning rather than focusing on the individual learner and they also need to concentrate on proactively identifying the needs of communities for ICT provision so that it supports social objectives. The evaluation concluded that there needs to be a paradigm shift with library services developing their ICT use and management so that it supports community activity, active citizenship and democratic participation rather than just conceiving ICT as a source of information transmission and retrieval. One way in which this could be achieved, it is suggested, is through greater user involvement in the planning and design of services.

Conclusion

The above evidence suggests that there are conflicting discourses about the impact and success of the People's Network in public libraries. This was also highlighted by Sommerlad et al. (2004) in their final evaluation of the People's Network project and the ICT training for staff. They highlighted the paradox of 'competing stories' (p. 129) about the People's Network stating that, on the one hand, there had been a good deal of energetic activity, change and acceptance of digital technologies. On the other hand, though, a recurring theme of their investigations had been 'wariness, inertia and sometimes resistance' (p. 130). Change has been 'slow and incremental' not a 'big bang' transforming the public library landscape (p. 125).

The management of the installation of the People's Network, and the staff training which followed it, was undoubtedly a success. The formal evaluations and study participants often commented, with some satisfaction, on the scale of the programme and the fact that it had been delivered on time and within budget. Similarly, there was evidence that, at a strategic level, the profile of the library service within the local authority had been enhanced through a demonstration that libraries could manage effectively a programme of the magnitude of the People's Network and also because the ICT facilities now available through the public library network has enabled them to link into a range of priority policy agendas at local level. Official programme evaluations and study participants were generally equally enthusiastic about the influx of new and different users attracted to public libraries by the People's Network facilities. Participants put forward a range of anecdotal evidence suggesting that the People's Network had been successful in drawing new people into the library and, in the process, introducing them to the other services provided. Others were more sceptical, however, unconvinced that former non-users, especially those from socially excluded groups, were now coming to the library to use the People's Network services and that they were going on to use other library facilities.

The discourse of conflict between 'new' and 'traditional' users, highlighted in Chapter 4, was once again evidenced in discussions around the People's Network and its use. To a certain extent, the library and, in particular, the area around the People's Network computers had become a site of conflict in some instances. Participants suggested that this conflict often had a generational aspect to it but there were suggestions that it also revolved around notions of 'insiders' and 'outsiders'; insiders being those who were local residents and were, and perhaps had long been, habitual users of a range of library services, while outsiders were characterized as newcomers to either the local area or the library and were perhaps transient workers or inhabitants, taking advantage of the free Internet access available in public libraries to maintain contact with friends and family at home. While interview participants were generally welcoming to these new users, whether resident or not, other users, the insiders, could become resentful.

The other prominent negative discourse surrounding discussions of the People's Network was whether it was being used effectively to fulfil the vision established in *New Library: the People's Network* (Library and Information Commission, 1997) and whether it was encouraging the strategic change necessary to enable public libraries to become a key player in the digital inclusion agenda. Providing access was all very well, it was argued (although some participants doubted whether even this was being achieved satisfactorily), but now public libraries had to move on from facilitating access to finding more creative and dynamic uses for the network so that they can play their full part in ensuring an inclusive information society. This is not just about access to technology but relies on using that technology as a channel to improve people's quality of life and life chances through digital citizenship.

Notes

1 NHS Direct is at URL: http://www.nhsdirect.nhs.uk [17.11.05].
2 Worktrain is at URL: http://www.worktrain.gov.uk [17.11.05].
3 Universities and Colleges Admission Service is at URL: http://www.ucas.ac.uk [17.11.05].
4 ChildcareLink is at URL: http://www.childcarelink.gov.uk/index.asp [17.11.05].
5 Planning Portal is at URL: http://www.planningportal.gov.uk/wps/portal/action/ChangePage/.pg/6e/.reqid/1?section=HOME&PpAction=location_uri&select_location=N5090 [17.11.05].
6 The UK Public Libraries Page is at URL: http://dspace.dial.pipex.com/town/square/ac940/weblibs.html [17.11.05].
7 The New Opportunities Fund merged with the lottery's Community Fund in June 2004 to create the Big Lottery Fund
8 Learndirect is at URL: http://www.learndirect.co.uk/ [17.11.05].
9 National Grid for Learning is at URL: http://www.ngfl.gov.uk/ [17.11.05].
10 EnrichUK is at URL: http://www.nof-digitise.org/ [17.11.05].
11 Powys Digital History Project is at URL: http://history.powys.org.uk/history/intro/menus.html [17.11.05].
12 Staffordshire Past Track is available at URL: http://www.staffspasttrack.org.uk/ [18.11.05].
13 Directgov is at: http://www.direct.gov.uk/Homepage/fs/en [18.11.05].

14 Results from the General Household Survey are available at URL: http://www.statistics.gov.uk/CCI/SearchRes.asp?term=general+household+survey [18.11.05].

15 An evaluation of the ELFNI project, including an outline of its background, can be found at: http://www.niauditoffice.gov.uk/pubs/ElectronicLibrariesforNI/FullReport.pdf [18.11.05].

Chapter 7

Regenerating Communities

The Policy Context: Neighbourhood Renewal

As outlined in Chapter 1, the UK has its fair share of social problems and the New Labour Government came to power in 1997 declaring its intention to tackle the worst of them. The Government's strategy of neighbourhood renewal aims to address the problems of poor neighbourhoods blighted by poverty, unemployment, poor health, educational underachievement, poor housing and crime. Focusing on Britain's most deprived neighbourhoods, the Government wants to tackle what has been termed 'postcode poverty' where 44 per cent of those living in the10 per cent most deprived electoral wards are on means tested benefits, 60 per cent of children live in families who are on means tested benefits and 25 per cent of adults of working age are out of work (compared with 8 per cent, 9 per cent and 4 per cent respectively of those living in the 10 per cent least deprived wards) (Neighbourhood Renewal Unit, 2004). The Government's first strategy for neighbourhood renewal, published in September 1998 by the Social Exclusion Unit, defined the problems facing areas of intense deprivation, detailed the action the Government had taken to date and outlined its future plans for dealing with area deprivation (Social Exclusion Unit, 1998). The second strategy action plan published in 2001 identified work and enterprise, crime, education and skills, health and housing and the physical environment as the areas which would be targeted in order to improve disadvantaged areas and a range of commitments were made in these key policy areas (Social Exclusion Unit, 2001a). It also emphasized that it was essential to develop a coordinated response across the public, private and voluntary sectors, depending on the needs of each community, and that local people should be empowered so that they are actively involved in neighbourhood renewal.

To drive the Government's strategy forward, the Neighbourhood Renewal Unit was established in 2001 to lead on and monitor the 80 commitments made in the 2001 strategy action plan.[1] Its task is to coordinate, and in some cases manage, a range of strategies, initiatives and schemes related to the whole area of neighbourhood regeneration including the New Deal for Communities, Local Strategic Partnerships and Neighbourhood Management and Warden Teams. There is also funding available for the 88 Neighbourhood Regeneration Fund Areas, the most deprived wards in England, through the Community Chest, Community Learning Chests and Community Empowerment Fund, amongst others, to support neighbourhood renewal activity.

It should be noted that the remits of the Social Exclusion Unit and Neighbourhood Renewal Unit cover England only although close links are maintained with the devolved administrations in Wales, Scotland and Northern Ireland and much of its work is relevant throughout the UK. Similarly, the national neighbourhood renewal strategies apply to England only although the point is made that they will be drawn upon by the devolved administrations in the other three home countries when compiling their own distinctive strategies. In Wales, the Welsh Assembly Government has committed itself to taking action on social justice and, as in England, has a focus on supporting communities to help themselves (Welsh Assembly Government, 2003). The Assembly's *Communities First* programme aims to foster social inclusion and community development in over a hundred deprived communities in Wales. In Northern Ireland, the *New Targeting Social Need* (or New TSN) policy is the Government's main strategy for tackling poverty and social exclusion[2] while in Scotland, the Scottish Executive's Social Justice Strategy focuses on the three aspects of closing the opportunity gap, tackling child poverty and promoting social inclusion.[3] The regeneration strategies in all four home countries focus on trying to prevent social exclusion occurring and also on building capacity within communities to identify, prioritize and resolve their most pressing problems.

Tackling Social Exclusion

Parker et al. (2002, p. 67) state that, '[n]eighbourhood renewal and social inclusion should be viewed as integral concepts' and assert that social exclusion is 'a vital aspect of neighbourhood renewal'. The New Labour Government came into power pledging to combat social exclusion and, concluding that the complex problems of deprivation and poverty demanded a co-ordinated strategic approach across government and external agencies, established the Social Exclusion Unit in England in 1997.[4] Statistics show that Britain has one of the highest levels of social exclusion in Europe and ranks poorly compared with other European nations in terms of children living in low income households, workless households, literacy and numeracy, 18 year olds in education, teenage pregnancy, drug use and crime (Social Exclusion Unit, 2001b), all indicators of social exclusion. Recognizing that social exclusion has high human, social and economic costs, the SEU has the task of helping address these issues and reduce social exclusion by producing 'joined-up solutions to joined-up problems' (Social Exclusion Unit, 2004, online resource), working in a number of key areas to: improve opportunities for socially excluded children; tackle the problems of deprived neighbourhoods including poor health, housing, low skills, high unemployment and crime; reduce homelessness and rough sleeping; and cut the rates of re-offending by ex-prisoners. The role of the SEU is to undertake research and formulate policy changes in these priority areas and set targets which are implemented by other government departments or cross departmental units.

Many definitions and explanations of the term 'social exclusion' have been advanced since it was first coined in the 1970s by French researchers describing the way in which the most disadvantaged fell through society's safety net (Roche,

2003). The SEU defines social exclusion as 'a shorthand term for what can happen when people or areas suffer from a combination of linked problems such as unemployment, poor skills, low incomes, poor housing, high crime, bad health and family breakdown' (Social Exclusion Unit, 2001b, online resource), but whatever the precise wording of the definition, social exclusion is generally recognized as primarily an economic phenomenon which has important social and political consequences. John Pateman (2004a) draws a distinction between social exclusion, social inclusion and social cohesion, suggesting that these three terms are often confused and, erroneously, used interchangeably although they are, in fact, on a continuum; policy makers and service providers should start by tackling social exclusion before moving on to promote social inclusion and, ultimately, build social cohesion. Harris and Dudley (2005) dispute this notion of a linear or sequential process, however, suggesting that communities can be excluded but still cohesive. They envisage a role for public libraries in promoting social cohesion through their resources, staff expertise and the library as a place and a symbol. They also note, however, that their research revealed little significant activity in public libraries and suggest that the concept of social cohesion is not well understood.

The Government advocates a three point approach to tackling exclusion (Social Exclusion Unit, 2001b). The first task is to prevent social exclusion from occurring in the first place by working with those at risk and targeting events which can trigger exclusion such as family poverty or low educational achievement. Secondly, those already excluded need assistance to help them become reintegrated into society. This might include basic skills support or work with rough sleepers. Thirdly, public services in the most deprived areas must improve their delivery and work to raise standards. Services in the most socially excluded neighbourhoods have sometimes failed local people although these are often the communities where need is greatest. Public library services have a potential role to play in all three of these strategies but perhaps the last point about public services is the key to their engagement in the social exclusion agenda. Public services can prevent social exclusion in a number of important ways: they can keep vulnerable people connected to mainstream society; they are often the only physical embodiment of civil society in excluded areas; and they can provide vital support to vulnerable families and children at risk (Page, 2000). By developing and improving services, libraries can play their part in both preventing social exclusion and helping socially excluded individuals and communities connect or re-connect with the rest of society.

Approaches to neighbourhood renewal in the UK have two key inter-related aspects, therefore: tackling the causes of social exclusion; and providing funds and support to develop and implement local, community-based initiatives. This chapter and the next will explore how public libraries are supporting both strands: firstly, in this chapter, how they are engaging with the social exclusion agenda to help address the worst problems that exist in the most deprived neighbourhoods; and secondly, in Chapter 8, the role they are playing in community building or development, working in partnership to empower communities to resolve their own issues and pursue joint concerns.

Public Libraries and Social Exclusion

The public library sector quickly identified a role for its services in responding to the social exclusion agenda set by the New Labour Government on its election in 1997. The first mention of public libraries and social exclusion in UK librarianship literature (according to the LISA bibliographic database) is, perhaps unsurprisingly, by John Pateman who, in an article for LASER Link in 1998, analysed how public libraries in the United Kingdom were contributing to the social exclusion debate (Pateman, 1998). Making the point that public libraries have always played their part in tackling social problems, culminating in the community librarianship movement of the 1970s and 1980s, he nevertheless asserted that services could do more, a theme he returned to in his interview for the study on which this book is based.

Policy and Research

Public libraries are often portrayed by those in the field as being committed to addressing the needs of the socially disadvantaged by developing services designed to address the needs of a range of 'special' groups. Free at the point of delivery, the services that public libraries provide including lifelong learning opportunities, access to information, books and resources in many community languages and different formats, services to the housebound, residential homes, prisons and hospitals, all delivered through the skills of trained staff, are often used to illustrate how libraries promote social inclusion and equality (Department of Culture, Arts and Leisure, 2002). They are considered to have a 'reach' which enables them to make a particular contribution to local regeneration (Linley, 2004).

The DCMS was quick to articulate the inclusive qualities of public libraries which make them well placed to combat social exclusion in guidance issued to local authorities in 1999 (Department for Culture, Media and Sport, 1999). The document, *Libraries for All*, highlighted public library services' role in establishing and sustaining the flow of information within excluded groups and communities and in providing access to ICT for personal and community development. Concerns were also raised, though, about the 40 per cent of the population who do not use public libraries and a range of obstacles were listed which prevented their socially inclusive use including institutional barriers such as restrictive opening hours, unnecessary rules and regulations and inappropriate staff attitudes and behaviour; personal and social barriers such as lack of basic skills, lack of confidence and poverty; perceptions and awareness causing difficulties for people who do not think libraries are relevant to their needs or who do not know about the facilities and services and how to use them; and environmental barriers including poor transport links, isolation and difficult physical access. To overcome some of these challenges, the DCMS set out a range of policy objectives, representing elements of good practice, which could help individual library authorities put tackling social exclusion at the heart of their development and services. The recommendations focused on mainstreaming social inclusion as a policy priority, developing services in consultation with socially excluded groups to ensure libraries were meeting their needs, considering accessibility issues and engaging in local and regional partnerships. It was acknowledged, though, that taking the recommendations forward would involve a cultural change within libraries and raised significant resourcing issues.

The Library and Information Commission (one of the predecessor bodies of MLA) was similarly positive about public libraries' inclusivity, declaring that they were 'the essence of inclusion' which epitomized the concept 'in their values and activities; and by their presence in local communities' (Library and Information Commission, 2000, online resource). The Commission described how libraries embody the values which underpin an inclusive society including accessibility, neutrality, freedom and citizenship. They are safe places where people meet on equal terms and which provide the infrastructure for inclusion through resources for learning and creativity, space for personal growth and enjoyment and access to community identity and sharing. This document also acknowledged there were challenges to address before the potential of libraries in this area was recognized and optimized, however.

How ready public libraries were to undertake the policy and cultural shift outlined by the DCMS was the focus of *Open to All*, a research project focusing on the capacity of public libraries in the UK to tackle exclusion (Muddiman et al., 2000). The authors suggested that the notion of public libraries having a long and honourable history in providing for disadvantaged sections of society had been overstated and that, in reality, they had often been inclusive in a limited sense only, adopting 'weak, voluntary and "take it or leave it" approaches to social inclusion' (p. viii). Because of this, the authors argued, libraries were underused by working class people and other excluded groups; there was a lack of knowledge about the needs of these groups; and there was a range of barriers which excluded many disadvantaged people. The research found that activity relevant to social inclusion in libraries across the UK was patchy and uneven and while a lack of resources was often to blame for the development of services and initiatives to tackle exclusion, there were also challenges relating to the internal procedures, cultures and traditions of library services. The report concluded that public libraries had the potential to play a key role in addressing social exclusion but would need to undergo a fundamental transformation to fully realize that potential and would need to change radically their strategies, practices and policies in all areas including planning, resourcing, staffing and marketing.

Drawing on the *Open to All* research among other studies, the DCMS issued new guidance in 2001 for libraries, museums and archives which built on its 1999 publication, further developed the policy priorities established there and grouped them into three: access; outreach/audience development; and agents of social change (Department for Culture, Media and Sport, 2001a). The document emphasized the importance of the second of these, outreach, to ensure that socially excluded people are consulted and involved in developing services. It also stressed the important role that partnerships can play in bringing in specialist knowledge, advice and experience. Despite this apparent commitment from the DCMS to ensuring that tackling social exclusion was at the heart of public library policy and service development, the original public library standards also published in 2001 seemed to shy away from enforcing action on social exclusion from public library authorities (Department for Culture Media and Sport, 2001b). None of the public library standards specifically mentioned social inclusion, nor were there any standards covering the provision of services to those in the community with special needs. Public library authorities were instructed instead to include local targets for services to specific groups in their Annual Library Plans and the standards listed six principles for tackling social exclusion which authorities were 'strongly encouraged' to implement. Considering the Government's social inclusion agenda and DCMS recognition of the role that public libraries could play in this area, it is perhaps surprising that more explicit standards on social exclusion were not formulated. The new 'streamlined' Public Library Service Standards similarly do not include standards addressing social exclusion which was frustrating for many participants, as John Vincent explained:

> In a way, if it had been spelt out more clearly across all of the standards so there didn't necessarily have to be a separate one [for social exclusion] but that there was something in most of them about targeting non-users, looking at barriers, that would have been great… And I think there's a mixed message coming in that MLA feature tackling social exclusion really highly on their agenda but it's not coming out in everything that comes out from them and similarly from the DCMS. (John Vincent)

John Dolan was also disappointed that there was no standard covering social exclusion specifically although he conceded that a national standard would have been difficult to define, illustrating his point with some statistics about the population of Birmingham:

> We have 44 per cent of the population of this city is under 30 years of age, there are 50 languages spoken at least, there's 20 per cent plus illiteracy, 60 per cent of the population are on or below the poverty line, 25 per cent of the population is under 16 years of age, there are 2,000 children in public care, 60 people a month come to Birmingham who are homeless. Now if that doesn't reflect the kind of complexity of dealing with social inclusion issues, I don't know what does. And, therefore, on the one hand I accept that it's not easy to produce a standard but at the same time, I think the standards in this regard have to be related to the place you're delivering it. (John Dolan)

Resource (now MLA) commissioned another piece of research in 2002, this time investigating the role of museums, archives and libraries in neighbourhood renewal and social inclusion (Parker et al., 2002) although the research did not distinguish between the two concepts of neighbourhood renewal on the one hand and social inclusion on the other. Suggesting that there is no clear understanding of what the former means, the research focused primarily on the extent of involvement in social inclusion initiatives by museums, archives and libraries. The researchers concluded that there had been a positive response from the sector to tackle the social inclusion agenda but there was still a need for the different domains to raise their profile and clarify and promote vigorously what they could offer potential partners.

The 2001 guidance from DCMS still forms the basis for MLA's approach to tackling social inclusion today, leading to the development of its *Access for All* toolkit designed 'to help museums, libraries and archives make access for everyone an essential part of their culture and practice' (MLA, 2004, p. 2). This is a self-assessment tool which public libraries can use to audit their own policies, practices and procedures with the aim of removing the barriers to collections, services and facilities which some disadvantaged groups and individuals experience. MLA also wants it to be used as the basis for advocacy, enabling libraries to demonstrate their commitment to equality of access, chart their progress towards an accessible service and identify areas for improvement that would benefit from extra funding. Additional 'access checklists' covering excluded groups such as disabled people and people from ethnic minority groups are also being developed to cover the specific needs of particular groups in depth.

The MLA toolkit draws upon its *Inspiring Learning for All* framework discussed in more detail in the next chapter (MLA, 2003). For the MLA, learning and access are part of the same agenda as people cannot engage with the learning opportunities provided by public libraries (and museums and archives) unless they have full access to them which, in their terms, includes physical, sensory, intellectual, financial and cultural access. One of the key principles of *Inspiring Learning for All* is that of 'creating inspiring and accessible learning environments', focusing on reaching out to those who do not use services by ensuring that those services are welcoming, available and stimulating. This involves developing an appropriate environment; developing staff skills so they are user oriented and supportive; and promoting the library as a space and resource for use by all members of the community.

In Wales, LISC (Wales), commissioned a study mapping the extent of activity on social exclusion in publicly-funded libraries in the country. For public libraries, the report found that there had been many improvements in meeting the needs of disadvantaged groups and there were many examples of good practice (Library and Information Services Council (Wales), 2003). There were still issues to address, though, around partnership working, access, staffing and training, the profile of libraries and measuring impact. CyMAL's initial prospectus emphasizes access and audience development to reach non-users, especially those in socially disadvantaged communities (CyMAL, 2004) and, similarly, its strategic library development programme lists 'promoting library services to everyone in Wales' and 'working in partnership to deliver better services' as key objectives (CyMAL, 2005).

The 2005 Select Committee Report reinforces previous policy statements, suggesting that public libraries should offer a variety of programmes and services designed to combat social exclusion (Culture, Media and Sport Committee, 2005) and there has also been increasing interest in how culture contributes to regeneration. A report commissioned by the DCMS (Evans and Shaw, 2004) suggests that cultural activity (including libraries) can impact on regeneration in three areas: environmental, economic and social. The report gives numerous examples of how public libraries have contributed to all three areas but also suggests that there is a lack of understanding and recognition of cultural impacts in relation to regeneration and it is often, therefore, overlooked. Similarly, a report commissioned by MLA into the social impact of museums, libraries and archives concluded that there were major weaknesses in the current evidence base of how these institutions contribute to social inclusion, neighbourhood renewal, community cohesion, cultural diversity, health and regeneration (Burns Owens Partnership, 2005). Nonetheless, a DCMS (Department for Culture, Media and Sport, 2004) consultation paper suggests that culture is *At the Heart of Regeneration* and singles out libraries for providing new local landmarks, extending their use, joining up with other local services and providing a wide range of resources for community use. The paper states that libraries can have a significant impact on the culture of a community through their physical presence and through the provision of a wide range of cultural and learning opportunities.

This body of policy pronouncements and research findings into social exclusion in public libraries generally support the notion that public libraries contribute to social inclusion and community regeneration, therefore, while acknowledging that services and facilities are not used to the extent that they could be by certain groups and individuals including disabled people, people from ethnic minority backgrounds and those on low incomes. As highlighted in Chapter 4, although much is made of the cross-section of the population who use public libraries, those who make the best use of their services and benefit the most from their facilities represent quite a narrow segment of society. Public libraries are aware of the need to reach out and diversify their user base for ethical, legal and business reasons and some services are making vigorous efforts to engage those who do not use public libraries to the extent that they could. Nevertheless, that policy and culture shift considered so vital by the DCMS and stressed in the *Open to All?* study seems to be a long time coming for others.

The need for public libraries to promote policies, services and facilities which promote social inclusion runs through much of *Framework for the Future* but is perhaps most evident in the 'community and civic values' strand where the importance of reaching out to non-users is stressed (Department for Culture, Media and Sport, 2003). John Pateman suggested in interview that commitment to this strand of *Framework* was not all that it could be, however, and that this had an impact on the regulatory framework for public libraries and, consequently, the effort that individual public library services expended on tackling social exclusion:

> I think if you look at how this work has been approached, it's related to the three strands in *Framework for the Future*. There's been a lot of focus on books, learning and reader development, massive investment there, all kinds of publications and conferences and what not. Second strand, e-government, People's Network – massive investment again and focus. But when you come to the third strand which is the social inclusion strand, they call it civic values or whatever, there has been no focus, no money, no investment. It is the poor relation of the three. So that is then reflected in the standards so the standards measure books and learning, the standards measure e-government; they don't measure social exclusion. (John Pateman)

John Vincent agreed and suspected that at the root of this relative neglect of the social exclusion agenda was a fear of appearing negative:

> If you talk to people from DCMS, they're very committed to tackling social exclusion but it's not being reflected in things. I'm not quite sure why that is. The only thing I can think (this is something I've picked up from some fairly senior people in Cilip) is that talking about social inclusion or exclusion is actually all jolly negative and what we need to be doing is looking at all the positives about public libraries and I don't agree with that. (John Vincent)

Framework for the Future suggests that to engage hard-to-reach groups and individuals, public libraries need to rethink their strategies on delivering services so that user needs are at the heart of everything they do. Services should then be designed so that they are inclusive. The role of staff in understanding users' needs and having the skills to engage positively with them is also highlighted as important. These three factors, strategy, services and skills, will be the focus for the discussion which follows, outlining how public libraries could engage with the social exclusion agenda, reviewing elements of good practice in service development and delivery and analysing the challenges that many services face which prevent them playing a key role in this important priority area.

Strategy

Public libraries could be viewed as having been complacent in the past about their inclusivity. Because they are free at the point of use, because anybody can walk off the street and use their services and because they have delivered services to groups perceived as excluded, it might have been taken for granted that public libraries are inclusive by their very nature. Just because libraries are theoretically open to all, though, does not mean that everybody uses them equally and although services to people with special needs are provided, not all those for whom they are intended take advantage because of the physical and psychological barriers identified in *Libraries for All* (Department for Culture, Media and Sport, 1999). It is now recognized that a more strategic approach is needed if public libraries are to play the role that they could in combating social exclusion.

Strategic approaches The DCMs policy guidance, *Libraries for All*, stressed the need for social exclusion to be explicitly mainstreamed as a policy priority for public libraries (Department for Culture, Media and Sport, 1999). *Open for All* reiterated this but found that most (around 60 per cent) of public library authorities had 'less than comprehensive strategies' (Muddiman et al., 2000, p. 29). The report acknowledged that the majority of services reported new policy and strategy activity, with 97 per cent of authorities aiming to include mention of social exclusion in their next Annual Library Plan. The researchers noted, however, that this apparent commitment was rarely supported by the designation of resources specifically aimed at tackling social exclusion. In Wales, 89 per cent of the public libraries participating in the LISC (Wales) survey stated that social inclusion related objectives were specifically incorporated into library service plans (Library and Information Services Council (Wales), 2003). The Welsh standards, though, like the English ones, do not specifically mention social inclusion. Research suggests that the most common strategy that libraries use to tackle social exclusion issues is to target client groups considered excluded, for example, disabled people, rather than taking a whole service approach. Although many useful and valuable services to 'special' groups have been developed over the years, this piecemeal approach to tackling the issue of social exclusion is no longer considered sufficient. In interview, John Pateman was very critical of some services' approach to exclusion:

> My view is that libraries are being forced to become more inclusive, they are not doing it by choice. They are not suddenly saying 'we must reach out', they are being forced to and I don't think a lot of library staff understand the differences between inclusion, exclusion and cohesion which isn't a good starting point, and the different strategies required on which approach you use. As a result, I think there is a lot of lip service paid to social exclusion. I think the word is bandied around very loosely. I think exclusion is still dealt with at the margins of what we do; it is clearly not mainstreamed. (John Pateman)

Mainstreaming means that ensuing equality of access to services must be at the heart of everything public libraries do and this demands a complete and thorough understanding of the needs of groups and individuals within the community served (Resource, 2001). Furthermore, this means the needs of all users and potential users and so libraries need to find ways of engaging local people, especially non-users, and finding out what they want from their public libraries and how they can become more inclusive as highlighted in Chapter 4.

Consultation Chapter 2 has already noted that the Best Value regime demands that local authority services consult local people and although Chapter 4 raised some concerns about the nature and effect of the consultation taking place in local authorities, commentators and interview participants agree that it is only through engaging with communities that their real, as opposed to perceived, needs will be established, as Bob McKee suggested.

> There needs to be a much stronger dialogue with local communities about what local library services could be. The key driver should be the Community Strategy and to make that work we have to get better… at engaging with local people about what they really feel about library services, not just superficial stuff like [Cipfa] Plus but really proper market research. (Bob McKee)

As he indicates, public libraries have been criticized in the past for consulting only those who use their services, through the Cipfa Plus (*Public Library User Survey)*, for example. The easy option, this, according to Pateman (2004a), reinforces the status quo as users tend to ask for more of what is already provided which clearly does not meet the needs of the 40 per cent of people who do not use public libraries. To try to make contact with and connect with those hard to reach groups who do not use public libraries and are often the most excluded, some library services are developing new methods and mechanisms for consultation and involvement as outlined in Chapter 4. Although in 2002 the Audit Commission noted that half of the Best Value reviews of public library services concluded that consultation with users and non-users was inadequate (Audit Commission, 2002), public libraries are making considerable efforts to engage excluded groups, leading to what Harris and Dudley (2005) call a 'consultation culture' (p. 31).

Communication with library users can help staff engage more closely with users' needs and increase users' confidence of the service and study participants explained how a variety of forms of user consultation was having the effect of bringing a wider range of people into the library and reaching socially excluded groups. Shiraz Durrani noted that Merton public libraries had developed a youth library forum to establish the needs of the young people of the borough resulting in youth spaces in libraries and an increase in support from this demographic as a consequence. In Nottinghamshire, Kath Owen explained that one of the senior librarians there had worked with homeless people, 'talking to them about how they perceive libraries, how they would like to see libraries' (Kath Owen). In these ways, public libraries aim to establish the needs of those who do not use public libraries and develop programmes to encourage their use of facilities and services.

Needs-based services Having established needs through consultation, therefore, public libraries must then develop needs-based services through being responsive to local needs. Many interviewees, when asked to articulate their vision of public library services in the future, stressed the importance of developing services so that they meet the communities' needs and gave examples of where this had been successful:

> I still think that the best community inclusion work is in Ferguslie Park in Paisley. I have not seen anything else in Scotland that measure up to that. Now that's because the books are there and the books are core but around that they've shaped their services so that conforms as far as possible to the demands of the community in terms of, well, the simple stuff like times of opening but behaviour patterns and splitting behaviour patterns by hours of opening. (Alan Hasson)

Another head of service explained how the branch or community libraries in her service had been made available as meeting spaces for local community groups within and outside library opening hours. Although some of the staff had been worried that books would go missing from unstaffed libraries, none had and the provision of a meeting area had been welcomed in socially excluded areas which often lack communal spaces.

The strategy of developing services that meet users' needs may seem obvious but some argue that public librarians have hitherto ignored the needs of a large proportion of the local population, perhaps those who need public library services the most but use them the least, and focused instead on satisfying the needs of those who already make good use of services, even though they often have the means to find other ways of meeting those needs. *Framework for the Future* urges library authorities to focus particularly on the needs of non-users, suggesting that they could benefit disproportionately from the services offered and in interview John Pateman agreed, saying of non-users and lapsed users:

> They use us the least but actually need us the most and the strategy we need to adopt for that is a social exclusion strategy with the passive and the lapsed users. (John Pateman)

The Network, in its evidence to the 2000 House of Commons Select Committee on Public Libraries (Culture, Media and Sport Committee, 2000), commented that there was opposition from 'traditional' library users when it was suggested that resources should be diverted into services tackling social exclusion but in interview John Vincent suggested that this is a false dichotomy and that public libraries need to engage with all their local communities, users and potential users.

> My vision would be one that begins to engage seriously with all its local communities, not ditching the people it's got already, which is a common assumption when we're talking about social inclusion work we mean getting rid of all the people we serve now and getting a load of new people in. So it's being skilled enough and being understanding of the tensions in any community to try to balance the two things. (John Vincent)

He also outlined his experiences when he worked in Lambeth in the 1970s when the public library service had shifted resources away from best sellers and satisfying requests within a few days towards promoting materials for socially excluded groups in the borough. As he commented, those who felt they were now losing out were the most vocal and this led to:

> …a whole lot of lobbying of elected members around the failure of the library service to deliver books within a certain time, and of course the standards tend to bear that out as well. And so we were actually heavily criticized in the end by the council for spending money on books for unemployed people and the black community and community languages whereas, to provide a service to those parts of the community, I think we were doing the right thing. (John Vincent)

He felt that this was a debate that the public library community had never really grappled with but, until it did, the tension between what he called the 'loud shouters' and the majority of people would never be resolved. Shiraz Durrani similarly felt that there was a lack of political will at both local and national levels to tackle the question of resource redirection and that made it very difficult to achieve development, especially when there was a 'constant battle between providing the current service which provides a service to a small group of people' (Shiraz Durrani) and providing innovative services to tackle social exclusion.

The real skill seems to be balancing the needs and demands of all the public library's different stakeholders although Shiraz Durrani felt that resources needed to be devoted to those services which achieved the best social outcome for the majority of the community, believing that, 'unless we change and challenge the way we do things, it's the same class of people, same group of people who know how to make user of it' (Shiraz Durrani). Like Shiraz Durrani, John Pateman was unapologetic about targeting specific groups:

> Some of us argue that we need to focus and target and base it on needs but that doesn't sit comfortably with a lot of white middle class librarians who think that is somehow unfair; they misunderstand the difference between equal opportunities and equal equity, they get the two confused. They think they have got to treat everybody exactly the same even though when people walk through the door they are not the same because of their life experiences for a start, their education and their background. All these migrant workers are not the same as people who have been born and bred and have got nice jobs in Lincolnshire. That underlies a lot of the thinking I think. (John Pateman)

He insisted, though, that in providing services which meet the needs of the socially excluded, the needs of the already included are also met:

> …it's not a case of taking away from one and giving to another. In developing a more inclusive service you are making services better for everybody, whether they are existing users, non-users or lapsed users (John Pateman).

To ensure that opposition like that at Lambeth does not arise when redirecting resources, library services need to consult and communicate with all the library's stakeholders (Pateman, 2004a). Services need to gather relevant information about local communities to ensure that decisions taken and policy arguments made are supported by appropriate evidence (Carpenter, 2004).

In two articles in *Library and Information Update*, John Pateman outlines the importance of public libraries developing a needs-based service and the steps they need to take to achieve this (Pateman, 2004a and 2004b). Fundamental changes to strategy, practices and staffing are recommended to transform library services from 'the more traditional, provider-driven service to a proactive, needs-based, community-driven service' (Pateman, 2004a, p. 37). Interviewees often commented that not enough public library services were taking up this challenge and that commitment to tackling social exclusion within public libraries was 'patchy' and often tokenistic when what is really needed is a fundamental shift of values to put tackling social exclusion at the heart of service development. Despite this doubt about the commitment of some public library services to address exclusion issues, about 100 public library authorities are members of *The Network*,[5] an organization committed to tackling social exclusion in libraries, museums, archives and galleries. Co-ordinated by John Vincent, the Network organizes courses, seminars and conferences designed to support organizations within the cultural sector develop policy and practices to target social exclusion. Even within The Network, though, Vincent felt that a lot of the work was at a 'very elementary level' (John Vincent). He explained:

> I think that lots of services take the view that there's such a huge agenda out there for public libraries, they don't really engage with it all except in a rather tokenistic way at top level. From my training experience, I don't think I've been anywhere yet that there's a

> perception from front line librarians and library assistants of what this is all about. (John Vincent)

And added:

> There's a kind of culture of, 'We've got quite enough to do already thank you and we don't need all this' or 'It's all political and it's nothing to do with us' and/or 'if we keep our heads down long enough it will all go away again' kind of view. (John Vincent)

Some commentators and study participants have questioned the level of commitment to and understanding of exclusion issues within the public library field, therefore. Nevertheless, many services have developed initiatives and services designed to reach out to those perceived as socially excluded.

Services

Sally Middleton gives the following clear definition of social exclusion which seems to capture the underlying rationale of much of the exclusion work taking place in public libraries:

> Social exclusion is when individuals, groups or whole communities are either deliberately excluded from access to mainstream services, or when they face barriers to using those services (Middleton, 2003).

The focus in most library services, therefore, is on increasing access by un-represented or under-represented groups and communities although Newman and McClean (2004) have asserted that there is a confusion between the terms access and audience development which results in the failure of many social inclusion activities. Parker et al. (2002) noted that libraries, museums and archives aim to build a more inclusive society, and demonstrate their role in this process, through work with specific minority groups rather than through whole-community approaches. *Framework for the Future* seemed to endorse this strategy, suggesting that library services first establish the needs of excluded communities and then redesign programmes and activities to ensure there are no barriers to access and use. Although Pateman and others are disappointed with the extent of commitment shown to tackling social exclusion by public library services, many have devoted resources to try to meet the needs of socially excluded groups and individuals within their communities. The website for *The Network* gives details of good practice in many authorities trying to improve services for a range of excluded groups. Similarly the Cilip/LiS *Libraries Changes Lives* award gives recognition to those authorities who have been successful in reaching out to excluded groups.[6]

A comprehensive account of activities cannot be given here and some will be, or already have been, discussed in other chapters; services and programmes aimed at tackling social exclusion based around the use of ICT were explored in Chapter 6, for example. Some examples of good practice will be given, however, primarily to illustrate that the key to increasing the use of public libraries by socially excluded groups, following the development of services which meet their needs, is the removal of barriers to use. An analysis of general issues around the development of services for socially excluded people is followed by a discussion of how services are being developed to overcome some of the barriers to use identified in *Libraries for All* (Department for Culture, Media and Sport, 1999).

Targeting and prioritizing Targeting specific groups perceived as socially excluded or at risk of social exclusion is an important aspect of opening up services but perhaps public libraries need to be clearer about the groups they are aiming services at and the extent to which some of the services perceived as tackling social exclusion do just that. In Wales, a survey of public libraries asked participants to identify groups considered disadvantaged (Library and Information Services Council (Wales), 2003). In response, services listed a range of groups and individuals considered at risk of physical, mental, economic or locational exclusion with some at risk of more than one. People with a physical or mental disability was the group identified by most of the authorities as excluded but the list also included the unemployed, elderly people, those living in deprived communities, those living in rural areas, single parent families, ethnic minorities, travellers, asylum seekers, full-time workers in communities without extended opening hours, excluded children and hospital patients. Public libraries have tended to focus on these 'traditional disadvantaged groups' (Library and Information Services Council (Wales), 2003, p. 9) which perhaps is understandable because as the Social Exclusion Unit makes clear, 'certain groups .... are disproportionately at risk of social exclusion' (Social Exclusion Unit, 2001b, online resource) and specific groups like young people in care, those living in low income households and those who do not attend school have been prioritized for attention by the Government. Asked for examples of specific services provided to the groups identified as disadvantaged, the LISC (Wales) survey participants listed services to the housebound, mobile library services, late night and Sunday opening, concessionary charges, basic skills tuition, specialist stock, adaptive technology for the disabled and reading clubs among others. Many, if not all, of these undoubtedly make access to services easier for people who are socially excluded but the extent to which some are deliberately targeting socially excluded people is, in some cases, open to question.

An issue about interpretation of the term social exclusion arises here. As John Vincent commented in interview, 'nobody's very bothered about definitions' (John Vincent) suggesting that in many cases public librarians try to give what they are doing a social exclusion perspective without really being clear about just how their services address it. Vincent gave the example of story-telling in a park which may very well be targeting children from socially excluded backgrounds but equally might not. Many would acknowledge that not all elderly people are socially excluded and nor are all those who use a mobile library service or live in rural areas although services to these groups are often represented as tackling social exclusion. As Vincent commented, in some cases they are and in some they are not. By Middleton's definition, though, these groups would be excluded. Those living in rural areas but working full-time elsewhere, for example, have little opportunity to use their local public library service whether through a community library or a mobile library. By all other measures, economic, political or physical, many are not disadvantaged but because there are barriers to them using services, they are excluded. Ultimately, though, it does not matter very much whether services, activities or initiatives designed to overcome social exclusion benefit those who are not disadvantaged, as long as services are more accessible for those who are. This reinforces the point made by John Pateman above that by improving provision for socially excluded people, services are enhanced for everybody.

Perhaps the issue of public libraries' response to the social exclusion agenda, which according to some interviewees is inadequate in many cases, does not hinge around interpretation or definition after all but is more a question of prioritization. Rather than tinkering around the edges, recasting their programmes to put a social exclusion gloss on them, some interviewees felt that public libraries should focus their efforts and budgets on developing services designed to reach out to the most socially excluded in their communities. In this model, people living in wealthy, rural, commuter villages would not be a priority because they are likely to have the means to satisfy their library-related needs in other ways. There is a danger, though, as discussed above and in previous chapters, that in trying to reach out to new groups, libraries alienate existing and long-time users of their services but Pateman (2004a) believes that information and communication are the keys to getting them on board. This is particularly important when services must take tough decisions about diverting resources into services designed to tackle the worst problem of social exclusion.

In some parts of the UK, developing services and committing resources to tackle social exclusion are more complicated that in others. One participant from Northern Ireland explained the difficulties her service faced:

> Targeting Social Need is essentially about poverty. Whereas before I came here I would have seen social exclusion as poverty but also about minority ethnic groups, travellers, people who would be excluded for a number of reasons, asylum seekers, older people, etc., here we have very, very sophisticated equality legislation spanning from the Good Friday Agreement whereby there are nine equality groups, the standard ones around gender and age and race and disability but also sexual orientation, whether someone's a carer or not, religion or perceived religion and political belief and that all has the weight of legislation behind it. The Targeting Social Need in terms of poverty is just a government agenda and the two are almost in opposition in some cases. Put bluntly, in [this area] the most deprived areas tend to be Catholic [but] skewing our resources into those areas does not meet the equality legislation. (Anon)

Even in those areas that do not face problems like these, library managers still face dilemmas about how best to distribute resources to meet the needs of the community and although those like John Pateman and Shiraz Durrani are convinced that the needs of the socially excluded and non-users should be prioritized because these constitute the majority of the population and have most need, others have queried whether public libraries should be spending resources on 'outreach to non users or to developing reading skills among those who are disadvantaged' with the effect that 'the majority are being neglected in the pursuit of the minority' (Coates, 2003, p. 6). Clearly, there are differences in the definition of which groups of users or potential users constitute 'the majority' and whose needs should be paramount.

Demonstrating value One of the problems that public libraries face in developing and justifying services for socially excluded groups is that much of the most valuable work is very staff and resource intensive and reaches relatively small numbers. In interview, John Vincent gave the example of the work with looked-after children funded by the Paul Hamlyn Foundation which he said was, 'immensely valuable but it's never going to be huge numbers' (John Vincent). He also mentioned that he had been working with six year eight boys, trying to encourage them to read and use the library. A successful programme, it was nevertheless very demanding and did not have significant quantitative results in terms of numbers reached nor impact on issue figures. Difficulties like these perhaps lead public libraries to trumpet the social exclusion aspects of initiatives like the People's Network which has reportedly reached thousands of users although, as Chapter 6 suggested, questions about the extent of its success with socially excluded groups have been raised. The success of other schemes to reach the socially excluded are perhaps less controversial. Bookstart and Sure Start activities in libraries, for example, discussed in more detail in Chapter 9, have enabled library services to target hard to reach groups more effectively. John Vincent maintained that activity around Sure Start was 'bringing in people from outside that mainstream' (John Vincent). Hopefully, the impact factors being developed by MLA will give public libraries more evidence with which to demonstrate the value of their services for socially excluded groups, individuals and communities. First, though, they need to make sure that they are reaching excluded groups by addressing the various factors preventing their use.

Overcoming institutional barriers – opening hours Some authorities have been creative in trying to break down the barriers identified in *Libraries for All* (Department for Culture, Media and Sport, 1999) and open up access to services for excluded groups. To overcome the institutional barriers which authorities, libraries and staff may create that discourage or restrict use by sections of the community, services have examined policies, procedures and services and in some cases extended or revised them to open up access. The 2005 Select Committee report on public libraries stated that there was evidence of extension of opening hours overall but noted that this was generally confined to large service points with only a minority of library authorities extending hours in most of their libraries (Culture, Media and Sport Committee, 2005). The issue of opening hours is a vexed one, as suggested in Chapter 4, with user satisfaction with this aspect of public library service declining. Tim Coates (2004) identified short and inconvenient opening hours as one reason for declining use and suggested that libraries benchmark their opening hours against nearby shops, supermarkets and restaurants some of which are open for more than 60 hours per week. The 2005 Select Committee report on public libraries also examined the issue of opening hours, suggesting that the Public Library Service Standard relating to opening hours was 'too blunt' an instrument to encourage libraries to extend their opening hours in response to public demand (Culture, Media and Sport Committee, 2005).

The interview data suggested that, despite these ongoing criticisms, there have been improvements in accessibility in terms of opening hours. This is supported by an analysis by Nick Moore who found that, following years of decline, the number of libraries open for more that 60 hours per week rose by 120 per cent and the number of those open for 30–59 hours per week rose by five per cent between 2001–02 and 2002–03 (the most recent figures available) (Moore, unpub.). For those interviewed, perhaps more important than this across the board increase was the systematic and user-focused way in which the hours had been extended. Interview participants frequently described how library services had reviewed opening hours in consultation with the communities served, for example, and although some had been given extra funds by the local authority to increase opening hours to meet the public library standards, others had simply changed them so that they are more suitable for their users. In Mansfield in Nottinghamshire, for example, staff's local knowledge convinced them that an earlier start in the morning would suit many users' shopping patterns. A trial was organized, although the Chief Librarian needed to be convinced. The staff was proved correct, however, with people queuing at 8.30 a.m. to enter the library.

Sunday opening is also becoming more widespread in response to user demand and although there are those who object on religious grounds (see, for example, Bakewell, 2001; Hedges, 2002), visiting the library on a Sunday has proved particularly popular with families, especially in smaller and rural communities and, again, public consultation has shown that Sundays are one of the few times that families have the time to visit the library together. Those public library services able to fund Sunday opening have witnessed large increases in use with Sundays often among their busiest times, suggesting that they are successfully aligning their opening hours with the needs of the community (Kempster, 2000). For some of those interview participants working in authorities where the libraries do not open on Sundays, this should be a priority as one librarian commented:

> Our opening hours need to change, we're the only public building in [City], just about, that's closed on a Sunday, so many more libraries are open on Sundays now. (Anon)

One head of service whose service does open libraries on Sundays explained that while users may welcome the move, staff are often opposed:

> So we opened on a Sunday [but] getting that through the staff wasn't easy. I had to do one to one interviews with all of them. There were a lot of genuine reasons for why people didn't want to work Sundays. We have lay preachers, people with families, but in the end everyone works one in six Sundays. And we achieved that with no extra revenue. (Anon)

Interview respondents often commented that addressing opening hours must be a priority for public libraries, therefore, but many felt that merely extending them was not always the answer. Rather, as in Mansfield, opening when convenient for the community and when use would be maximized should be the main concern. Thus, in Wrexham, although the central library is open long hours, over 60 hours a week as Mr Coates advocates, there is a policy of opening the small community libraries at times best suited to their users' needs, in this case when schools finish for the day. This may seem common sense but there is a perception that for too long opening hours have been arranged for the convenience of staff rather than users. To remedy this, the needs of the community must be established through consultation. In socially excluded neighbourhoods, for example, fear of crime or poor transport links may affect when people use public libraries. One head of libraries working in a borough characterized by social deprivation described how staff surveyed people in a shopping centre in an attempt to reach non-users as well as those already using the service. This consultation resulted in a slight increase in opening hours for the central library in both the mornings and the evenings but no radical extension of hours at night as this was not demanded by the community, few of whom were likely to venture in the town centre in the evening because of fear of crime and lack of reason to do so.

This declining use of town and city centres is a matter of concern for local and national policy makers. The development of out-of-town shopping and business developments threaten the vitality of many town and city centres while crime and anti-social behaviour can make them virtual no-go areas (Williams and Green, 2001). For public libraries, the alienating and uninviting character of many of Britain's town centres raises another important issue; that of library location. In socially excluded neighbourhoods, fear of crime or poor transport links may affect where and when people use public libraries and so the type of consultation with the community described above is essential. The co-location of public libraries with other services is advocated as an important method of reaching excluded groups and is one way in which libraries are sharing resources and extending opening hours. Analysis of the implications of the policy of co-location is included in the discussion of library buildings in Chapter 8 but these kinds of developments were, according to Chris Smith, the key to reaching groups of non- or infrequent users:

> I think if I had one wish, it would be for library services to think innovatively about how to open themselves up more readily to the public: longer opening hours, more accessible location and so on. I remember visiting… a library that was next to a sports centre, it was part of the same building and it was staffed during normal hours on a self-policing basis and people had a swipe card that let them in and that they then used on a reader to record the fact that they were borrowing a book. (Chris Smith)

Enabling access in this way is undoubtedly important but other perhaps less obvious obtacles many also deter potential users.

Overcoming institutional barriers – rules and regulations Linley and Usherwood (1998) have suggested that the rules and regulations surrounding library membership and use can intimidate potential users and act as a psychological barrier limiting access for some sections of the community. For some, perceptions of culture and atmosphere can be off-putting while others may face practical difficulties. A 1995 study found that 25 per cent of adults tested on their ability to fill out a form could only give very basic information such as name and address, for example (Gregory, 1996). It is vital, therefore, that joining procedures are as simple and accessible as possible to promote equity. Interviewees often agreed that many of the rules around library membership and use can be off-putting and many authorities are reviewing and revising theirs to make the library seem less unapproachable and daunting. Some library services are addressing the issue either by offering confidential joining schemes through which people can get help filling in forms or by making it standard practice for library staff to fill in the membership on behalf of library users, removing the need for them to ask for assistance. Others are trying to make joining the library generally less bureaucratic. In Wrexham, for example, children no longer need a parent's signature to join the library as Alan Watkin explained:

> We abolished [the need for a parental signature] overnight. So we take away a complete barrier to kids, particularly for kids from deprived areas where they'd say 'My Dad won't let me have that because he doesn't want to sign for anything'. It doesn't matter any more. (Alan Watkin)

In addition and as an added incentive to encourage them to become library members, children under 16 with a library card can access the free swimming facilities now available across Wales in the summer holidays.

In the past, those without a permanent address, such as travellers or homeless people, and those without the means to prove it, such as a utility bill, have often been excluded from library membership. Again, though, some library authorities are trying to overcome this obstacle to library use by experimenting with schemes extending membership to groups who have previously been excluded because of their inability to comply with library joining regulations. Kath Owen acknowledged that bureaucratic joining procedures could be off-putting for some sections of the community and Nottinghamshire public libraries were trying to address this:

> The homeless was one particular area that we've looked at a lot and I think we're not the only authority where rules and regulations mitigate against homeless people joining the library because we ask for ID; we've been looking at ways around that. (Kath Owen)

In Enfield, the *Welcome to Your Library* (WTYL) project identified the difficulties that refugees and asylum seekers faced when they wanted to become library members. Libraries often require two pieces of identification but people from these groups usually have only one, paperwork from the National Asylum Support Service (Carpenter, 2004). Procedures in Enfield have been simplified so that only one piece of ID is now needed. Other library services have gone down a similar path. One interview participant explained the steps her library service had taken to try to make the library more accessible:

> Libraries make it very difficult for people to join. We let people join on a limited membership, until they come in next time.. So we looked at issues like that, which was putting people off, because basically we want to encourage them in. That was, I think, quite difficult for a lot of staff. (Anon)

The WTYL project gave some other straightforward advice for libraries looking to make joining procedures simpler: translate forms to meet local needs; take a flexible approach to enlist membership at community events or groups; encourage the participation of local refugee organizations when designing joining packs; ensure all staff are aware of the barriers faced and produce guidelines to ensure consistency in the way in which joining procedures are administered; ensure joining procedures enable the library to gather relevant management information to target needs and improve services. Although there are examples of good practice in this area, John Vincent felt that libraries were still too wedded to outdated procedures:

> I do a lot of training with librarians and library assistants [and] they're actually doing the same old processes that I remember doing when I started working in libraries in the '60s. Somebody was telling me the other day, she'd spent the whole of her previous working day looking at people who'd defaulted [on fines] and deciding whether to 'blacklist' them or not. And so I'm not sure we've looked at all our processes. If you look at all the barriers around joining, all the forms of ID, there are some now like Essex and Wrexham which are starting to do away with all that but even so, we get bogged down with past procedures. (John Vincent)

Another participant acknowledged, though, that changes like these introduced to make the library more accessible and open were not always easy for staff to come to terms with:

> We took down all the prohibitory notices that we had, because instead of welcoming people in you are sort of putting people off, that was a hard thing to get across to the staff. (Anon)

Overcoming institutional barriers – book stock policies The importance of ensuring book stocks and other materials reflect the needs of the community and are in appropriate formats is emphasized in *Libraries for All* (Department for Culture, Media and Sport, 1999). A survey of public library services undertaken by the *Network* found that the majority of responding authorities did have an allocation for the purchase of materials for socially excluded groups but few based this on a thorough needs analysis, most basing their allocation on the previous year's figures (Vincent, 2002). The majority of authorities who responded included specific mention of socially excluded groups in their stock selection policies but generally their focus was on the 'traditional' socially excluded groups such as children and young people or elderly people, not all of whom may be excluded anyway as discussed above. *The Network* survey concluded that there was little or no stock policy development for some key socially excluded groups such as travellers or homeless people. Public libraries are better at meeting the resource needs of some socially excluded groups than others, therefore. Public libraries in the UK have a long history of providing resources in community languages, for example, although the WTYL project stressed the need to keep management information up to date to ensure that the needs of newcomers as well as long established communities are met (Carpenter, 2004). This was also emphasized by an interview participant explaining how social inclusion policies impacts on the stock held by the library:

> You only have to look around at immigration, for a start. Where do you find literature in Serbo-Croat? We don't have a huge number [of immigrants in this area] I must admit but in a lot of authorities, it's a huge part of their population. (Anon)

The identification and selection of stock for excluded groups can be difficult and time consuming. Library suppliers are generally good at supplying mainstream material but librarians working with excluded groups often have to find other ways of meeting their specific needs. There are specialist services such as CILLA (The Co-operative of Indic Language Library Authorities) but personal contacts, recommendations and strategies such as Internet searching are also important for sourcing suitable material, according to *The Network* survey (Vincent, 2002). Co-operation between library authorities is another important way of improving coverage of various community languages. The WTYL report stressed that involving the refugee and asylum communities is key to ensuring stock is relevant and that holds true for all excluded groups (Carpenter, 2004). As noted above, some authorities are making a concerted effort to consult with those perceived as excluded and those who do not currently use the library and this consultation often involves participation in stock selection. The result is a book stock which better reflects the needs of the local community. Another method of making the stock more relevant for excluded groups is to involve communities in actually producing material. The National Literacy Trust, as part of its National Reading Campaign, has gathered case studies of *Telling Tales* projects; work involving libraries which gathers stories from different cultures and generations and makes them available to a wider audience.[7]

Overcoming personal and social barriers Individuals' personal circumstances can make them reluctant to use public library services. Those with poor basic skills, for example, can find services based around reading, writing and communication very daunting although some library services are linking with partners within the community to provide services for basic skills learners in recognition that community libraries can be less threatening, formal or distracting than a school or college. Nevertheless, as institutions based primarily around the written word, libraries do need to convince those with learning difficulties or basic skills needs that the library has something to offer them. Those on low incomes can also be reluctant to use library services perhaps not realizing that most services are free at the point of use or because they are fearful about accumulating fees and fines which they will be unable to pay. All libraries have free or concessionary rates for users on low incomes including children, elderly people and those on benefits although these vary depending on the authority. Perhaps more important is the need for staff to be flexible about charges and fees and for management to allow them to use their discretion to waive fines when they feel it is appropriate. One interview participant believed that empowering the staff was often the key to making the library a more welcoming place. She explained how the regulations governing library membership and use had been revised following local government reorganization and the establishment of the unitary authority and its own library service:

> What we did in effect was throw away the rule books that come with a big organization and really looked at what the needs of the community were. To organize a huge county you do need rule books and the staff had a great tendency to hide behind those rule books. …What we tried to do was look at what the needs of the community were, which we did in a few ways, but also empowered the staff to make decisions on small issues and some perhaps fairly complex issues for librarians / library assistants. Like making decisions on letting people off fines, something they had never done before (Anon)

Jan Holden agreed that staff attitude was often the key to opening up services to hard to reach groups. Unlike the participant above, she felt rules were important but needed to be interpreted flexibly:

> From a user's point of view, we have changed the way that our staff interact with customers and I think that has made an incredible amount of difference to the range of people who use the library. So we haven't thrown away the rule book, any large organization still needs to work with rules but it's about staff having the willingness to negotiate the rules with people and to treat people like grown ups and to treat them as individuals with an individual's needs. (Jan Holden)

She acknowledged, though, that this involved a lot of training and support of staff.

People from socially excluded groups may also suffer from direct and indirect discrimination which can hinder their library use. Evidence suggests that libraries are under-used by people from minority ethnic backgrounds, for example, the collections and services available not always fully reflecting the diversity of the communities they serve. Roach and Morrison (1998) suggested that ethnic minority communities often experience disadvantage and discrimination in access to public services because of their nature, size, traditions and modes of operation and, like many other public services, the public library has been guilty of excluding ethnic minority groups. This kind of institutionalized racism can only be addressed by changing the culture of the organization, according to Durrani (2001) but, at the moment, many Black and minority ethnic groups feel they have no stake in the library service.

The experience of these kinds of personal and social barriers can lead to the formation of a general perception that libraries are 'not for the likes of us'.

Overcoming perception and awareness barriers Those without a tradition of using library services may feel intimidated by the environment and the experience of the public library. Roach and Morrison (1998) found that the library was not culturally relevant for many minority ethnic groups, for example. In interview, John Pateman was adamant that a significant proportion of the population still believes that libraries are not for them:

> I know a lot of people who have never used libraries, generations of families who have never used libraries, they have never thought it was for them in the same way that the opera house isn't for them or the ballet isn't for them. They think you have to pay to use them, for example, they think you have to be brainy, academic, you have to be 'boffs', as the young people call it, and libraries are definitely not cool or sexy. (John Pateman)

The image of public libraries can be off-putting for socially excluded people, therefore. Once persuaded through the doors, some may change their views, however. Many of the basic skills learners who participated in the *Quick Reads* project, designed to support their reading for pleasure, felt that significant cultural changes had taken place in library services since many of them had last visited their local library (Train, 2003). Through the project, they also became more aware of the services provided by the library and of their actual or potential relevance to their lives.

Ethnic and youth cultures can also shape perceptions about the relevance and value of the library according to Roach and Morrison (1998) although some authorities are making strenuous efforts to reposition the library service. The issue of relevance is vital; unless socially excluded people can see that libraries are relevant to their needs, they are not likely to use them. The WTYL project report made the point that when people are struggling with day to day survival, a visit to the library will probably be the last thing on their minds (Carpenter, 2004). In fact, as the report makes clear, the public library can help them access opportunities for information, learning and reading to support them in improving their position and circumstances. Developing an understanding and awareness of the role of the library through outreach work is essential in these circumstances. The WTYL project also found that refugees and asylum seekers often lacked the confidence to make use of the library and its services even though some of them attended meetings of groups on library premises. Poor spoken English meant they lacked the confidence to use the library's facilities. In other cases, poor literacy in their own languages meant that they had little reason to use the library. Family literacy projects, working in partnership with refugee community groups, seemed to be a good way of reaching these groups, through Sure Start, for example, or homework clubs.

Overcoming environmental barriers The kinds of psychological barriers outlined above can cause significant difficulties which prevent individuals and groups accessing public library services; others face very practical physical obstacles which can leave them excluded, although there is legislation designed to help prevent this. The Disability and Discrimination Act (DDA), passed in 1995, has important implications for public libraries in the UK. Passed to end the discrimination that many disabled people encounter in employment, education and access to goods and services, the Act has been phased in over the last five years so that since 2 December 1996 it has been unlawful for service providers to treat disabled people less favourably for a reason relating to their disability. Since 1 October 1999 service providers have had to make 'reasonable adjustments' for disabled people, such as providing extra help or making changes to the way they provide their services. Finally, since October 2004 service providers have had to make 'reasonable adjustments' to the physical features of their premises to overcome physical barriers to access (Disability Rights Commission, 2004).

The disability organization Scope, in its memorandum submitted to the 2000 Select Committee on public libraries, highlighted the potentially serious results of a lack of access to public library services for disabled people:

> Denying access to a public library puts a barrier in the way of disabled people in accessing key local, regional and national information which enables them to practice their human and civil rights (Culture, Media and Sport Committee, 2000 Appendix 8).

There is a perception that public libraries have a good record of providing services to and for disabled people although concern has been expressed that some types of disabilities, visual impairment for example, are better addressed than others (Culture, Media and Sport Committee, 2000). Users seem generally satisfied with physical access to public libraries, with around 85 per cent responding that ease of access both entering and within the library were either very good or good in the Cipfa PLUS survey (Cipfa, no date). It must be remembered, though, that this is a survey of users only and therefore does not include those who perhaps have been deterred from using the library because of access difficulties.

A survey undertaken in 2001 found that libraries, museums and archives were aware of the requirements of users but that provision was uneven and there was still a long way to go before all were compliant with the DDA (Solon Consultants, 2001). Similarly, a study focusing on public libraries alone found that the public libraries participating in the research were aware of many of the more obvious physical access needs of disabled people such as the need for ramps, lifts etc, and were trying to respond positively to the requirements of the DDA but physical access issues that were perhaps less obvious to able-bodied people such as shelving, table and counter proportions, were not consistently addressed (McCaskill and Goulding, 2001). Funding the necessary improvements was identified as the key challenge especially in buildings which, as Cilip, acknowledges, were often built before 'there was any awareness of the needs and rights of disabled people to have full access to library services' (Cilip, 2003, online resource). Another more recent study found that physical access to public libraries for people for disabilites was generally good although not all were fully DDA compliant at the time of the survey (early 2004).[8] Problems remaining included libraries on multiple levels and heavy doors but the participating authorities seemed to be making genuine efforts to become accessible for disabled people. In Cornwall, for example, the County Council made £500,000 available to bring library buildings in line with the DDA standards, including the installation of ramps, lifts and toilets. Accesibility details for individual libraries are generally posted on library websites for those with access to the Internet.

Some people find it difficult to reach the library altogether, however, with those in rural communities at particular risk of exclusion and isolation. The common perception that social exclusion is a problem confined to urban England was challenged by a Countryside Agency report which provided insight into the lives and hardships experienced by individuals in rural areas (Countryside Agency, 2000). The Local Government Association also outlined the distinctive nature of rural social exclusion highlighting the lack of access to opportunities (including jobs, learning and training), to services (including health care, education, shops, leisure and cultural services), and to information (including welfare advice and information); transport poverty (greater reliance on public transport but comparative lack and infrequency of transport); under-employment, seasonal, casual and temporary employment and low wages and the high costs of housing relative to local wage levels (Moor & Whitworth, 2001). Although the difficulties faced by the socially excluded in rural areas can be shrouded by the power and affluence of the wider rural community, *Libraries for All* (Department for Culture, Media and Sport, 1999, p. 9) acknowledged that exclusion was not geographically limited, 'embracing rural, urban and suburban areas alike' and noting that the 'isolation problems experienced by rural communities' were one barrier preventing people from using public libraries. In interview, John Pateman agreed that lying behind the picturesque scenes of country life were problems of real disadvantage and although his move in 2004 from the inner-city London borough of Merton to rural Lincolnshire might be seen as quite a change, many of the problems of exclusion remain the same and are often exacerbated by isolation.

Mobile libraries have long been used to provide public library services to communities with easy access to static libraries. The mobile system has served the rural population reasonably well over the years but it has been suggested that this provision is now insufficient and a more flexible approach is required (Hicken, 2002) although technological advances have enabled the adaptation of mobile libraries to provide computers and Internet access. The Derbyshire Mobile Library Project, for example, delivers Internet access to rural communities through the mobile library service.[9] The mobile van, which has a receiver, parks within the range of local public buildings with fixed ISDN lines fitted with transmitters. In North Derbyshire and the Peak District, the service operates at 18 locations with host buildings, including village halls and local shops, receiving a small payment for their assistance. The project is designed to broaden 'the appeal and relevance of the library service' and offer lifelong learning opportunities and information about public services. Other authorities are exploring alternatives to mobile library services. One study found that social inclusion objectives were a significant motivating factor for much of the development of different library service delivery mechanisms in rural areas, especially in the formation of partnerships designed to extend services to hard to reach groups (Benstead et al., 2004). In Cornwall, for example, the library service was working with Sure Start to provide a mobile toy library service to rural communities. The location and integration of library services points with other local services or amenities was also considered vital to extending services to isolated and excluded communities, an issue pointed out by many interview participants as discussed below.

Challenges

Despite the evidence of good work in the area of social exclusion illustrated by examples of good practice above, challenges remain. The WTYL project report identified the problem of 'fragmented and maginalized' work with socially excluded groups as hindering the effectiveness of public library activities aimed at socially excluded groups (Carpenter, 2004, p. 10). The word 'patchy' was used by many of those interviewed to describe the level of commitment by public library services to tackling social exclusion. Interviewees also complained that much of the work was based around short-term projects which were often not sustained and not mainstreamed. Resourcing is clearly problematic and few authorities seem entirely willing to prioritize the needs of excluded people and communities and redirect substantial resources into meeting those needs with the result that action is uneven across the country with some library services still finding it difficult to engage with hard-to-reach excluded groups. This may be related to a lack of understanding among staff or a reluctance to change established processes and behaviour to welcome new groups as suggested above.

Staffing

The widening of the library remit, illustrated by the examples of new and innovative services described above, raises urgent questions about the staffing of public libraries and the qualifications and skills needed by staff. Inappropriate staff attitudes, values, beliefs and behaviour are perceived as serious institutional barriers which can hamper the development of a more inclusive service. Although some interview participants praised their staff's commitment and capacity to take on new challenges and embrace the social exclusion agenda, others were critical of some colleagues' willingness to involve themselves with it.

The role and skills of public library staff are considered vital to delivering on social exclusion objectives. *Libraries for All* (Department for Culture, Media and Sport, 1999) emphasized the importance of communicating with library staff about the development of services to tackle social exclusion and the need to equip them with the skills, knowledge and competences to deliver those services. Although diversity and equalities training has been a feature of many library services' training programmes, John Vincent suggested in interview that, in his experience of leading training in library services, staff often do not really understand the key issues around social exclusion. He suggested that this was not always necessarily their fault and that library service management had not been particularly good at involving staff and informing them of developments such as *Inspiring Learning for All*, for example. He added, though, that many individual staff members also did not seem very engaged and did not want to become engaged, thinking that such issues were nothing to do with them and harking back to a time when libraries 'just lent books and you provided information from the reference library' (John Vincent). John Pateman agreed that, generally, staff did not want to be challenged to provide new services or deal with users others than those they were used to. He commented that library staff were often in 'a cosy and comfortable relationship' with users with whom they share backgrounds, attitudes, interests, values, beliefs and behaviours. People coming into the library who do not fit that norm because of their age, ethnicity or social background disturb that comfortable relationship and staff often do not know how to react. Alan Watkin also acknowledged that although staff in Wrexham libraries have excellent customer care skills, they were nervous when people that they did not recognize as 'people like themselves' entered the library. In some cases, it seems they have good reason to be anxious and he gave the example of another library authority where the biggest problem in its centres of deprivation is the fear staff have and the physical assaults they suffer. Nevertheless, the progress of the social exclusion agenda can only be hindered when 'so many of the groups we're talking about seem to be, at first sight, an antagonistic grouping to the people who are providing the service' (Alan Watkin).

In contrast, Martin Molloy was much more positive about the capacity and dedication of staff in Derbyshire to deliver the library service's objectives. Although not talking about social exclusion specifically, he reinforced the points made by John Vincent about communication and involvement and asserted that it is the responsibility of the management of the library service to ensure that staff are on board, cautioning:

> What we can't do is betray the staff, it's no good thinking they're going to do this by osmosis or something, you have got to make it clear to them what the challenge is and why the challenge exists. But these are clever people, you know, they're not fools, you need to explain to them why things are politically important, why we've got to do this thing in a particular way. And then you've got to give them proper training and you've got to make sure it covers all your staff so the relief staff, the drivers, everybody, that everybody's involved in this (Martin Molloy).

In this way, he believed that staff would become advocates for the service. John Pateman also believed that staff must and could become advocates:

> We need staff who are… advocates for the communities they serve. If you are going to build a community you need to have advocacy and we are too passive, too kind of neutral. That means championing, actually championing, for example, the rights of excluded groups such as travellers and refugees. (John Pateman)

He felt that this was not just about staff approach and training but also needed more radical action to encourage the appointment of new staff with the qualifications, experience and attitude relevant to working with excluded groups. In Lincolnshire he felt that the skills and confidence to work with socially excluded groups were not necessarily to be found in the current staffing establishment dominated by, 'mostly women and mostly elderly women, mostly middle class women and that isn't the profile of the population' (John Pateman).

Trying to ensure that the staff more accurately reflects the local community is a challenge already raised in Chapter 5. Failure to do so can seriously hamper library services' success in tackling social exclusion and interviewees often stressed the need to diversify the staff base. Ayub Khan, for example, commented that although a lot of attention had been paid to the design of library buildings to make them more welcoming, and rightly so, what went on inside those buildings was also important to opening up access to excluded groups. As suggested in Chapter 5, this including paying attention to the profile of the people working there, with age, sex and cultural backgrounds particularly relevant. In email correspondence, David Jones, Head of Camden Libraries, suggested that targeting users is a good way of recruiting staff from an ethnically diverse background. He noted that Camden had been successful in encouraging learners who accessed services for activities such as Basic Skills, English as a Second Overseas Language or Internet taster sessions to apply for posts in the service and they had recruited several Bengali and Somali employees that way.

The importance of a culturally sensitive personal contact to make socially excluded people feel comfortable in the library is recognized by many authorities and some are taking steps to make the staffing profile more representative of the local population. In Camden, work placements for refugees are being trialled as a way of diversifying the profile of library staff and building links with refugee communities. Aimed at those from the borough's Somali and Congolese refugee communities, the project aims to give refugees 12 week's experience of working in libraries on a year's rolling programme. Six refugees will be on placement at any one time. Applicants will have to fill in a standard application form so that they receive real experience of applying for and holding a job. Those successful will then undergo the library service's standard induction programme and be given the opportunity to work on projects within the community. It is hoped that the project will benefit the service, the community and the individual refugee by involving the refugee community and refugee community groups in the project with a view to ensuring that libraries more closely reflect the make-up of their neighbourhoods.[10]

As mentioned in Chapter 5, the use of volunteers is also increasingly seen as a useful way of diversifying the library workforce and of promoting library work as a career to communities who may not have considered it previously. John Pateman said in interview that he was keen to attract volunteers from the traveller community to work in libraries and become advocates for the services within those groups. He admitted, though, that in his experience it was easy to find white, middle class volunteers but encouraging people from the Black community, particularly young people, and other excluded groups to volunteer was much more difficult.

Outreach work by staff who understand the communities they are working with is another important way of making services more accessible for excluded groups. Authorities like Newham, an inner London borough, have community outreach teams taking services to individuals and community venues in an attempt to reach some of society's most disadvantaged groups. Sure Start has given many library services a platform from which to become involved with a range of excluded groups as Kath Owen explained:

> [With] things like Sure Start, the Children's Coordinators are doing a huge amount of work out in the communities. We've got Sure Start workers who are coming into libraries

on a regular basis, doing work with projects with groups of under fives and their carers with Boots Books for Babies… I think that's another very strong aspect of our work in the future, not only in being more inclusive and welcoming people into the library but also going full circle, I suppose, back to outreach work which I think, because of things like NOF, have perhaps declined. (Kath Owen)

In his interview, though, Shiraz Durrani raised the question of whether developing specialist posts or teams to take forward the social exclusion agenda or deliver services to specific excluded groups was the best way to tackle the issue. He felt that there was a danger that in creating specialist teams for, for example, work with Black and minority ethnic groups or for equal access, marginalized the work and gave other staff an excuse not to become involved themselves but instead pass enquiries or issues on to the special team. The whole concept of outreach has also been questioned. Outreach services can be seen as condescending and paternalistic, giving the impression that these types of activities are marginal, not mainstream, and are part of a handout culture (Hererra, no date).

As we saw in Chapter 5, another issue raised in interview related to staffing for services designed to tackle social exclusion was whether professional librarians were the best people to undertake this type of work. David Jones noted that although most public library services in multicultural boroughs do not experience difficulties recruiting staff from minority ethnic groups for support staff positions, at middle management and senior levels it is more difficult. His solution was not to insist on a professional qualification in all instances but to require either a professional qualification or relevant experience, supported by ongoing training and support. He felt that this enables unqualified operational staff to move beyond the glass ceiling and not only promotes a more diverse workforce but also fully utilizes the customer care and business planning skills that many operational staff have.

Conclusion

The public library community's commitment to, and potential role in, tackling social exclusion has been established in a range of policy and strategy documents and the evidence suggests that public libraries are making a significant contribution and engaging with the social exclusion agenda although activity and commitment is more developed in some library authorities than in others. A lack of real commitment from policy makers was identified by some participants as an obstacle to the development of strategy and activity in more public library services, however. In England, although the DCMS and MLA have highlighted the role that public libraries can play in overcoming exclusion, there is some feeling that their words are not always supported by actions and that, if they really want to make this a priority, a public library standard needs to be developed which will encourage library services to review their policies and activities in this area. Until then, library authorities that feel that they do not have the capacity, skills or resources to devote to social exclusion work will continue to avoid reviewing services and policies from a social exclusion perspective. Some would argue, though, that until the standards are put on a more formal or even statutory basis, library services and local authorities will not take them seriously anyway.

Discourses of prioritization and targeting were prominent in discussions of social exclusion, from both interview participants and other commentators, with some dispute over who 'the majority' of users or potential users are and how best to reach them. As highlighted in Chapter 4, commentators like Tim Coates seem to suggest that public libraries have gone too far in trying to attract users from those sections of society that have not been heavy users of public libraries in the past. In so doing, it is suggested, they are in danger of alienating the mainstays of public libraries, generally characterized as those wanting a good read. Study participants, though, recognized the need to attract a wider range of people into public libraries for ethical and policy priority reasons, emphasizing that this necessarily had an impact on services provided and activities developed. This often led to discussions of a conflict of interest between serving these new users and other, more long-standing library members. With limited resources, public libraries have to prioritise and there has been some debate about how the needs of 'the majority' are being neglected to serve the narrow, sectional interests of 'the minority'. But while most of the interviewees who raised this subject believed that 'the majority' are those beyond the regular, library-using public, commentators like Coates are adamant that 'the majority' *is* the regular, library-using public. Establishing the needs of the community and developing mechanisms and services to ensure they are met is acknowledged as essential but, in this context, there is some question about whose needs and how these should be prioritized.

Aside from resources, the other main challenge raised in the interviews was that of staffing. Staffing needs to be appropriate for the community being served and there was some concern expressed that the current staffing establishment in many public library services was not suited to pursuing social inclusion goals. While some participants seemed to feel that a clean sweep was necessary, others were convinced that staff already in post were adaptable and capable of taking on new duties and altering their behaviour and attitudes in ways which would welcome those nervous or unsure about entering the public library. It was acknowledged, though, that this often involved changes to organizational culture, ethos, practices and conduct which some staff found difficult to accept. The key, according to some participants, was support, training and trust from the top. Staff could not be expected to change attitudes or adapt to new procedures overnight but needed an understanding, first of all, of why things were changing and then consistent and ongoing encouragement and backing.

A good number of years of development and engagement with the social exclusion agenda (more pronounced, perhaps, in some library services than others) means that there is now a large body of good practice and experience helping identify which delivery mechanisms, initiatives and interventions meet the needs of socially excluded groups and are successful in reaching out to those from disadvantaged communities. The key to much of this activity is effective multi-agency working, engaging in partnerships with other local organizations, bodies and groups so that the needs of the community, and vulnerable groups within it, are considered in a holistic, joined-up way. This leads us to a discussion of libraries working in partnership for community development in the next chapter.

Notes

1 The Neighbourhood Renewal Unit website is at URL: http://www.neighbourhood.gov.uk/ [24.11.05].
2 New TSN website is at URL: http://www.newtsnni.gov.uk/index.htm [24.11.05].
3 Further information available at URL: http://www.scotland.gov.uk/Topics/People/Social-Inclusion [24.11.05].
4 The Social Exclusion Unit website is at URL: http://www.socialexclusionunit.gov.uk/ [24.11.05].
5 The Network website is at URL: http://www.seapn.org.uk/index.html [24.11.05].
6 Further information about the Libraries Change Lives Award is available at URL: http://www.cilip.org.uk/aboutcilip/medalsandawards/LibrariesChangeLives [24.11.05].
7 Further information about *Telling Tales* case studies is available at URL: http://www.literacytrust.org.uk/campaign/tellingtales.html [24.11.05].
8 Further information about the Biblioformeda project is available at URL: http://www.lboro.ac.uk/departments/dis/disresearch/bibliomeda.html [24.11.05]. Not all results have yet been published.
9 Further information is available at URL: http://getconnected.ngfl.gov.uk/ index.php?s=case_derby [24.11.05].
10 Email correspondence with David Jones, Head of Libraries, Camden Council.

Chapter 8

Building Communities

The Policy Context: Community Development

The previous chapter makes it clear that both individuals and/or communities can be socially excluded but an individual's problems are often related to problems within the locality where they live as well as to personal circumstances. Efforts to confront and halt social exclusion have therefore focused on community activities and development as well as helping individuals and their families. According to the Community Development Foundation, '[s]ocial inclusion and community development are two sides of the same coin' (Community Development Foundation, 2004a, online resource) because community development initiatives work with the most marginalized, enabling them to participate in their local communities, in association with statutory and voluntary organizations, to improve community life. The Government's 2001 neighbourhood renewal strategy action plan stresses that better coordination of local initiatives and action and the involvement of the local community are key to tackling the problems of disadvantaged areas (Social Exclusion Unit, 2001). This means building new partnerships at local level to coordinate area-based action and fostering community participation.

Partnership working is a vital aspect of the Government's modernizing agenda for local authorities. It is hoped that greater powers to engage in partnership arrangements with other bodies, organizations and agencies will lead to actions and initiatives which advance the economic, social and environmental well-being of the community. Best Value, with its emphasis on policy cohesion, has also encouraged the spread of partnership working. At the basis of this is the perception that government departments, agencies or organizations working alone cannot make a significant difference to the quality of life of a local area and that partnership working, with a strategic co-ordination of services, can eliminate wasteful duplication, make more effective use of resources and avoid gaps in services. Partnerships are also advocated as a way of responding to public demands for 'all-in-one' services or 'one-stop-shops' that no single service can provide alone (Holt, 1999). These kinds of 'joined-up' approaches, the Government argues, will correct some of the inefficiencies and general muddle arising from the previous Conservative administration introduction of the market into public services which resulted in the fragmentation and complexity of service delivery (Rouse, 2001). As an example, part 1 of the Local Government Act 2000 requires local authorities to produce a long term local community strategy focusing on the promotion of the well-being of the community, enhancing quality of life and contributing to sustainable development. The strategy should be taken forward by a Local Strategic Partnership (LSP) bringing together representatives from the public, private, community and voluntary sectors operating within the community with the aim of tackling fundamental and complex cross-cutting issues requiring a coherent and integrated response from a range of different bodies. LSPs are considered key to tackling the complex problems of regeneration and those in the most deprived neighbourhoods receive additional funding to assist their work.

Community participation in decision making at a local level is a key element of community development and government policy increasingly is to involve local people in identifying the issues which matter to their community, set priorities and design solutions. There is an emphasis on consulting and listening to communities and the national strategy for neighbourhood renewal makes the point that this can include 'communities of interest' such as Black and minority ethnic groups or disabled people as well as the more conventional geographically-based communities (Social Exclusion Unit, 2001). It is expected that local residents will sit on LSPs which will have to undertake extensive outreach work to ensure people from local communities understand that they have the opportunity to participate although it is recognized that activity at a very local, sub-community level with specific groups, especially those perceived as hard to reach, may be necessary as will training and support. The national strategy also makes the point that, for many, involvement in community self-help and mutual support activity will be the form that much community engagement takes place rather than through formal decision making bodies and processes. This aspect of community development, activities which improve local conditions through local people pursuing a common cause or sharing common interests, can strengthen communities by encouraging connections between people – the basis of social capital. Although the Community Development Foundation stresses that community activity must be neither bought nor coerced but truly voluntary and largely self-created, its extent and effectiveness are critically affected by deliberate development and local services have a role to play in enabling community activity and providing opportunities which support it (Community Development Foundation, 2004b). The focus on community learning for community development has been particularly strong in Scotland. The approach of the Scottish Executive emphasizes both learning in the community and community learning, that is, 'people engaging with each other to bring about changes that enhance local life' (Smith, 2004, online resource). This is an approach that libraries could usefully adopt.

Public Libraries and Community Development

The themes of community development and transformation have become increasingly prominent in statements from MLA and the DCMS. A recent pamphlet stressed that libraries (and museums and archives) lie at the heart of communities where they can act as catalysts for the creation of human and social capital (MLA, 2005). The *Framework for the Future* marketing programme which has focused on finding a message or theme around which the public library community could unite and which could be used to demonstrate the role and value of public libraries to the public and to government, has decided on 'heart of the community' as exemplifying a range of key ideas relating to public libraries, including:

- a place that feels good and that makes people proud
- an idea that's grounded in our lives
- focusing on people and where they live
- based on the relationships that staff build and the services that are developed
- a unique space.[1]

Themes around the idea of community and how public libraries can facilitate community building are becoming increasingly apparent in policy documents, therefore. Lord Andrew McIntosh in his written answer highlighted this role:

> All public libraries have real potential to become hubs of their communities and one of the main aims of the *Framework* strategy is to encourage that potential to be realised more widely. (Lord Andrew McIntosh)

As outlined in the introduction to this chapter, there are two key elements to community development which the Government is keen to pursue. One is the importance of multi-agency working so that the skills and energies of a range of relevant partners are engaged in finding solutions to the often complex problems facing excluded communities. The second is supporting communities themselves in resolving problems in their locality and implementing solutions. Public libraries can and are playing a role in both aspects. Firstly, partnership working was a key theme of the interviews for the study on which this book is based, confirming that multi-agency working is extensive and accepted as part of the culture. Secondly, public libraries are considered to have an important supportive role to play in enabling community involvement, cohesion and capacity building through the provision of public, neutral, community space in which local groups can meet and also where individuals can encounter and interact with others from the local area. These two aspects are the focus for our discussion of public library involvement in community development.

Partnership Working

The regeneration agenda, as articulated by the Government, demands a co-ordinated approach across the local authority and with external private and voluntary agencies to build inclusive communities. New bodies to take forward the various strategies are being established and public libraries need to ensure that they are involved and engaged as multi-agency partnerships support the local authority's work in many different areas including for cultural and education purposes as well as for economic and social regeneration. This approach, of considering community needs in a more holistic way, means that public libraries must, and increasingly are entering into strategic partnerships and working with other local and central government departments and agencies as well as with voluntary and private sector partners. The Government is keen to encourage this; *Framework for the Future* mentions partnerships in a variety of contexts, stressing that modern library services increasingly depend on working in cooperation with a range of agencies and departments (Department for Culture, Media and Sport, 2003). Similarly, the Annual Library Plans required public libraries to state the nature of partnerships developed, suggesting that those assessing the plans would consider the extent to which public libraries were actively fostering alliances for service development. The Library Position Statements also obliged library services to provide a list of partnerships in place and proposed.

Clearly, then, Whitehall pressure to engage in partnership working is increasing and although public library services have always worked with others both inside and outside the council as illustrated in Chapters 2 and 3, the modernizing government agenda has facilitated closer working relationships, often engaging public libraries in a range of programmes and activities central to the local authority's community strategy and social and economic priorities. Partnership working is not new for public libraries but perhaps what is new is the emphasis now given to formal partnerships and the range of issues and policy areas they are now addressing. The number of partnerships that public libraries are engaged in is increasing, therefore, as is their range and scope, and they are playing an important role in promoting the contribution of libraries to the wider social policy agenda.

Delivering Services in Partnership

As well as demonstrating how public libraries can deliver key priorities in a range of priority policy areas, partnership working is now also considered vital to a range of services provided by the public library. There was a general acceptance among interview participants that, in the words of Margaret Watson, no public library service can operate in a vacuum now, a view reinforced by another participant who commented:

> [Libraries] can't do anything these days that's worth doing without working in cooperation and partnership with someone and the days of library services operating alone and getting away with it, even though they weren't doing anything terribly valuable half the time, have long since gone. (Anon)

Libraries' work with children and young people has been greatly enhanced through cooperation with youth services, childcare providers, education and health care providers and has led to a range of innovative initiatives such as Bookstart and homework clubs or study support centres. Similarly, partnership is often the key to public library work on social inclusion including contacts with local community groups and other council departments such as Social Services and also with voluntary groups and associations or charities serving a range of excluded people while partnership with commercial companies have assisted public libraries in their literature development work and in the provision of ICT.[2] Martin Molloy commented that those outside libraries are often surprised at the extent of their partnership working:

DCMS asked us to go through a process of identifying all the partnerships that libraries were involved with to deliver services across the county council and the Chief Exec was knocked out by the scale of what we were involved in. That was a big eye-opener to him and I suspect it would be a big eye-opener to other people. (Martin Molloy)

Bob Janes agreed that libraries were open to partnership whenever a suitable opportunity arose:

As a department, as opposed to just libraries, we will work with anybody who has a common agenda, there isn't a limit. There are limits in terms of funding, there are limits in terms of staffing – those are good, solid, practical reasons for not being able to do everything but the philosophical approach is that if they are pointing in the same direction and they've got something to offer, we'll share it with them. (Cllr Bob Janes)

In some areas of the UK, partnership working is more advanced and more necessary than others. In Northern Ireland, for example, the fact that library services were under the responsibility of the Education and Library Boards meant that, in the words of one participant from the province:

…nearly everybody is an external partner and that's always that bit more difficult than working, say, within a unitary authority. I'm not saying internal partnerships are always easy but they're definitely easier than external partnerships. (Anon)

Another participant felt that unitary status made partnerships much easier to forge and maintain:

It is easier to do partnerships with other parts of the authority because there are just fewer people to relate with and we have a much, much better relationship with the museums service and the arts service and the sports service than most other authorities. Most other librarians would never get to see an Arts Officer on a yearly basis; we meet weekly. So it does make things easier, you can work together much more easily. (Anon)

In 2001, the Government's Beacon Council Scheme, which was established in 1999 to reward those local authorities considered to be demonstrating best practice,[3] turned its attention to public libraries. One of the themes of round three of the Beacon Scheme was *Libraries as a Community Resource*, aiming to identify those authorities which recognized the key role that public libraries could play in improving the quality of daily life of communities by fostering community development, promoting community identity and developing social inclusion. As well as demonstrating that the library service was at the heart of the council's priorities, that it had a clear vision and strategy for development and that it had responsive consultation processes, to receive Beacon status for its library service an authority also had to show that it had adopted a holistic approach to delivering services, working in new, innovative and effective ways in partnership with other organizations.

Eight councils won Beacon status for their library services: Liverpool, Barnet, Blackburn with Darwen, Leeds, Stockton on Tees, Suffolk, Sunderland and Sutton. Some examples of the types of partnerships they are now engaged in demonstrates the importance of these arrangements for library services and also the range of organizations with which they are working. Stockton's partnerships with Education colleagues, local businesses such as Safeway, Sainsbury's, W.H. Smith, publishers and authors have led to imaginative schemes such as Stockton Children's Book of the Year and Junior & Young Librarian scheme. Co-location with other community facilities such as housing, police, education, leisure and health are also being encouraged to facilitate wider access to learning and citizen information. A Public Finance Initiative (PFI) bid for a new community library facility in a growing residential estate combines the library with a school resource centre and ICT suite. In fact, the list of partnerships with which Stockton-on-Tees library service is involved runs to 13 pages. In Barnet, a Multimedia Centre with *Learndirect* provision at Hendon Library was the result of partnerships with a range of other local education providers including Middlesex University, Barnet College, the London North Learning and Skills Council and Prospects Careers Services. Work with the council's Equality Team is helping the library service deliver cultural and community events such as Black History Month, International Women's Day and International Day of Disabled People as well as strategies to promote the use and development of the council's multicultural resources collection. In Suffolk, Library Links is piloting new ways of providing library services to rural communities featuring mini-libraries of books and a PC in 8 village locations including a shop and post office while a partnership with the Employment Service is giving people access to the details of 400,000 jobs through the *Worktrain* website.

These partnerships are undoubtedly benefiting users and raising the profile of the library services concerned but there is a question of whether, and if so how, partnership working has led to a refocus of public library aims and objectives away from 'traditional' professional matters to a concern with wider policy objectives. Participation in partnerships is likely to have extended the scope of public libraries beyond what many view as the 'traditional' core services of book lending and information provision. While many welcome the widening of the social role of the public library service, some have voiced fears that the agenda could be skewed in a way that does not suit the library or its users as one participant acknowledged:

> We have to work [in partnership] wherever we can. We work very closely with Education on a lot of issues. We work with Social Services. Departments like that have a different set of priorities and a different set of outcomes and that makes it difficult for us and costly for us in staff time. In the end you can be using up a lot of staff time chasing small numbers. (Anon)

Joyce Little also conceded that there was sometimes a danger of losing sight of the end goal when bidding for funding and building partnerships, which often went hand in hand:

> We quickly realized that we couldn't just be chasing funding; it had to fit in with what we saw the purpose of the library as being... We learnt that you don't create a group of partners just to access funding that is perhaps peripheral to what you see as the main business, it's taking away resources and staff and management time and the results might be very good but it might be for a very small group of people, perhaps. So we've learnt to become cuter both with external funding and with partners. (Joyce Little)

To avoid these problems, Jan Holden said that it was important to work with partners 'whose aims and objectives are the same as yours to get an advantageous outcome' (Jan Holden). Other participants were equally clear that their services had not entered into partnerships just for the sake of it and that, before embarking on any partnerships, they were sure of what the service and its users would gain:

> Any partnership you take on, you need to show the benefit for the library's public users. You're not just doing it because it suits the other partner; you'll end up doing all the work and not getting any benefits. You have to be very careful about what you do. There has to be a purpose and there has to be a deliverable for the library public before we can do it because otherwise we are at full stretch. (Anon)

Another participant picked up on the issue of resources, especially staffing resources, stressing that it was imperative that any partnership entered into was productive for the library service:

> We try not to get ourselves embroiled in partnerships that, really, we'd be better placed not to. You have to acknowledge that there are those that you really steer away from because you would just end up going to meeting after meeting after meeting. We are so open, I think, in the library service to actually not just being a partner but being a very proactive one that our staff end up getting the jobs and the tasks and everything, which is fine but we are bound by targets and indicators and really want to give a really good service ourselves. (Andrea Barker)

Effective Partnership Working

Despite these concerns, library managers and policy makers generally stress the benefits of working in partnership. These kinds of partnerships enable libraries to obtain external funding and appropriate practical support to introduce new services and develop libraries as a community resource promoting inclusion, a better quality of life and opportunities for lifelong learning for the whole community. Closer working with other council departments and agencies has improved staff morale in some instances. Study participants identified a range of benefits that they felt had arisen from working in partnership with internal, authority partners and external partners. Martin Molloy, for example, felt that the exposure given to libraries through partnership with the BBC gave a major boost to promotion efforts:

> Some of the work we're starting to do with the BBC nationally with libraries is tremendous and, over the next few years, is going to transform how libraries appear, I think. We will have the support of the major communicator in the country in terms of radio and television, we will have that behind us in a partnership. We're going to have to

deliver; the BBC aren't going to do nothing for nothing, but we have that capacity, we can do that. (Martin Molloy)

Another participant also talked of how partnerships could raise the profile of the library service, within the authority and beyond, and the benefits this has for the community:

Partnership working does give librarians the opportunity to work across a whole range of sectors that may otherwise be difficult to access and this raises the profile for professional librarians and raises the status of the borough. A lot of the people we try and work with are constantly restructuring and this has been particularly evident with the primary care trust but we have achieved a sound partnership with their health visitors in the distribution of *Bookstart* packs and this has had a very positive impact in the community. (Anon)

Other participants talked of the access to additional funding that working in partnership often facilitated, as one explained:

I think having a partnership agreement in place actually reinforces any external funds that you're going for. A lot of the time it's a pre-requisite with many of the funding bids that you do have a partnership agreement rather than be on your own and it can be extremely beneficial because there's a lot of funding libraries can't go for, being a statutory service. So we can go in the back door and hook some money in that way as well. (Anon)

Joyce Little ran through the advantages of partnership working as she såw them, stressing the value of the relationships formed through partnerships:

[Partnership working] can give access to funding, it can give access to client groups that perhaps you're wanting to target. Providing something's successful, it establishes a relationship that can really be quite a strong bond that will then continue so that even if it's only a letter of support you ask for in the future, you can just phone somebody up and say, 'Can you do this for me?' (Joyce Little)

Working on a range of initiatives with partners from across the local authority and outside it which address key policy areas can have multiple benefits for the library service, therefore. Working successfully in partnerships is not easy, however. It requires time, effort and resources as Helen Connolly recognized:

I think one of the biggest problems is not that people have a problem with cooperation *per se* or partnership working, it's the amount of partnership, it's almost overwhelming, the range of people they should be talking to. Let's face it, they could spend their entire working week catching up with the various people in the community, locally, regionally, nationally, and not get an ounce of other work done. You could spend your entire life trying to map and work and collaborate and try and find ways of not reinventing the wheel and trying to have economies of scale and all these good reasons why we say partnership working is great and why it must be done. But at the end of the day, they have to draw a line and they have to spend some time working with other people and they have to get the job done as well. I think that's what people are struggling with; it's not the notion of actually doing it, it's managing it… I think people have moved beyond the struggle mentally of why they have to do it, I think it's just managing it and getting on with it and balancing it with their other work priorities. (Helen Connolly)

Other barriers to public libraries forging closer relationships with potential partners also remain, including a lack of knowledge about libraries and the ways in which they work, a lack of effective networking and perhaps even the image of the public library. Libraries need to convince policy makers and colleagues within the local authority as well as external organizations and other potential partners that they can help them deliver on a whole range of cross-cutting issues although this was not always easy according to one participant who seemed to question how far libraries could participate in community regeneration activities:

We have a lot of partnerships, we have worked hard at partnerships, but I would say there are a lot of government initiatives that have come out, like the Pathfinders, and Neighbourhood Renewal, which it's not easy for libraries to link in with. We are not community development officers. So we do work with partners but there is a limit to what we can do. If the service has a low profile within the authority it is difficult to get involved in things like Local Strategic Partnerships. We do, but a lot of the time we are picking up crumbs from the table because it's all about the priorities being different. (Anon)

A report on partnerships between libraries and arts organizations found that the latter still considered public libraries and librarians dull and uninspiring which inhibited opportunities to work together (Liddle et al., 1999). Librarians' weak networking and cultural differences between the two types of organizations also hampered partnerships, with arts organizations feeling that libraries were slow to respond and that their perceived bureaucratic and hierarchical structures made them inflexible. Library services might have a job to do, therefore, in convincing potential partners of their ability to contribute and play a role in community initiatives. One interview participant felt that libraries were 'just not key players' (Anon) and another commented that, despite developments like the People's Network, libraries still had to push for involvement in projects and programmes:

I still think it's a case of knocking on doors. It is a case of actually proving the business case for libraries and demonstrating that you are a professional service with credibility in the wider world. The partnerships that we have established take a lot of diplomacy and a lot of work for people to actually sign up to working with you. (Anon)

Another participant disagreed, however, suggesting that the library service had become an increasingly attractive partner for a range of other departments and organizations:

I think there's been more and more partnerships in recent years and certainly more agencies have been coming to us, seeking us out and also being more receptive to our approaches when we say, 'Look, we can do this for you'. (Anon)

Parker et al. (2002, p. 33) asserted that the contribution of public libraries to wider policy areas, 'has been under-estimated or overlooked' because of poor partnership working and a tendency to be inward-looking. Because of this, they can miss out on initiatives to which they could make a real contribution and which could be important sources of funding. In Wales, for example, the Learning Partnerships Initiative for 14-19 year olds made little reference to library and information services, nor did the Assembly's Communities First initiative, focusing on regeneration in areas of social exclusion (Ede, 2003).

The key to involvement in community development initiatives, according to Carpenter (2004), is for public libraries to be clear about their role and be able to promote and communicate this effectively at local level. The Cilip Executive Advisory Group on Social Inclusion agreed that advocacy of the role and contribution of library services in tackling social exclusion must be a priority and added that the workforce needed to improve its negotiating and influencing skills if they were 'to be seen as part of the answer to a more inclusive society, rather than a worthy add-on' (Social Inclusion Executive Advisory Group to Cilip, 2002, p. 7). Some interview participants questioned whether librarians were sufficiently trained or even psychologically prepared for partnership working. Frances Hendrix, for example, commented that librarians were not good at making partnerships either within the local authority or outside the library sector and another participant felt that the uncertainty that often comes with partnership working was difficult for some librarians to cope with:

> Some people are better at [working in partnership]. It worries some people more than it worries other people. Some people just can't cope with it because they maybe think that they have to control it all the while. I think if you're a control freak then partnership working is probably a bit difficult. (Anon)

With a stronger steer from the DCMS on the direction in which public libraries should be moving, national and local priorities and initiatives may conflict and this could stifle their flexibility and ability to engage in multi-agency working. Partners may not share the same objectives, priorities and time-scales and even those services who display and have been rewarded for best practice in this area have had difficulties resolving some of the more intractable problems surrounding partnership working. Nevertheless, partnership working is considered essential to ensure that public libraries play their full role in local and national policy agendas and is considered particularly important to community regeneration and development. The other principal way in which public libraries are involved in community building is in the provision of public space through their networks of buildings and service points.

The Library Building as a Community Resource

Discussion around the role, function and condition of public library buildings often arose unprompted in interview, suggesting that this was an issue of high concern for those working in and with public libraries. The two discourses prominent in discussions of the physical library focused on, firstly, the potential for the public library to become a focus for community activity and support community capacity building and, secondly, how this could be achieved through the refurbishment, redesign and relocation of buildings. Unfortunately, discussion around both discourses often concluded that the potential of the library building to become a dynamic community space would never be fully realized while so much of the building stock is old, tired and off-putting to potential users.

The Potential of the Public Library Space

> Public libraries contribute to community development by offering one of the few free community spaces where people, individually or in groups, can develop themselves through reading and informal learning. Their neutrality in a divided society is well recognised and highly prized by both service managers and users (Department of Culture, Arts and Leisure, 2002, p.8).

Reinforcing this idea that the environment of the public library can assist community development, interview participants often suggested that the presence of a public library within a community had a symbolic as well as practical value because of its capacity to offer, according to Bill Macnaught, 'a friendly, neutral space', a much underestimated characteristic in his opinion. An analysis of the extent to which public libraries could be considered successful public spaces concluded that they are generally perceived as welcoming, accessible and neutral spaces, open to all comers and within which people are treated as citizens rather than consumers (Goulding, 2005). It also suggested, though, that they are not as socially inclusive as they might be and sometimes struggle to meet their aim of being strong community facilities open to all because of some of the barriers to use outlined in the discussion of social exclusion in Chapter 7.

Nevertheless, many claims have been made for the ability of the public library to underpin community development and building by supporting a range of group or community experiences and activities. Similarly, it is said that they offer individuals the opportunity to engage with others from the locality including those from different backgrounds and different social circles to themselves (for example, Linley and Usherwood, 1998). For the isolated, in particular, the library can play a hugely important role, providing opportunities for them to make contact with others from their community and become more integrated. In fact, even when users are not necessarily interacting with one another, the mere fact of being in other people's company is sufficient for some to appreciate the public library as a community space. Undertaking personal activities in a public setting surrounded by others from the local community doing the same, combines individuality with communality and can promote tolerance, diversity and social cohesion (Salmon, 2002). *Tomorrow's Libraries* emphasized that libraries in Northern Ireland were places where 'all sections of the community intermingle freely', for example (Department of Culture, Arts and Leisure, 2002, p. 8). More formal or organized group activities taking place in the library also often draw their membership from across the local community and can build bonds between individuals as well as help give people a say in how their communities are run through community meetings, MPs' surgeries and local consultation discussions (MLA, 2005).

Social capital The kinds of associations outlined above are important in building social capital, the relationships among persons, groups and communities which engender trust and/or mutual obligations. These relationships, expectancies and trusting obligations between people function as a kind of social glue enabling them to act more effectively, making society more efficient and making life generally more rewarding. The potential of public libraries to build social capital through the fostering of social links which bind the community together was recently highlighted by Bryson, Usherwood and Proctor (2003) and, for many commentators, libraries act as community fora, with the potential to renew communities by building social capital and encouraging civic engagement through the development of community partnerships, the facilitation of local dialogue and the dissemination of local information (Kranich, 2004). As public spaces, it is said that public libraries are conducive to interpersonal relationships and solidarity, encouraging a sense of belonging and community and, by providing public space for people to share interests, experiences, views and outlook, it is suggested that libraries can promote and sustain community identity, dialogue and collaboration (see, for example, Leckie & Hopkins, 2002).

The much celebrated neutrality of the public library space was considered by participants to be a very positive attribute which enabled people from a wide range of backgrounds to come together and feel comfortable in the public library space. Other participants commented that public libraries play an important role in connecting people: connecting individuals with one another, connecting people with their local communities, and connecting communities with wider society. This is seen as particularly important at a time of increasing social fragmentation. Alan Watkin stressed that people need a community focus, saying of Wales:

> Even more than in England some of the traditional foci have disappeared. Chapels have disappeared by the score and in this area all our traditional industry disappeared so the work's club, the union gathering, they've all gone as well. So all those traditional points where people for other reasons grouped have disappeared. (Alan Watkin)

He also made the point that there had been significant migration into the area which had changed the population profile. All these trends had the result of people being pulled apart from one another but many of those interviewed felt that the public library could give communities something to focus on and fill the gap left by many of the traditional meeting places. In this scenario, libraries become community focal points and also access points to other local authority or agency services. At a basic level, libraries often offer space to different groups within the local area, enabling them to give information, advice and advocacy to members of the community. As mentioned, MPs often hold their surgeries in public libraries, for example, and housing or welfare rights advice agencies make themselves available at regular times in libraries as do Citizens' Advice Bureaux.

Because of activities like these, there was a perception, articulated in many of the interviews, that the diversity of people coming into the library had widened in recent years. An increase in organized library-led activities such as reading groups, family and local history associations, homework help clubs and children's programmes as well as the increased incidence of community groups using the library as a meeting place for a range of activities from slimming clubs to adult education classes, means that libraries are used by a wide cross-section of the local population. New facilities and resources have also attracted those who were reluctant to use public libraries in the past. While this increased and diverse use is very welcome for library services eager to prove their relevance and worth to local and national politicians as well as the local population, it raises issues of territorialism and how easily public library space can accommodate users seeking quite different experiences from their use of that space and with differing attitudes to acceptable behaviour within it, as discussed in Chapter 4.

As also highlighted in Chapter 4, the term 'traditional user' was used often to refer to those who use the public library on a regular basis for its book lending and reference services, in contrast to 'new users' often attracted to the library by the ICT and other facilities on offer because although the spotlight has been on the impact that ICT has had on the use made of public library space and the atmosphere inside the library, it is not just technology that has had the effect of bringing new users into public libraries. As libraries have sought to embed themselves within the community, they have often become a focus for many diverse community activities, one head of service noting:

> We have not been precious in terms of what we have used our libraries for. If we think that there is a synergy and a partnership to be had with individuals in the community or other sectors, we have really built upon that opportunity. (Anon)

Most public libraries also put on events themselves which attract people from across the community including author visits, local history groups, reading circles or the many children's activities throughout the summer vacations. In these ways, it was felt that public libraries offer individuals the opportunity to engage with others from the locality. But apart from these special events, the library in its day-to-day use also had a social aspect as Joyce Little emphasized:

> We've always been a meeting place for people and the heart of our traditional use is the older person, often retired, visiting the library on a certain day, once a week. [This] is part of their social life and they will meet other friends. And that is something that we have to take into account in our new library development, we've got to ensure we have meeting space. In some places we have refreshments, making sure there are places that they can meet and feel comfortable. (Joyce Little)

Many of the librarians interviewed expressed a desire to make their libraries more welcoming, informal spaces where people can go and meet their friends and others from the community and they often try to build this into new buildings and refurbishments when they have the money. One head of service commented that one of the key messages to emerge from the public consultation his library service undertook when considering building new libraries or refurbishing existing sites was that people wanted a place to meet and a sense of place. This kind of consultation was considered very important in giving communities a sense of ownership and pride in their local public library facilities and, according to one interview participant, can create a real sense of ownership. Talking about the library refurbishment programme in his borough he said:

> They've all been done very much in consultation with the local communities, the Friends groups, local councillors and they've all been taken through the plans, they've all had the opportunity to input into it, their ideas have been taken on board when they can be and they've come out the other end with ownership of it. I've been to all the re-openings and I'm quite struck with the ownership and pride that the library users have in their library and in their contribution to how it looks. (Cllr Graham Tope)

Again, there have been questions raised about the impact some developments may have on their more long-standing users and whether the transformation of the library into a 'meeting place, performance space and group learning site was compatible with the traditional need for quiet reflection and solitary study' (Building Centre Trust, 2000). One head of service noted:

> When we began to provide certain kinds of activities in libraries, some of our residents did not approve of the noise and bustle that they created e.g. events such as book sales, craft fairs, exercise classes. But at the end of the day people came round to these ideas and they accepted them. I think you do have to take a bit of risk. (Anon)

In trying to accommodate new uses within the public library space, therefore, there is a danger that the more established will be driven away, restricting its ability to act as a dynamic meeting place. To resolve the worst of the problems there is a move towards zoning. Worpole (2004) has suggested, for example, that libraries could have a quiet zone, a study zone, a more sociable or meeting area, a separate area for ICT etc. Others are looking at time zoning so that perhaps Wednesday afternoons will be a quiet time while Saturday mornings are more sociable. This seems to minimize the potential of the library as a meeting space, however and, as we have seen, both the library literature and interview participants have stressed how the public library can facilitate connections between people with a range of backgrounds and experiences. The idea of zoning seems to mitigate against that with, as Ayub Khab said, a danger of compartmentalizing people. Although some felt that it was important, in the words of one librarian, 'to keep our traditional users happy' (Anon), others were concerned that these core users were in older age groups and that if public libraries were not made welcoming and attractive to younger people, the service would lose its purpose and most of its users within a couple of decades. One interview participant commented:

> People get upset that [the library is] not the quiet, studious, temple of culture that they want it to be. But in this day and age, if you provided that then nobody would come through the door. (Anon)

An Australian research project report concluded that public libraries build social capital by establishing and nurturing links between people, by encouraging trust through social inclusion and through encouraging greater tolerance and understanding of diversity (New Focus, 2003). The report made the point, though, that social interactions between individuals do not automatically lead to the building of social capital and the strengthening of community bonds or effective collective action on shared problems. The challenge for local services like public libraries is to provide structures and processes which take naturally occurring interactions and transform them into community development opportunities because although public libraries are based in communities, the extent to which they are community-based has been questioned (Harris, 1998).

Community capacity building John Pateman suggested in interview that libraries are too passive and neutral, a quality that has traditionally been viewed as a strength of public libraries. He argued, though, that staff need to be more interventionist and act as advocates for communities although he doubted whether many had the appropriate skills. Similarly, although many of those working within and for public libraries emphasize their role as a community resource, the LISC (Wales) report makes the point that just providing space for individuals or community groups to meet is essentially a passive form of social exclusion or community development work (Library and Information Services Council (Wales), 2003). To become fully involved in community development work, public libraries should be involved in supporting local people to become involved in neighborhood renewal. This might entail capacity building, enabling individuals and groups to acquire the skills, competencies and tools required for them to resolve the issues facing the community as well as providing the space in which they can meet. Harris and Dudley (2005) suggest that public libraries need to consider how they contribute to social interactions at local level and how they can guide and support the development of linkages, networks and capacity for communication, self-help and mutual support within libraries. They assert that there are three clear roles for libraries: promoting information sharing; providing spaces and occasions for groups to meet; stimulating the use of virtual spaces for networking, broadcasting information and presenting community memory.

When discussing the role of public libraries in community development, interview participants primarily stressed how the provision of space could bring individuals and groups together. The importance of the physical library building giving a community a sense of place was also emphasized in many of the interviews and discussions. Alan Watkin asserted, for example:

> I do obviously believe that to be a librarian you don't have to be sitting in the middle of the library but people recognize and need a community focus. (Alan Watkin)

Furthermore, the public library was considered to have advantages over many of the other public or semi-public places available to local people as another head of service made clear:

> The public library is seen as a neutral space. It's somewhere that people can go, not be questioned why they're there, they can just come in and sit. If they want to come in out of the rain, that's fine. (Joyce Little)

Those interviewed frequently commented on the friendliness and non-judgemental nature of the public libraries often giving examples of users who were reluctant to enter a school or college to take courses on email and Internet use but who were happy to come to the library for the same purpose. The public library is also, strangely, often not considered by people to be part of local government which again adds to its image of neutrality:

> I think what libraries are able to do is to offer that sort of element of neutrality. People coming in to use our service don't often see us as the rest of the city council, they see us as slightly apart although they can remind you constantly that they're paying our wages! (Anon)

While staff attitude and approachability must have an impact on people's view of the library as a welcoming place where they can go without fear of being criticized or judged, many of those interviewed felt that the environment of the library building was also important, Bill Macnaught suggesting that the space had a 'civilizing' effect on people. He also asserted that this function of the library is frequently undervalued and others have similarly commented that the provision of a public building into which people can go free of charge, for quite extensive hours, feel safe and have a positive experience is of real, although generally underestimated, value for communities (Culture, Media and Sport Committee, 2004a). Although, as discussed in Chapter 4, some dispute the rather positive gloss often given to official library use statistics and insist that the library using public is uniform in terms of race, class and age, others insist that the open, neutral nature of the public library encourages a wide range of users through its doors and that this has important, beneficial consequences for the community and society as a whole. Bill Macnaught explained:

> You know, nobody's challenging you when you walk into a public library and interrogating you about your views and your values and your political persuasion and all this sort of stuff. It is genuinely a melting pot for all sorts of different beliefs … but I don't think local government generally values the contribution that public libraries make to a tolerant society. And it's not just through reading the books, although that contributes as well [by] broadening people's thinking, I think it's about the physical space. (Bill Macnaught)

The important role that the public library plays in connecting communities to the wider society and connecting individuals with opportunities was discussed above and was also emphasized by the Community Development Foundation in their memorandum to the 2000 Select Committee on Public Libraries in which it also expressed concern about the closure of many community libraries (Culture, Media and Sport Committee, 2000). Proposals to close libraries are invariably accompanied by campaigns bringing together a range of community groups concerned about the loss of the facility and the services it provides. Proctor et al. (1998) documented the impact of library closures on local communities, concluding that closure had a significant impact on users with one in five denied access altogether following the closure of their local library and young children particularly badly affected.

Chief librarians are often frustrated at the refusal of community and friends groups to contemplate the closure of a library, however, even when that building no longer meets the needs of the community it was once designed to serve. In fact, in some cases, that community has ceased to exist or has changed so dramatically that the library needs to be closed or relocated to continue to serve its purpose. In other cases, refurbishment and renewal are necessary to ensure that the library is an attractive and viable location for community activity. Although there is evidence of some activity on this front in public libraries in the UK, interviewees often commented on the necessity of refreshing the public library environment.

Buildings Old and New

There has been considerable attention focused on new public library buildings in recent years with the *Better Public Libraries* and *21st Century Libraries* reports presenting the diverse range of best practice taking place in the sector (Cabe, 2003; Worpole, 2004). In 2003 the new Bournemouth central library won the Prime Minister's *Better Public Buildings* award, Peckham library won the Stirling prize for best new building in Britain in 2000 and others, such as the re-built Norfolk Millennium Library and the Ideas Store in Tower Hamlets, are seen as excellent practice in civic design and a vital element in their areas' regeneration, an acknowledgement that public library buildings can make an important contribution to the quality of life of an area. The economic stringencies of the 1980s and 1990s outlined in Chapter 1, meant that funds for building maintenance or renewal were not generous, however, and many libraries have become quite run down.

The importance of presenting a welcoming, functional space to users and potential users was emphasized by many interview participants. As mentioned above, interviewees invariably brought up the issue of library buildings when considering the challenges facing public library services, often suggesting that many public library buildings were not suitable for the provision of a modern public library service, reinforcing the point made by the 2005 Select Committee report that 'shabby buildings' were a significant barrier to use (Culture, Media and Sport Committee, 2005, p. 31). The report condemned the poor condition of the physical infrastructure as 'a scandal that must be rectified' (p. 32). The problems identified by interview participants were generally related to a lack of resources to make changes which many considered vital to attract non-users, to ensure that the best use could be made of the resources and facilities the library now offers and to encourage community involvement. The 2005 Select Committee report estimates that between £240 million and £650 million will be needed to refurbish England's libraries and recommended a plan of action involving assistance from a partnership of local and central government supplemented by Lottery funding and PFI projects (Culture, Media and Sport Committee, 2005).

Despite problems with funding capital projects like new library buildings, many library services have had building and refurbishment programmes over the last few years and some have been successful in obtaining funding from a combination of sources including their local authorities although interview participants often stressed that the capital programme of local councils did not stretch as far as the library service. A new library at Birmingham is planned and the focus there, as Ayub Khan explained, is to make the library transparent both physically and psychologically. It is hoped that by using a lot of glass in the design, people can see what goes on in the library and those who are not regular library users, in particular, can see that there are people like them in there. In this way it is hoped that a wide range of people, including those who do not generally use the public library, will be encouraged to enter, so increasing the diversity of people passing through the doors. As we saw in Chapter 7, there are concerns that public libraries are not as socially inclusive as they might be and that people are deterred from entering the library because of a range of barriers to use. In this respect, building design can also be a barrier, as one librarian interviewed commented:

> The actual libraries themselves need to be brightened up…. Public expectation has changed enormously; they don't want to go into tatty, dark, dingy places. (Anon)

To overcome this, many library services have established a refurbishment programme and those interviewed often commented that this encouraged new and lapsed users into the building. One librarian explained:

> You refurbish a library, people are interested and they'll come in…., there's press coverage, a lot of press releases, we have events to launch it and it's the whole package. (Anon)

Despite the optimism and positive experiences of interview participants who had witnessed the interest in new or refurbished spaces, there was a common perception among those interviewed that many potential users were deterred by the condition of many public library buildings. Many commented that the interior space can be refreshed and upgraded quite cheaply and many libraries had benefited from an internal renovation. The outside of libraries often left 'something to be desired' (Anon), however. One head of service commented, '[a]s our Chief Executive says, what you do inside the libraries is wonderful, it's a shame about the outside' (Andrea Barker). This sentiment was echoed by many of those interviewed, another remarking:

> [M]ost facades of libraries are not welcoming and that's not the fault of the librarian but they've got a building that they've got to try and encourage people in… And I think, unfortunately, from a librarian's point of view, they are stuck with those sorts of buildings. (Anon)

Although some library services had been successful in gaining funds for new builds and refurbishment, others were struggling and in many places, the buildings are just no longer appropriate. One head of service said:

> We have had a big debate about the *Who's in Charge* report. I know this has caused a furore but some aspects of what Mr Coates is saying is exactly right. We know the buildings are not fit for purpose. In [this authority] they are all different designs, built in different decades of the 20th century and all requiring different levels of maintenance. (Anon)

The situation throughout the UK seems to be very patchy so that while some authorities have buildings that are state of the art, others are more state of the ark. It can be variable within individual public library services too. Many authorities still have remnants of the old Carnegie Foundation libraries built in the nineteenth and early twentieth centuries, for example. Although some interviewees admitted retaining a nagging fondness for these rather grand, formal, municipal buildings, they are not appropriate for the delivery of a modern public library service and can be off putting. Victorian design was considered inappropriate, then, but it was also noted that modern architecture could similarly deter users, as one librarian working in a new library commented:

> I think the design of spaces is really important and that shouldn't be underestimated in this building. It's not a traditional looking building, the customers we have are not traditional library customers and to many people who are traditional library customers, they don't like that. (Jan Holden)

Although many authorities are manifestly struggling to meet the expectations of today's library users for a modern, bright library environment, others have managed to find solutions to the problems of ageing building stocks and outdated, shabby interiors. The two Cabe reports mentioned above give examples of innovative approaches to the design of public library buildings and interview participants also gave their experiences of designing or re-designing library spaces to meet the needs of their users and communities. Through new builds and refurbishments, libraries have been trying consciously to change their image to appeal to non-users and lapsed users. Many in the public library community feel that the image that many of the public have of the public library, especially those who do not use it, is a false one, formed by their experiences of using the library as a child and popular media stereotypes. Those interviewed often expressed the opinion that local people generally do not realize or understand the extent of the services on offer in public libraries. There was concern that people's image of the public library is still rooted in the reading rooms of the 1950s and that many do not appreciate the changes that have taken place in public libraries with the installation of networks and ICT and the provision of leisure, information and learning resources in many different formats. The image of the public library as a middling service for middle-aged and middle-class people is enduring although there was little agreement among interview participants as to its truth.

Some library services in the UK have tried to communicate the developments that have taken place in public libraries by 're-branding' which in practice has often meant abandoning the term 'library' in favour of a name designed to appeal to those unlikely to enter a building designated as a library. Thus, in Tower Hamlets in inner-city London 'Idea Stores' have appeared (Wills, 2003) while in the counties of Kent and Hampshire 'Discovery Centres' are being established (Ward, 2003). Although losing 'the L word' has been the trend for some time in academic libraries, it is a relatively recent phenomenon in public libraries in the UK and many are unsure about its validity, one national politician remarking recently:

> [W]e will lie down in the streets and blockade the libraries if any attempt is made to rename them 'resource centres' or anything like that. (Culture, Media and Sport Committee, 2004b, Q. 71)

The 2005 Select Committee Report regretted that, 'the word "library" seems to have accreted such negative overtones' (Culture, Media and Sport Committee, 2005, p. 17) and suggested that re-invigoration rather than re-branding would be preferable.

Interview participants were often similarly ambivalent about losing the name 'library', one head of service commenting:

> I don't want us to end up branding like [nationwide supermarket chains] Sainsburys or Tescos or anybody else. Or to lose our identity. You know 'library' does have a meaning and a connotation, it is a strong brand name. You may well be able to get away with 'The Ideas Store' in parts of the country where the majority of the population do not have a history of public libraries so therefore 'library' does not carry weight but for the majority of this country, actually, 'public library' does have weight, it is an important brand, we shouldn't give it up. (Martin Molloy)

Another made the point that changing the name of the building does not alter the nature of the service:

> I have difficulties with the occasional view that emerges [that says], 'well this has so many things in it and it's so interesting, shouldn't we call it something else?' Certainly my experience is that the most vibrant libraries are places which have many things going on at any one time and to me that's what a library is, that's what it should be and we'll worry about the name later when people have stopped coming in. (John Dolan)

The point made above by Martin Molloy, though, that communities vary and have different characteristics and therefore react differently to new models of provision, is important. While the library users in one area may favour a more conventional model, others will embrace change. Some interviewees certainly felt that public libraries needed a radical image overhaul to attract those who do not use them and that one of the main ways of achieving this is through a change of name alongside refurbishment and a fresh look. Arguing that there is a need to reach out to lapsed and non-users and encourage them to use public libraries, John Pateman commented that part of the problem was the design of library buildings which can make people reluctant to cross the threshold. Talking about the central library of his service he said:

> They took a decision 10 years ago before I arrived to build a new central library and they chose to build it in the style of a Carnegie library which to me was mad... You go inside of it; it has all the whizzy new things that you'd find in the modern library, but the exterior it says academia, municipality, it says pay your council tax or go to jail, it's full of negative connotations if you like. I think that was a missed opportunity. (John Pateman)

Some interview participants felt, then, that because of their design, libraries in the UK often 'struggle with image' (Worpole, 2004, p. 9) deterring those who most need their services.

Others, as indicated above, believed that it is what goes on in the library, the services, facilities and assistance provided, that will encourage increased use not a name change or branding. While acknowledging that much of the public library building stock in the UK is not fit for purpose with investment needed on a large scale, Bill Macnaught felt that it is what goes on inside the library, rather than its design or condition, that makes the library space special. Arguing that even the most unprepossessing of places can draw people in, he said:

> You see, what's interesting for me is not the big new glossy buildings, it's the little local run-down buildings which, however run-down, still offer that friendly, neutral space. (Bill Macnaught)

Marketing and promotion are still important, though, to communicate with users and potential users about the changes taking place in public libraries and the range of services now provided. Nevertheless, despite the insistence of many interviewed that libraries throughout the country were developing new services and new ways of operating which would appeal to all sections of society, one head of service asserted that the stereotype of libraries as book-lined institutions for the intelligent and middle classes was, in fact, still very much the reality in most places:

> The fundamental operation of a public library hasn't changed in 150 years. Therefore, this is an enduring stereotype that's got more reality attached to it than perception and that is a pretty unshakeable image to move. I think the only way of doing that is re-branding it as an Ideas Store, like Tower Hamlets, or coming up with a really radical design to a building like Peckham, Bournemouth or Norwich. (John Pateman)

He agreed that the word 'library' 'continues to exert a very strong behavioural power' (Worpole, 2004, p. 12) but, in his opinion, it was generally a negative one, especially for those in socially excluded groups who the public library service was seeking to attract. Whether grounded in reality or not, the image of the public library as a formal, municipal institution which is part of the establishment can be a psychological barrier to use and can impact on the receptivity of the space, effectively limiting its accessibility.

Co-location Many of the developments of new libraries discussed above involved public libraries sharing space with other facilities or services. This was for practical as well as policy imperatives. On the practical side, the sharing of costs was considered beneficial for all partners involved. It was also noted that people attracted to a building by one service or facility would be likely to use others located in the same place, potentially increasing the use of all partners sharing the site. On the policy side, the Government is keen to see the development of one-stop shops for local government services and information to engage groups and individuals perceived as hard to reach (Department for Culture, Media and Sport, 2003). One head of service interviewed articulated both the practical, financial and the strategic policy aspects of co-location. Stressing the challenge of securing funds to invest in capital projects he commented:

> I think the years are gone, or should be going, where we are just thinking of library replacements. I think there should be a vision built around cross-cutting service delivery … built around information, advice and access. (Anon)

The interviews confirmed that public libraries are increasingly sharing premises with a range of other services including other local government services such as housing or social services, with schools, with other leisure and cultural facilities such as museums and within community centres. They have also been placed within shopping centres and retail developments. The examples given in the interviews illustrate different models of provision between and even within library services, confirming that local needs and local patterns of use must be the priority when considering co-location. Some heads of service interviewed were keen to be involved with a variety of different service providers. One, saying that her service was 'up for co-location if and when the opportunity comes' (Andrea Barker), gave examples of library facilities in her borough co-located with a school, a leisure centre and a neighbourhood centre.

Other interview respondents raised the issue of whether some partnerships were more effective or even more desirable than others, given the mission of the public library. Commenting on the importance of having a presence in the community, one head of service said:

> Ideally we would favour high street locations with libraries co-located with those sectors where we identify a synergy and opportunities for a strong community presence and shared sense of purpose, e.g. retail, health, education and voluntary sector. (Anon)

Another, commenting on the increasing move towards co-location, noted:

> I believe the trick there is the library to be part of a wider complex of facilities so you've almost got a sort of civic core … that people want to use. (Alan Watkin)

The word 'want' here is significant; people use the public library out of choice, not because they are compelled to through need or unfortunate circumstances as with so many other public services, as one head of service commented:

> We're a service they choose to use rather than they have to use. They might have to use social services, they might have to use housing or they have to use education if they've got children attending school. I think, because they see us as something different, we can use that to embed ourselves into the local communities we're serving much more and easier and from that we can start developing those communities. (Anon)

In Alan Watkin's opinion, this had implications for the kinds of other services or agencies with which libraries should be located. Discussing the type of facilities with which he would be content or eager to share premises he said:

> I don't mind clinics so much; I'm not sure about doctors' surgeries. You usually go into a clinic because it's to do with wellness as opposed to sickness. I suppose what I'm saying is that there's an advantage to being grouped with things which give a positive message to people as opposed to a negative message. (Alan Watkin)

He was also unsure about public libraries being sited in shopping centres. Although Morris and Brown (2004) found that shopping centre locations can benefit libraries and have often been very successful in helping increase footfall to the public library, they can have a consumerist air which does not always fit well with the public library image as free, neutral and accessible to all. In fact, shopping centres are often cited as exemplifying the way in which public space has become privatized and, in some cases, sanitized of certain elements such as homeless people or large groups of young people, the very people that public libraries are trying to attract. For Alan Watkin, though, the objections were also practical:

> So often, libraries don't have resources to compete in terms of presentation with commercial premises so they always look like a charity shop. (Alan Watkin)

Others advocate caution in relation to co-location more generally. The 2005 Select Committee report, for example, recommends co-location where possible but advises that the circumstances of particular communities must be evaluated. The report recognizes the potential of co-located services to meet a wide range of community needs also warns that libraries should not be over-loaded with objectives or expectations (Culture, Media and Sport Committee, 2005).

The dilapidated condition of many library buildings, the lack of local authority funds for new builds and refurbishment programmes and the era of 'joined-up' government (Pollitt, 2003) has encouraged public libraries to co-locate with a wide range of other public services and facilities, therefore, and while there are undoubtedly both sound financial and strategic advantages to this policy, the impact on the character of the library space needs to be considered carefully. One study found that public libraries sited in schools can face problems when trying to serve two quite diverse communities in the same space, for example (McNicol,

2003). Lord Andrew Macintosh stated in his written response that he recognized the concerns that some have about libraries being placed within or adjacent to formal educational institutions, stressing that there must be a feeling of community ownership of the facilities. In trying to be innovative and attract new people into the library, more established library users may be alienated and there may be advantages to libraries maintaining a distinct identity although this is not necessarily precluded by sharing premises with other services.

Conclusion

The research interview data suggest that the 'heart of the community' marketing message is a reflection of service developments in local public library services throughout the UK (and not just in English public libraries for which the message was developed). Currently, though, it is perhaps only a partially accurate reflection. Increasingly, the public library is being positioned not just as a place to borrow or read books or even to access digital material but as a key community resource and facility which can act as a venue for community events and as an access point, connecting local people with each other and with wider society. A cynic may argue that a decline in many of their conventional services, such as the book lending service, has left public libraries struggling to justify their continued existence and funding from the public purse and that this has led them to articulate their connections with, and importance to, the idea of community. It will also strike a chord with politicians increasingly concerned about a perceived decline of community and the social disorder, incivility, and alienation which are seen as inevitable consequences. The result is that the public library is increasingly represented as embedded within the community, symbolizing civic life and values in an era of increasing privatization and consumerism.

The role of partnership working is emphasized in many discussions of community development and building and public libraries are taking part in many co-operative arrangements which are attempting to improve the quality of life and opportunities within communities. Information about a range of partnerships arose in the interviews, suggesting that public libraries recognize the importance of working across the local authority and outside it for maximum impact. The importance of partnerships for raising the profile of the library service and for providing a good service to users was a clear discourse but another discourse centred around the difficultly of forming productive partnerships in some circumstances was equally prominent. Public libraries were not always considered when partnerships were formed although they could often make a useful contribution and it seemed that it was more difficult to convince some potential partners that libraries could be a valuable part of a project, programme or activity than it was to work with others. As we will see in the next chapter, relations with the Education department of the local authority were often described as difficult, for example.

The other key area of discourse around public libraries' role in community building is related to their provision of neutral, community space. Although, as suggested above, public library buildings suffer a number of problems that must be rectified, interview participants were keen to press the case for libraries to act as public community spaces where people can meet and interact with the aim of facilitating more positive and extensive connections within the neighbourhood. Community building must be more proactive than merely providing a physical space for local people to use of course, but the presence of a library in the neighbourhood was considered an important way of fostering community capacity building. The role that local institutions can play in supporting community capacity building by helping bring communities together has been acknowledged (Kearns and Turok, 2004) and interview respondents often talked of how public libraries were achieving this through different activities, programmes and the simple provision of publicly available, free space. In public libraries, the range of services provided, often criticized as betraying a lack of focus, means that a variety of people are brought together under the public library's roof. The sense of engagement and common purpose this stimulates can be an important, if underrated, source of social support.

The role of the public library space in acting as a community meeting place is gaining in importance and emphasis in the UK, therefore. The success of the strategy of highlighting this aspect of public library service is dependent on a number of key developments and variables, however, the most important of which is funding. As we have seen, those participating in the study often commented that much of the public library building stock in the UK is not appropriate for a modern public library service and that, because of their experiences of retail environments, public expectations have changed so that they are often deterred by the condition of many public library buildings. Many also commented on the huge increases in use when new libraries were built or when older premises were refurbished. The importance of redesigning and freshening up libraries so that they were welcoming spaces was often stressed by interview participants and although the services provided, the ownership people feel and the atmosphere generated by staff is probably more important in creating a successful community space than attractive, contemporary decor, people do not want to go into 'tatty, dark, dingy places' in the words the librarian quoted above. Upgrading public library buildings throughout the UK will take enormous investment after years of under-funding and although some library services have managed to establish building and refurbishment programmes, accessing funding from a variety of private and public sources, the issue of the building stock really needs to be addressed as a matter of urgency at a national level because, as one head of service remarked:

> To make a national claim for the library being at the heart of the community, some investment is going to have to be made. (John Dolan)

Notes

1 The presentation to the 2004 Public Library Authorities Conference setting out the background and rationale for the 'heart of the community' message can be found at

URL: http://www.mla.gov.uk/documents/powerpoint/fff_presentation_hotc_files/frame.html [29.06.05].

2 Individual authorities' Public Library Position Statements give a good overview of the range of partnership working in English public libraries. See URL: http://www.libplans.ws/ [06.12.05].

3 For more information about the Beacon Scheme see URL: http://www.odpm.gov.uk/index.asp?id=1135596 [06.12.05].

Chapter 9

Libraries and Learning

The Policy Context: Up-skilling the United Kingdom

Tony Blair came into office in 1997 famously declaring that the three priorities for the New Labour Government would be 'education, education, education'. Referring primarily to formal, school-based education for those aged 18 and under, lifelong learning has also been a priority for successive New Labour Governments although some have argued that 'education, education, education' actually means 'schools, schools, schools' (Culture, Media and Sport Committee, 2000, para. 59). Raising standards in schools and increasing the numbers going into higher education have been the highest profile features of the Government's education policy but there are signs that vocational education and adult learning are moving up the agenda. In a speech in 2004, for example, Tony Blair said that adults wanting to return to education would be assisted through free tuition for those with low levels of skills (BBC, 2004). As indicated in Chapter 1, lifelong learning is seen by the Government as closely linked to both social exclusion and the nation's economic prosperity. The 1998 Green Paper, *The Learning Age: a Renaissance for a New Britain*, defined lifelong learning as 'the continuous development of the skills, knowledge and understanding that are essential for employability and fulfilment' (Department for Education and Employment, 1998, para. 16), and stressed that, whilst valuable in itself, lifelong learning is a fundamental part of the process of getting people into employment or advancing their work situation, a means to 'up-skill' the nation in order to improve the country's economic performance and its global position.

The Government's reform agenda for education first targeted schools, however. The changes to and reorganization of the school system in the UK (primarily England and Wales) since 1997 are too extensive and too complex to detail here but curricula, qualifications, assessment methods and attainment systems have all been reviewed and revised. The focus for New Labour's education reforms in schools has been continuous improvement. This involves setting high standards through a national curriculum and school inspections, league tables and 'naming and shaming' so-called 'failing schools', and more freedom for schools to set their own budgets. The structure of education provision has also been transformed with the development of specialist schools, academies and the concept of choice high on the agenda. Early years provision has been extended and a strong focus on developing literacy, numeracy, ICT and generic skills has been a key feature of the curriculum at all levels of the formal education system.

Improving the basic skills of adults has also been a priority. *Skills for Life* set out the Government's strategy for improving the literacy and numeracy skills of the estimated seven million adults in England with basic skills needs (Department for Education and Employment, 2001). The strategy lists a number of groups, including those both in and out of work, which will be targeted to reduce the number of adults with literacy and numeracy to the level of the UK's international competitors, who generally have lower levels of people with poor basic skills. Tackling the literacy and numeracy problems of the country would benefit the economy, it is argued, as well as the individual. The strategy claims that poor literacy and numeracy skills cost the country £10 billion a year while, for the individual, financial costs can be accompanied by low self esteem, low motivation, health problems and social exclusion. There is also evidence that the children of those with poor basic skills are likely to struggle with reading, writing and numeracy at school. The Government's commitment to improving the skills levels of those outside the formal education system was reinforced in its Skills Strategy published in 2003: *21st Century Skills: Realising Our Potential* (Department for Education and Skills, 2003). The strategy set out the Government's main issue of concern; that although progress had been made on reforming education for children and young people at school and in higher or further education, skills levels within the workforce were lagging behind those of the UK's main international competitors. The percentage of the workforce qualified to intermediate skill levels (apprenticeship, skilled craft and technician level) in the UK is low: 28 per cent compared with 51 per cent in France and 65 per cent in Germany. Gaps in basic skills for employability such as literacy, numeracy and use of IT were also identified as challenges hindering the UK's economic productivity and competitiveness as were the poor mathematical and the leadership and management skills of the current workforce.

The Treasury has also expressed concern about the poor productivity of the British workforce compared with its major competitors and much of the problem, it feels, lies with the relatively low level of skills in the UK (Learning and Skills Council, 2004). The vocational education and training systems of many of Britain's rivals in the global economy are considered to be more advanced and more successful at developing the skilled workers necessary for strong productivity and prosperity. There are clear benefits for the economic well-being of the country, therefore, in investing in education, skills and training at all levels. For the individual, too, there are significant gains. Higher earnings and a more stable, secure work history are likely for those with formal qualifications while those without are more likely to experience long periods of unemployment and worklessness and the related problems of poverty, poor health, and social isolation. There are two imperatives behind the Government's determination to raise standards of education and skills, therefore: firstly, to improve the productivity and therefore competitiveness of British industry; and secondly, to reduce the numbers of those dependent on benefits and at risk of social exclusion. To achieve this, the Government's priorities as established in the Skills Strategy are to: enable adults without qualifications to gain skills for employability by entitling them to free learning opportunities; financially support those working for qualifications or reskilling in the priority skills areas identified; and ensure that there is 'a varied range of learning opportunities for personal fulfilment, community development and active citizenship' (p. 27). The ultimate aim of the Government in pursing its Skills Strategy is to, 'ensure that everyone has the skills they need to become more employable and adaptable' (Department for Education and Skills, 2003, p. 12).

It should be noted that *21st Century Skills* is primarily a strategy for England; Scotland, Wales and Northern Ireland have each developed its own strategies for basic skills and lifelong learning.[1] Some elements of the English strategy do have implications for the Devolved Administrations, though, as certain bodies have a UK-wide remit. Furthermore, the strategy was developed in consultation with them and is consistent with the direction of their policies for skills. In Scotland, for example, a focus on community learning has developed as an important strand of the Executive's agenda as indicated in the previous chapter and this could be a useful concept with which public libraries could demonstrate their value to the government's education and lifelong learning agendas.

Community Learning and Informal Learning

Although not focused only on adults, community learning is generally defined as those learning activities taking place outside the classroom and educational institutions which often, therefore, primarily target adults. Community learning programmes and activities also often prioritize adult learning although connecting with the young people of the community through youth work and the youth service is another important feature. The Scottish Executive's (2004) guidance for community learning and development, for example, lists its three national priority areas as being adult learning, focusing on core literacy, numeracy, ICT and personal effectiveness skills; young people's learning to facilitate their personal and education development and their civic engagement; and building community capacity so that local people have the ability to participate in decision making about local services, as discussed in Chapter 8. An earlier report of a Scottish Office working group, though, stressed the lifelong nature of community learning and its importance to improving the quality of life of individuals and groups of all ages (Scottish Office, 1999).

Smith (2004a) summarizes Stephen Brookfield's (1983) approach to community learning which emphasizes that it is deliberate and purposeful with learners seeking to acquire knowledge and skills. Nevertheless, there may not be closely specified goals. It occurs outside formal educational establishments and receives no institutional accreditation or validation but is voluntary, self-motivated and self-generating although the point is made that the stimulus for the learning may be a crisis outside the learner's control. Smith feels that Brookfield's definition has strengths but is also rather constraining. Firstly, he makes the point that educational institutions like schools are important features of communities and, secondly, Brookfield focuses solely on gaining skills and knowledge neglecting to mention the important role of acquiring attitudes and values which can enhance the learning process and provide stimulation for new learning.

Much of the learning that takes place through community learning is informal learning: the 'unorganized, unsystematic and even unintentional' (Coombes and Ahmed, 1974, p. 8) learning which occurs daily. Although Smith (1999) is largely sceptical of the usefulness of the notion of informal learning, feeling that the dichotomy between formal and informal learning is primarily an administrative one, he acknowledges that interest in informal learning is growing and cites a variety of commentators in the adult education and lifelong learning fields who stress the value of this type of learning. What is perceived as a government fixation with testing, qualifications, accreditation and skills for employability is increasingly being challenged by a backlash of opinion insisting that informal learning is not an inferior form of learning and is valuable in its own right as a way of developing capabilities such as problem solving, initiative, creativity and the desire to continue learning. The National Curriculum's focus on testing and assessment has been criticized as stifling young people's desire to learn and particularly to read. Lord Chris Smith, first Secretary of State for Culture, Media and Sport and Chair of the 2004 Man Booker Prize for fiction, condemned the 'focus on the mechanics of numeracy and literacy' in schools which he felt had 'driven out the sense of joy that comes from creative activity' (Smith, 2004b, online resource). He also criticized local authorities for shutting public libraries, suggesting that he considers them important vehicles for the type of informal learning facilitated by reading and engagement through the literature and the other resources they hold for public access.

Learning in Libraries

Many commentators and practitioners in the public library field are excited about the role public libraries can play in helping deliver the Government's learning agenda, seeing it as a way of raising the profile of the public library service, so attracting more attention and, hopefully, more funding. Others view public library involvement in learning as returning to the roots of the public library movement, with the potential to enhance the standing, relevance and credibility of public libraries within the community. Lancashire County Council, for example, in its memorandum of evidence to the 2000 Select Committee on Public Libraries suggested:

> In many respects the Lifelong Learning role takes the public library service back to its roots contained within the 1850 Act, where it was seen as a significant element of the drive for the wider availability of educational opportunities (Culture, Media and Sport Committee, 2000, online resource)

The library community's understanding of learning, especially lifelong learning, seems to be much wider than that laid out in many Government publications and policy statements, however. Firstly, the Government's policies on lifelong learning focus almost exclusively on those aged 16 and over.[2] There is an acknowledgement that children of all ages need to develop the skills which will enable them to continue learning throughout their lives, but the Government's lifelong learning priorities target the 16-19 age group, adult basic skills and employment market skills (Library Association, 2001a). This last point, skills for employability, is the second major difference of emphasis between most Government statements on lifelong learning and how many in public libraries approach the issue of learning. In 2001, the Library Association (now Cilip) questioned whether the Government's policy on lifelong learning was just a policy on employability (Library Association, 2001a) and although the 2003 Skills Strategy notes that people undertake learning for personal fulfilment as well as for qualifications, it clearly prioritizes work-related skills (Department for Education and Skills, 2003).

For many in the public library field, however, lifelong learning should be just that: lifelong, from cradle to grave or 'womb to tomb' in the words of Glenys Willars in interview. The Library Association emphasized that, '[l]ifelong learning must encompass pre-16 (including pre-school) education as well as post-16 education' (Library Association, 2001a, p. 7). Similarly, many would reject the prominence given to the acquisition of qualifications and employability skills. While the learning taking place in public libraries may very well be relevant to employment at times, at others it may have no relevance at all but is still necessary and valuable in its own right. The evaluation of the People's Network project reported, however, that libraries had, to some extent, 'bought into' the Government's 'upskilling of the workforce' agenda with much public library activity focusing on training and education rather than lifelong learning in its broadest sense (Sommerlad et al., 2004, p. 72). *Inspiring Learning for All* is MLA's vision for developing accessible learning in libraries, museums and archives which proposes the following very broad definition of learning:

> Learning is a process of active engagement with experience. It is what people do when they want to make sense of the world. It may involve the development or deepening of skills, knowledge, understanding, awareness, values, ideas and feelings, or an increase in the capacity to reflect. Effective learning leads to change, development and the desire to learn more. (MLA, 2003, section 1)

Interview participants generally had a similarly wide conception of the learning that takes place in public libraries and Glenys Willars suggested that libraries had to promote themselves as learning organizations:

> The library has always been a learning organization but I think what we're looking at now is how we enable other people, the public out there, to understand that it's a learning organization. I think if we think about learning in its broadest definition, and not formal learning or doing a course or coming to a learning session, and we think about all the things we do in different aspects of learning, people using their brains in different ways, then I think that the library is a learning organization. (Glenys Willars)

Supporters of public libraries claim that the public library is the ideal environment for learning activities, both formal and informal, to take place, its key attributes including its accessibility (in all senses), its wealth of resources (including staff, space and ICT facilities) and its non-threatening nature (Library Association, 2001a). Public libraries have a tradition of providing for broad-based educational needs and many regard them as study oriented, providing space for reading, writing, thinking, viewing, word processing and Internet access. They are accessible, located within the heart of the community and often considered a focal point within that community. They also have a record of personal service, impartiality and independence. Although, as we have seen, opening hours have been cut in some authorities, public libraries are open for longer hours than many other study centres, including evenings and Saturdays for those at work. Trained staff are available in public libraries who are able to relate supply to demand, provide access to information, have knowledge of information sources and can advise on access to resources in other libraries. User-focused staff thus provide a supportive environment for learners. Moreover, they are part of many local networks and have links within their own community which are often the key to opening up access to learning resources and expertise. *New Library: The People's Network* (Library and Information Commission, 1997) emphasized how the use of the Internet in public libraries will open up learning opportunities for all and many *learndirect* centres have been established in libraries, confirming their role as providers of resources and support for learners. A recent review of adult learning provision inside and outside public libraries identified a range of key strengths which made public libraries important adult learning providers including their open environment, their knowledgeable and trained staff, their flexibility, their partnerships with other learning providers and other libraries, their provision of public access ICT facilities and their ability to supply outreach services through mobile libraries, housebound services and in community venues (Ashcroft et al., 2005).

Despite the enthusiasm for characterizing public libraries as centres of learning, there are barriers to fully realizing their role in this area, however. One study of the role that public libraries could play in supporting learning suggested that they retained a largely traditional outlook based on providing access to resources rather than engaging fully with the new learning agenda and becoming learning providers (McNicol and Dalton, 2003). The same study also suggested that, '[m]any staff lack the training, confidence and time to support learners fully' (p. 4). Staff skills and expertise need to be thought through carefully as there are often limits to how far library staff can help learners as suggested in Chapter 5. They are not usually trained tutors and may not have the required learning support skills or the time to assist users in their learning activities. The issue of staff training was also highlighted by Ashcroft et al. (2005). Their report confirmed that although a range of staff training had taken place in public libraries, this had focused primarily on ICT proficiency and suggested that further training to support those with basic skills needs or those taking NVQ courses, as well as general customer care training, was still required.

Funding is another key issue as most public library authorities are unlikely to have the resources to help all users. Cooperation and partnership should be the answer here but links with the formal education sector are not always easy to forge. *Empowering the Learning Community* (Library and Information Commission,

2000), a study investigating the links between libraries serving the formal education system and public libraries, found that cooperation was inadequate. Although some progress has been made, the *Inspire* scheme, for example, enables learners to access public, academic and national libraries across England,[3] building constructive relationships with organizations and agencies outside the library domain has proved even more difficult perhaps partly because public libraries are scarcely mentioned in many education and skills development debates. The Government's Skills Strategy refers to libraries only twice, for example, once in the context of IAG (information, advice and guidance) provision and once when discussing adult and community learning programmes which support learning that does not lead to a qualification. *Skills for Life*, the strategy for improving adult literacy and numeracy in England, does make numerous references to libraries, however, suggesting that they are, 'a preferred place of learning for many adults' (Department for Education and Employment, 2001, p. 32). The strategy also notes, though, that libraries are one of the, 'parts of government which do not have education and training as part of their core business' (p. 38), a statement with which many in public libraries would disagree. The extent and nature of the role of libraries in the skills and learning strategies of the other home countries varies considerably. In Northern Ireland and Wales, the emphasis is on public libraries enabling access to ICT to open up learning opportunities. In Scotland, public libraries are envisaged as part of a network encouraging community-based learning.

Margaret Bennett, Head of Lifelong Learning & Technologies at the DfES, confirmed the lack of reference to the role of libraries in major policy initiatives in the lifelong learning area and, coming from a library background, expressed surprise that their contribution was not recognized (Bennett, 2001). Interview participants also often commented on the difficulty of gaining recognition for the role of public libraries in the learning agenda, suggesting that the formal education sector (the local authority's Education department, schools and colleges etc.) was sometimes slow to acknowledge the contribution that libraries could and were making in this area. Bill Macnaught felt that this was partly due to the narrow conception of lifelong learning that other stakeholders held:

> There is a strong resistance from the DfES sector, nationally and locally, to anybody else intervening. [They think] the only people who know about this stuff are the educationalists. I think that the biggest challenge facing libraries in providing services is getting recognition from DfES and from colleagues at a LEA level that libraries have got a serious part to play… I suspect there are still teachers and others in the LEA in some posts who still see lifelong learning being maybe up to 25 years old so it's beyond school, it's maybe 16-25… And I think that's extremely unhelpful and you really do need to see it conceptually that it starts as a child and never stops. (Bill Macnaught)

Julia Field was more optimistic, however, feeling that libraries were gaining more recognition but this seemed to be because of circumstance rather than anything else:

> I think we've always worked very well with Adult and Community Education. A lot of this I think is down to location but we used to be in the same building as the Adult and Community Education managers whereas Education as a whole is over in Keynsham so there's just that meeting over coffee, sort of thing. But I think now we've got our lifelong learning person and also one of our librarians was seconded into Education to do Best Value work and subsequently stayed permanently so it helps having a librarian planted over there, it's changed people's perceptions. (Julia Field)

The presence of Charles Clarke, Secretary of State for Education, at the launch for *Inspiring Learning for All* was taken as a sign that government is willing to support libraries' role in lifelong learning and also that it had adapted to new educational theories valuing informal learning (Library and Information Update, 2004) and perhaps part of the problem public libraries have faced in the past in trying to carve out a more influential role in the learning agenda is their difficulty in collecting and presenting evidence of their impact on learning. As part of the *Inspiring Learning for All* vision, the Research Centre for Museums and Galleries developed five Generic Learning Outcomes (GLOs) to measure the impact of learning in museums, archives and galleries (Research Centre for Museums and Galleries, 2003). The GLOs group what learners have learnt into broad categories, showing the richness and depth of learning possible in cultural organizations. These include: an increase in knowledge and understanding; an increase in skills; a change in attitudes or values; evidence of enjoyment, inspiration and creativity; evidence of activity, behaviour, progression. This conceptual framework is important for organizations like public libraries that have been hampered in the past by their lack of evidence of how they contribute to users' learning. The *Inspiring Learning for All* GLOs give public libraries a common language and framework to use when talking about learning to others, particularly useful when trying to build partnerships for community learning although John Dolan still felt this was an uphill battle because of the difficulties libraries faced in monitoring and quantifying the contribution that libraries make:

> I think library learning is characterized by people who supplement formal learning or learn independently in a way that probably no other service really supports but it's very difficult to evidence that and the people who distribute funding…, because there's a whole funding regime that drives this that is to do with short-term programmes, targets and such like, that kind of learning that the library enables or delivers isn't easily matched with those sorts of objectives, which I think is unfortunate. (John Dolan)

Bill Macnaught agreed that measuring the impact of libraries on learning was difficult but should be pursued:

> We need to work with the supportive colleagues in DfES, in LEAs who will argue that, whether we can measure it or not, they are entirely convinced that we do make a positive contribution and just because it's difficult to measure, we shouldn't underestimate the contribution that we make. (Bill Macnaught)

Many of the *Inspiring Learning for All* GLOs are 'soft' outcomes, such as attitudes, values, emotions and beliefs, in contrast to 'hard' facts and skills. Although the *Inspiring Learning for All* framework does give public libraries a way of demonstrating their impact on learning, the current focus on qualifications and accredited learning may still mean that libraries are by-passed as partners in local Learning Partnerships. First established in 1999, Learning Partnerships are designed to promote cooperation among the many providers working in post-16 learning in a geographical area and although many public library services are members, the current emphasis on vocational learning can mean that their contribution to the learning agenda is overlooked, as discussed more fully below. But although the Department for Education and Skills' lifelong learning agenda focuses on improving the levels of skills for employability and qualifications of those over 16 years of age, other government departments recognize the importance of less formal learning for enhancing individuals' quality of life and strengthening their involvement in society. In *Framework for the Future*, the Department for Culture, Media and Sport notes that learning has to start before school and extend beyond it, creating a learning culture:

> …in which people expect and want to learn, pursue their hobbies and interests, develop their information literacy skills, be creative and gain inspiration, develop vocational and non-vocational skills, well after they have left formal education. (Department for Culture, Media and Sport, 2003, p. 28)

Framework for the Future suggests that public libraries should focus their activities on three main areas: supporting early learning; supporting pupils and students; and supporting older students. This chapter will review public library activity in all three areas. *Framework for the Future* also makes the point that public library activities which promote reading play a key role in supporting learning. It explicitly links reading and learning and discusses them together as one of the three key areas of activities which should be at the heart of libraries' modern mission. Bob McKee suggested in interview, however, that learning should be a separate strand and that is the approach taken here so while this chapter will discuss some of the developments around reading development taking place in public libraries, particularly those supporting early years reading, Chapter 10 contains the main analysis of how public libraries promote reading to both adults and young people.

Supporting Early Learning

Although children were not initially welcome in the first public libraries, separate children's libraries began to be widely established in thc 1880s and ever since services to children have been one of the cornerstones of public library provision in the United Kingdom. Greenhalgh and Worpole (1995) write of the 'symbolic value' of children's library tickets, reporting that parents considered a library ticket to be 'one of the child's first links to a wider society and one of the first ways of being recognized as an individual citizen' (p. 90). Even though they may not use the public library themselves, the British people are generally very supportive of the role the library plays for children and young people. There seems to be an acceptance that libraries are a sound investment which can help children acquire vital life skills and give them a sense of belonging to a broader community which takes its responsibility for their development seriously. Public libraries have responded by establishing a range of services and activities designed to support young children's learning and language development. Ninety six per cent of public libraries in the UK offer story and rhyme sessions for young children (Creaser and Maynard, 2003), for example, designed to help develop children's language and reading skills and also support parents in reading and communicating with their children. These kinds of activities, while long a feature of public library services to children, are becoming more important and more closely organized according to Glenys Willars:

> As far as story time goes that, over the last few years, well probably always, has been quite ad hoc and not necessarily happening on a regular basis but in our service plan for next year, every library has got to have at least one story time every week. In fact, I think all large libraries have to and even the smallest libraries must have one once a month. We've never had that guidance before. Every library has got to have at least one class visit or nursery visit once a week, something like that. We've never had that kind of target before and I think there will be more children who benefit from the service through that. (Glenys Willars)

Research has shown that the pre-school children of parents participating in programmes to develop their skills of communicating with their children exhibited greater developmental progress (Evangelou and Sylva, 2003). Other research suggests that babies' early experiences with books can have a significant effect on their literacy development provided they receive sufficient support and encouragement (Wade and Moore, 1996) and there is general acceptance that the earlier children learn to read the better they will do in later life (Culture, Media and Sport Committee, 2005). In fact, Professor Kathy Sylva, who is leading the Eppe[4] research into pre-school education, when asked by the Parliamentary Select Committee on Education what single thing a carer should do to support their children's learning replied, 'Take them to the library' (Education and Employment Committee, 2000, para. 387). Many activities in public libraries aim at encouraging parents in early language and literacy activities with their very young children, therefore, and focus increasingly on those at risk of social exclusion in an attempt to improve the life chances of those living in poverty. Research demonstrating the key role that library and reading can play in young people's lives is confirming the importance of children's services in public libraries for young people's development as are policy statements from government.

Children's and Young People's Services in Public Libraries: Research and Policy

The role that public libraries can play in improving children's and their carers' quality of life has been the focus of considerable research in the UK. *A Place for Children* was a large research project investigating services to children in public libraries funded by the British Library Research and Innovation Centre from 1996 to 1998 (Elkin and Kinnell, 2000). The report gives a comprehensive account of the impact of public libraries on children and their reading development. *Start with the Child* was another piece of research investigating children's use of libraries, museums and archives, commissioned by Resource and Cilip. It reviews existing research into children's and young people's needs, motivations and attitudes and the implications of these for the various cultural institutions (Morris Hargreaves McIntyre, 2002). Taking the results of the research, the Cilip Working Group on Library Provision for Children and Young People (2002) produced their own report detailing the services that libraries of all types currently provide to their young users and how those services could and should develop.

This chapter will not reproduce detailed findings of these research projects here but will instead give an overview of some key developments in public library services to children since they reported. In summary, though, *A Place For Children* illustrated how public libraries support children's development by improving their reading skills and helping them to grow intellectually, socially and culturally (Elkin and Kinnell, 2000). It also reported, however, that although many of the parents, children, librarians and teachers interviewed endorsed the important role of libraries, decision makers responsible for educational and literacy initiatives often ignored the role of the public library or did not fully understand its potential. The research showed that the number of children's librarians in public libraries had fallen and that there had also been a decline in expenditure on materials. Despite these resource restrictions, though, public librarians were still making huge efforts to promote children's reading and develop activities and resources to stimulate children's enthusiasm and passion for reading. *Start With The Child* noted that although the development needs of children have not changed, the context in which children grow and learn is now radically different with new media and new leisure pursuits demanding their attention and a greater variety of information sources and services available (Morris Hargreaves McIntyre, 2002). One interview participant said that the main impact of the research, for her, had been to make her:

> …stop and think about where kids see their lives going now and all the complexities of their lives really and how libraries must fit in somewhere or we're lost. So we've got to really look at the lives of kids, what drives them, the language they use, the scene they choose to function in and all those complexities go into making young people what they are today and we have to be up there with them. (Anon)

The Cilip working group concluded that library services wanting to reach out to children and young people must consider how they can develop appropriate environments and services; ensure those services are relevant and responsive; develop appropriate forms of help for young people and those who support them;

and work in partnerships within the community to provide services of benefit to young people and their families (Cilip Working Group on Library Provision for Children and Young People, 2002).

In setting out a vision for public library services in England, *Framework for the Future* (Department for Culture, Media and Sport, 2003) acknowledged the role of public libraries in supporting early learning and its action plan highlighted how public libraries could enable and encourage children and young people to become enthusiastic learners and readers. One of the most recent policy documents on young people and public libraries to emerge is *Fulfilling Their Potential* (The Reading Agency, 2004). As part of *Framework for the Future*, *Fulfilling Their Potential* proposed the 'national offers' that should be developed in public libraries for young people and recommended that they should be given access to: the library as *the* space in the community for young people; inspiring, relevant reading including creative reading activities; the chance to get involved and shape the library service; the library as the place to participate in the wider community and in democracy; and the library as the independent place for information and study support.

Public library services to children are clearly a priority, then, and recent events and policy initiatives have put them even higher up the agenda. There is a determination at both local and national government levels to improve early years services, prompted partly by some tragic cases in which public services failed individual children but also by the recognition that quality early years services can improve children's life chances and reduce their risk of social exclusion. In response to perceived problems with the current administration of children's and young people's services, the Government established the cross-departmental Children and Young People's Unit[5] to coordinate services and information sharing with the ultimate aim of opening opportunities for all children and ensuring all achieve their potential.

Early learning is considered central to this and seen to be inextricably linked with health, the creation of stable communities and social inclusion (Library Association, 2001b). The Labour Government's 2003 green paper *Every Child Matters* (2003) set out a framework for improving services to children and their families and was the basis for the Children's Bill which received Royal Assent in November 2004. The Bill created an independent Children's Commissioner to protect the rights of children and young people and, at the local level, required that social services and local authority education for children is overseen by a Director of Children's Services. In addition, relevant agencies in local areas must make arrangements to promote co-operation to: safeguard children's physical and mental health; protect them from harm and neglect; support their education and training; enable them to make a contribution to society; and promote their social and economic well-being. Cross-departmental working is considered essential for good early years services, therefore, but some public library services are finding it easier to involve themselves in this than others although Bob McKee commented that libraries would seem to be an obvious partner:

> The merging and integrating of children's services…, well the first public service that young children experience, apart from the health service, is the public library service, or should be. (Bob McKee)

Nevertheless, one participant said that libraries were not at present involved in the new Children's Directorate that had been established in the borough but added, 'that's not to say they won't be' (Anon).

Increased funding has followed these developments in children's services with the Chancellor announcing an extra £100 million to establish Children's Centres in the most deprived wards and plans to extend free childcare, or 'educare', to under-fives in disadvantaged areas. As a result of the Government's early years initiatives, activity in public libraries aimed at young children has intensified, much of it focused on helping deliver the Sure Start programme.

Sure Start

Sure Start is a Government programme which aims to tackle social exclusion and child poverty by improving the health, educational and emotional development of young children and their families in England.[6] The focus is on providing joined-up services in those areas where high proportions of children live in poverty. There are four main objectives for Sure Start: improving social and emotional development; improving health; improving the ability to learn; and strengthening families and communities. Public libraries have a potential role to play in all areas and are specifically mentioned in the Sure Start Delivery Guidance as supporting a positive home learning environment (Sure Start, 2003a). Furthermore, local authorities are encouraged to increase the use of libraries by families with young children and are given a Service Delivery Agreement target to achieve this (Sure Start, 2003b).

As the Library Association commented, 'Sure Start offers libraries an unprecedented mechanism for effectively targeting children most in need of our services' (Library Association, 2001b, para. 3.1) and many public library services have used Sure Start to build effective local partnerships and reach children and parents they might previously have had difficulty contacting. An audit of library services' involvement with Sure Start by the Early Years Library Network (EYLN) found that the Sure Start library target was highly valued by many library authorities in helping them build partnerships with other early years service providers and gaining funding for library posts designed to help local Sure Start programmes achieve the target (Early Years Library Network, 2004a). Library authorities often commented in their audit returns that before the target was established, convincing other providers that libraries had a contribution to make to early years development was frequently an uphill struggle and although some were still disappointed with their level of engagement, many commented that the target had been invaluable in supporting their involvement and had enabled them to become members of their local Early Years Development and Childcare Partnerships (EYDCPs), for example, which draw together representatives of all the relevant early years interests in the community. Previously, some library services had been excluded from EYDCPs as their contribution had been considered irrelevant although others had managed to find a role, and secure funding, as providers of printed resources and toys to those with special needs (Library Association, 2001b).

The EYLN audit of Sure Start activity in public libraries found that of the 99 library authorities responding, 86 were involved in Sure Start partnerships and the levels of activity were impressive. Percentage increases in active use of library services by Sure Start children aged up to four varied but in some authorities were remarkable with a huge 500 per cent increase in library use in one programme in East Sussex. Issues of books and other resources to Sure Start families also registered increases. Regular library activities such as story-time and singing and rhyming sessions for Sure Start families had been developed too, often run by library staff funded through local Sure Start programmes; the audit returns found that 175 library posts had been funded by Sure Start in 66 authorities and the actual figure across the country was likely to be higher. The activity and funding provided through Sure Start was also found to have a wide impact on libraries participating in the programmes enabling them to refurbish their children's libraries and improve the quality of books and materials available for the benefit of all users although as Moira Arthur pointed out in interview, Sure Start funding is not accessible to all libraries, only those in socially excluded areas. She nevertheless agreed that the funding had had a significant impact on those public libraries benefiting and, as a consequence, on library supply although she was concerned about the long term continuity of the funding:

> Sure Start schemes have impacted on us because we've seen such a rise in that funding and that spending. Where libraries have been able to get access to that it's had a huge impact which has meant [libraries buying] things like cloth books, board books, things like that that libraries would not traditionally have bought. And publishers are reacting to that by publishing more of that material as well which can be good. But when that funding stops, where do we go from there? Because libraries could potentially be expected to fund that themselves, they'll have to find the funding from somewhere. (Moira Arthur)

Sure Start has also encouraged many library services to think more strategically about their early years provision and has raised the awareness of staff of the needs of young children and their families according to Glenys Willars in interview who felt that Sure Start, along with research like *Start with the Child*, had made children's service a higher priority. In many cases, Sure Start activity is linked with Bookstart,[7] another national initiative focusing on children's early years development.

Bookstart

First established as a local scheme in Birmingham in 1992, Bookstart developed into the first national baby book-giving programme in the world. Designed to introduce books to children at the earliest age and, perhaps more importantly, encourage parents to share reading and books with their children, Bookstart is usually administered through the public library service but delivered by the local health authority through health visitors. At every child's seven to nine-month health check, parents are given a free Bookstart pack; a canvas bag containing two baby books, a booklet explaining how and why to share books with young children, a booklist and an invitation to join the local library. Bookstart has had a range of sponsors since its inception and has had various funding crises over the years leading it to seek new partners. Now in a cooperative arrangement with a range of publishers, suppliers, manufacturers, artists, designers and printers, the future of Bookstart looks more secure especially as the Chancellor of the Exchequer announced extra funding for the scheme through Sure Start in the Government's 2004 spending review. In July 2005 an extension of the scheme was announced so that children in Sure Start areas will now receive three gifts of books and related material, their first before they are one, the second between their first and second birthdays and their third when they are aged three to four (Bookstart, 2005).

Before 2002, Bookstart packs were free for local schemes to distribute in their communities but the funding crisis the initiative experienced in 2001 means that Booktrust, the charity which administers Bookstart, now charges local schemes £2.50 per pack. Local authorities therefore have to find ways of funding the material and many have done this through their EYDCP. Once again, then, public libraries are being brought into contact with other early year providers, a development which can only help them secure recognition of the role of libraries in early years provision. In fact, multi-agency approaches are key to Bookstart, involving close cooperation between the library and health authorities in an area and there should be mutually beneficial outcomes for all involved. EYDCPs, for example, have found Bookstart packs to be a useful way of distributing child care information directly into the home of new parents and library authorities have been able to develop new partnerships and embed libraries' work into local early years activity (Library Association, 2001c)

The national Bookstart initiative was launched in 1999 and has grown exponentially. According to the Bookstart website, 2,601,000 Bookstart books have been distributed and 5,000 libraries are involved in promoting schemes. Bookstart Plus, for children at 18 months, has also been launched and My Bookstart Treasure Box for three year olds is being piloted in Sure Start areas. An evaluation of the programme undertaken in 2001 found that parents and carers had better book-sharing skills, read more and read more often with their children after participating in Bookstart (National Centre for Research in Children's Literature, 2001). Library membership and library visits among Bookstart families increased and parents and carers often said they were more confident about reading to their children. *Start With The Child* noted anecdotal evidence from public librarians suggesting that Bookstart had not delivered the large increases in library use anticipated, however (Cilip Working Group on Library Provision for Children and Young People, 2002). Nevertheless, Bookstart is generally considered an excellent pre-literacy strategy and health visitors have endorsed the scheme as an aid to positive parenting, helping to build strong and loving relationships and develop language acquisition and listening skills. There is also evidence that Bookstart children achieved higher scores in all areas of baseline testing when they started school than a selected control group and displayed more positive behaviour during book sharing sessions such as showing a keen interest in the text and asking questions (Wade and Moore, 1998).

Bookstart has thus become 'a key element within libraries' early years activity' (Library Association, 2001c, para. 7), with research evidence of its impact on children's literacy and language development enabling public libraries to build partnerships and position themselves as significant players in early years provision. McElwee (2004) suggests that before Bookstart, many library services made welcoming noises to encourage carers with their pre-school children into libraries but actually offered them few services. Bookstart, she argues, has been the catalyst for the development of new services aimed at this user group such as Rhymetimes, interactive sessions using nursery rhymes, songs and action rhymes which encourage interaction between parent and baby and so develop communication, bonding and enjoyment.

One participant, taking issue with Tim Coates' view that public libraries are abandoning books and reading in favour of ICT provision and other services, highlighted this kind of scheme as proof that libraries were still focused on book-related services:

> We are investing in children that can't read now but clearly gain advantage in terms of social communication and even educational skills as they enter into formal education, through exposure to books, story telling and reading. If we don't believe there is a future for libraries and books and reading, why would we be doing that and why would we have tens of thousands of parents with babies engaging in this programme? (Anon)

Young children's learning has undoubtedly benefited from library-based schemes like Sure Start and Bookstart, then, and these initiatives have also had an impact on their families as, very often, they have prompted parents and carers to examine their own literacy needs and seek support as a consequence.

Family Learning

Public libraries are becoming increasingly involved in family learning and family literacy initiatives, often through Sure Start. Family learning is defined by Ofsted thus:

> Family learning … brings together different family members to work on a common theme. [T]he focus is on planned activity, in which adults and children come together, to work and learn collaboratively (Ofsted, 2000, p. 5)

Support to families is provided on the basis that as children spend only 15 per cent of their time at school, the home and family can have a huge impact on their learning and development (Cilip Working Group on Library Provision for Children and Young People, 2002). For their parents or carers, family learning programmes are viewed as a non-threatening first step to literacy, language and numeracy programmes as well as to a range of other learning opportunities (NIACE, 2003).

Family learning and literacy activity in the UK takes place mainly in schools with parents accompanying their children to nursery or pre-school care and to primary school classes. For the adults involved, family literacy has been found to improve understanding of child development; improve competency in such key skill areas as literacy, numeracy and parenting; increase parents' or carers' confidence in their dealings with schools; support progression to higher education; and improve parents' or carers' relationship with their children (Ofsted, 2000). Children participating successfully in family learning programmes have demonstrated accelerated development of oracy and pre-literacy skills; improvements in literacy and numeracy; better behaviour and attitudes; higher confidence and self-esteem because of the interest their parents or carers were showing in their progress; and an awareness that learning is an ongoing activity that adults as well as children engage in.

The Ofsted survey of family learning provision noted that government efforts have focused on literacy within the formal education system but drew attention to some innovative and effective work taking place in public libraries, often in partnership with other providers within the local authority and voluntary sector. NIACE (2003) research found that 71 per cent of local education authorities (LEAs) responding to their survey delivered family literacy programmes through libraries and museums, the third most common delivery mechanism after schools (94 per cent) and directly by the LEA (76 per cent). Non-governmental agencies operating in the area of learning and family policy have emphasized the need for family learning to be viewed in a broader context, with better recognition given to the kind of informal learning that takes place in public libraries (Kirk et al., 2004). Kirk et al. (2004) note that, for public libraries, 'the concept of families learning together is not entirely new' (p. 178) and suggest that the case for family literacy activity in public libraries has been well made for some time. In recent years, public library activities focusing on providing advice and support for parents on sharing books with young children have frequently led to other library-based family learning activities promoting basic skills, for example, or ICT skills.

A small survey by Kirk et al. (2004) found that some libraries are playing a key role in family learning with services often targeted at areas where social exclusion is a problem. *Start With The Child* made the point that public library activity in this area often focuses on early years provision with few activities for older children although there are notable exceptions (Cilip Working Group on Library Provision for Children and Young People, 2002). The survey by Kirk et al. (2004) found, though, that their respondents often identified homework support as a family learning activity which presumably targets older children. The other activities identified were ICT learning sessions, family history activities, literacy activities, arts and crafts sessions and numeracy development. This preliminary survey does not give detailed information about the activities but shows that activity is increasing and is likely to be an area of considerable development in coming years and is of real value according to one interview participant who, talking about the people using the libraries in the most deprived estates of the borough, said:

> People come in with their children and start to do family learning programmes and really benefit from this. It takes an awful lot of courage to do this but once they do begin to use the library they are signed up for life. We have seen families really engaging with this process, the parents are improving their skills at the same time as their children are improving their reading and doing their homework in the library. It makes a huge difference to a community to engage in these activities. (Anon)

Challenges

Initiatives like Sure Start and Bookstart have undoubtedly helped public libraries demonstrate their value for early learning and family learning but some library authorities report that it is still difficult to convince other early years partners that they have a valuable contribution to make. Although the Sure Start target on library use has helped matters, authorities responding to the EYLN Sure Start audit often reported that relationships with other providers were still developing (Early Years Library Network, 2004a). It will be interesting to see the extent to which public libraries are involved in the new Children's Centres, designed to bring education, care, family support and health service together. The EYLN suggests that the depth and nature of involvement varies considerably, with some local authorities recognizing the importance of libraries' contribution and establishing Children's Centres with libraries as a key partner (Early Years Library Network, 2004b). In others, funding, for example for library staff to act as outreach workers in Centres, is uncertain. Public library involvement in the family learning area is also dependent on their ability to convince other key players that they have a role to play, as suggested above. Although the NIACE (2003) survey suggests that LEAs recognize the value of public library learning activities and approaches, funding comes from the DfEE through the LSCs and so public libraries must make an impact at this level.

The other main challenge identified both in the literature and by interview participants was the issue of staffing. *Start With The Child* emphasized the importance of providing young people and their families with appropriate help through staff skilled in promoting reading and encouraging children to engage with books (Cilip Working Group on Library Provision for Children and Young People, 2002). As noted above, *A Place for Children* reported that the number of specialist children's librarians had fallen. On the other hand, the number of library posts for early years specialists has increased through schemes like Sure Start although these are not necessarily librarians and are often reliant on short-term or project funding. Glenys Willars felt, though, that libraries should be taking advantage of staff with a range of skills:

> We have got people like the community outreach workers for early years and Sure Start, they're children people. The heresy there is that none of them are librarians. In fact, when we appointed the first one we said you do not need to be a teacher or a librarian,

you've got to want to work with children and their parents and their families. (Glenys Willars)

Another interview participant disagreed, suggesting that a qualification in librarianship gives people a wider conception of the role of libraries in the learning and development processes:

I do worry about children's librarians. I worry that when I did my degree I studied children's librarianship and children's literature and you always did that. Now I know there has to be change [but] I still think a library qualification is very important because it helps you see the bigger picture, having had an education gives you that bigger picture, deeper understanding of why things are the way they are, how we can move forward. (Anon)

There still seems to be some debate about the need for specialist positions as highlighted in Chapter 5, however. Although there is no dispute that specific skills are needed to work with young people and their families, there is a question about whether the best way of developing these skills is to continue to have children's librarians to focus specifically on these user groups, or whether children's work should be part of every library worker's remit, so mainstreaming work with children. *Start With The Child* stated that the loss of specialist staff is cause for concern but also stressed that, '[l]ibrary services should be doing everything possible to ensure that all staff are confident and competent in supporting children and young people' (Cilip Working Group on Library Provision for Children and Young People, 2002, p. 19) recommending that '[t]he recruitment process for all new staff should include criteria which demand evidence of a positive attitude towards children and young people' (p. 23).

In interview, Glenys Willars agreed, commenting:

If you'd spoken to me in the past I wouldn't have said this but I do now think that we don't want children's specialists in our libraries because what I think we need is every single member of our staff to be able to work with children. I don't care if they're not interested, a lot of the children's librarians weren't interested, but they could do it. And no more should we ever have anybody going into a library and meeting somebody on an enquiry desk who says, 'Oh no, sorry, I can't help you there because the children's librarian isn't in'. Never again. (Glenys Willars)

Moira Arthur disagreed, however, expressing the opinion in interview that the reduction in the number of children's specialists had had a negative impact on children's services in public libraries and adding:

I don't necessarily believe that you've got to be a children's specialist to order children's books but I do think a lot of the people in the adult sphere are not interested in children's books so it's having an interest which is the point and I think when you have generalists, something will give and the thing that will give is the thing that you're not that interested in and often that's children's books. (Moira Arthur)

Supporting Young People's Development

A lot of the work with young people in public libraries focuses on encouraging them to read so that they can make positive use of their leisure time and so that their life chances are improved through higher literacy levels and an interest in learning. Reader development is the focus of the next chapter and so this type of activity is not considered here. Rather, this section considers how public libraries complement the learning that takes place within the formal education system and how they support the improvement of young people's life chances through working in partnership with other local providers and agencies. In fact, public library reader development and literature promotion work with children and young people also supports the work of schools by encouraging children to read and continue their learning outside the formal education environment and the symbiotic relationship of reading and learning is clear. Many library-based activities centred around books and literature and the spoken and written word help to develop the higher learning skills of creativity, critical reasoning and self-expression, providing a firm basis for young people to continue their studies into further and higher education and beyond (Local Government Association, 2003). Nevertheless, for convenience they are treated separately.

As well as proposing a national programme for the development of services to young people, *Fulfilling Their Potential* (The Reading Agency, 2004) also considered how libraries can deliver on the Government's agenda for improving young people's lives established in *Every Child Matters*. Although it found that libraries engage substantially with 11-19 year olds, *Fulfilling Their Potential* asserted that the public library service has the potential to reach out to this age group even more and noted that it has many strengths including its unique community presence; a space that is not home nor school; a source of support for wide reading experiences; support for life skills and personal development; the ability to support parents; the capacity to support improved standards in reading, ICT and information literacy; and the ability to work successfully in partnership with other agencies to support disaffected young people. Young people themselves often focused on the capacity of the public library to provide them with a good range of free reading material and support in finding suitable resources; access to ICT; help with homework; helpful staff; and '[s]omewhere to chill away from home' (p. 23). They also found things to criticize, however, including dark, dull and daunting environments; inadequate book stocks; too few computers; and unwelcoming staff.

Many library services are aware that they need to address a range of these issues if they are to achieve their full potential in serving the needs of young people and are developing initiatives and activities designed to raise the profile of public libraries with this important user group. Indeed, the importance of engaging with children and young people was highlighted by many interview participants including John Dolan:

> If you invest in children, you'll get literate adults and we're probably already trying to deal with children who are the children of the last generation missed. That's a view I hold

> both about here and nationally, generally. If we don't start to reach children soon, we'll be dealing with a second generation of adults whose children we're trying to attract. (John Dolan)

Another participant also talked of a lost generation of potential public library users and the importance of trying to connect with children and young people:

> [We need to create] this image now of being more cool and the place where young people want to hang out because I think we've missed a generation in a sense, we've missed [people in their] 20s, 30s and 40s, some of them have passed us by so we've really got to focus more than ever on our young people. (Anon)

Some of the ways in which public libraries are trying to connect with this group of users are outlined below.

Support for the Formal School Curriculum

While support for pre-school learning has long been a priority for public libraries, assistance to those in schools has not traditionally been considered a key role. In fact, the relationship between public libraries and formal education in the past has been described as 'uneasy' (Heeks, 1996, p. 139). Education legislation in the 1980s, including the introduction of the National Curriculum and local management of schools, had a significant impact on public library services and their relationship with school students, however. The increase in continuous assessment and project work in the National Curriculum often highlighted the inadequacy of many school libraries which led students to turn to the public library to fulfil their reference and research needs. Similarly, reductions in School Library Services and the opting out of many schools from their subscription services put increased pressure on the non-fiction collections of public libraries and meant that they took on renewed importance as adjuncts and partners to schools. The cumulative result of all the changes to the education system in the 1980s was:

> … large increases in the number of school students who were coming into the library on a regular basis to do project work, use the reference section, ask librarians the answers to all their homework questions, occupy the seats and tables, and generally make their presence felt in mostly pleasant (but occasionally disruptive) ways. (Greenhalgh and Worpole, 1995, p. 26)

Public library services support the school curriculum in many ways, therefore, and one of the most important to emerge in recent years is study support through homework clubs. According to MLA, six out of ten libraries provide out-of-school study support (MLA, 2004a) and *Fulfilling Our Potential* states that 80 per cent of library authorities run homework clubs (The Reading Agency, 2004). Helping children with their homework was a feature of public library work before the education reforms set out above, but in the 1980s and 1990s the amount of time spent supporting children's school work in public libraries increased significantly following various government initiatives. Homework help in public libraries is not new, therefore, but homework help clubs have been 'seized on in the library press, by service heads and local politicians, not to mention many national politicians, as an excellent way of helping young people help themselves' (London Borough of Southwark, 1997, no page number).

Many homework support initiatives have been established in public libraries serving socially excluded neighbourhoods in recognition that children in schools which perform poorly in league tables generally have few study or information skills, their homes often lack space or resources with which to study and the level of parental support can also be comparatively weak (Bevin and Goulding, 1999). A study of homework clubs in public libraries in the UK reported that structured study support in public libraries works extremely well and had benefits beyond their educational role, easing the transition from primary to secondary education, helping young people to assert their individuality, and providing support and pastoral care which might not be available from the home or school environments (Train et al., 2000).

There are many examples of good practice in study support available across public library services in the UK. In Enfield, for example, Study Zones are open for sessions after school, on Saturday mornings and during some holidays. They are heavily used by pupils from local schools and are open exclusively one morning a week for pupils who have been excluded from school and those at risk of exclusion. The support that libraries provide to the formal education sector is not always as organized as homework clubs but can develop more organically. Alan Watkin outlined how support for school children had developed in one of the libraries in Wrexham in an urban village called Cefn Mawr:

> Our library is across the road from the two schools, one Welsh, one English primary school and going back 3 years, the odd kid would drift into the library. We gained money to set up an ICT suite before the NOF money but, more importantly, three year funding from the charity for a specialist worker to work with the kids who actually was a librarian but who really had a real aptitude to work with that age group. And in consequence, there's 35 to 40 kids go straight from school to the library every night. (Alan Watkin)

Joyce Little explained that these kind of initiatives could be hard work:

> It's been a big struggle for us in some libraries because children, in some areas of Liverpool, do not readily wish to have anything to do with schools out of school. So it's using carrots to encourage children to come in and it's been quite informal but they are supporting their learning. (Joyce Little)

In other areas of the city, though, out-of-school activities were more formally organized by study workers and other library services were also taking a more formal approach as Glenys Willars explained:

> All our libraries, if somebody went in with their homework, staff would be expected to support them… But what we're developing is a strategy for study support so that every large library will have certain levels of designated time so that if you come at that time you'll get more specialist help. We might work with the Education department on that as

well but they want to do things in a slightly different way to the way a public library might want to because we want it to be open to anybody who wants homework support and some of the education funding is targeted very much at children who need particular support and they get specialist support from teachers who can work with that individual. But they're interested in using library spaces as venues to do that work. Middle-sized libraries will probably not have designated times and the smallest ones may or may not but it may only be two hours each week. (Glenys Willars)

Many services have been successful in establishing homework clubs or study support in their libraries, therefore, but there are also challenges associated with this kind of provision. Glenys Willars felt that the space available for children's services, in general, and for study support in particular was often restricted and this could be a problem, especially in smaller libraries:

> Even in the smallest library there has to be a defined space. There are challenges, I suppose, in things like the provision for giving homework support, the space they've got available and, again, the staff being able to give the kind of support we might want them to. (Glenys Willars)

Because of this, some services have turned to education and youth services to provide staffing although Glenys Willars felt that library staff could provide support perfectly well:

> We would hope that library staff could do it and, again, they may need training. I don't necessarily think they have to be trained as teachers because I don't necessarily think somebody coming in to do their homework, unless it was targeted at particular children for particular reasons, they just need somebody who can help them think through what they've got to do and find the resources to support them and do it which I think is a librarian role really. (Glenys Willars)

Another challenge for public libraries wanting to increase their profile with regard to children's learning was, according to Bill Macnaught, to obtain recognition of the way in which libraries supported their formal and informal learning:

> School age children and young people, the work that we do in the library to support their learning; how do we illustrate the impact that's had? There's a lot of work going on to try to do that but… at the moment DfES or for that matter DCMS will only be convinced about the work that we're doing if we can demonstrate the outcomes and so if you're talking about education attainment being strong, they'll say, 'Well where's the exam results evidence of that?' (Bill Macnaught)

Joyce Little also felt that the role that libraries could play in supporting children's formal learning went unrecognized by many educationalists. Explaining how the library service had to take a lead and apply for external funding to support the study support centres in Liverpool she said:

> I don't think that the schools recognized the value of having somewhere out of school [for study support]. They would see that the main location for the homework club was after school in their school. (Joyce Little)

As Glenys Willars, suggested above, once again working in partnership is often the key to success with study support. Bevin and Goulding (1999) in their study of the early days of public library-based homework clubs found that cooperation with other local authority departments and agencies was vital to maximize the potential of the study support provided. Cooperation with the local education authority, the schools library service and the youth service were all common to ensure that sufficient funding, staffing and other resources were available to the young people using the facility. This model of integrated services is also recommended as a way of reaching out to young people and encouraging them to use the library for purposes other than study support.

Enhancing Young People's Life Chances

Working in partnership with local authority youth services and Connexions, the Government's one-stop support service for 13 to 19 year olds in England, among others, public libraries are contributing to young people's personal and social development. Public libraries can offer young people information about training, volunteering and work opportunities as well as a place away from home and school to meet friends and spend their leisure time. *Fulfilling Their Potential* notes that young people increasingly feel monitored and recorded with their progress being closely tracked by school and agencies like Connexions (The Reading Agency, 2004). It suggests that public libraries, on the other hand, are welcoming, safe, non-judgmental and neutral, 'where people's information needs, reading habits and opinion are treated with respect and confidentiality and their achievements and progress are not a matter of record' (p. 11). Whether young people view public libraries as quite so welcoming is another matter, however, and, as noted above, the report also found that young people were often less than complimentary about them.

Initiatives to encourage young people to engage with public library services are increasingly focusing on involving them in decisions about the services that they are likely to use. *Fulfilling Their Potential* stresses that young people want to be consulted about the services they use and those which affect them. It also gives some examples of good practice, describing the work in Shropshire County Libraries designed to improve library membership among 15 to 24 year olds. As well as involving young people in stock decisions, they were also recruited as 'mystery shoppers' and involved in other aspects of the service's marketing strategy. As outlined in Chapter 7, some library services are making strenuous efforts to consult groups perceived as hard to reach and excluded and that often includes young people although one participant admitted that, although young people were consulted:

> ...one thing we're not very good at is coming back to kids and saying 'This is what you told us, this is what we're going to do'... There's still room for improvement there. (Anon)

Encouraging young people to become involved in making decisions about their local public library is seen by The Reading Agency and MLA who commissioned *Fulfilling Their Potential* as a valuable initial step in fostering their civic engagement (MLA, 2004b). Involvement in the planning and service development of the library could foster a wider connection with the community and, more generally, society. A wide range of schemes has been developed to encourage young people into libraries. These generally focus on reading and books and are discussed in more detail in the next chapter. They are often funded under government initiatives designed to equip young people with new skills, reduce youth offending and support community cohesion. The Positive Activities for Young People (PAYP) scheme, for example, is a £25 million programme for England funded by the DCMS, DfES, the Home Office and the New Opportunities Fund. Targeting young people at risk, the scheme runs in the school holidays, aiming to provide quality developmental sports, arts and creative activities through which young people are supported to return or stay in education, develop their personal skills, learn tolerance and respect for others from different backgrounds and communities and contribute to their communities. Working in partnership with youth services and youth offending teams, public libraries have played an active role in developing literature and reader development activities which meet PAYP objectives. In Liverpool, for example, creative writing session, craft sessions and a photography scheme where young people took pictures of things that made them happy or unhappy and then wrote about them all encouraged young people to think about their communities and their place within it.

The availability of the Internet and access to other computing facilities is also attracting young people into public libraries in increasing numbers and this is welcomed by those in the public library community although, as indicated in Chapters 4 and 6, large numbers of young people can cause difficulties for other users and staff. The free access to computers and the Internet in public libraries has undoubtedly proved very popular with children and young people, giving them access to resources to support their school-based studies and also supporting their informal learning. For adults, too, the provision of ICT resources in public libraries is positioning libraries as key players on the lifelong learning and post-compulsory education scene, as discussed in Chapter 6, while their involvement with Sure Start and family learning is establishing a role for them in basic skills provision.

Adult Learners

Chapter 6 outlined how many of the public library services to adult learners are focusing on extending their ICT skills and breaking down the digital divide but beyond their development as ICT learning centres, public libraries are establishing programmes and activities which enable their users to develop skills to support their formal and informal learning needs. Remembering the very broad definition of learning given in *Inspiring Learning for All* (MLA, 2003), most of the activities which take place in public libraries can be seen as supporting people's learning. The PricewaterhouseCoopers (2005) study on the impact of public libraries reported that the services provided by public libraries had an impact on a number of the Government's adult education policy themes. Activities and services provided were judged to be both enjoyable and valuable for skills development. As with children and young people, reader development work with adults enables them to develop knowledge and understanding as well as encouraging them to explore their feelings, beliefs and values. People can also pursue pastimes or hobbies for their own interest, enabling informal, individual learning as well as more formal group learning activities or courses so that, according to *Framework for the Future*:

> '[t]he self-motivated learning which libraries promote is central to the creation of a lifelong learning culture in which people expect and want to learn throughout their lifetime'. (Department for Culture, Media and Sport, 2003, p. 8)

Here, the understanding in the library community of learning as focused around the 'the creativity and inspiration and enjoyment agenda as well as knowledge and skills' (Sue Wilkinson) is clear.

As noted above, Chapter 10 focuses on the literature development work taking place in public libraries designed to support people's creativity, enjoyment and development through interaction with books and reading. This section will focus on the aspects of learning in public libraries which have recently been emphasized by policy makers and by those participating in the research interviews for this study: work with 'first-steppers'; connecting people with learning opportunities; and work with adult basic skills learners.

Libraries as a First Step to Learning

The Local Government Association (2003) notes that, for many people, the biggest obstacle to accessing learning and training opportunities is taking the first step back to learning. The Association suggests that cultural organizations like libraries can provide a second chance for people by offering a neutral, informal environment catering for a whole range of learning needs. Many in the public library community would support these points. *Framework for the Future* describes public libraries as 'learning start up organizations' (Department for Culture, Media and Sport, 2003, p. 29), suggesting that those with poor previous experience of formal education may need extra encouragement to return to learning and libraries are in an ideal position to help them. The 2000 Select Committee on Public Libraries also emphasized that public libraries are well placed to support the learning of those deterred by activities which are too formal or provided in a conventional educational setting (Culture, Media and Sport Committee, 2000). Public libraries are considered to be ideal vehicles for giving people a simpler introduction to learning than they might otherwise experience in a formal education setting. They can also reach out to those who might be deterred by the cost of a formal course or who may just want to learn a specific skill, to use email, for example, rather than take a complete ICT course (Laird, 2004). In some cases, users may be 'learning by stealth' (Ashcroft et al., 2005, p. 41); accessing learning materials and support without them realizing it.

The capacity of public libraries to provide a safe, welcoming and supportive learning environment for nervous or hesitant learners is well established in the public library literature, therefore, and was also a key theme of the research interviews, picking up on many of the points raised in the last chapter related to the idea of the library as a neutral, non-threatening space. Jan Holden highlighted this aspect of public library learning provision:

> We've done loads of focus group work with excluded groups about where people go for information, where they go for information about learning and in most cases people said they'd come to this library to find things out because it's not as threatening as other places. (Jan Holden)

Alan Watkin outlined the Routes project, funded by NOF and running in four library services in Wales, explaining that groups and individuals were introduced to ICT learning which enabled them to become informal learners in the library setting. He also commented that many of the people who had taken up learning opportunities offered by the Routes project (discussed below) also felt 'very unhappy about thinking of going into some form of formal college class' (Alan Watkin). Similarly, another participant said,

> If you're trying to encourage somebody back into learning, they don't always want to go to an education establishment but coming into a library and actually being able to enrol onto a course means that you don't actually lose them. Because I have a feeling that if we said, 'You can do this course 3 miles up the road at the centre for the college' they might not necessarily make that 3 mile journey when they were in that initial stage of needing confidence because they were returning to learning for the first time. (Anon)

Although Martin Molloy agreed that this showed that the public library had the public's confidence and that this was very gratifying, he was also concerned that libraries were not equipped to support people's more complex learning needs. Connecting people with appropriate learning opportunities was not always easy, though, and he thought that this indicated that other parts of the education system had problems that they needed to address:

> [Libraries are] not geared up to teach people [more advanced] skills in the library, that's not what the library staff are there for. But when we recommend going to an education suite, things like that, it's 'Oh no, I don't like education' and you know that their memories of school means that they don't want to do it and the number of people who say, 'I like the library, it's friendly, nobody judges you', that's great in a way but it does show we've got problems elsewhere. (Martin Molloy)

Libraries should be able to capitalize on the view of the library as an appropriate and welcoming place to take the first step back to learning but they also need to be able to direct people on to appropriate higher level learning opportunities when the time comes.

The Next Step

Public libraries across the UK are trying to support those who have been successful at returning to learning and want to move on to develop their skills, knowledge or interests. The Library Association in its memorandum of evidence submitted to the 2000 Select Committee on Public Libraries noted the potential for public libraries to act as a gateway, leading people from informal learning to accredited learning programmes resulting in qualifications (Culture, Media and Sport Committee, 2000). Similarly, McNicol and Dalton (2003) reported that participants in their study commented that one of main advantages of the public library was its ability to link informal and formal learning, helping and inspiring people to progress from informal learning to more formal courses and identifying suitable opportunities. Ashcroft et al. (2005) confirmed that public library services provide a wide range of courses and services for adult learning, some of which appeal to all learner groups and others which target a particular community such as English language learners. John Dolan was concerned, though, that much of the learning agenda was narrowly focused on ICT skills and libraries were missing an opportunity to become involved with learning in its broadest sense:

> The ICT clearly has a part to play both in accessing information about learning as well as accessing learning itself. But it's early days for that; you can access the Internet but the amount of online learning programmes, programmed learning, is limited, but that's beginning to take off. (John Dolan)

Alyson Harbour felt, though, that public libraries should continue to concentrate on informal learning while providing connections to more formal opportunities within the local area:

> I think it's absolutely critical that libraries stay as the informal sector of education and not the formal [although] I think it's really good to provide avenues into formal education. (Alyson Harbour)

Partnership with other learning providers is often the key here and many public library services are engaged in cooperative schemes with other local providers to support those studying for qualifications, as distance learners, part-time learners or full-time students. In Medway, for example, an adult education centre has been opened in Lordswood library in a partnership between the public library service and the adult and community learning service. In Liverpool, Joyce Little explained how the library service was supported by the Adult and Community Learning service which provided tutors to deliver learning services to the public. Ashcroft et al. (2005) list a range of partnerships activities which the case study libraries in their research had engaged in, concluding that the advantages of partnership included the sharing of costs, facilities and marketing.

There is no doubt that many learners like to have their progress recorded, monitored and recognized through the award of a qualification or certificate and through partnerships with other learning organizations, public libraries can help them achieve this. Many others pursue informal learning for pleasure, though, and gaining recognition of the important role that this kind of learning plays in many people's lives and, additionally, how public libraries facilitate it is often an uphill battle. One Head of Service participating in the formal evaluation of the People's Network project suggested that the Learning and Skills Council had not been a good partner because it was just not interested in informal or community learning, only in accredited or formal learning (Sommerlad et al., 2004) This was reinforced by participants in this study, one commenting that the Education department in the authority had not been interested in linking with libraries on the lifelong learning agenda:

> …until they realized the number of people that actually do come into libraries and people like using libraries; they're a non-threatening environment for the public. The relationship [with Education] has changed and changed for the better but all the time we are fighting a different set of priorities and a different set of outcomes. I think very often their outcomes will involve either getting people back into work or on to education; that isn't the outcome for libraries. (Anon)

Another participant agreed that 'we don't integrate particularly well' (Anon) with the lifelong learning section of the local authority which John Dolan attributed to a preoccupation with employability and accreditation on the part of many of the key stakeholders:

> I don't think the powerful players in the lifelong learning community at national and regional level find it very easy to understand the library role. And I think that's partly because the understanding of lifelong learning is now heavily invested in an ambition to get people into work and therefore to give learning accreditation. And the concepts of… good, self-learning and self-motivated learning and independent learning have been pushed aside a bit to be replaced by learning programmes and structured learning. (John Dolan)

Alan Watkin felt that, in these circumstances, establishing productive partnerships to take forward the lifelong learning agenda was sometimes difficult:

> I think we've had one or two disappointments in that libraries aren't identified by partners as being as important as they should be. Education [department] is an example of that and I think that's because they've been forced down this route of certain performance indicators and targets… So they're very school centred and very conventionally education centred so, in effect, in something like literacy, we've lost ground over the years. (Alan Watkin)

Nevertheless, many public library services are trying to establish services aimed at supporting literacy learners.

Supporting Basic Skills Learners

As indicated in the Introduction to this chapter, there is general acceptance that the ability to read and write is vital, valued as a skill in its own right and for the access it provides to other benefits including employment, earning power and the capacity to participate fully in society. Literacy increases individuals' life chances, enabling them to reach their full potential and play their full role as citizens. The consequences of poor literacy skills are also well documented and include powerlessness, poverty, low participation in community life and reduced confidence and self-esteem. Society and the economy as a whole will also suffer if some citizens lack the skills to participate and contribute fully (Hartley, 1990). The British Government has responded to concern about literacy rates in the UK with a number of major initiatives[8] but surveys of the nation's literacy suggest that the UK cannot afford to be complacent about literacy rates. The Moser report estimated that 7 million British adults had literacy levels below that of an average 11 year old and that one in five adults were functionally illiterate; they could not find the page for plumbers, for example, if given the Yellow Pages (Working Group on Post 16 Basic Skills, 1999).

Literacy issues are closely linked to, and in some cases underpin, a whole range of key government programmes including the education and lifelong learning agendas, the development of the information society and knowledge economy and the drive to promote citizenship and tackle social exclusion through neighbourhood renewal and rural development. A discussion paper from the National Literacy Trust provides a clear overview of the links between literacy and social exclusion (Bird, 2004). It suggests that children of parents with poor literacy and communication skills start school at a disadvantage and often find it difficult to catch up so that they become 'caught in the spiral of self-doubt and sense of failure' (p. 4). Adults with low levels of literacy are often unskilled, have sporadic employment records, low aspirations and are more likely to be depressed and engaged in criminal activity. They are also less likely to be active citizens. For the state, this means higher social and welfare costs and crowded prisons.

Chapter 7 suggested that those with literacy difficulties may find institutions centred around the written word intimidating but within the public library community there is a strong belief that public libraries can assist those with basic skills needs. *Framework for the Future*, for example, states that, '[l]ibraries are ideally placed to recognise and support people who might benefit from tuition' (Department for Culture, Media and Sport, 2003, p. 8). Because of the impact of poor literacy on so many areas of life, there is also a growing realization that action to tackle literacy must be multi-agency. Initiatives such as Bookstart prove that the public library can widen its sphere of influence and work in a co-ordinated and integrated manner across the local authority and with voluntary and community-based organizations to improve children's and their carers' life chances. One participant explained how this was happening in her authority:

> We do a lot, through IT, a lot of basic skills [work]. We work in partnership with the College and with other sixth form colleges on basic skills. We do a lot of reading development, we actually work outside libraries in community centres, the traditional sorts of places you would expect, but also in pubs. We are not precious about where the building is based. We have run reading groups for Asian women and those Asian women have gone on to do further qualifications and are now taking reading clubs into their community with our help. That end of literacy is important. (Anon)

Public library commentators and practitioners suggest that public library involvement in adult literacy provision will give adult learners greater opportunity and flexibility to become involved in literacy-related activities and perhaps then on to other learning activities as one participant suggested:

> The college is very keen to develop opportunities for residents to access basic skills education because they want to get more of the adult community involved at the college. They see the libraries, particularly in areas of special need and very deprived communities, as being a gateway to getting people enrolled into further education and that's been very successful for us. (Anon)

Once again, their community location and welcoming, neutral image is said to be attractive to those with basic skills needs although, as established in Chapter 7, those needing help may well be deterred by a variety of barriers to use, a problem noted by one participant in the *Mapping the Territory* project who suggested:

> The library remains the street-corner learning centre, a role enhanced in the digital era through free access to the net and learning resources. However I believe those with basic skills problems lack the confidence/awareness, and would not see libraries as a useful place. (Barzey, 2003, p. 38)

The *Mapping the Territory* project investigated the provision of adult basic skills services in libraries, archives and museums and highlighted the fact that although individual library authorities were at different stages at embarking on work with adults with basic skills needs, overall libraries led the field in the cultural sector and, importantly, recognized that this is an area in which they should be developing services. The research found little support or direct provision for formal basic skills learning, though, with just five museums, archives and libraries (2 per cent) supporting a formal literacy certificate, six (2 per cent) supporting a numeracy certificate and the same number and percentage supporting an English as a Second Overseas Language (ESOL) certificate. The emphasis in all the cultural services was on informal learning, concentrating on family learning, literacy and research skills. the report identified the main challenges for the sector as formal staff training, staff capacity and funding. It was noted, though, that many seemed willing to support this area of government policy and that libraries, in particular, were making a contribution. The author concluded that this was in part due to the People's Network and the presence of *learndirect* centres in public libraries but also because of the intrinsic connection between libraries and reading. Reader development activities which support reading for pleasure were acknowledged in the research as a form of informal basic skills learning and a reader development approach has been found to be valuable in work with adult basic skills learners.

The *Vital Link* programme, led by The Reading Agency in partnership with the National Literacy Trust and the National Reading Campaign, confirms a support role for public libraries in addressing adult literacy, focusing on the identification and provision of resources and the delivery of reader development approaches to encourage reading amongst emergent readers.[9] Emergent readers are identified as those who have progressed beyond adult basic skills collections but who often lack confidence in choosing books that they will find accessible and therefore enjoy reading. The programme has developed collections for adults with a reading age of between 9 and 14 and also produces promotional materials for libraries to publicize the collections. The evaluation of the pilot stage of the programme found widespread acceptance of the role of the public library in basic skills learning from library staff, basic skills tutors and learners themselves but this acceptance was by no means universal and barriers including charges, inadequate signage and inappropriate location and display of suitable stock were problems preventing wider use by the target group (Train et al., no date).

Interview participants frequently picked up on many of the themes identified by previous studies. The environment of the library, for example, was often cited as an advantage, one participant saying, 'it's a comforting environment for people, not going into a learning environment' (Laurayne Featherstone). Similarly the importance of partnerships in this area was highlighted:

> Libraries that have worked successfully with basic skills providers are not necessarily turning themselves into basic skills tutors, they're finding the basic skills providers and saying, 'You could do it here, you could do it with our resources.' (Sue Wilkinson)

The public library could become an appropriate site for basic skills activity to take place, then, working in co-operation with basic skills providers although some of the barriers to the use of public libraries by the target group, such as those discussed in the previous chapter, would need to be addressed.

Conclusion

The literature and research interviews exposed a number of key discourses focused around the learning role of public libraries. Public libraries are portrayed as having a learning tradition; they support a range of learning needs and are study focused, providing resources, facilities and staff assistance. They were also characterized within the literature and by interview participants as accessible focal points within communities, providing a neutral, impartial and supportive learning environment. Trained, user-focused staff are available and help create an encouraging and non-threatening environment for learners, facilitating access to information and suitable learning resources. The research suggests, however, that despite evidence of their value to the learning process, public libraries often struggle to clarify their role in the learning process, with the consequence that they are often over-looked when initiatives and policies are launched and when funding is distributed. Internal, organizational failings, including staff skills and confidence and a lack of funding, can mean that they fail to convince potential partners that they have much to contribute to the learning process. The current political environment with its emphasis on learning for employability and on formal qualifications and accreditation can also leave public libraries, which tend to focus on informal learning, out in the cold. An analysis of the research interviews identifies discourses of frustration and of feeling hard done by as a result which not only seems to be leading to disappointment and demoralization, but can also cause practical resourcing difficulties if libraries are missing out on funding which could enhance their services to learners.

There does seem to be considerable scope for public libraries to be involved in formal, informal and community-based learning although their success at staking a claim within the learning agenda seems to be heavily dependent on the local context and the extent to which the library service can convince other local learning providers that they have a valuable contribution to make. Collaboration and partnership in local learning agendas and partnerships seems to be more advanced at some levels than at others. Thus, while the Sure Start and Bookstart programmes have enabled library services to build a range of positive relationships at early years level, full participation in local adult learning activities and initiatives seems to be more difficult because of the different priorities of the more formal education or learning providers. Even at early years level, some library authorities have found it easier than others to be accepted as a partner with an important contribution to make to EYDCPs.

Ashcroft et al. (2005) suggested that the public library services participating in their study had responded positively to the vision set out in *Framework for the Future* by planning and developing services and initiatives to support learners generally and particularly to support adult learners. Their report concluded that the public library services in their sample had succeeded in reaching out to a range of different social groups, working with partners to provide the services needed by their communities and innovating in the face of some serious constraints. Sommerlad et al. (2004) are more cautious in their praise, however, suggesting that public libraries are not really engaging with models of community and informal learning which they have so much to offer as social environments. Instead, they report, 'the individual learner remains the dominant paradigm' (p. 135). They feel that the 'learning communities' concept is one which public libraries could usefully explore.

In the United States, Ronald McCabe (2001) fears that public librarians are rejecting the serious agenda of social education in favour of a libertarian approach which emphasizes access to information for individuals. Asserting that, '[e]ducation for a demoncratic society is the great narrative behind the public library as an institution' (p. 99), he warns of the dangers of adhering to a new mission of providing access to individuals. Not only does he feel that this new mission will fail to inspire support for public libraries but he also comments that it is a tactical error to base the rationale for public libraries on access to information in an information-rich environment. In contrast, he argues, education is desperately needed, partly to help people make sense of the huge amounts of information now available. The evidence from the UK literature and the interviews for this study would suggest that public libraries here are not neglecting the learning agenda and, if anything, would want to be even more closely involved in opening up learning opportunities for individuals and communities. Persuading other learning providers that they have a contribution to make in this area seems to be their biggest challenge.

Notes

1 Scottish Executive (2003), *Life Through Learning; Learning Through Life: A Strategy for Lifelong Learning*, Scottish Executive, Edinburgh, (URL: http://www.scotland.gov.uk/library5/lifelong/llsm-00.asp) [09.12.05]; Welsh Assembly Government (2001), *The Learning Country*, Welsh Assembly Government, Cardiff, (http://www.wales.gov.uk/subieducationtraining/content/learningcountry/tlc-contents-e.htm) [09.12.05]; Department for Employment and Learning (2003), *Essential Skills for Living*, Department for Employment and Learning, Belfast, (URL: http://www.delni.gov.uk/docs/PDF/4622%20DEL%20Essential%20Skills.pdf) [09.12.05].

2 See, for example, the Government's website for lifelong learners: (URL: http://www.lifelonglearning.co.uk/) [09.12.05].

3 Inspire website: (URL: http://www.inspire.gov.uk/) [09.12.05].

4 Eppe research: (URL: http://k1.ioe.ac.uk/schools/ecpe/eppe/index.htm) [09.12.05].

5 Children and Young People's Unit website: (URL: http://www.cypu.gov.uk/) [09.12.05].

6 Sure Start website: (URL: http://www.surestart.gov.uk/) [09.12.05].

7 Bookstart website: (URL: http://bookstart.co.uk/) [09.12.05].

8 For example, the National Literacy Strategy: (URL: http://www.standards.dfes.gov.uk/literacy/) [09.12.05]; the Moser report, *Improving Literacy and Numeracy: a Fresh Start*: (URL: http://www.lifelonglearning.co.uk/mosergroup/index.htm) [09.12.05].

9 Vital Link website: (URL: http://www.readingagency.co.uk/html/whatWeDo03.cfm?projectID=40&loc=projects) [09.12.05].

Chapter 10

Books and Reading

The Policy Context: The National Literacy Strategy

The New Labour Government launched the National Literacy Strategy for England on coming to office in 1997.[1] Designed to raise the standards of literacy in primary schools over a five to ten year period, this has involved the setting of targets and the introduction of a daily Literacy Hour in schools. The impetus behind the National Literacy Strategy was concern that Britain was not performing well in international comparisons of children's reading, holding a below average position in international literacy league tables, outperformed by a range of countries including Finland, the United States, Sweden, France, Italy, New Zealand and Norway (Literacy Taskforce, 1997). Particularly worrying was the long 'tail' of underachievement with the performance of lower ability students substantially below that of other countries.

The Literacy Taskforce, established when New Labour was in opposition to produce recommendations on the content and structure of a national strategy for tackling the country's literacy problems, documented the extent and cause of 'this evidently unacceptable state of affairs' in a preliminary report published in 1997 (Literacy Taskforce, 1997, para. 34). It noted that concerns about literacy had been expressed since the 1970s but no systematic attempt to address them had been made, with practice varying from school to school and the cultures of voluntarism and professional autonomy firmly embedded. Teaching methods and content were not consistent and there was no mechanism for sharing excellent practice. That changed with the Education Reform Act of 1988 and the introduction of the National Curriculum but the Literacy Taskforce suggested that this, while solving the problem of varying practices, introduced new difficulties with the broad nature of the curriculum distracting teachers from the three 'Rs'. It therefore recommended a strategy for raising the standards of literacy based on a national target that, by 2002, 80 per cent of 11 year olds should reach the standard expected for their age in English. This was to be achieved through a teaching framework which set out termly teaching objectives, introduced the Literacy Hour and gave additional guidance for children with special needs (Beard, 1998).

Despite failing to meet the above target, there is some evidence that the National Literacy Strategy is having a beneficial impact on children's literacy. The PIRLS (Progress in International Reading Literacy Study) research from 2001 put English children among the most able readers in the world at around age ten (Twist et al., 2003), below only Sweden and the Netherlands for overall reading achievement. Within that rating, England scored particularly well for reading for literacy experience (the highest score along with Sweden) and fifth (below Sweden, the Netherlands, Bulgaria and Latvia) for reading for informational purposes. Despite these encouraging results, there is still evidence that the range of children's reading ability in England is very wide, in fact it has one of the largest ranges. When considering the three international achievement benchmarks established by the PIRLS research, England has the highest proportion of pupils in the top 10 per cent internationally, the second highest proportion in the top 25 per cent and the third highest proportion in the top 50 per cent indicating that 'the top performing pupils in England are among the best in the world' (Twist et al., 2003, p. 20). As the report makes clear, however, 'the reading performance of lower scoring pupils is not as encouraging' (p. 20) with a substantial difference between the achievement of high and low scoring pupils. Nevertheless, the report concludes that 'there does appear to be a marked increase in the international standing of England from the mid-1990s to PIRLS 2001' (p. 22), suggesting that the National Literacy Strategy has had its successes.

Although targeted at primary schools, the philosophy underpinning the National Literacy Strategy acknowledges the importance of reading and the opportunities it brings for all. The previous chapter outlined the Government's view of the role of literacy in economic and social prosperity, noting that there is an economic imperative behind the Government's basic skills agenda. In interview, Martin Molloy also stressed the benefits of reading for the individual and society and the economy:

> We want to be building new readers, we want to be making a reading nation because the more literate and numerate we are, the more opportunities there are for our workforce. Whether you like it or not, we're in a capitalist system, we're competing with other countries and libraries have got a role to play in helping develop an interested, articulate, educated workforce and that's significant. (Martin Molloy)

There is also acknowledgement of the other benefits that literacy can bring for all ages, however. In a report setting out the findings of relevant research and other evidence, Roger Beard (1998) discusses the policy and strategic considerations behind the National Literacy Strategy suggesting that literacy makes a valuable contribution to individuals' personal growth through reading and responding to literature and from the use of information. The thought processes that reading demands develops critical and analytical thinking, enabling us to make judgements about the world and other people. Literature, it is claimed,

> 'helps to shape the personality, refine the sensibility, sharpen the critical intelligence; … it is a powerful instrument for empathy and a medium through which children can acquire their values' (Beard, 1998, p. 8).

Others similarly document how reading can contribute to people's quality of life. Usherwood and Toyne's (2002) study of the value and impact of public library book reading explored the role that reading fiction played in people's lives, finding that it was valued as a way of escaping and relaxing but also as a means of instruction for developing practical knowledge and as an instrument for establishing personal identity and self-knowledge. Within reader response theory, readers are no longer viewed as passive absorbers of texts but as agents who interact with works of fiction, finding their own interpretations and meanings in the words of an author (Suleiman and Crosman, 1980). Holden (2004) suggests that reading is a creative process through which:

> We do not only gain knowledge from reading, we acquire emotional depth and subtlety of response. We can become more empathetic, and we can also heal ourselves. (Holden, 2004, p. 7)

The central importance of reading for literacy, learning, quality of life and the personal development of individuals is clearly stated in many government sponsored publications and policy statements, therefore, and is recognized as a crucial, if not *the* crucial, life skill. Happily, there is evidence that the United Kingdom is a nation of readers. As indicated in Chapter 1, reading is a popular cultural activity with 72 per cent of women and 58 per cent of men having read a book in the four weeks prior to the General Household Survey in 2002 (Fox and Rickards, 2004). Similarly, nationwide televised initiatives based around books and reading have proved immensely popular as have locally based reading groups and reading circles. Once again, though, the divide between those able to participate in and enjoy these events and activities and those who are unable to because of their lack of reading ability is stark; the OECD's International Adult Literacy Survey indicated that literacy skills in the UK were very polarized with large proportions of people at both the highest and lowest levels (OECD, 2000). Nevertheless, the number and popularity of reading and literature activities in the UK in recent years does indicate a healthy interest in books and reading.

A Reading Renaissance

Despite the challenge of radio, cinema, television and the Internet, books have retained their power and position as cultural objects and a source of knowledge, inspiration, escape and comfort for millions of people in the UK. In fact, television and the publishing industry have now started to work very successfully together and, as Miranda McKearney, Director of The Reading Agency suggested in interview, 'it's really exciting that television is waking up to the fact that reading attracts huge audiences'. The popularity of the BBC's *Big Read* and Richard and Judy's BookClub as well as 'the Harry Potter phenomenon' are all cited as evidence of a renewed interest in and passion for reading in Britain and the scale of activity is impressive. 125,000 new titles a year are published in the UK, more than in the US and the number of books sold has also risen by 20 per cent since 1997 (Coates, 2004). World Book Day is celebrated each year by reading related activities and events in schools and libraries across the country and with the distribution of twelve million book tokens to school children.

As part of the National Literacy Strategy, the National Year of Reading ran from September 1998 to August 1999. Funded by the Government and administered by the National Literacy Trust, the National Year of Reading was designed to involve the whole community in developing literacy skills and the joy of reading, focusing particularly on increasing the number of children and young people reading regularly, especially with their families, and encouraging more people to read for pleasure and discuss their reading choices. The National Year of Reading became a platform for the development of reading related activities across the country with funding being granted to organizations including local community groups and voluntary associations, prisons, libraries and schools for reading and writing projects. An evaluation of public library participation in the Year was judged an outstanding success overall with benefits including an enhanced profile for the library service, the formation of new partnerships and an acknowledgement of the importance of reading and libraries' role in providing and promoting reading materials (Streatfield et al., 2000). The work of the National Year of Reading is continued by the National Reading Campaign.[2]

The other recent development which suggests sustained or even increasing interest in the UK in books and reading is the huge growth of reading groups. Although, as Jenny Hartley (2001) points out, group-based reading has existed for as long as reading and, in fact, was probably more common before the era of printing and cheap books, the number of reading groups or circles in the UK has increased dramatically in recent years. In fact, The Reading Agency describes their rapid development and popularity as 'not so much a tide as a tidal wave' (The Reading Agency, 2004a, p.8). Apart from the well publicized national reading groups, run through the Richard and Judy television show and Radio 4's Bookclub programme, local groups are also thriving while Internet based groups give those who are geographically isolated or confined close to home for a variety of reasons the opportunity to share their thoughts on reading and books.

Public libraries have not been slow to capitalize upon and become involved with all the activity going on nationally and locally aimed at encouraging people to read more, read more widely, think about and discuss their reactions to books. They were often lead partners in National Year of Reading activities which, as indicated above, frequently served to re-energize and refocus their book and reading related services, and thousands of reading groups around the UK are supported by library services.[3] Bob McKee suggested in interview that all the activity and awareness around books and reading in the UK could only benefit public libraries and that, importantly, they were taking advantage of developments:

> There's this phenomenally wonderful public interest in books and reading again, you know, all these things like the *Big Read* and the hoo-ha over literary prizes, it's great. People talk about an information society but we've sort of turned into a books and reading society again and that's just great and libraries are benefiting from that. (Bob McKee)

This chapter will focus on a range of issues facing public libraries in their essential activities of acquiring and storing books and making them available for use. It will analyse how they are adapting their collection management strategies and methods in the light of recent evidence about the performance of public library book borrowing services and will explore the impact of reader development initiatives in public libraries.

Public Libraries and Books

> Public librarians are the unsung heroes of the book trade. Few people realise the amount of time and attention they devote to promoting books: from careful consideration of which fiction to buy to tracing down obscure non-fiction material that can be purloined from other branches. And they are devoted to maintaining these services. (Baverstock, 1997, p. 224)

User statistics show that most people visit the public library to borrow books and surveys confirm that users and non-users associate the public library first and foremost with the lending of books (see, for example, Mori, 2002). According to some commentators, books bestow the library with a quasi-religious aura which is the basis for the 'libraryness' factor (Greenhalgh and Worpole, 1995, p. 51). Books and printed material are also the foundation of what in the United States is called the 'library faith', that is, a belief in the virtue of the printed word and a conviction that reading is in itself good and the reading of books is moral and useful and so libraries contribute to society (Bostwick, 1910). This attitude towards reading and the book can also be seen in recent reports commissioned in the UK. In *Framework for the Future*, for example, literacy and reading are considered essential pre-requisites for cultural and social change as they stimulate learning, thinking and enquiring (Department for Culture, Media and Sport, 2003).

A Public Library Borrowing Crisis

Although public libraries today are about so much more than books, the book lending and reference services that they provide still define much of what the public library service does in the eyes of both the public and policy makers. Lord MacIntosh, in the 2004 DCMS report to parliament on library matters, confirmed that the core purpose of public libraries is books (Department for Culture, Media and Sport, 2004). Similarly, the 2005 Culture, Media and Sport Parliamentary Select Committee asserted:

> We are in no doubt that, while libraries are about more than books (and newspapers and journals), these traditional materials must be the bedrock upon which the library services rest no matter how the institution is refreshed or re-branded in the light of local consultation. (Culture, Media and Sport Committee, 2005, p. 18)

The Committee also stressed that although a local authority may choose to offer a range of services and facilities from a public library site, 'within this plethora of services, the notion of simply reading for pleasure must be fundamental' (Culture, Media and Sport Committee, 2005, pp. 18 - 19). A recent PricewaterhouseCoopers (2005) report on the impact of public libraries, though, questioned this view, suggesting that 'book borrowing indicators should not be used as the prime measure of how libraries contribute to local and national priorities' (p. 4) and recommending that libraries should not be viewed primarily as free bookshops or warehouses. Many research participants agreed with the sentiment expressed in the report that 'Books are not everything' (p. 4) but nevertheless argued for a reinvigoration of book and reading-based services.

Lord Andrew McIntosh in his written response articulated this opinion clearly: 'Despite the exciting changes to libraries in recent years, I believe books and reading remain at the heart of everything that libraries are about' (Lord Andrew McIntosh). Graham Tope made very similar points:

> I think lending books is the core business and always will be. I'm not one of those who believes that it will all disappear and end in whatever time period you want to say. I think that is the core business. (Lord Graham Tope)

Another interview participant felt that libraries had to develop services to appeal to a wider constituency but also agreed that books and reading should remain at the heart of the public library service message:

> I think you do have to take a bit of a risk but what I wouldn't like to see diminished is the whole brand of what a library is. As a profession and a sector we don't actually market that brand well at present and the *Framework for the Future* Action Plan is about building on what we do best. This includes provision of books, reading, literacy and the promotion of all that activity as a life enhancer and learning experience. We don't do enough to promote that brand and if we did, we would probably get more partnerships and more take-up of services as a result. (Anon)

Picking up on surveys that show that most people associate public libraries with books, Miranda McKearney felt that public libraries were not always in tune with their users and potential users:

> I think it's a really, really big issue, a really fundamental one of what public libraries think they're there to do and it's something The Reading Agency has been going on about for ages; putting reading very centrally back at the heart of what libraries think they're there for. Because there's this very strange mis-match [between] what all the research tells you users want from their libraries, which is a decent selection of books amongst other things, and the kind of perception within bits of the library service that that actually isn't their core purpose. (Miranda McKearney)

The importance of the book and the reading related services which public libraries offer is being emphasized by politicians and practitioners, therefore. But recent evidence suggests that public libraries are not performing as well as they could in this respect. Although the statistics detailed above indicate that reading, as a leisure pursuit, plays a central part in many people's lives, the borrowing of books from public libraries has been in decline since the mid 1980s. Nick Moore (unpub.) has tracked the fall in loans from English public libraries since the mid 1970s (Table 10.1) and others have also drawn attention to the 'dramatic rate of decline' (Coates, 2004, p.5; see also Audit Commission, 2002), predicting that if it is not arrested, libraries will no longer be used in 20 years time.

Table 10.1 Loans from English public libraries

Year	75–76	80–81	85–86	90–91	95–96	00–01	02–03
Loans (000s)	532,760	550,776	540,028	475,527	437,158	342,914	305,112
Loans per head of pop.	11.47	12.05	11.46	10.25	9.27	6.86	6.16

Source: Adapted from: Moore, N., unpub.

The 2005 Select Committee report emphasized the serious nature of the situation stating that the overall picture was 'one of decline – both in provision and usage – especially in the provision of books which many see as a key library function' (Culture, Media and Sport Committee, 2005, p. 14). As suggested above, reading remains a popular pastime and, if anything, the interest in books and reading is growing so it is unlikely that people are turning away from public library lending services because of factors associated with the book as a medium in itself or reading as entertainment but rather because of something to do with their experiences of borrowing from the public library. The importance of a welcoming, comfortable building for attracting increased use was highlighted in Chapter 8 and it has been suggested that public libraries could usefully adopt some of the design and marketing techniques of bookshops (see, for example, Cabe, 2003). Although interview participants often insisted that libraries were not bookshops, wary of a wholesale implementation of a retail model, many services were using some of their promotional methods. One participant explained:

> We have done quite innovative things, for example, merging the reference library with the lending library and putting the adult non-fiction books into broader subject categories, just as if you walked into a Waterstone's bookshop. We still have the Dewey decimal system which staff are very precious about; the public aren't, it's meaningless to the public. As a result, what we have done here is make a more welcoming space. (Anon)

She also explained how a 'Quick Choice' section had been established near the front entrance of the central library, 'a bit like an airport bookshop' (Anon). Other participants, while agreeing that the retail sector had some good ideas about how to create a comfortable public environment felt that bookshops did not necessarily have all the answers as Miranda McKearney commented:

> I don't think we should be misled to think that bookshops have all the answers because I think we have some very, very powerful marketing tools and, of course, there's a lot

of debate in the book trade that the principle marketing tools that booksellers use is price. Libraries have loads of other things that they use. (Miranda McKearney)

Other participants agreed that public libraries and bookshops 'are not the same beasts' (Jan Holden), had different purposes and were not actually in competition with one another. One interviewee, commenting on the *Who's in Charge* report explained:

> I think [Tim Coates] is setting up libraries and bookshops as competitors and my view has always been, no, they're not, they're complementary. We've got all the evidence and research which [shows that] the majority of people who buy books [also] borrow books. It isn't a conflict. We have had some really good managers in our Waterstones on the corner there and when we've had good managers the synergy has been great because they've sent people to us, 'No, sorry that book's out of print but the chances are the library's got it' and we've said, 'No, that's a brand new book but if you don't want to wait, go to Waterstones'. So I've always seen there's been that synergy between the two and by working more closely together it could benefit a lot of people. (Anon)

Many of those participating in the research interviews acknowledged that falling issue figures were not good news for a service whose core purpose, or public and political perception of its core purpose, was related to the borrowing of books. It was often acknowledged, for example, that Tim Coates had been correct to raise the decline in issue figures the main challenge facing the public library service, one participant saying:

> I think [Tim Coates] is right, we do have to worry about issues declining because at the heart of the public library service is the book operation so if issues are going down dramatically all the time then it's a cause for concern. (Anon)

Nevertheless, while not complacent about declining issue figures, participants also stressed that issue figures were a very crude measurement of performance in this regard. One interviewee, echoing the opinion of the PricewaterhouseCoopers (2005) report that books are not everything, said:

> Libraries are about so much more that just issuing books so whilst it's a cause for concern, it's not necessarily an indication of, say, a failing library service because you've got simple things like virtual visits. What about the number of virtual visits? Probably increasing. And if you put the two together, you've probably got increased use; you can easily demonstrate increased use of the library service compared with ten years ago. And then, of course, you've got all the other things that libraries do, that people go in to use them for. So it's a balanced situation. Yes, we can't be complacent about book issues but, on the other hand, it's not the whole story. (Anon)

Other participants felt that issue figures did not reflect the quality of work that public libraries did around books and reading as Miranda McKearney pointed out:

> Are book issues the only way we want to measure the value of what public libraries are doing with reading? Which comes back to what you think they're there for. There's been

> a lot of work going on, consultation sessions around the country, about a SCL-led piece of work on a vision for libraries' work with readers and you've got library staff saying they want to see in that vision combating illiteracy as a key role. And, of course, very often that involves working with small groups of socially excluded people, incredibly intensive but it's a bit like preventative medicine. How do you measure the value of that work? (Miranda McKearney)

Others felt that issue figure did not adequately address people's patterns of use of books or of the library either, Geoffrey Smith going as far as to say, 'issue figures don't bother me that much because they reflect the whole pattern of people's reading and use of books and so on and so I'm not so worried about it' (Geoffrey Smith) while Moira Arthur pointed out that people use the book stock of the library in ways other that just borrowing:

> I don't know if issues are the main thing. I think [libraries] have felt that was the only way they could measure how successful they are and I know within quite a number of library authorities, they buy a lot of non-fiction; about 30 per cent of the stock is non-fiction. But the issues for non-fiction are much lower because kids might go into the library and then just look at the book in the library and not borrow it so it's actually quite difficult to estimate how much use these books are getting. (Moira Arthur)

Practical, logistical difficulties such as shorter opening hours have been offered as reasons why people are borrowing less from public libraries but others have suggested that it could be the quality of the book stock which deters people because, as reported in *Framework for the Future*, only 59 per cent of users find the book they came to the library to borrow or use. Similarly, the Audit Commission (2002) has suggested that user satisfaction figures raise the question of whether libraries have enough copies of the books that people want. Surveys of non-users invariably highlight stock quality and stock choice as reasons that people do not use public libraries although, as discussed in Chapter 4, lack of interest and need are generally the principal reasons for non-use. The most recent Select Committee enquiry into public libraries suggested that people are buying more books and borrowing fewer from public libraries because of the combination of the reduced price of books from a variety of different outlets on the one hand and the poor quality of book stocks in many public libraries on the other (Culture, Media and Sport Committee, 2005). The quality and quantity of supply would seem, on the face of it, to be clearly related to funding. The decline in the value of the book fund has been documented by LISU (Creaser et al., 2004) and the argument is often made that when savings are necessary, the book budget is an easy target. According to LISU, books now account for less than nine per cent of total public library expenditure compared with 17 to 18 per cent in the 1980s although 2002-03 saw an average increase of almost five per cent in expenditure. Nevertheless, the situation was considered so grave by the 2005 Select Committee on public libraries that it recommended that a 'substantial increase in the percentage of funding spent by each library authority on books should be a priority' (Culture, Media and Sport Committee, 2005, p. 20). Alan Hasson certainly believed that the link between declining issues and shrinking book funds was clear: 'The traditional core business, that's the lending of books, has been falling dramatically but it's been falling dramatically because the book fund has been cut dramatically' (Alan Hasson). Another participant agreed but was unsure whether an increase in the books funds of public libraries would increase book issues:

> Whether [higher spending on books] would reverse the trend I don't know. It probably would, we don't really know. It certainly doesn't help when you don't buy books; your issues are bound to go down… If you reduce the book fund so it's not so good, after about two years of course the stock gets very tired and stale and people are discouraged from coming and using it. It is important to keep buying new books, basically. (Anon)

It is interesting to note, though, that book issues began declining in the 1980s before severe cuts to the book fund began. Grindlay and Morris's (2004) statistical analysis of trends in public library borrowing and financing suggested that the decline in public library borrowing in the 1980s could not have been caused by cutbacks in book funds although they state that declining book issues in the 1990s did correspond with decreased expenditure on new library book stock. They further suggest that 'extrinsic factors' such as increasing affluence within society and households also play a major role in the decline of borrowing from public libraries. As suggested in Chapter 4, lifestyle trends were identified by many of those participating in the research interviews as a causal factor in declining library use and their impact on book borrowing and, therefore, issue figures was often highlighted.

One research participant suggested, 'I don't think it's as simple as just buying more books although I'd argue [for that] forever' (Anon) and a lot of discussion around this topic focused on the fact that as a society and as individuals, we are becoming increasingly affluent and acquisitive:

> The middle class and the affluent, we buy our books. I don't want a book that somebody else has mucked about with and hasn't been cleaned, I don't want to have to drive to the nearest library. (Frances Hendrix)

John Pateman agreed that increased affluence combined with better bookshops meant that 'we are not going to get [the public] back into the library queuing up for books'. Other developments in the book industry were also considered to have had an impact on public library borrowing as one participant explained, referring to Tim Coates' report which included a list of books which he felt all public libraries should stock:

> There has been a cultural shift. People are more acquisitive, better off, more people buy books and the evidence is there in the increasing book sales… And I thought it was very telling that in the *Who's in Charge?* report, these 10 books, litmus test kind of books, one of them was Jane Austen's *Sense and Sensibility*. Well, you could go into any of the bookshops and buy a copy for £1.20 which is roughly the reservation fee. The fact is I know that if I want to read classic literature, I go and buy a Penguin Classic for £1.20, I wouldn't dream of borrowing it from the library. They look nice on the shelves, they're quite attractive aren't they? I'm afraid that's the culture we're in; we're owners. When

> you look at the affordability factor, there was something the other day that compared the price of a popular novel 100 years ago [and] the average working man and how long it took him to earn it. Well, if we're talking about a paperback for £5 or £6, currently we're talking about an hour and half to earn that. A comparable figure in 1904 was something like 10 hours. Therefore, I think the public library service gets too hung up on the number of books it's issuing. (Anon)

Other participants, while accepting that there had been a cultural shift in people's attitude to books, felt that public libraries should not be defeatist, one saying:

> I think books have now become a commodity that people see, that they go out and buy rather than borrow. I think we need to remind people that they're paying for these services already and that we can offer a far greater choice than any bookshop can. (Anon)

Although there is a perception in some circles that public libraries have been abandoning books in favour of ICT provision and the pursuit of other policy priorities (see Coates, 2004, for example), *Framework for the Future* and work arising from its Action Plan confirms that books and reading should be at the heart of the public library's purpose. For Miranda McKearney this is reassuring but in some ways also exasperating and astonishing that a case has to be made for books and reading to be at the core of a vision of public libraries. In interview, talking about *Framework for the Future*, she said, 'I found it absolutely extraordinary that things have reached the stage where it was a relief to see books and reading there as a core purpose'. She also suggested that there was work to be done on showing public libraries how reading could help them deliver on many national and local government priorities and how it could be an advocacy tool for them. She gave the example of how the reading challenges and activities that take place in public libraries throughout the year but especially during vacations can help improve young people's life chances, encouraging them to engage with literature and so raising their achievement in schools. Lord Andrew McIntosh felt that demonstrating how this kind of activity contributed to policy priorities was one way of protecting the book fund. In his written response he explained:

> It is sad but, I fear, true that some authorities have seen the book fund as a soft option when savings are being sought. Getting local politicians to understand the importance of, for example, reading programmes undertaken by libraries is one part of our approach to this difficulty. (Lord Andrew McIntosh)

Some of these points have been picked up on by MLA in their leaflet *A Quiet Revolution* (MLA, 2004a). Here, the value of reading and how it contributes to the Shared Priorities agreed between local and national government is made clear. Public library work with young people and books, encouraging them to see reading as empowering, relevant and fun, can help raise standards in schools. Reading can improve the quality of life for a range of socially excluded groups and promote a sense of well-being as well as provide valuable advice of a range of health and lifestyle related topics, so promoting healthier communities and reducing health inequalities. By stressing the importance of reading and books, MLA is validating the valuable work undertaken over the years by organizations such as The Reading Agency and Opening the Book. It also serves as a springboard for further work and interest in books and reading, establishing public libraries as 'the foremost mediators of fiction' (Greenhalgh and Worpole, 1995, p. 132). To that end, MLA has also commissioned research into different stock procurement models to analyse whether public libraries can acquire stock more efficiently and effectively.

Stock Management in Public Libraries

The importance of holding the right quality and quantity of stock for users' needs cannot be underestimated. Stock is, according to the National Acquisitions Group (1998, p. 4), 'the lifeblood of a public library service'. As the library's stock is its key asset, its selection and subsequent management should be of the utmost priority. Librarians do not have a free hand, of course, in deciding what their libraries should stock. Selection decisions must meet the needs of the community, first and foremost, and, because they are a public service, they must also be taken in the light of local and national political priorities. Unfortunately, there seems to have been little evidence of such a systematic approach to stock management in public libraries over the years. The Audit Commission (1997) urged public libraries to focus on users' needs rather than pursuing 'the Holy Grail of comprehensive coverage' as Anne Ollier put it in interview but many of the judgements made about stock are taken quickly (Opening the Book, 2004) and many 'are still made, to a large extent, intuitively' (Kerr, 2001, p. 3). Although the days are over when, according to Anne Ollier, you could tell a lot about the branch librarian's personal interests by looking at the book stock in that library, stock management in some library services is still quite unmethodical.

Interview participants were divided on this issue. Cuts to the book budget have resulted in services trying to make the stock they are able to buy work harder. Reader development work is relevant here and is discussed more fully below but stock rotation was also the key to more effective and efficient use of the book stock for many participants, one explaining:

> We're using the books we buy more sensibly. A lot of that is to do with the development of library management systems and the ability to circulate stock so we're buying a wider range; because you circulate it, you can take risks. Our system will tell you after six months. You check in and it says this book is due to move to so and so. Five to six thousand books a week move that way. (Anon)

There are still concerns, however, that public library stock management and particularly selection is inefficient and an in-depth review of public library stock procurement in English public libraries, funded by MLA has been undertaken by consultants PKF who were appointed to review the supply chain for acquiring books in libraries, establish the real cost of stock supply in public libraries, analyse the costs and benefits of models currently used and suggest best practice models (PKF, 2005). Their report concluded that 'efficiency gains and better value for money could be found, largely by library services throughout the country adopting the same processes and by purchasing books together' (p. 4). A paper from Bertram's Library Services also suggested that there was considerable scope for efficiency savings through the outsourcing of various library supply operations (Bertram Library Services, 2005). By using supplier selection (discussed below), supplier-maintained information systems, delivery directly to branches rather than a central point and stock supplied in standard format, Bertram's estimates that library services could make saving of 50–100 per cent of their book funds annually in areas such as staffing, transport, information systems and stock processing. Such conclusions from a company whose business is to service public libraries and their stock needs are hardly surprising, though. Tim Coates was also very critical of stock acquisition and management processes in *Who's in Charge* (Coates, 2004), calling them 'extremely cumbersome' (p. 21) and suggesting that they adopt the systems of the commercial bookselling industry. Anne Ollier suggested in interview, though, that there were different constraints on public libraries:

> One of the frequent criticisms is that [public libraries] don't get their books on the shelves on time [but]... we have to prepare them for loan, they can't just put these books out without having the date stamp or whatever in. That's a very typical constraint. Also, there's a growing trend in the publishing world now, and I'm focusing on fiction, to place embargoes for the public [library sector] so we don't stand a cat's chance in hell in getting them to people by publication date. Now, we're offering special services to over-ride that but they do come at a price because they have a cost to us, of course. So we try desperately and we'll continue to try desperately to compete with the bookshops in terms of speed of supply. (Anne Ollier)

As well as being as efficient as possible, the selection of stock in public libraries must be responsive to users needs but one study estimated that as much as 50 per cent of library services did not have or did not use market data and information when making selection decisions (Muir and Fishwick, 2000). This view was supported by some participants and although, as we have seen in previous chapters, some library services are making a real effort to involve members of the community in decisions about their local library services, Miranda McKearney still felt that the picture was 'patchy' although she did acknowledge that, 'there are examples where authorities are working closely with their users to look very radically really at the stock' and added:

> Time and time again when library authorities take young people on book buying expeditions, they're amazed by the depth of thought and responsibility that even very, very disaffected young people show. So [there's a] big message there about being able to trust your users. (Miranda McKearney)

For public library services today, stock means so much more than just books, of course. CDs, DVDs, videos and computer games are all available for loan alongside the fiction and non-fiction books. Although these developments may be lamented by those who, according to Greenhalgh and Worpole (1995), regret the move that libraries have made into stocking other media formats fearing books will be 'edged out by videos and compact discs' (p. 141), the incorporation of new forms of communication is a logical development for a service seeking to remain relevant to a variety of communities and their needs. In fact, the 1964 Act states that public libraries should provide a wide range of materials for the public to borrow including:

> …books and other printed materials and pictures, gramophone records, films and other materials, sufficient in number, range and quality to meet the general requirements and any special requirements both of adults and children. (Great Britain, 1964, section 7(2)(a))

This chapter will focus on public library work with books and reading material, though, in recognition of the attention paid recently to this aspect of the service and developments in public libraries' approach to reader development as well as the ongoing debate about the kinds of reading material public libraries should stock.

The 'Fiction Question'

Concern about the 'fiction question' or 'fiction nuisance' is as old as public libraries themselves. The first public librarians' disquiet about the public's appetite for novels, generally regarded as a trivial and inferior form of reading material (Sturges and Barr, 1992), remained a feature of professional debate throughout the twentieth century. In the 1950s, Hoggart questioned what proportions of public library issues were 'of worthless fiction' (Hoggart, 1958, p. 276), noting that between 75 and 80 per cent of public library issues were fiction and adding, 'most librarians would say, I think, that much of this fiction is of a very poor kind' (p. 276). In 1995, Robert Snape's account of *Leisure and the Rise of the Public Library* tracked the origins and development of the 'fiction question', suggesting that it had had a significant effect on the development of the public library services and that it was still unresolved (Snape, 1995). Although there might still be some concerns about the provision of light, recreational fiction in public libraries today, few would question the presence of large stocks of fiction books in libraries and the reader development movement has legitimized the reading of a whole range of different materials, stressing the benefits that individuals can gain from books which speak personally to them. The 2005 Select Committee report, for example, stresses that, for public library services, 'the notion of simply reading for pleasure must be fundamental' (Culture, Media and Sport Committee, 2005, p. 19). Greenhalgh and Worpole (1995) suggest, though, that, '[t]he overwhelming popularity of genre fiction … continues to cause embarrassment among some librarians' (p. 130).

The key issue, according to some, is whether the public library book lending service should be quality or demand driven. Although this debate was of enormous concern to the pioneers of the public library service in the United Kingdom in the late nineteenth and early twentieth centuries, it does not seem to have been the focus of attention here in recent times and was not mentioned in many of the interviews for this study although one participant did question the stock buying policies of some public library services, saying:

> OK, put more money in books but [libraries] keep buying Mills and Boon and stupid fiction. OK, it's good to read but is it always good for people to read more of what they always read? (Shiraz Durrani)

Another, though, felt that librarians should not make a distinction between 'good' and 'bad' types of reading:

> There's been a slightly snobby divide, I think, between [users of ICT] and people who read 'proper' books and I think what we need to be looking at is beginning to bridge that gap so that people who read online aren't seen as lesser citizens than people who read books or people who read fiction. (John Vincent)

The lack of recent focus on the 'fiction question' in the UK is in stark contrast to professional debates taking place in the United States where the libertarian approach to public library services is increasingly questioned. McCabe (2001), while acknowledging that popular fiction has an important community building function, also stresses that its role should be balanced with the public library's educational functions, commenting, '[a] simple surrender to the demand approach to selection will clearly degrade the mission of the public library' (p. 150). Defining 'quality' in relation to the public library book stock is difficult and controversial. In the United States, there is an ongoing debate in the library profession and more widely about what people should be reading with some in favour of the value of traditional, 'serious literature' (Hafner and Mick, 1993, p. 67). Accepting that the literary canon is ethnocentric and 'codifies, perpetuates and privileges the values of an Anglo-American male elite' (Folker and Hafner, 1993, p. 57), some commentators nevertheless maintain the value of 'great books' which 'participate in humanity's great conversation about the questions of the human mind and the longings of the human heart' (Hafner and Mick, 1993, p. 67).

As suggested above, these debates have not been a strong feature of recent discussions around public library book stock in the United Kingdom although the issue of quality has been raised. The 2001 Public Library Standards promised the development of 'quality' indicators for public library book stocks, for example. These did not transpire and instead, library services are being encouraged to use the *Stock Quality Health Check*, developed by the reader development training and consultation firm Opening the Book. In the UK, the debate over quality seems to revolve increasingly around the depth, breadth and variety of the book stock and the stock selection policies and practices needed to ensure that libraries hold books which appeal to a broad range of users.

A Balanced Collection

Opening the Book developed the *Stock Quality Health Check* on behalf of the Audit Commission in 2000. Used initially for Best Value inspections, the *Stock*

Quality Health Check has been updated and adapted into a self-assessment tool, enabling public libraries to evaluate 'the relevance, depth and range of stock they hold in relation to the profile of the communities they serve' (Audit Commission, 2004, p. 2). The tool aims to assist public libraries develop a balanced book stock which caters for all audiences. Rather than relying on a 'literary merit' definition of quality, the *Stock Quality Health Check* defines a quality collection as 'as one which covers the whole range of fiction' (Opening the Book, 2004, p. 7). The *Health Check* supplies a list of sample titles and, by checking the range of those titles available on its catalogue and the number of copies available, a library service should obtain a clear picture of the balance of its collection. The *Health Check* makes it clear that the list of individual titles should not be seen as a 'definitive' list or literary canon that every library should stock. Rather, it has been compiled to test certain aspects of collections to see where collections are falling short or where certain audiences are being neglected, for example.

The library services which participated in piloting the *Health Check* reported positive results (Audit Commission, 2004). The analysis proved helpful in providing an overview of stock held and imbalances in collections, showing in which areas of stock or genres services were overbuying and under buying and also for demonstrating the breadth of reading interest within the library-using public. All the pilot library authorities cited by the Audit Commission (2004) stressed the need to widen the range of fiction provided as the *Health Check* gave them hard evidence that there was over-provision of some types of fiction within their collection. As suggested above, it has been said that public library stock policies are unadventurous, designed to satisfy the needs of existing users rather than trying to attract new ones. Opening the Book (2004) comments that '[m]any stock policies are rather bland summaries which provide little help in practice' (p. 21). This can result in cautious selection as can selection processes. According to Opening the Book (2004), the results of the *Health Check* can provide library services with much food for thought including an examination of who undertakes stock selection, how and from where and suggests that a variety of practices can lead to conservatism in selection.

One interview participant felt, though, that lack of money and public demand channelled through branch library staff rather than selection practices led to narrow public library book stocks. She explained:

> I think if we had more money we'd take more risks but we can't afford to trim back [on best sellers] because [the public] expect the new books at the same time as [WH] Smiths. And every library will say, 'we need our own copy of this' and it's a real argument to say, 'no, sorry, we've got to provide a range', [when staff say], 'our readers don't want a range, they want the latest copy sitting in their library.' (Anon)

Moira Arthur agreed that public libraries were working within a range of constraints which were not applicable to bookshops, saying:

> I spoke to Tim Coates last week and I said to him then it's OK saying [libraries] should be more like a bookshop but bookshops can be as daring as they like, they can take anything

> and everything and what doesn't sell, they just ship it right back to the publisher. Libraries can't do that. So from the actual selection viewpoint, they've got to be much more focused, I think, they can't just buy everything and anything. (Moira Arthur)

Although a lot of attention has been focused on the selection of new stock, libraries hold a huge range of resources which perhaps could be used to better effect.

The Back Catalogue

The focus on acquiring new stock and current titles which will appeal to those who might have abandoned the public library because of its lack of up-to-date stock might have an impact on the back catalogue of public libraries. Chapman, Creaser and Spiller (2000) found that the vast majority of acquisitions (75 to 85 per cent) was made in the year of publication or the year following and that the proportion of 'older' material acquired by public libraries was small and 'rather disconcerting' (p. 309). Citing research evidence that many of the books sought by the public from public libraries were standard works with a long history, the authors suggested that stock revision should draw on the whole range of titles available, not just new stock, but concluded that little stock revision is actually going on at all in public libraries.

It has also been suggested that libraries should perhaps give up on trying to compete with bookshops on the provision of a wide range of contemporary literary fiction and instead focus on providing for those who want something out of the ordinary. The public library service, with its local and national networks, has access to a huge backlist of out of date, out of print and out of fashion material and some would argue that instead of obsessing about providing a balanced bookstock of sufficient depth and breadth and providing the newest best sellers, the public library service should concentrate its efforts on capitalizing on this valuable resource.

Interview participants, while agreeing with some elements of this argument, generally rejected this view, however, and felt that public libraries must continue to try to provide a breadth of reading material to meet the needs of all in the community. Geoffrey Smith insisted that such a strategy would not 'match the expectations of the user' who expected to see 'the out of print stuff but on the other hand they want to see the Booker prize winners and an ever changing collection of interesting books on the shelves, not dry as dust stuff' (Geoffrey Smith). Martin Molloy suggested that public libraries had a duty to provide access to as wide a range of fiction as possible:

> When you're talking, particularly, about new fiction especially hardback, some of it, unless it's picked up by something like Quality Paperback is never going to appear anywhere other than in hardback. If you didn't have libraries providing that, whole chunks of the population would never read anything. (Martin Molloy)

Miranda McKearney agreed that libraries had to capitalize on their Unique Selling Propositions (USPs) but that, 'library USPs around reading shouldn't reside in not having contemporary literature' (Miranda McKearney), Another interview participant similarly insisted that public libraries had to try to provide a wide a range of stock within funding constraints:

> We've had huge success with schemes like On Approval where we've got multiple popular paperbacks but they're not the top 30 [in the fiction bestsellers lists]. And actually, if you looked at the top 30, they're not the highest issues in our libraries and people want the breadth. If we focused all our money into these top 30 we would lose the breadth of the stock that we have that actually appeals to such a diverse community and we would, like many bookshops, only get a small proportion of the population in them and the rest go to specialist booksellers because they're after specialist books. (Anon)

Anne Ollier also felt that, as far as the provision of books was concerned, public libraries should continue to try to be all things to all people and that librarians should try to make links between new titles and existing stock:

> As a bookseller, I do have a biased view on this! I think there's a role for both. I think if libraries are going to encourage people in, they've got to do something better than just have odd stuff in, if they're going to grow their usage. I think they can entice people in by proving that they're up to date and can supply what the public want and use that as a springboard then, to persuade people to go and look at different things. This is the role of librarians, knowing what their book stock is and being able to guide people and say, 'Well, you enjoyed this one, how about having a look at this? This author writes in a very similar way'. (Anne Ollier)

Selection Practices

In response to criticisms from the Audit Commission as well as internal pressures to make the most of their book funds, public libraries have sought to increase the effectiveness and efficiency of their selection methods. The traditional approvals method, by which large numbers of new titles are physically transported to the local authority for librarians to choose which they would like to add to stock, is increasingly being supplemented, if not replaced, by methods considered more efficient. In 1998, an investigation by Capital Planning Information (CPI) revealed that although public libraries were using approvals for a high proportion of their stock, librarians felt that there were other viable and more efficient alternatives for many categories of books (Capital Planning Information, 1998). At the time, it was still considered important to personally view adult non-fiction and children's books before purchase although many of those participating in the CPI study felt that 80 per cent of what they were buying was 'inescapable' (p. 9), that is, the vast majority of their purchases were best sellers and genre fiction that they had to buy to meet customer expectations. In these cases, they were keen to find more efficient methods of making those inevitable purchases, so leaving them more time to devote to the remaining 20 per cent of stock which demanded closer scrutiny.

Selection by CD-Rom and the Internet The CPI study was undertaken some time ago now and, given the increasing interest in public library stock management, the pressure of the book fund and the comments made above about balance of stock and over-provision in some areas, it is likely that librarians are no longer quite so complacent about that 80 per cent of 'inescapable' stock. Nevertheless, librarians are still keen to find more cost-effective methods of selecting new books and this has led to the development of selection by CD-Rom, online selection via the Internet and supplier selection. The first two of these work on the same premise; that instead of physically seeing the book in an approvals collections or in a library supplier's showroom, images of the title and information about it are made available on a computer screen. Development of the technology has been rapid so that the conclusions of a report from 2000 on book purchasing by public libraries already seem very outdated in some respects (Muir and Fishwick, 2000). Then, the authors concluded that the relative cost of approvals versus selection by CD-Rom for libraries was impossible to calculate but, as much of the cost derived from the time taken to actually view and select books, there was unlikely to be a great deal of difference between selecting a book on screen and from an approvals collection. It was suggested that other savings, in staff time to pack and unpack books and in travelling to meetings, would probably be more than made up for by the cost of IT development and networking. For the suppliers, the researchers concluded that any savings made in ceasing to transport approvals could be lost as library services demanded larger discounts, although these were by no means guaranteed.

The development and wider availability of technology since the publication of this report is likely to have had a huge impact on practice. Selection at a distance, without physically seeing and handling the books, is now widely accepted. When first introduced, many librarians were opposed to the concept, believing that there was no substitute for hands-on selection and that the information provided on the CD-Rom was insufficient to make informed judgements. Others argued that the amount of time a librarian making a selection from an approvals collection could spend looking at each individual title was very limited anyway and at least on the CD-Rom, information was standardized and readily available. Some still maintain that it is important to evaluate some categories of books, for example children's books, in person but, generally, opposition has dissipated, probably as the technology has developed and improved. In fact, CD-Rom is now old technology. In interview, Anne Ollier of Holt Jackson Library Services said that she had discontinued their CD-Rom selection service in 2003 because they could offer a better service through their website. She felt that this type of selection could free librarians to focus on more interesting aspects of stock work:

> We've taken a lot of the drudgery out of the acquisitions processes and also selection processes as well. Our website brings selection and acquisition together into one role and that could create savings for our customers to focus more. As a librarian, I was never quite sure what my role was in the library. I felt we were trying to do so many things and you spread yourself too thin. Maybe librarians could focus on this promotion of reading as a core role for them to take on [and] there are signs that this is happening. (Anne Ollier)

Supplier selection Supplier selection is another method through which library services are trying to increase the efficiency of their selection processes. Not without controversy, supplier selection entails library services engaging the services of the supplier to choose certain areas of new stock for them. According to a paper from Bertram's Library Services, supplier selection entails library services trusting suppliers to do 'what they do best – and what they do best includes selecting and sourcing the most appropriate product range for their customers' (Bertram Library Services, 2005, p. 5). This was endorsed by the PKF (2005) report on public library stock procurement which recommended that suppliers select books for public libraries so that 'all but a very small amount of materials should be selected by suppliers (who employ professional librarians) with library services holding back minimal sums for additional local items' (p. 5).

When selecting books for public libraries, suppliers are guided by community or site profiles and detailed specifications for stock requirements which lay out exactly how many books are required, in what category and format. A study which investigated the feasibility and potential advantages of supplier selection at the end of the 1990s concluded that supplier selection was practicable but robust planning and policy mechanisms were essential (Capital Planning Information, 1999). The study found that those library services participating in pilot supplier selection schemes anticipated a range of benefits including the release of staff time from the selection of current titles, enabling them to focus on other stock management work. It was also hoped that the suppliers' selectors had access to better information through their contacts with publishers and that this would enable them to place orders early enough to guarantee supply ahead of release date. This last anticipated benefit did not transpire and although, overall, it was concluded that supplier selection could work, neither of the two authorities participating in the pilot continued with it at the time.

Since the late 1990s, though, many authorities have adopted supplier selection for all or part of their stock and have experienced a range of benefits. Bertram Library Services suggests that suppliers are 'better placed than any individual librarian to understand current and future trends in publishing and reading' (Bertram Library Services, 2005, p. 9). Liverpool public library service, for example, which uses Bertram's for supplier selection and piloted the *Stock Quality Health Check*, attributed much of its success with the model to its use of supplier selection, commenting that the range and depth of coverage of adult fiction on those areas of stock selected by their supplier (independent publishers and male appeal) were impressive. It was also found that those areas of stock still selected in-house did not perform as well in the *Health Check* (Branching Out, no date). Aside from the *Health Check*, Liverpool libraries have had a 24 per cent increase in issues since Bertram's has managed their stock selection and the number of readers' requests satisfied from libraries within Liverpool has risen significantly (Bertram Library Services, 2005). The paper from Bertram's concludes (perhaps unsurprisingly) that supplier selection has been a success for Liverpool library service which was able to redirect resources to extend opening hours and allow staff to spend more time with users.

Others are more wary of supplier selection and are concerned about the practice from both professional and practical viewpoints. While many argue that the practice leaves public library staff free to concentrate on developmental work, others would protest that the quality control of selection decisions is now out of the hands of staff trained to provide a varied stock and who have intimate knowledge of their local community and its needs. The move towards supplier selection may have intensified the trend towards the purchase of newer material as established by Chapman et al. (2000), for example, and may also favour certain subject areas, such as biographies, potentially leading to an unbalanced stock. One participant disagreed with the notion that supplier selection was more cost efficient for her service and, whilst acknowledging that some services were very happy with the practice, said that her library service could select stock more cheaply. Miranda McKearney also felt that the use of supplier selection could lead to a conservative range of books within the public library, saying that she felt that some services were 'constrained by contracts with suppliers putting in mainstream stuff' (Miranda McKearney).

Geoffrey Smith was of the opinion that supplier selection had 'loosened up' the relationship between suppliers and librarians, adding, 'if nothing else, it's shown selectors, particularly fiction selectors, that librarians haven't necessarily got all the information or ideas' (Geoffrey Smith). Other developments in the book and library supply industries have also changed the relationship between suppliers and libraries.

Relationships with Library Suppliers

The library supply sector has been experiencing upheaval since the 1990s. Although many cite the end of the Net Book Agreement (NBA) in 1995 as a turning point in library/supplier relations, Gray (1998) states that UK library supply was in turmoil before this with retrenchment, mergers and a search for efficiency gains on both sides of the supplier chain. The ending of the NBA, which supported a system of resale price maintenance on books preventing bookshops selling books below the price fixed by the publishers, has had a profound effect on the relationship between library suppliers and their customers. The most dramatic effect has been in the nature of the discounts now demanded by library customers, under pressure to make the most of their book funds. The competition this price-driven market has stimulated within the library supply sector has been too fierce for some to weather leading to closures and mergers with the result that there are now just five or six main library suppliers in the UK.

Geoffrey Smith was clear that the end of the NBA had:

> '…forced the issue of discounting. It was really the Net Book Agreement that forced the change. It was tentative before but with the Net Book Agreement going, well, you get what you pay for and now librarians are beginning to realize that.' (Geoffrey Smith)

One librarian participating in the interviews confirmed this, saying that the abolition of the NBA had not been 'as disastrous as had been thought' and adding that, as a result of discounts, libraries had lost:

> …those little things that library suppliers churned out and thought you wanted. Now it's much more business-like, quite fun really. It makes you think about what you want [because] you have to pay for it. So, yes, [the abolition of the NBA] had an effect but I think we are getting better value for money now. (Anon)

This participant also said that she had the impression that discounts were now levelling out and Moira Arthur said that, from the library supplier's point of view, something had to give:

> We turn up at review meetings and authorities will say to us, 'Right, what about reader development? What can you do for us? We want author events, we want these authors, we want you to pay for them, you'll pay their expenses won't you?' And we say, 'Well, no, that's why you're getting extra discounts'… And what we're finding is that discounts have risen but libraries still want promotions and in fact they want us to be very pro-active and, to be honest, there is no extra for that. (Moira Arthur)

The search for ever larger discounts to make the book fund stretch further has also led to the forming of purchasing consortia which can be a mixed blessing for the library suppliers. On the one hand, winning a consortium tender to supply books can give a supplier a contract worth millions of pounds of business. On the other hand, because of the business the consortium is giving the supplier, ever larger discounts are demanded. A study of library purchasing consortia in the UK reported that most consortia seem to command a minimum 20 per cent discount on UK-published books which could rise to 30 per cent, a level considered unviable by some in the book trade (Ball and Friend, 2001). The relationship between suppliers and customers has changed significantly with the establishment of consortia and is now increasingly based around a short-term contract approach rather than long-term, guaranteed customer loyalty (Ball and Pye, 2000). Bertram Library Services (2005) which supplies the Central Buying Consortium (CBC), the largest local authority purchasing consortium in the UK, asserts that there is a range of benefits to be gained by library services working in a consortium. Larger discounts are possible and the speed of supply is increased so that those titles in stock at the supplier can be processed, despatched and delivered to the customer within 72 hours of being ordered, comparable, they suggest, to retail sector replenishment timescales.

Consortia should, and in some cases do, lower costs for both suppliers and library services but, according to Moira Arthur in interview, most of the public library consortia are not actually true consortia but a group of library authorities who have got together for the purpose of acquiring larger discounts:

> A consortium, in library terms, is a group of libraries who get together to work exactly in the way that they have done in the past individually but then turn up with a tender that

> says, 'We've got X million pounds to spend' so then they want more discount, 'We deserve extra discount.' (Moira Arthur)

Each member of the consortium still maintains its own servicing instructions (e.g. reinforcing, adding bar codes, categorization or classification schemes etc.), processing requirements, delivery points and promotion requirements, all of which raise costs for the supplier. Although the National Acquisitions Group (NAG) has worked hard to promote the concept of a single national standard for book servicing (National Acquisitions Group, 2003), it has had mixed success. The PKF (2005) report on public library procurement insisted that 'it is essential that library services adopt standard processes if any real efficiency gains are to be made' (p. 5) and also recommended that, in the absence of a national purchasing agency, all library services should join consortia to benefit from the best available discounts.

Lord Andrew McIntosh in his written response said that the DCMS was keen 'to try to ensure that authorities get the best value they can for their "buck"' (Lord Andrew McIntosh) and combining with other library services in consortia or partnership is one way that library services feel they can achieve this. One participant clarified the savings this allowed the library service he worked for and also explained the anger he felt when commentators like Tim Coates complained about the inefficiency of public library stock management processes:

> Because we've got the buying power of [a large neighbouring authority] alongside us, we command much bigger discounts than we would otherwise so it's something we always feel a bit cross about when we read national reports such as from the Audit Commission and the recent Libri one saying, 'Oh libraries are spending an awful lot of money per item'. We actually get very large discounts and we're making very effective use of the book fund. (Anon)

Some participants felt that purchasing consortia were a mixed blessing for the library supply industry and therefore for public libraries, one interviewee explaining:

> The consortia thing concerns me. Large consortia, if they move their business away from [a supplier], that leaves the supplier going under, effectively, and there's not a lot of them left anyway and you need that competition. (Anon)

As Anne Ollier suggested, 'it makes it a difficult, volatile market that you're operating in now with the forming of consortia' (Anne Ollier).

The other development that has transformed library supply is EDI (electronic data interchange). Public library services are turning to EDI for book ordering in increasing numbers for efficiency and effectiveness reasons, a very different situation from just a few years ago when Muir (2000, p. 224) concluded that, 'the use of EDI remains at very low levels in the public library sector'. EDI enables a library service to send standard order information directly to a supplier's system without the need for the supplier to manually re-input that information. Similarly, once an order has been fulfilled, the supplier can send invoice information directly to the library service as well as full bibliographic details which, again, can be transferred directly onto the library's system without the need to re-key the information. Moira Arthur, in an email following her interview, suggested that the number of authorities with no EDI capability now 'could almost be counted on the fingers of one hand'. Similarly, Anne Ollier reported that there has been a rapid take up of EDI messaging driven by the growing adoption of web based selection tools. There are still constraints on the use of EDI, however, the main one being the capability of the library management system used because not all can support the full suite of messages. Moira Arthur also indicated that there is quite a wide variation in library services' ability to take advantage of all the services offered so that while some are just using EDI to transmit orders, others, albeit a minority, are moving on to the 'Quotes' message which enables them to add order information to their acquisitions systems, potentially saving them a lot of work. EDI invoicing is also in the pipeline and although in its infancy, Moira Arthur said that she envisaged that quite a number of library authorities would be moving to EDI invoicing in the very near future.

Despite the low take up reported in 2000, the benefits for both public libraries and suppliers were clear in Muir's study even at that time and although some system problems remain, the falling cost of the hardware and software necessary to support EDI must have made the benefits even clearer. Muir (2000) concluded that library services could make substantial savings through the use of EDI through simplifying the administration of orders, deliveries and payments and through savings in labour costs. In fact, Anne Ollier said in interview that one library service had calculated that it had saved the equivalent of four staff years in their acquisitions department, that is, four people over one year. Another participant estimated that EDI saved her service a week in ordering time. For library suppliers there are also staff savings to be made in not having to re-key order information received from customers (Muir, 2000). The speed and accuracy of EDI, the access to more up-to-date information and the closer links between customers and suppliers that EDI facilitate were also mentioned by Muir (2000) as substantial benefits to be gained from using the technology.

The above discussion has outlined all the ways in which library services and library suppliers are trying to make stock available for public libraries users. Increasingly, though, as book funds become squeezed, library services also need to exploit that stock to its full potential and that is where reader development has a role to play.

Reader Development

Reader development and stock promotion activities are an increasingly important part of stock management but they are treated separately here for convenience. According to MLA (2004b, slide 9), '[r]eading or reader development describes the active way libraries and others work to create the best possible reading experience for everyone'. As we have seen, public library fiction lending services have the overwhelming support of the general public and are of real value as evidenced by Usherwood and Toyne (2002) among others. It could be argued that appreciation of this very important aspect of public library service was a little unclear in the early and mid 1990s, however, with the increasing focus on ICT. The claim seemed to be that facilitating public access to information and communications technology would be the saviour of the public library service in the United Kingdom, and falling issue figures seemed to confirm the prognosis that public libraries needed more than just books to attract the public through the door. A variety of witnesses to the 2005 Select Committee Inquiry into public libraries (Culture, Media and Sport Committee, 2005), for example, argued that public librarians have been focusing their attention and spending on ICT services to the detriment of book-related services and facilities. This is actually far from the truth and although there is concern that all the focus on ICT had diverted attention away from the core business of books, there has been enormous interest and even government money going into fiction promotion and reader development activities over the last decade too.

The DCMS/Wolfson Public Libraries Challenge Fund was established in July 1997 and ran for five years, funding a range of innovative projects designed to enhance the facilities and services of public libraries in England. In 1998/99 and 1999/2000 the awards focused on developing their ICT facilities but in 2000/2001 and 2001/2002, projects focusing on reader development activities and initiatives were funded. Thirty-three awards were made in 2000/2001 and 16 in 2001/2002, funding projects which aimed to enhance libraries' traditional strength in promoting reading as a skill and a pleasure and also to reach new audiences, particularly socially excluded groups.[4] An evaluation of the 2000/2001 scheme concluded that it had been extremely successful at stimulating new reader development initiatives and services in the short-term but that sustainability and long-term funding was a problem facing many of the projects (Wallis et al., 2002). The report also suggested that there was evidence that the reader development work being funded by the Challenge Fund was not being embedded in mainstream library activity. A follow-up impact study undertaken in 2003 painted a more optimistic picture, however, finding that many of the benefits emerging from the projects such as reaching new audiences, increasing library use, developing partnership and staff development had been sustained by most of those participating (Book Marketing Limited, 2003). Only a third of respondents to the study felt that reader development work had increased or had become more mainstream in their services as a result of the projects, though. As well as government investment in this area, other external funding has also been important in developing activities and initiatives. The Paul Hamlyn Foundation established a Reading and Library Challenge Fund in 2002 to 'try to affect long term change to the way libraries and other institutions work with young people and others with limited access to books, reading and other library services' (Paul Hamlyn Foundation, 2005, online resource). Focusing on socially excluded groups such as children in care, asylum seekers and refugees, young people at risk and prisoners, the scheme will run until 2006 and expects to award £3 million over the period 2003–2006.

Study participants were enthusiastic about reader development work in public libraries and were committed to maintaining and extending it. Martin Molloy, for example, when asked whether he thought reader development activity had led to a renaissance in the way public libraries approach fiction replied:

> Definitely, there's no question of that. I think the sad thing is that it's taken people who are not librarians to lead us back to where we were. I could go on about this for a long time because I always believe this is bizarre, that librarians who were very good at telling people about books because they read the books, suddenly abandoned that because they became managers and they thought, 'Well managers don't do this'. We gave away our strength really. (Martin Molloy)

Another participant similarly felt that public libraries were rediscovering a purpose that had become lost:

> In the sense of reader development coming back in, well it's rather heartening for old fashioned librarians like me, it's heartening to see libraries returning to their roots really because a few years ago, ten years ago I suppose, they didn't do any of this reader development stuff and yet that is at the core and that's got to be important for a literate nation. (Anon)

Substantial effort and investment is going into work with books in public libraries, therefore, and this section will first review some developments in public libraries' work with adult readers before considering how they are reaching out to a younger audience.

Developing Adult Readers

Although the development of ICT systems and services has undoubtedly become a very important issue for public libraries in the UK, the expansion of reader development and fiction promotion work has also continued apace. There is a perception, though, that until recently library staff working with adult fiction have been slightly reluctant to promote fiction as dynamically as children's librarians have long been doing. The disinclination to approach fiction promotion and the development of adult readers' breadth of reading material in a similar way to that of children's may be the result of a number of perceptions on the part of librarians working with adult users. They may feel that reading is a very private activity, for example, and worry about patronizing readers by suggesting alternative reading material. The wide choice of reading matter in public libraries can be bewildering for adult readers, though, and, increasingly, public librarians are realizing that development activities can help those who do not know what they want to read find something they are willing to try. The widespread recognition that public libraries have a lot of valuable experience to offer in this regard has led to something of a sea change (Niven, 1992) in the way that librarians think about their work with adult readers of fiction. In conjunction with organizations such as MLA, Opening the Book and The Reading Agency, public libraries have been developing innovative methods of encouraging people to widen their horizons through the reading of fiction and also developing a clear vision of their role in the reading agenda and how that role can be realized. One interview participant echoed the comments made above about libraries rediscovering their role in this area and also highlighted the strategic approach that library services were taking towards this aspect of their service, taking a side swipe at Tim Coates' suggestion that libraries were abandoning their book-related activities, in the process:

> Where has the man been if he has missed the commitment to reader development and reading development? I think that's the ground we have recovered in the last five or six years. We were, I think, probably the first public library to appoint a Reader Development Officer, we have two now. But we have also embedded reading development and book promotion in the operational teams. We have always done a pretty good job with children's literature but the trick has been to move it into adult and harder-to-reach categories. (Anon)

Policy and strategy Much of the work around reading development has focused on developing and supporting national reading-related initiatives in public libraries as well as producing advocacy material and training library staff in key aspects of reader development work. Training is considered essential as proactively promoting fiction to adult readers is quite a new venture for many public library staff. Although promotion in the form of displays, book lists and author visits have long been common methods that public librarians have used in an attempt to attract interest for their collections, lean times for public services have meant that librarians have had to make their book stock work harder and this has led to increasing interest in innovative ways of engaging the reading public and so improving the circulation of stock. Economy and efficiency are not the only imperatives behind the rising interest in reader development work, however, and The Reading Agency's report on the development of reading groups lists the value of reading groups for individual readers and for libraries, many of which apply to reader development work more generally (The Reading Agency, 2004b). For the individual, public libraries have a mission to facilitate access to works of the imagination for individuals' personal development and to promote reading as a meaningful and satisfying recreational activity. For libraries, reader development work can help them serve the community better and develop the library audience, raise their profile, challenge stereotypes and deliver on a range of policy agendas including literacy, learning, creativity, community cohesion and healthy living.

As noted above, *Framework for the Future* emphasized that the ability to read brings with it a range of practical and psychological benefits (Department for Culture, Media and Sport, 2003) and its Action Plan sets out a number of objectives and priorities for public libraries to ensure that awareness of the support public libraries can offer readers is widespread and that they build and take advantage of partnerships to 'provide stimulating and contemporary reading experiences for adults' (MLA, 2004c, p. 18). A range of partners and stakeholders are listed as having a contribution to make to this element of the Action Plan including the Arts Council, the Learning and Skills Trust and the National Literacy Trust, and The Reading Agency takes the lead on many of the actions listed including establishing partnerships with the media and the book trade and the development of reading groups. As with all the *Framework* actions, there is an emphasis on the concept of 'national offers' – standard programmes of reading development activities, supported by collections and promotional material, which local library staff can use in their own library services. National offers or programmes are considered an essential element in the transformation of public library services, helping overcome the 'fragmentation' 'patchiness' and 'postcode lottery' of service provision by offering an agreed minimum level of activity to all users wherever they live. The Reading Agency (2004b) lists a range of benefits which results from national programmes of reader development including a better use of resources, the production of high-quality support materials, the dissemination of good practice and effective workforce development. This approach is also considered important to raise the profile of the public library service as a national network, providing a firm infrastructure for public-sector involvement and investment, facilitating partnership working and supporting advocacy efforts by raising the profile of the public library contribution to a range of key policy agendas.

A vision for reader development has been produced which is designed to support public libraries in their work with readers, giving a common framework, understanding and definitions of what reader development is all about and how libraries can demonstrate the key role they play in delivering the national reading agenda to their stakeholders (MLA, 2004b). Based upon the mission statement, 'To bring reading to the heart of every community' (MLA, 2004b, slide 3), the aims of public libraries' reader development work are listed as being to: enhance people's pleasure and build their confidence; improve learning and literacy; strengthen communities; open up choice; encourage health and well being; and stimulate creativity and support culture. To achieve these, strategies have been developed which include national reading offers, workforce development and advocacy supported by evidence of the impact of public library reading activities. The vision also lists a range of benefits of reading, designed to assist library staff articulate the importance of reading and the value of public library activities in this area, focusing on how reading can build learning and life chances, creativity, quality of life and health and well-being. The vision also describes libraries' USPs or the unique contribution they make to delivering the reading agenda and how their work with readers supports national and local political priorities, all designed to assist libraries in their advocacy efforts.

A report into public library consultation on the original version of this vision gives an interesting insight into approaches to work with readers in public libraries (Valentine, 2004). The terms 'reader development' and 'readers' group', for example, were felt to be ill understood outside the profession and also rather patronizing, as if something was 'being done' to participants. For these reasons, 'reading development' and 'reading groups' were preferred although the first of these was still considered quite impenetrable and something more accessible was sought. The consultation proved that there is a great deal of excitement about the role that public libraries can play in the reading agenda. An appendix to the report listing hopes and dreams for the future of reading development in public libraries runs to 31 pages and envisages a thriving reading development environment in which reading is more popular than ever, leading to better library use which facilitates increased funding and highlights the recognition of the value of reading and libraries' role in promoting it. The appendix also lists fears and challenges facing public libraries in developing their work in this area, though, and these also cover 18 pages focusing primarily on the availability of adequate funding and staff time to support and sustain reader development activities. In addition, there was concern that this type of activity was 'flavour of the month' with policy makers and politicians and a fad which, once past, would leave libraries struggling to deliver services without adequate funding or support. A shortage of staff skills and confidence to engage with readers was another challenge identified and it was felt that new approaches to training and recruitment practices were needed to address the problem. The whole concept of 'national offers' was also questioned, with fears that national prescription would stifle local innovation and that local needs might not be met through national programmes. Miranda McKearney felt, though, that a combination of action at national and local levels was the ideal.

The emphasis on national offers in this chapter is essentially on those developed in England through *Framework for the Future* and its action plan. The other home nations have their own approaches to reader development and one participant in Scotland felt that libraries there were lagging behind their English counterparts although activity had increased. He explained:

> Within the last year or so, we've done more reader development, there's more happening, there's some national funding coming through for that. So I think the picture is shifting. It's still an issue and something we've got to address and try to get a better balance. The problem there is, or was, a lot of ICT funding and much less book funding. Certainly I think there's less up here than there is down south. Nationally, we've got some Arts Council money but Hamlyn Foundation money, we don't have that, for example, so there's much less reader development money here than there is down south. (Anon)

Activities and initiatives for adults Activities designed to fulfil the strategy and vision set out above are focusing on a number of key areas. Although there are some concerns that national offers may be too prescriptive and inflexible, there is a wide acceptance of the concept with strong backing for programmes that will target stock, staff and promotions (Valentine, 2004). In addition, activities to develop and support reading groups play a central role in many library services' work with readers. To sustain and support these activities, the brokering of partnerships with a range of agencies and organizations in both the public and private sectors is considered essential and this is inextricably linked to advocacy and marketing which should ensure that the role that public libraries can play in the national reading agenda is recognized and understood. These three activity areas of national offers, reading groups and partnerships and advocacy will be examined in turn although it is often difficult to discuss one without the other; many of the promotional activities, for example, are undertaken in partnership.

As outlined above, the concept of national offers is firmly established in *Framework for the Future* (Department for Culture, Media and Sport, 2003) and, in relation to work with books and reading, these are generally focused around national promotions to reach new audiences and emphasize the range and depth of the public library book stock. In addition, many library services have developed their own local initiatives and activities either independently or in co-operation with neighbouring library authorities. It is difficult to do justice here to the vast number of initiatives and promotions underway and the creativity that library authorities and their partners are investing in them but the *Branching Out* website organized by Opening the Book gives an indication of the range and scale of activity. Its 'project search' facility enables those organizing reader development activities to search on a variety of categories to gain inspiration from previous projects and promotions, from 'raising the profile of Indic writing' to 'targeting male readers who can't get to the library'.[5]

To support library staff in their reader development activities, training has been identified as essential (Valentine, 2004). The *Branching Out* website offers a range of training exercises to develop staff skills and confidence in engaging with readers.[6] It also offers an online reader development training course, *Frontline*, designed to improve staff skills at encouraging readers to try out new book choices and increase their enjoyment of reading.[7] Similarly, The Reading Agency offers a range of training opportunities and many library services also arrange their own internal or co-operative training to develop and share good, innovative practice. Other staffing practices and policies also need to be addressed to ensure reader development work is fully embedded into library service activities. Participants in the reader development vision consultation stressed that this kind of work should be regarded as a core activity and all staff should be committed to it (Valentine, 2004). This may involve the rewriting of job descriptions and job adverts so that a positive attitude to reading and engaging with readers becomes a core element of all customer-facing positions in public libraries.

A positive approach to ICT and how it can be used to promote reading is also required because, reinforcing the point made above that books and ICT can complement one another rather than being in competition, the use of ICT to support reader development activities is widespread, both to support library staff to engage with readers and through direct connections with readers. Many interview participants agreed that books and ICT were natural partners, not opponents as often portrayed:

> I think one of the great things The Reading Agency has done is to show how you can link IT and reading in a very imaginative way, in a way that develops library use, encourages people to come and do interesting things. (Martin Molloy)

The People's Network final evaluation report notes that there had been a noticeable increase in the use of ICT to support reader development, ranging from simply signposting readers to relevant websites to using interactive technologies to inform readers' choices (Sommerlad et al., 2004). The East Midlands Reader and Library Development project's *So What Do You Fancy Tonight* website, for example, again designed and hosted by Opening the Book, targets 16 to 24 year olds and gives them a range of ideas for books and videos available from their local libraries, including a mystery 'blind date' book which is reserved and waiting for them.[8] The other common type of ICT-based reader development work is when readers recommend or review books and these are made available through the Internet. The *Ask Chris* website developed by Essex County Library Service currently contains 2538 books and 7361 reviews written by individuals and reading groups, for example.[9] There are also national reading sites such as the Big Lottery funded *Whichbook.net* which enables readers to find books which suit their mood by selecting the kind of book they would like to read on a range of emotional criteria such as happy or sad, optimistic or bleak as well as whether they would like a long or short book or an easy or demanding read.[10] The site contains extracts of the works and enables users to check whether titles are available in their local library by connecting them with library service catalogues. All these literature promotion activities are designed to connect readers with books and encourage them to expand their reading horizons. The same is true of reading groups.

One strand of the *Framework for the Future* Action Plan includes the development of a strategic approach to reading group provision in public libraries (MLA, 2004c). The Reading Agency is leading this work and has produced a national public library development programme for reading groups which establishes the case for a national approach and outlines the kind of provision public libraries may provide (The Reading Agency, 2004b). The report on the strategy includes the results of a mapping survey which found that libraries currently offer a range of services to support reading groups including group loans, free reservations, newsletters, staff to run the groups, free meeting space in the library, and author events and activities. The results of the survey suggested that public library reading group activity is flourishing and inclusive and that the infrastructure for a national development programme is already in place. It was also reported that many reading groups serve a specific demographic audience of readers focusing on, for example, families, gender-based groups or groups defined by ethnicity. They can be comprised of readers with specific reading needs such as listening groups, those reading large print or Braille, people with basic skills or those with dyslexia. By catering for a wide range of needs, reading groups can target 'hard to reach' groups and help make the library service more inclusive.

Despite the benefits to be gained from reading groups by individual readers, communities and library services, The Reading Agency acknowledges a variety of challenges to the implementation of a national reading group strategy. One of the most important is the demands made on the library service in the servicing of groups including pressure on staff skills and time. Valentine (2004) reported that those consulted on the national vision for reader development were unenthusiastic about the prospect of library staff running reading groups. Although reading groups were perceived to be an important part of reader development, especially if they could target 'hard to reach' groups, they were not considered core, not central to it and there were widespread concerns about the availability of staffing and financial resources to maintain existing groups and develop more. It was felt, though, that public libraries could offer advice, information and support to reading groups and assist those seeking to establish a reading group. The development of national support materials, training and activities for libraries operating reading groups was also considered appropriate. These could be developed in partnership and The Reading Agency identified a range of potential partners with which public libraries could work in developing and supporting reading groups (The Reading Agency, 2004b). Such partnerships have already proved beneficial in other areas of reader development work.

A glance at The Reading Agency's website gives an indication of the range of partners with which public libraries work to develop innovation approaches to reader development including media organizations, publishers and arts and educational organizations at both national and local levels. Too numerous to detail here, this section will focus on some recent national initiatives, supported by *Framework for the Future*. Work with the broadcast media has been a feature of recent initiatives. The BBC's *Big Read* in 2003, to find Britain's favourite book, stimulated enormous interest in books and reading and many public libraries ran reading groups and activities based around the programme. A new partnership led by The Reading Agency and supported by the Arts Council and MLA is focusing on working with BBC radio, specifically BBC Radio 4 and BBC7. Through this partnership, a new post has been created, BBC Radio and Libraries Co-ordinator, and the project is exploring the way that radio and libraries can work together to give readers and listeners new reading experiences and build audiences on both sides of the partnership. The creation of reading and library-related content in radio output is being explored accompanied by the development of supporting material for libraries as well as online reader content.

The other major national partnership being developed through *Framework for the Future* is with publishers – the *Reading Partners* initiative. Led again by The Reading Agency, this initiative has the support of seven leading adult publishers, keen to take advantage of the access to readers which libraries can provide, as well as the Public Lending Right (PLR).[11] According to Rickett (2005, online resource) '[p]ublishers, struggling to get their wares into the front of bookshops, have realised that libraries provide a wonderful alternative route to readers'. For the libraries involved, the initiative can offer them high quality book promotion materials, timely information about new publications and promotions as well as access to authors, designers and editors. The first pilot promotion resulting from the *Reading Partners* programme was the *Borrowers Recommend* promotion launched in February 2005. Based on the PLR's public library borrowing figures for 2003-04, the promotion took a selection of 21 books representing some of the best issuing titles by emerging writers as highlighted by the PLR figures. Intended to be an annual event, this pilot promotion was adopted by 125 library authorities nationwide who were provided with relevant point of lend material supported by a website.[12] According to one librarian interviewed this kind of scheme was extending the range of stock in public libraries and she felt there was a lot of value in 'doing things together and sharing and tossing ideas around' (Anon). Anne Ollier agreed that activities like these had been very successful so that every week Askews was sending out over 1,000 sets of their 'Bestsellers Service' – new entrants to the bestsellers list. For her, this proved that public libraries were keen to respond to users' demands for up-to-date and in demand material.

Through a range of reader development activities with adults, public libraries are trying to enhance people's reading experiences, encouraging them to read more and read more widely. As suggested above, children's librarians have a strong track record of doing this and although some participants in the reader development vision consultation were worried that it could become an adult-driven agenda with children's needs becoming sidelined (Valentine, 2004), the huge amount of activity taking place in public libraries encouraging children to become engaged with reading and books would indicate that this is not an imminent threat.

Developing Young Readers

The value of reading for children's learning was outlined in Chapter 9 but despite educational and government recognition of the clear benefits to be gained from engaging with books and reading and the considerable resources being focused on fostering children's literacy skills in schools, research suggests that children's enjoyment of reading has declined significantly since 1998 (Sainsbury, 2003). The Progress in International Literacy Study (PIRLS) study similarly indicated that pupils in England read very well in comparison with children from other countries but their enjoyment of reading was poor in comparison (Mullis et al., 2003). NFER research in 2003, in contrast, found that 70 per cent of children in years four and six (aged about nine and eleven years respectively) said that they enjoyed reading, liked reading silently by themselves, read at home most days and did not think reading was boring (Sainsbury, 2003). A survey of teenagers also found that a majority enjoyed reading and were enthusiastic about it, seeing it as relaxing and fun (Mori, 2003). In both the Mori and the NFER surveys, girls were more avid readers than boys and, in the NFER study, younger age groups were more positive than older children (Sainsbury, 2003). The NFER survey was also undertaken in 1998 and the 2003 results indicated that children's confidence in reading had increased significantly; they were less likely to find reading difficult and less likely to want an adult's help with reading. Their enjoyment of reading had declined, however, and this was particularly true of older boys. Compared with children in 1998, children in 2003 were less likely to enjoy reading stories, poems or information books, were more likely to prefer watching television to reading and were less likely to enjoy going to the library.

Sainsbury (2003) suggested that part of the problem could lie with the Literacy Hour in schools which, in some cases, has become a 'literature hour' with less emphasis on developing reading skills and more on appreciating literature. The reading material for the Literacy Hour is chosen by the teacher and is used to develop specific reading skills. Some teachers have found it difficult to fire children's enthusiasm for reading which might involve encouraging them to explore their own reading preferences and react emotionally as well as cognitively. Alan Watkin felt that this made it difficult to persuade young people, especially those from challenging backgrounds, to read for pleasure:

> I keep arguing that a word I never hear about reading from the educationalists is 'enjoyment'. So is it any wonder in an area where kids are coming from some degree of impoverishment and lack of a home environment where books are important or reading's important or perhaps the parents can't even read, that [reading] is a task, it's not something they get enjoyment from? (Alan Watkin)

The focus for public library reading activities, in contrast, is on reading for enjoyment and creativity outside the formal school curriculum and although there is a strong emphasis on how library-based reading activities can support educational achievement in schools, reading activities with children and young people in public libraries are primarily designed to create enthusiastic readers by giving them the opportunity to experience a wide range of reading material, targeting educational and quality of life benefits. Below, we first consider the approach being taken to reader development activities with children and young people before a review of some of the key activities in this area.

Policy and strategy In the *Framework for the Future* Action Plan (MLA, 2004c), the audience for children's reading development activities is divided into a number of key audiences: early years (children under five years old and their families), school age children and young people although the last two are not mutually exclusive. The link between reading and learning is made clearly in the Action Plan and the programmes in this area focus on enhancing the literacy skills of children and their parents and encouraging them to view the public library as a key supporter of reading development. Details of *Fulfilling Their Potential* (The Reading Agency, 2004c), the strategy to develop young people's engagement with society through reading, were given in Chapter 9 and the kinds of activities this is generating will be outlined below. For younger children, the *Serving Families Well* report investigated awareness, usage and opinions of library services for children aged 0–5, and recommended how all three might be improved (Book Marketing Limited, 2004). The survey found that only about half of those with children in the 0–5 age range surveyed had visited a public library in the last year and only 40 per cent had done so in connection with services for their child(ren). Younger parents and those from lower social classes were less likely to visit the library than older parents from more affluent backgrounds. Lack of time was the main barrier to use overall but the biggest reason that non-users did not use the library was because they just never thought of it as an activity that they could participate in with their child(ren). Non-users had quite poor perceptions of public library buildings and the facilities they offered and of the friendliness or welcoming attitude of staff. Many were concerned about library rules and regulations, particularly fines and charges for lost or damaged books. The report recommended a national marketing campaign to promote libraries as welcoming places which offer valuable and fun activities for young children. It also recommended that this kind of activity should be considered a core part of the service and that staff should be trained to deliver it effectively. Library facilities, especially toilets and changing areas, also needed to be upgraded according to the report. Based on the findings of the *Serving Families Well* research, a 'family friendly' national offer is being developed by MLA and the Early Years Library Network (EYLN).

As with work with adult readers, individual library authorities are engaged in a lot of creative work at the local level and, increasingly, this is being supplemented by initiatives organized at a national level which local services can use and adapt to suit their own particular circumstances. The Book Start scheme was outlined in Chapter 9 and its success suggests that national schemes, supplemented by local information and activities, can have an important impact on the incidence of library visiting (National Centre for Research in Children's Literature, 2001). The nationwide Summer Reading Challenges started in 1999 have proved equally popular and address children's learning needs through helping them maintain their literacy skills throughout the summer holidays as well as encouraging them to enjoy and engage with books in a supportive environment. In both cases, the professional and polished nature of the materials developed for the initiatives are considered key to the success of these national schemes. *Start with the Child* suggested that children of all ages are increasingly consumerist and the marketing and production of resources must be of the highest quality (Cilip Working Group on Library Provision for Children and Young People, 2002). This has led to the trend of organizing fewer high quality initiatives in partnership rather than more local, lower quality, small scale productions. Some of the highest profile initiatives are considered below.

Activities and initiatives for children and young people The Summer Reading Challenge is perhaps the best established national reading development promotion for children. Launched in 1999 and now run annually by The Reading Agency, the Challenge is the largest national reading development initiative for children with participation from 90 per cent of library authorities in the UK. Appealing to children's love of collecting, the Summer Reading Challenge is a personal challenge, encouraging primary school children to use the library and read throughout the summer holidays. The Challenge has a different theme every year and supporting materials reflect this theme. For 2005, the theme was the *Reading Voyage* based around a nautical theme with participating children given their own personal ship's reading log to plot their achievements over the summer. As an incentive to stretch themselves and engage with a wide range of books and reading material, children are given 'rewards' to collect such as stickers, certificates and a medal for completing the Challenge. Libraries can order a range of resources including posters, stickers, bookmarks, banners and pencils to promote the Challenge and capture children's interest. Interactive online support materials are also now playing an increasingly important role in encouraging children's participation in the Challenge and fostering their creativity and engagement with the Challenge books through puzzles, quizzes and features about characters and authors.

An evaluation of the 2003 Reading Challenge, the *Reading Maze*, found that children taking part gained a range of benefits from their participation (product perceptions ltd, 2003). Sixty-six per cent of children surveyed said they had read more in the summer holidays because of the Challenge than they would have if they had not participated and it also seemed to widen their reading horizons with 45 per cent reading a book they would not have wanted to have read otherwise. The Challenge also had a positive impact on their views of the library with 12 per cent joining the library just to participate in the challenge and 99 per cent saying that they enjoyed visiting the library. The evaluation concluded that the Summer

Reading Challenge had a positive impact on the five Generic Learning Outcomes identified by the *Inspiring Learning for All* tool-kit, discussed in Chapter 9. As importantly, though, especially considering the decline in children's enjoyment of reading described above, the Challenge seemed to encourage children to read for pleasure. PricewaterhouseCoopers' (2005) study of the impact of public libraries reported that summer reading schemes promote children's enjoyment, confidence and motivation and reading ability, all of which link clearly to national themes and priorities set out in the government green paper *Every Child Matters* (2003).

Another national initiative trying to inspire young people to read more adventurously and gain confidence in expressing their opinions about books is *Chatterbooks*. An Orange Prize for Fiction Educational Initiative, *Chatterbooks* is a national network of reading groups for four to twelve year-olds started in 2001. *Chatterbooks* is co-ordinated by The Reading Agency and in 2004 ran in 116 authorities throughout the UK involving 266 library based groups (The Reading Agency, 2005). The 2004 evaluation of *Chatterbooks* reported that the children participating experienced a range of benefits including enjoying reading, enjoying talking about books, reading more widely and becoming more confident about themselves as readers (The Reading Agency, 2005). Libraries have benefited from the scheme too. The initiative is supported by high quality publicity material and training sessions and notes and the training, as well as involvement in organizing and running the groups, has helped library staff become more skilled and confident in talking to children and their carers about books, according to 90 per cent of authorities responding to the 2004 evaluation. Sixty per cent said that *Chatterbooks* also helped increase library use, either by targeted groups or overall. *Chatterbooks* is considered a model of good practice in libraries/business partnership with telecoms company Orange sponsoring the packs provided to children which consist of a *Chatterbooks* back-pack containing a reading diary, stickers, note pads, games and bookmarks. The importance of partnerships for this area of public library work is clear once again, therefore, and, in this case, the activities have also enabled libraries to build partnerships with schools.

Turning to older children, and again demonstrating the value of partnerships, YouthBOOX was a collaboration between librarians and youth workers co-ordinated by The Reading Agency and the National Youth Agency. Targeting socially excluded young people, the project aimed to overcome some of the negative perceptions they have about libraries, encourage their participation in planning library services and choosing resources and promote reading for pleasure. Supporting this initiative was the magazine BOOX and its associated website which had book and magazine reviews written by young people, features and quizzes. The success of the programme led to a further project called YouthBOOX Moving On, supported by the Paul Hamlyn Foundation. Aimed at emerging readers, the programme tried to 'create palatable routes back into reading' for socially excluded youngsters (The Reading Agency, no date, p. 3) and specifically target those with low literacy skills. The project developed a new reading promotion, *txt*, for young people with a low reading age but high interest level and local libraries in partnership with youth workers and basic skills agencies organized a range of activities around reading, writing and other creative activities.

As with the adult initiatives, all these programmes aimed at children and young people are supported by web-based resources. There are also reading development projects which are Internet-led such as *Stories from the Web*.[13] Managed by Birmingham public libraries, *Stories from the Web* is a website and reader development programme aimed at children from eight to fourteen years of age. Split into two, one area for eight to eleven year olds and the other for eleven to fourteen year olds, the website hosts a range of reviews, features, stories and children's own writing to try to encourage children to interact creatively with ICT. In addition, *Stories from the Web* clubs are organized in public libraries which combine book promotion and reader development activities with computer-related activities, all in a shared situation.

Once again, staff training is an essential part of the success of many of the initiatives described above. The YouthBOOX programme was supported by a range of training opportunities for library staff to develop their confidence in working with young people. Similarly, *Their Reading Futures*, funded by the DCMS through MLA, is a programme of training and support led by The Reading Agency to help front line library staff build their skills and confidence in engaging with young people about books and reading.[14] Training sessions have taken place across the regions and the website also provides support.

Conclusion

Tim Coates (2004) gives a damning account of public library stock management in *Who's in Charge* but the evidence presented above suggests that there is a lot of activity in areas of stock management and reader development to reach out to new audiences and try to manage stocks better for existing users and those who do not use the public library because they do not feel it meets their reading related needs. There is no doubt that there are problems with the declining issues of books from public libraries and one message from the statistical analyses that have been carried out is clear; book issues from public libraries, especially issues of adult fiction, have been declining since the mid 1980s and the rate of decline has intensified during the 1990s. Other messages are perhaps not so clear cut, though, and, as Creaser et al. (2004, p. 14) point out, the statistics raise 'complex questions of cause and effect over which debate will continue for some time'. There was some resignation among interview participants that society and people's leisure and consumer related behaviour had changed in ways that meant that public libraries would be unable or unlikely to ever again achieve the high issue figures of the early 1980s. Coates puts the blame for declining issues firmly at the door of cuts in the book fund and there was an acknowledgement among interview participants that this had certainly played a part in the decline in the range and quality of the stock and, therefore, loans but this was considered to be just one factor in the downward trend for issues, albeit a very important one.

Many of those participating in the research interviews felt that those like Coates, the Audit Commission and the DCMS were too preoccupied with issues anyway as a measure of public library effectiveness. The temptation to retort, 'they would say that wouldn't they?' is strong but it is not just public library practitioners who feel that library issue figures do not give a clear picture of public library use and success. Others connected with, but not a part of, the public library profession similarly feel that issue figures are a very crude mechanism for evaluating the achievements of public libraries. Interview participants such as Miranda McKearney, Moira Arthur and Geoffrey Smith, all of whom were critical of other aspects of the public library approach to stock management, agreed with the PricewaterhouseCoopers report, convinced that there were other more valuable ways to assess the impact that book provision and lending services were having on communities and individuals. An outcomes, rather than outputs, approach was favoured which puts the emphasis on what users have gained from public library book-related services rather than the number of books issued by the library.

While certainly not complacent about declining issues, a shift from a focus on the quantity of books issued to a focus on the quality of the use of public library book stocks was therefore advocated by many of those participating in the research interviews. In this scenario, public libraries cease to be mere suppliers of reading material and turn their attention to helping people engage with a wide range of literature in an attempt to reignite some of the enthusiasm for reading and books which seems to have become lost in the drive to raise practical literacy skills. Discourses of rediscovery were prominent around discussion of reader development during the research interviews, especially with regard to work with adult readers. There was a sense that the role of facilitating enjoyment and engagement with books and reading had been lost to some extent or perhaps had never been a priority for older users but that now public libraries had developed a range of initiatives, such as reading groups, to assist people with their reading choices and with helping them benefit from the creativity associated with reading. There was a recognition and some embarrassment, though, that it had taken people from outside the public library profession, generally literature promotion and development organizations, to galvanize activity and development in this area.

Cuts to the book fund have meant that library services have had to examine their stock management processes to try to ensure that the stock that they do buy has maximum impact. This is partly achieved through reader development activities and also through a re-examination of processes and practices associated with selection and acquisition. The literature and interview participants agreed that there is scope for improving procedures although action was being taken on several fronts. The *Stock Quality Health Check*, for example, was encouraging library services to take a more systematic approach to stock revision and various innovations in stock rotation were also being trialled. The use of EDI was speeding up acquisitions although the release of bestsellers onto library shelves was still hampered by publishers' embargoes in some cases. The quest for discounts and value for money was driving the adoption of new approaches to selection too and the establishment of purchasing consortia which some felt were a mixed blessing for both library services and library suppliers. The stock management practices and costs presented in *Who's in Charge* give the impression of complacency and profligacy within public library services, although they were based on the experiences of just one library authority. Many of those participating in the research interviews disputed this picture and, although not a representative sample of library service practitioners, instead suggested that library services were doing all they could do drive costs down and find solutions to some of the stock related issues facing them. As one participant said, 'the image of libraries just sitting there and festering is a totally false one' (Anon).

Notes

1 National Literacy Strategy website URL: http://www.standards.dfes.gov.uk/primary/literacy/ [16.12.05].
2 National Reading Campaign website URL: http://www.literacytrust.org.uk/campaign/welcome.html [16.12.05].
3 The Reading Agency estimates that 4,500 library reading groups are in operation.
4 Details of the projects funded and other information about the fund can be found at URL: http://www.mla.gov.uk/action/dcmswolf/00dcmswo.asp [16.12.05].
5 Branching Out website URL: http://www.branching-out.net/branching-out/search.asp [16.12.05].
6 Branching Out training website URL: http://www.branching-out.net/branching-out/page2.asp?idno=616 [16.12.05].
7 Frontline website URL: http://www.branching-out.net/branching-out/page2.asp?idno=910 [16.12.05].
8 'So What Do You Fancy Tonight' website URL: http://www.whatareyouuptotonight.com/welcome/ [16.12.05].
9 Ask Chris URL: http://askchris.essexcc.gov.uk/ [16.12.05].
10 Whichbook.net URL: http://www.whichbook.net/index.jsp [16.12.05].
11 'PLR was established by the Public Lending Right Act 1979 which gave British authors a legal right to receive payment for the free lending of their books by public libraries. Under the Act funding is provided by Central Government and payments are made to eligible authors in accordance with how often their books are lent out from a selected sample of UK public libraries.' Public Lending Right website URL: http://www.plr.uk.com/enhancedindex.htm [16.12.05].
12 Borrowers Recommend website URL: http://www.borrowersrecommend.co.uk/ [16.12.05].
13 Stories from the Web website URL: http://www.storiesfromtheweb.org/ sfwhomepage.htm [16.12.05].
14 Their Reading Futures URL: http://www.theirreadingfutures.org.uk [16.12.05].

Chapter 11

Discourses of Public Library Futures

Strategic Direction

The public library at the beginning of the twentieth century is undoubtedly very different from the public library 150, 100 or 50 years ago and that is perhaps the secret of its enduring success and the reason why it continues to be held in affection and valued by the British people. As society has evolved, so the public library has reinvented itself, trying to establish itself as a vital tool in politicians' agendas for change. This chapter will discuss how successfully the public library has coped with and met the complex and countervailing pressures and demands placed on it during the early 21st century and whether it will be able to continue to do so in the future, drawing primarily on the research interviews.

A common criticism of public libraries is that they try to be 'all things to all people'. As we have seen, the 1964 *Public Libraries and Museums Act*, the legislation establishing public libraries as a statutory service which all local authorities in England and Wales must provide, demands that public library services be 'comprehensive and efficient'. The loose wording of the Act has arguably led public libraries to try to develop services aimed at meeting the reading, information, learning and recreational needs of as many in the community as possible. While for some this means that public library services lack focus and are floundering in an attempt to present a clear, coherent message, others interpret this diversity as a strength and represent its flexibility and adaptability as characteristics that make the public library service special. Leadbeater (2003) takes the former view, suggesting that public libraries lack a mission or purpose and should remedy this by focusing on a few 'inspirational goals' (p. 13). Greenhalgh and Worpole (1995) have similarly suggested that public libraries face 'an identity crisis' (p. 35) through which their focus, purpose and strategy have become unclear.

Framework for the Future (Department for Culture, Media and Sport, 2003) was an attempt to put some meat on the bones of the 1964 Act and develop a core set of programmes around which all public library services in England could unite. As highlighted in Chapter 2, the document met with a mixed response in the public library community, some welcoming the establishment of a national focus on the three core areas of books, reading and learning; digital citizenship; and community and civic values which it outlined, others disappointed that the vision presented was not more 'visionary' and aspirational. The three areas of activity established seemed uncontentious in themselves, however, and are also reflected in library strategies or statements of purpose from the other home countries. Thus, in

Northern Ireland, the *Tomorrow's Library* report suggested that public libraries in the province should focus on contributing to the Government's agenda through widening access and participation, targeting social need, supporting learning, encouraging creativity, contributing to the information age, reinforcing community and encouraging opportunities for new revenue raising (Department of Culture, Arts and Leisure, 2002). The report also suggested that themes of 'learning, information, heritage, cultural identity, creativity, diversity, cultural tourism, and employment' (p. 5) were common in discourses of public libraries. In interview, Alan Watkin agreed that a *Framework for the Future* for Wales would have 'pretty well' the same priorities although he thought that bilingualism and cultural inheritance would probably feature more strongly. Another Welsh participant felt that Welsh public libraries had different priorities, though, explaining:

> I was very impressed with *Framework for the Future*, [that's] a personal statement, I thought it was very comprehensive, very sensible but I think there are other models for us and I think to be honest, the Republic of Ireland strategy document is perhaps nearer for us because of scale, it's much more about integration and partnership and working together so I think that's probably more relevant... So I wouldn't argue with what *Framework for Future's* trying to do, and I'm sure for England it's entirely appropriate but for us it's probably too conceptual. We would probably want something that not only had the strategy but also had the action planning attached. I appreciate that in England they've had to take it in much longer tranches because, first of all, they've got to get everybody going in the same direction. Compared to the oil tanker that is England, we are much more of a sort of tug that can actually be more agile in the way that it responds and reacts and I think we have to play to our strengths. (Anon)

Similarly, in Scotland, one participant felt that any document with the same purpose as *Framework* 'wouldn't look like *Framework* at all' (Anon) suggesting that the manner of operationalizing and delivering initiatives (which might very well be similar to those contained in *Framework*) would be very different, taking a more bottom-up approach. Another Scottish participant made a similar point, saying:

> The Scottish climate is very different, the Scottish climate is much more consensual, if you like, so there is a greater resistance to imposition of standards. We're not very good at coming together I don't think, I think we all recognize the need for it but we haven't managed to achieve it yet. So I don't think the actual content would have been different but I think the approach would have been different. (Anon)

A common sense of role and purpose around public library services do seem to be shared, therefore, although the means of achieving those and their emphases will be different not just in the four home countries but also in the different parts of those countries and for different communities. With this in mind, we now turn to how study participants articulated their sense of the role and purpose of public libraries. This discussion will reinforce and summarize many of the themes and issues discussed in previous chapters to give an overview of the different understandings of public library role, scope and direction which emerged during the research.

Role and Purpose

As discussed above, *Framework for the Future* was an attempt to establish a common understanding of role and purpose for public library services in England and some participants felt that the document gave public libraries something tangible to organize around, to the extent that one said, 'the core vision is there and if libraries are still debating, it's rather a sad thing' (Anon). Bill Macnaught agreed that the benefits of Framework and its action plan was that 'there is a much stronger perception of us being an institution'. Others were more uncertain of whether the messages contained in *Framework* were strong enough or creative enough to take library services forward in a positive manner. Shiraz Durrani, for example, said:

> There doesn't seem to be a vision for libraries, someone looking ahead five years from now. There are no new ideas coming in, there is a lot of stagnation and people in positions of power are there to maintain their position, I think. The whole issue of what libraries are for is never seen as of interest. (Shiraz Durrani)

Frances Hendrix similarly suggested that public libraries did not have a clear role and purpose, commenting, 'It's a bit like Marks and Spencers, I think, it does not know now what it is supposed to be doing' (Frances Hendrix). John Vincent also felt that libraries lacked a core, unifying purpose, saying that he felt there needed to be a:

> …repositioning of libraries so we become clearer about what we're doing. I've got friends in authorities who bemoan the fact that we haven't got the stock funds that we had in the '70s, that you can't find, a bit like Tim Coates does, *Wuthering Heights* on every library shelf, or whatever it is. Is that actually what we're about or are we about delivering other services? (John Vincent)

He later added:

> From my experience, we kind of lost our way a bit in the '80s so if you asked me what my fundamental view of libraries and librarianship is, I think we've got a really powerful role to play but lots of people, for whatever reason, don't realize what the role is. And quite a lot of library staff seem to me to be searching for a bandwagon that they can get on. (John Vincent)

Like Leadbeater (2003) and Greenhalgh and Worpole (1995), some interview participants felt that public libraries had tried in the past to meet too many needs and, in doing so, had lost their focus and even their relevance. Some used the common phrase 'all things to all people', suggesting that this caused difficulties for the service. Francis Hendrix, for example, said:

> I think what has happened is that we have diversified and diversified, tried to be too many things to too many people and have lost our way. (Francis Hendrix)

Bill Macnaught agreed and felt that this made it difficult for libraries to promote themselves dynamically:

> The difficulty we've got is that in the last 30 years public libraries have gone in so many directions, the common accusation is all things to all people. Trying to agree now what are the key messages is actually quite difficult because right now, if you talked about what you could go into any library and find, you are probably back to [the fact that] you can borrow books free of charge and you'll get free or cheap (you can't even say free in every library service) access to the Internet. So if your message to people out there, the only message that we're all joined on, is that you can have free access to borrow books, well what's new about that? What's transformational about that? (Bill Macnaught)

Martin Molloy, though, felt that trying to be all things to all people made public libraries a strong and vibrant community resource:

> I like to feel that, here, we run some ground breaking IT services, we're right at the front end … but at the same time we've got a fantastic record for reader development and young people, things like Book Pushers… And that's how I'd like it to be, something for everyone, that kind of mix. (Martin Molloy)

Bob Janes agreed that libraries had 'to be prepared to bend and sway with community needs and adapt' (Cllr Bob Janes).

Some participants felt that public libraries were too eager to adapt and had been led down the road of too much diversity in the services they provided by striving too hard to make themselves relevant to government priorities. Frances Hendrix commented:

> The problem with the public library service is that it takes everybody else's agenda, it doesn't set its own and say, 'Right, this is what the public libraries is going to specialize in, it can't do everything, it's going to do this, this and this'. (Frances Hendrix)

Another participant agreed, explaining the difficulties that she felt this caused for public libraries:

> One of the problems of public libraries not setting their own agenda is that they're pushed from pillar to post, they're the victim of the ever-changing central government agenda and because they're always seeking funding, they feel as if they have to be… lifelong learning centres now, we have to be community spaces now, we have to be ICT cafes, we have to be bookstores. (Anon)

She later added that she felt that libraries had a 'reactive agenda' in which they chased the funding associated with particular initiatives and, as a result, lacked 'self-knowledge of what the public library stands for' (Anon). Others participants emphasized, though, that as a public service, paid for by the public purse, public libraries had a responsibility to support local and national government policies and were excited about how public libraries could contribute to a range of political and policy agendas, as one interviewee explained:

> The other things we're concerned with most of all is to place libraries into the bigger picture of corporate priorities and contributions to other things and part of this bigger picture of local government development because the library service can't just go on in a sort of silo. (Anon)

John Pateman also felt that this was of vital and urgent importance:

> We need a revolution, we don't have time for more evolution. We have been evolving for 150 years and we can't go on. In 15 years, the service could be dead, that is a serious possibility. We must be seen to be meeting those national, regional and corporate agendas; very explicitly connecting ourselves to those. Inclusion, regeneration and learning, with evidence, that to me is the modern public library service. (John Pateman)

Some participants explained which specific current or future agendas they felt were particularly relevant to public libraries, one saying:

> I think what we need to do at the moment is to look at other agendas that are happening nationally – the creativity agenda and the arts and we need to be working more closely with them because I think that before the creativity comes, the reading and the imagination is needed and I think we can support that agenda. (Anon)

Another said:

> I think it's a combination of the social policy or access agenda with the learning agenda with the e-government agenda, and it's the ability of libraries to respond to all of those initiatives which is going to be important. (Sue Wilkinson)

Some participants felt that, even in picking up on these new agendas, libraries were still fulfilling quite 'traditional' roles, 'education, information and recreation' (Glenys Willars), but using new terminology and new facilities and equipment to demonstrate their continuing value and contribution. Alan Hasson, for example, explained:

> The information role and the capacity building role is straight out of the old text books isn't it? It's nothing radical. It's simply saying you give people the opportunities, either as individuals or as a community, to become more engaged with the democratic process. (Alan Hasson)

He later added that the 'core business is access to information and entertainment. Now whether that's done through books or whatever else, that doesn't change' (Alan Hasson). Others agreed, Margaret Watson commenting:

> We have always been about knowledge and information. The fact that we have got different tools, we have got lots more resources, we have got globalization, it doesn't

> actually change from the original libraries that were set up. The public library was set up to support the working man and I don't think it has changed very much, but I do think the tools have. (Margaret Watson)

Alan Watkin also felt that public libraries were fulfilling much the same roles as they always had been but using different vocabulary:

> The vocabulary reflects that we must do those things slightly differently. So if you look at *Framework for the Future*, the headings they got there, you could transpose that into a different vocabulary of 50 years ago and virtually get a match, I think. (Alan Watkin)

Many participants articulated what they felt the core values of public library services were and these often centred around access to information, books and the learning that they facilitated. One interviewee said, for example, that libraries enabled 'individuals or groups of individuals unbiased access to books, computers, information, knowledge and works of the imagination' (Anon) while a participant from Northern Ireland said that she felt the role of public libraries was 'essentially education followed by culture' (Anon). Bill Macnaught said that he thought that 'libraries have always been about literature and information as our core products' (Bill Macnaught) and Jan Holden commented:

> From my point of view libraries are about reading and learning, they're about literacy, they're about literature, they're about enjoying finding out and the ability to go somewhere and move on in whatever way that you want to move on in terms of information. (Jan Holden)

The support for reading and books as being at the heart of the public library service from many participants must be heartening for those who feel that libraries have lost their way as far as books are concerned. Joyce Little, for example, said 'the core functions of libraries is providing reading and literature to people' (Joyce Little) and others emphasized the information function of libraries, facilitated by access to books but also other information resources.

Other discourses around role and purpose focused on the value of services for individuals and communities and their transformative power. One participant said, for example, that the fundamental vision of public libraries was 'about giving people skills, knowledge and empowerment' (Anon) and Bob McKee felt that ideas around the role and purpose of public libraries 'haven't changed in the last 150 years, [they] will never change. It's about giving people access to knowledge so that individuals, families, communities can reach their potential whether that's intellectual, creative, imaginative, personal potential' (Bob McKee). Discourses around quality of life issues were also prominent as was discussion around the values promoted by the public library services which contributed to people's quality of life. Bill Macnaught, for example, suggested that libraries were 'an essential part of a creative and tolerant society' and 'a force for good in society' (Bill Macnaught). Another participant similarly felt that it was important to talk about values, 'the value of the service to the public, what it can lead to rather than what it directly delivers' (Anon). Bob McKee summed up what he thought public libraries added to people's lives thus:

> Cultural enrichment, public value, tackling poverty of aspiration, providing something, a wellspring, that people can draw on throughout their lives. Libraries do all that. (Bob McKee)

In keeping with current agendas around community and regeneration, participants often focused on the community role of the public library which was frequently linked with inclusivity. One participant said:

> Libraries are at the heart of communities, they are part of the quality of life of the whole country and if you don't have a vibrant library in your community, it is lacking. (Anon)

Bob Janes felt that libraries were 'a clear community resource' which were 'at the heart of a lot of social regeneration of some communities' (Bob Janes). Some participants felt this community role could be achieved through facilitating access to citizenship information, one participant saying, 'the local public library should be seen as the first point of contact for the local community with the council' (Anon) and another that, 'we should also try and champion libraries as gateways to civic and community information, try and get people to be active citizens' (Anon). Lord Tope similarly felt that public libraries could be important agents of citizenship saying, 'I think that libraries have a very important role to play in, if you want a grand term, the democratic process in the widest sense, actually engaging with the local communities' (Cllr Graham Tope).

Vision of Future

As well as asking participants what they felt the current role and purpose of public libraries were and whether they felt ideas around these had changed radically in recent times, interviewees were also asked for their own personal vision for the future of public libraries. Some of those interviewed felt, like John Pateman quoted above, that public libraries would not have a future unless they changed fundamentally their outlook and organization. The predication by Tim Coates (2004), that public libraries will have ceased to be used entirely in 20 years unless problems with stock management are addressed was often cited and some participants were of the same opinion. Shiraz Durrani, for example, said, 'there's no guarantee of existence as far as libraries are concerned' (Shiraz Durrani) while Frances Hendrix said that she was not sure that libraries would have a role in the future and that she was 'quite pessimistic about it' (Frances Hendrix). Others were more optimistic, however, feeling that public libraries had weathered some challenging times but were now organizing and facing the future positively. Joyce Little, for example, suggested that 'the demise of the public library is very overstated' (Joyce Little) and Bob McKee said:

> I see a service which has come through a very challenging period and is actually shaping itself up in a very sensible way, not in a turmoil way at all but in a very sensible, strategic and structured way to deal with the issues that it faces. (Bob McKee)

Picking up on the points made above that the role and purpose of the public library had not changed dramatically over the years, participants often felt that the vision of what libraries had to offer had similarly remained relatively stable over the years. Again, though, it was agreed that the approach needed to change, Alan Hasson saying that his vision of the public library service was that it should 'continue to do well' that 'it's done well for 20 years with a patina of imagination' (Alan Hasson). Another participant commented, 'I suppose I'm quite a traditionalist because I see it as providing local access to information, learning and culture but obviously in a modern way' (Anon). Many participants when discussing their visions of the future emphasized elements laid out in *Framework for the Future* and particularly strong were visions around the public library as an inclusive, community facility. Jan Holden, for example, said that she wanted to see a:

> …melting down of this middle class bastion of librarians and libraries. It's about anybody being able to walk in off the street. That's what libraries were about when they first started, working people, ordinary people being able to use the resource to better themselves and I don't think we've lost that. Maybe we lost that a few years ago but I think that's what we're about now. (Jan Holden)

John Vincent's vision of the future also focused on trying to reach out to new users while retaining the loyalty of existing ones:

> My vision would be one that begins to engage seriously with all its local communities, not ditching the people that it's got already, which is a common assumption when we're talking about social inclusion work [that] we mean getting rid of all the people we serve now and getting a load of new people in. So it's being skilled enough and being understanding of the tensions in any community to try to balance the two things. (John Vincent)

Alan Watkin felt that accessibility and a community focus was the way forward for public libraries:

> We should be genuinely accessible to all. We are in theory accessible but that's the social inclusion agenda, so genuinely accessible. Secondly we should be seen as attractive and vibrant to the local community and thirdly we should then provide a range of services based on books, cultural products like information which actually meet the specific needs of that community. So, yes, we would provide the right reading materials, we would provide the right information resources and the library would be seen as being an essential element of any real community in Wales. (Alan Watkin)

Two key linked discourses were strong in discussions of the role of the public library within the community; firstly, the library as a physical community facility and, secondly, community engagement. The increasing importance placed on the physical library space was highlighted in Chapter 8 and this was often emphasized again in participants' vision of the future. Diana Edmonds, for example, said that, in her opinion, the library 'should be a learning space, it is above all a safe space and it should also be a vehicle into council facilities, council services. I really just think it's the place to be' (Diana Edmonds). Another participant agreed on the importance of the library building 'as a location within the community, somewhere that's attractive and good to visit' (Anon) while John Dolan also emphasized the importance of 'an environment that people will welcome being in, one that is physically attractive, contemporary, nobody likes old and dirty' (John Dolan).

Alongside discussions of the physical library building, participants' visions of a community facility also highlighted the importance of engaging with communities. Lord Tope said that he would like to see more development with the community engagement agenda, commenting:

> I'd like to see our libraries around the borough as a sort of focal point, both physically and also in sort of outreach, if you like, in the work they do actually promoting much more the community engagement. Not just come in and borrow a book or use the computer or borrow a DVD or whatever, but actually there's things happening there which engage with the local community more. (Cllr Graham Tope)

This engagement agenda was also highlighted by another participant who agreed that public libraries' role should be 'to connect people, to connect communities to connect people with local authorities, to connect people with information and skills' (Anon).

Associated with this discourse of community engagement was another related to the development of a needs-based service, because, as Margaret Watson explained, 'I think [the public library has] always been a part of the community but the community is changing and the needs that the community have are changing' (Margaret Watson). Another participant agreed that the needs of community must be paramount:

> [The public library's] role I think is very much being within the community, being that catalyst, if you like, for regeneration, for renewal, confidence building where needed but I think it's being responsive to local needs, working with those communities to identify what those needs are and being accountable at local level as well. (Anon)

To be successful in this respect, it was often felt by participants that public libraries needed to become part of the community and be 'very proactive in reaching out to communities' (Anon). Andrea Barker suggested that this was the aim of the library service in Stockton-on-Tees:

> Our vision is to meet the needs of our users. The work in hand is to keep up continuously, knowing and reshaping ourselves and refocusing… This is about community engagement. This is about libraries being at the heart of communities. If we have to change and shift to make [users] feel more comfortable coming in, like what they see when they get there and then come back, then that's the nub of it to me. (Andrea Barker)

Sue Wilkinson also emphasized the importance of responding to the community's needs, saying:

> The vision we've set out in *Inspiring Learning for All* is a service that is needs-driven, that works in partnership with a whole range of other institutions to deliver its agenda, that's an environment that is conducive to learning, that's proactive in reaching out to people, that sees itself as having some hugely important things to offer that will change people's lives, and I think it's there. (Sue Wilkinson)

Communicating the Vision

Research participants were able to articulate their ideas around the future direction of the public library service in the UK clearly but they often acknowledged that they were generally not as successful at communicating key messages about public libraries to the public or politicians, as highlighted in Chapter 3. The issue of changing the popular public perception of libraries was considered vital, though, by participants. One interviewee said of libraries, for example, 'these places are still like a mystery to the general public. We know and love them. We can understand them but the vast majority of the public don't' (Anon). Alan Watkin agreed 'the biggest issue is a marketing issue. To my mind, there's no other thing as important. How do we get the perception of what the library is now starting to look like again over to people?' (Alan Watkin). The terms 'marketing', 'promotion', 'advertising' and even 'branding' were often used interchangeably by participants and although they are actually distinct concepts and processes, the message coming from participants seemed to be that public libraries needed to raise their game and communicate more clearly and cleverly what libraries now could offer people.

Participants often commented that public library marketing and promotion was generally quite poor and that the messages libraries were trying to communicate were unclear or even contradictory. John Dolan said, for example, 'we don't market enough, we don't design our products sufficiently to meet the communities that we're trying to attract and serve' (John Dolan). Other participants felt that libraries were still trying to overcome an image problem, one participant saying:

> We're still struggling with this image problem. And [the fact] that people feel that they can just produce reports and they feel that they know what we're about suggests to me that we haven't got the marketing of what we're about right. (Anon)

As a result, many interviewees spoke of the need for marketing and there was considerable support for a national marketing campaign, rather than local, piecemeal efforts although it was recognized that MLA were making efforts in this respect. One Scottish participant said:

> It has to be national and I mean UK-wide, I don't mean national meaning Scotland. I think it's something that we need. If we gathered our combined resources together and really marketed our services, it really could make a terrific difference. (Anon)

Some participants felt that promotion was not only necessary to attract users but also potential partners, one saying:

> There is still a lot of marketing, communication, promotional activity to be done, less so within the council but certainly in terms of some of the other partners… There's still a role to do to get over some of the prejudices some people have. (Anon)

Joyce Little agreed that 'the main barrier is selling our message as to what we do and the opportunities that are there' (Joyce Little) among possible partners.

Some participants felts that the answer lay in transforming the image of the brand 'library'. As suggested in Chapter 8, some library authorities have re-branded some of their libraries as Ideas Stores or Discovery Centres. Others felt that a name change was insufficient and that the answer was to change people's perceptions of the term 'library', as one explained:

> I don't want to be an Idea Box. It's a library, why pretend to be something else? Why can't you say it's a library? If it's an image problem then we need to be dealing with the image. (Anon)

Bill Macnaught agreed, saying:

> A measure of success is every local authority would want to use the word library, not apologize and think of a different word, a synonym, whether it's Ideas Stores or Discovery Centres and so on. I think we really do want to rebuild the brand of library. (Bill Macnaught)

Another participant also felt that changing the public perception of libraries was a challenge but one which libraries must address if people were to start seeing them, 'as an organization with a can-do mentality that delivers' (Anon)

Conclusion

This final section will sum up the discussion above and also summarize some of the related key themes emerging from previous chapters, highlighting the prominent discourses which have emerged from the analysis. One of the objectives of the research on which this book is based was to analyse and explore the justifying ideologies around public libraries. Many of the discourses which emerged both in the literature and in interview were centred around the purpose and the clarity, or lack of clarity, of the role of the modern public library service. The vision and discourses of public library purpose for England set out in *Framework for the Future* were often the basis for exploring themes and issues associated with the legitimating of public libraries and their role in contemporary society. One of the principal discourses focused on the need for a strong vision which would engage users, local authority policymakers, potential partners in the public, private and voluntary sectors, and national government. A related discourse lay in the expressed need to clarify the 1964 *Public Libraries and Museums Act* and its demand that services be 'comprehensive and efficient'. A key element of this discourse was a commonly expressed perception that the loose wording of the Act had led public libraries to try to be all things to all people and, as a consequence, had lost its way somewhat. In relation to all these discourses there was a recognition that *Framework for the Future* was a clear attempt to focus public library services into core programme areas and give shape to their activities. Although there was a lack of agreement on how strong the vision it presented was, *Framework for the Future* was generally considered a positive move around which purpose and roles could be negotiated depending on the nature of the community served.

An exposition of professional, managerial and policy agendas was another objective of the research and these often arose around discussions of purpose and roles. A wide range of concerns was articulated, reflecting the far-reaching scope of the service, as indicated above, and its connection with a variety of quality of life and social issues. Through the elucidation of these agendas, discourses of values and value conflicts among stakeholders emerged. Professional discourses around the status and future of the book lending role of the public library service, for example, were common, often in reference to the *Who's in Charge* report. In an information rich society, the book lending function was now considered by some to be the public library's Unique Selling Proposition but there were many expressions of concern that the emphasis on books had been lost. There was a perception that in reaching out to groups who did not use the public library to borrow books, the needs of the book reading, library using public were being neglected. An opposing discourse focused on the fact that services were organized around the needs of the vocal middle classes who use libraries out of proportion to their presence within the population as a whole and that, to attract those who do not use public libraries regularly (the majority of the British public), they need to develop services designed to appeal to all.

Managerial discourses often revolved around funding and the accountability and efficiency measures introduced into local government over the last two decades. Performance indicators and standards had proved a double-edged sword; although they highlighted some quite alarming trends in public library use (issue figures, for example), they were also considered useful weapons in the battle to lever additional funding from local authority budgets. Discussions around policy agendas were characterized by discourses focusing on the shared priorities of local and national government. Although there was some disquiet that public libraries do not set their own agendas but ride the coat-tails of programmes of those developed by others, public libraries arc a local government services and the need for them to demonstrate how they contribute to the shared priorities and local policy agendas was the dominant discourse. Discourses around partnership working were also very strong with recognition that libraries are operating in a cross-cutting policy environment and that partnership can assist them in explicitly connecting with important political priorities, placing them at the heart of local, regional and national activities. That is not to say that public libraries adopt policy themes or initiatives wholesale without adapting them. Discussions of how public libraries can connect with national and local priorities illuminated different ideological positions on key delivery issues. Discourses around the populist nature of many of the services provided by public library services gave rise to opposing positions, a flavour of which is given above.

These examples of prominent discourses suggest that the social purpose and position of the contemporary public library service is still being negotiated. It is perhaps inevitable that a service with its history and sustained by public funding will provoke disagreements and disputes about value, purpose and direction. Recent policy initiatives as well as broad social, technological and economic developments have brought issues of impact and rationale into sharp relief and forced public librarians and their supporters to engage with the underlying principles and justification of public libraries. By revealing and explicating the discourses currently dominating discussions of public libraries, it is hoped that this research has encouraged those within and outside the public library community to engage in the ongoing debate about the place of public libraries within our national life.

Appendix 1

List of Research Participants

The list below includes the names of all those who agreed to be identified in the list of participants and/or in the text. Post titles and organizational affiliations were correct at the time of the interviews but may since have changed

Sue Anderson	Reading, Learning and Community Engagement Manager, Stockton Library Service
Moira Arthur	Managing Director, Peters Bookselling Services
Susan Atkinson	Borough Librarian, Hartlepool Borough Libraries
Andrea Barker	Head of Lifelong Learning, Stockton Library Service
Chris Batt	Chief Executive, Museums Libraries and Archives Council (MLA)
Margaret Bellamy	Head of Library Services, Leicestershire County Council
Linda Berube	Co-East Regional Manager
Janet Brisland	Manager, Centre for the Child, Central Library, Birmingham
Carol Campbell Hayes	Operations Manager, Libraries and Heritage, Derbyshire Cultural and Community Services
Robert Clayton	Library Services Manager, Rutland County Council
Helen Connolly	Network Adviser, Museums Libraries and Archives Council (MLA)
John Dolan	Assistant Director (Community Learning and Libraries), Birmingham City Council
Shiraz Durrani	Innovations and Development Manager, Library and Heritage Service, London Borough of Merton
Diana Edmonds	Head of Service, Haringey Public Libraries
Laurayn Featherstone	Performance, Promotion and People's Network Manager, Stockton Library Service
Julia Fieldhouse	Head of Customer Service, Libraries and Information, Bath and North East Somerset Council
Jo Grocott	Service Development Office, Stock Management and Promotion, Staffordshire Library and Information Services
Jane Hall	Assistant Head of Culture and Tourism – Libraries, Heritage and Information, Sunderland City Council

Alyson Harbour	Business Development Manager, Customer Service, Libraries and Information, Bath and North East Somerset Council
Alan Hasson	Head of Community Services, Scottish Borders Council
Frances Hendrix	
Jan Holden	Area Librarian, Norwich, Norfolk Library and Information Service
Linda Houston	Chief Librarian, Belfast Education and Library Board
Councillor Bob Janes	Cabinet Member Community Services, Derbyshire County Council
Ayub Khan	Quality and Operations Manager Warwickshire Library and Information Services (formally Principal Project Officer, Library of Birmingham, Birmingham City Council)
Roy Knight	Head of Cultural Services, Rutland County Council
Trevor Knight	Executive Head of Library, Heritage and Registration Services, London Borough of Sutton
David Lathrope	Deputy Director (Culture and Community), Nottingham City Council
Susan Law	Head of Library and Information Service, Blackburn with Darwen Borough Council
Joyce Little	Head of Libraries and Information Services, Liverpool City Council
Bill McNaught	Head of Cultural Development, Gateshead Council
Lord Andrew McIntosh	Minister for Culture, Media and Sport, DCMS
Miranda McKearney	Director, The Reading Agency
Dr Bob McKee	Chief Executive, Cilip
Ken McKinlay	Head of Cultural Services, East Renfrewshire Council
Moira Methven	Senior Manager, Dundee City Council Communities Department
Martin Molloy	Director of Cultural and Community Services, Derbyshire County Council
Anne Ollier	Director of Sales and Customer Care, Holt Jackson Co Ltd.
Helen Osborn	Chief Librarian, Western Education and Library Board
Kath Owen	Principal Librarian, Nottinghamshire County Council
John Pateman	Head of Libraries, Sport and Support Services, Lincolnshire County Council (personal capacity)
David Potts	Senior Network Adviser, Museums Libraries and Archives Council (MLA)
Linda Simpson	Director of Culture and Heritage, CIP Group of Companies
Rt Hon Chris Smith, MP	Former Secretary of State for Culture, Media and Sport (now Lord Chris Smith)
Geoff Smith	Consultant

Andrew Stevens	Senior Policy Adviser (Libraries), Museums, Libraries and Archives Council (MLA)
Anne Tingle	Performance and Improvement Co-ordinator, Stockton Library Service
Cllr Graham Tope CBE	Lead Councillor for Libraries, Heritage and Registration Services, London Borough of Sutton
Pam Usher	Head of Customer Care and Deputy Director of Economic and Community Development, London Borough of Barnet (personal capacity)
John Vincent	Networker, the Network – Tackling Social Exclusion
Geoff Warren	Development Director, MLA West Midlands
Alan Watkin	Chief Officer, Libraries, Leisure and Culture, Wrexham County Borough Council
Margaret Watson	Past President Cilip
Sarah Wilkie	Libraries Policy Adviser, Museums, Libraries and Archives Council (MLA)
Sue Wilkinson	Director: Learning, Access, Renaissance and Regions, Museums, Libraries and Archives Council (MLA)
Glenys Willars	Learning and Information Development Manager, Leicestershire Library Services

Appendix 2

Sample Interview Questions

It has been said that, unlike many other arts/cultural institutions, there is a lack of powerful government lobbying on behalf of public libraries. Do you think this is a fair criticism? What do you think should or could be done to campaign more effectively for public libraries?

What impact do you think other public library-specific accountability mechanisms (e.g. Public Library Standards, Annual Library Plans/Public Library Position Statements) have had on the profile of the public library service within the local authority?

Do you think the so-called 'bidding culture' has encouraged or constrained public library development?

A lot of the community work involves partnership with other agencies inside and outside the local authority. Have developments within public libraries (e.g. the People's Network) encouraged others to seek out public libraries as partners or is it still a case of 'knocking on doors'?

All the literature seems to suggest there is a real staffing crisis in public libraries. In your experience, is the situation as bleak as it is often painted? At all levels (support staff, new recruits to the profession, middle management and specialists, leadership)? What do you think are the key issues and main problems?

Although public libraries are still associated with books in most people's minds, recent evidence suggests that they are not performing as well as they could in this respect. Are you concerned about the decline in public library issue figures and the amount public library authorities spend on book stock? Can these trends be reversed? If so, how?

Recent reports (e.g. *Who's in Charge*, *Overdue*, reports from the Audit Commission etc.) have painted a picture of the public library service as an institution in turmoil, uncertain of its purpose and in danger of losing its 'traditional' users whilst being unable to reach out to new ones. Do you think this is an accurate reflection of the situation?

How would you sum up your vision of the role of the modern public library service?

Appendix 3

Glossary of Common Abbreviations

ACL	Advisory Council on Libraries
ALP	Annual Library Plan
BV	Best Value
Cilip	The Chartered Institute of Library and Information Professionals
Cipfa	The Chartered Institute of Public Finance and Accountancy
CONARLS	Circle of Officers of National and Regional Library Systems
COSLA	The Convention of Scottish Local Authorities
CPA	Comprehensive Performance Assessment
CyMAL	Museums, Libraries and Archives Wales
DCAL	The Department for Culture, Arts and Leisure
DCMS	The Department for Culture, Media and Sport
DDA	Disability Discrimination Act
DfEE	The Department for Education and Employment (now DfES)
DfES	The Department for Education and Skills
DTI	The Department for Trade and Industry
IFLA	International Federation of Library Associations
LA	Library Association (now Cilip)
LGR	Local Government Review
LIS	Library and Information Services
LISC (NI)	Library and Information Services Council Northern Ireland
LISC (Wales)	Library and Information Services Council Wales
LISU	Library and Information Statistics Unit
LSC	Learning and Skills Council
MLA	Council for Museums, Libraries and Archives
NOF	New Opportunities Fund
ODPM	Office of the Deputy Prime Minister
PFI	Public Finance Initiative
PLPS	Public Library Position Statements
PLUS	Public Library User Survey
PN	The People's Network
PSA	Public Services Agreement
SCL	Society of Chief Librarians
SEMLAC	South East Museum Libraries and Archives Council
SLIC	Scottish Library and Information Council
Wilip	The Wider Information and Libraries Issues Project

Bibliography

Aalto, M. and Knight, T. (1999), *Fundraising: Alternative Financial Support for Public Library Services*, Scarecrow Press, Lanham (Maryland).

Accenture (2001), *Rhetoric vs. Reality: Closing the Gap* (URL: http://www.accenture.com/xdoc/en/industries/government/final.pdf), [24.8.2005].

Allan, G. (2001), 'Can you Trust this Model?' *Library Association Record*, Vol. 103(12), pp. 754-755.

Ashcroft, L., Farrow, J., Matthews, G., McClelland, B., Watts, C. and Woolrych, R. (2005), *Provision for Adult Learners in Public Libraries in England*, MLA, London. (URL: http://www.mla.gov.uk/documents/fff_LJMU_adultlearners.doc), [15.8.2005].

Audit Commission (1997), *Due for Renewal*, Audit Commission, London.

Audit Commission (2002), *Building Better Library Services*, Audit Commission, London (URL: http://www.audit-commission.gov.uk/reports/), [21.11.2004].

Audit Commission (2002), *Building Better Library Services*, Audit Commission, London (URL: http://www.audit-commission.gov.uk/Products/NATIONAL-REPORT/9D0A0DD1-3BF9-4c52-9112-67D520E7C0AB/ACKLibrariesbr.pdf), [5.11.2004].

Audit Commission (2003), *Recruitment and Retention: A Public Service Workforce for the Twenty-First Century*, Audit Commission, London.

Audit Commission (2003), *User Focus and Citizen Engagement. Learning from Comprehensive Performance Assessment: Briefing 4*, Audit Commission, London (URL: http://www.audit-commission.gov.uk/cpa/furtherlearningstcc.asp), [23.8.2005].

Audit Commission (2004), *Public Libraries Stock Quality Health Check. Adult Fiction and Poetry*, Audit Commission, London.

Bagehot, 'Consuming Passions: Britain's Labour Party is as Confused as it is Divided', *The Economist*, 8th May, p. 29.

Bakewell, K. (2001), 'What do public libraries do on Sundays?', *Librarians' Christian Fellowship Newsletter*, Vol. 78, pp. 4-5.

Ball, D. and Friend, F. (2001), 'Library Purchasing Consortia in the UK', *Liber Quarterly*, Vol. 11(1), pp. 98-102.

Ball, D. and Pye, J. (2000), 'Library Purchasing Consortia: the UK Periodicals Supply Market', *Learned Publishing*, Vol. 13(1), pp. 25-35.

Barzey, A. (2003), *Mapping The Territory: A Baseline Study of The Ability Of Museums, Archives and Libraries to Contribute to the Government's Targets for Adult Basic Skills in England*, Resource, London (URL: http://www.literacytrust.org.uk/mapping/report.html), [15.8.2005].

Baverstock, A. (1997), *How to Market Books*, Kogan Page, London.

BBC (2004), 'Blair's Pledge to Older Learners', *BBC Online* (URL: http://news.bbc.co.uk/2/hi/uk_news/education/3712183.stm), [20.8.2005].

BBC News (12 March 2005), Libraries 'in scandalous state' (URL: http://news.bbc.co.uk/1/hi/uk/4334949.stm), [26.8.2005].

BBC News Online (2002), *'UK' Tops Literary Spending League: BBC News Online*, 8th November (URL: http://news.bbc.co.uk/1/hi/business/2416995.stm), [5.11.2004].

BBC News Online (2004), *Libraries Face Cash Crisis* (URL: http://news.bbc.co.uk/2/hi/uk_news/northern_ireland/3506206.stm), [6.12.2004].

BBC Press Office (2003), *The Big Read - the Final is on Saturday*, URL: http://www.bbc.tv/pressoffice/pressreleases/stories/2003/12_december/11/big_read_final.shtml), [8.11.2004].

BCS (2002), *BCS Press Release: Productivity Hit by Skills Gap* (URL: http://www1.bcs.org.uk/DocsRepository/04100/4125/skillsgap.htm), [23.11.2004].

Beard, R. (1998), *National Literacy Strategy. Review of Research and Other Related Evidence*, Department for Education and Employment, London.

Bennett, M. (2001), 'Reaching Those in Need', *Public Library Journal*, Vol. 16(4), pp. 105-107.

Benstead, K., Sapcey, R. and Goulding, A. (forthcoming), 'Changing Public Library Service Delivery to Rural Communities in England', *New Library World*, forthcoming.

Bertram Library Services (2005), *'More Books for their Buck': Practical Solution to the Challenges Facing UK Public Library Supply; a Perspective from Bertram Library Services* (URL: http://www.bertrams.com/Aboutus/Bertram%20Library%20Services%20Prospectus.pdf), [21.11.2004].

Bevin, D. and Goulding, A. (1999), 'Homework Clubs in Public Libraries', *New Library World*, Vol. 100(1147), pp. 49-59.

Bird, V. (2004), *Literacy and Social Exclusion: the Policy Challenge. A Discussion Paper* (URL: http://www.literacytrust.org.uk/), [21.11.2004].

Black, A. (1996), 'Local Politics and National Provision', in M. Kinnell and P. Sturges (eds), *Continuity and Innovation in the Public Library: The Development of a Social Institution*, Library Association Publishing, London, pp. 48-66.

Black, A. (2000), *The Public Library in Britain 1914-2000*, The British Library, London.

Bohme, S. and Spiller, D. (1999), *Perspectives of Public Library Use 2. A Compendium of Survey Information*, Library and Information Statistics Unit (LISU) & Book Marketing Ltd (BML), Loughborough and London.

Boissé, A.A. (1996), 'Adjusting the Horizontal Hold: Flattening the Organization', *Library Administration and Management*, Vol. 10(2), pp. 77-91.

Book Marketing Ltd (2000), *Reading the Situation: Book Reading, Buying and Borrowing Habits in Britain*, Book Marketing Ltd, London.

Book Marketing Limited (2003), *Evaluation of the Continuing Impact of the DCMS/Wolfson Public Library Challenge Fund, 2000-02*, Resource, London (URL: http://www.mla.gov.uk/action/dcmswolf/00dcmswo.asp), [11.11.2004].

Book Marketing Limited (2004), *Serving Families Well*, Book Marketing Limited, London (URL: http://www.mla.gov.uk/documents/fff_eyln_rep.doc), [13.8.2005].

Bookstart (2005), *Extending the National Bookstart Programme – 2005/06* (URL: http://www.bookstart.co.uk/bookstart/schemes/docs/Section1.pdf), [7.8.2005].

Bostwick, A. E. (1910), *The American Public Library*, Appleton, New York.

Branching Out (no date), 'Liverpool's Experience with the Stock Quality Health Check' (URL: http://www.branching-out.net/branching-out/page2.asp?idno=874), [13.8.2005].

Brookfield, S.D. (1883), Adult Learner, Adult Education and the Community, Open University Press, Milton Keynes, quoted in Smith, M. K. (2004), *Learning in the Community and Community Learning: The Encyclopaedia of Informal Education* (URL: http://infed.org/lifelonglearning/b-edcom.htm), [21.11.2004].

Brophy, P. (2002), *The People's Network: A Turning Point for Public Libraries. First Findings*, Resource, London (URL: http://www.resource.gov.uk/documents/pnreport.pdf), [23.11.2004].

Brophy, P. (2003), *The People's Network: A Turning Point for Public Libraries. First Findings*, Resource, London (URL: http://www.resource.gov.uk/documents/pnreport.pdf), [21.11.2004].

Brophy, P. (2004), *The People's Network: Moving Forward*, MLA, London (URL: http://www.mla.gov.uk/documents/id1414rep.pdf), [24.8.2005].

Bryson, J., Usherwood, B. and Proctor, R. (2003), *Libraries Must Also be Buildings? New Library Impact Study*, Resource, London (URL: http://cplis.shef.ac.uk/New%20Library%20Impact%20Study.pdf), [25.8.2005].

Bryson, J., Usherwood, B. and Proctor, R. (2003), *Libraries Must Also Be Buildings? New Library Impact Study*, CPLIS, Sheffield.

Buckley, J. (2003), 'E-service Quality and the Public Sector', *Managing Service Quality*, Vol. 13(6), pp. 453-462.

Building Centre Trust (2000), *Annual Review 1999-2000*, Building Centre Trust, London. Quoted in Bryson, J., Usherwood, B. and Proctor, R. (2003), *Libraries Must Also Be Buildings? New Library Impact Study*, CPLIS, Sheffield, p. 45.

Building Trust Centre (2000), Annual Review 1999-2000, Building Centre Trust, London. Quoted in Bryson J., Usherwood, B. and Proctor, R. (2003), *Libraries Must Also Be Buildings? New Library Impact Study*, Resource, London, p. 45.

Burns Owens Partnership (2005), *New Directions in Social Policy: Developing the Evidence Base for Museums, Libraries and Archives in England* (URL: www.mla.gov.uk/documents/ndsp_developing_evidence.doc), [31.8.2005].

Cabe (Commission for Architecture and the Built Environment) (2003), *Better Public Libraries*, Cabe and Resource, London (URL: http://www.mla.gov.uk/documents/id874rep.pdf), [31.8.2005].

Cabinet Office (1999), *Modernising Government*, The Stationary Office, London.

Capital Planning Information (1998), *A Matter of Choice: Information Used in Public Library Book Selection*, CPI, Bruton.

Capital Planning Information (1999), *Outsourcing Book Selection: Supplier Selection in Public Libraries*, CPI Ltd, Bruton.

Carpenter, H. (2005), *Welcome to Your Library Project: Development Public Library Services for Asylum Seekers and Refugees in the London Boroughs of Brent, Camden, Enfield, Merton, Newham. Final Report* (URL: http://www.llda.org.uk/files/WTYL_PC_FINAL_REPORT.pdf), [31.8.2005].

Central Office of Information (1998), *Our Information Age: the Government's Vision*, Central Office of Information, London.

Chadwick, A. and May, C. (2003), 'Interaction Between States and Citizens in the Age of the Internet: "E-government" in the United States, Britain and the European Union', *Governance*, Vol. 16(2), pp. 271-300.

Chapman, A., Creaser, C. and Spiller, D. (2000), 'Trends in Monograph Acquisitions in UK Libraries', *Library Management*, Vol. 21(6), pp. 307-315.

Child to Read Well (1997), The Literacy Task Force, London (URL: http://www.leeds.ac.uk/educol/documents/000000153.htm), [13.8.2005].

Cilip (2002), *The Comprehensive Performance Assessment Framework for Single Tier and County Councils The Audit Commission Consultation Papers. A Short Briefing Paper* (*URL:* http://www.cilip.org.uk/professionalguidance/lobbying/consultations2002/cpa/shortbriefing.htm), [22.5.2005].

Cilip (2003), *Cilip Framework of Qualifications: Consultation Document on the Proposed New Framework of Qualifications to be Introduced in Spring 2005*, Cilip, London.

Cilip (2003), *Library and Information Services for Disabled People* (URL: http://www.cilip.org.uk/professionalguidance/equalopportunities/briefings/Disability.htm), [30.8.2005].

Cilip News (2003), 'Clear Water Between Cilip and Minister on Public Library Resourcing', *Cilip News*, 19/03/03 (URL: http://www.cilip.org.uk/news/2003/190303.html), [28.11.2004].

Cilip News (2003), 'Essential Public Library Services Need Resources to Do the Job', *Cilip News*, 11/02/03 (URL: http://www.cilip.org.uk/news/2003/110203.html), [28.11.2004].

Cilip News (2004), 'Libraries in Spotlight as Government Acknowledges Challenges', *Cilip News*, 24/06/04 (URL: http://www.cilip.org.uk/news/2004/040624.html), [26.11.2004].

Cilip Working Group on Library Provision for Children and Young People (2002), *Start with the Child: Report of the Cilip Working Group on Library Provision for Children and Young People*, Cilip, London (URL: http://www.cilip.org.uk/NR/rdonlyres/D94ED35A-81DB-4421-9815-74F2B454A7AB/0/startwiththechild.pdf), [9.8.2005].

Cilip Working Group on Library Provision for Children and Young People (2002), *Start with the Child. Report of the Cilip Working Group on Library Provision for Children and Young People*, Cilip, London (URL: http://www.cilip.org.uk/professionalguidance/youngpeople/startwiththechild), [15.8.2005].

Cipfa (2003), *Public Library Statistics. 2001-02 Actuals*, Cipfa, London.

Cipfa (2004), *Public Library Statistics 2002/3: Actuals*, Cipfa, London.

Cipfa , *Public Library User Surveys (PLUS) National Report 2001–2002* (URL: http://www.ipf.co.uk/plus/plus_nationalreport_200102.pdf), [21.11.2004].

Circle of Officers of National and Regional Library Systems (CONARLS) (2000), *Carpe Diem. Modelling Futures for Library Regions in a Changing Cultural Environment*, Resource, London (Library and Information Commission Research Report 88).

Clive, S. (2003), *Getting it Together*, Resource, London (URL: http://www.mla.gov.uk/documents/engagerep.pdf), [22.8.2005].

Clore Leadership Programme Task Force (2002), *Cultural Leadership: The Clore Leadership Programme. Task Force Final Report, December 2002* (URL: http://www.clreleadership.org/full_report.htm), [26.8.2005].

Coates, T. (2004), *Who's in Charge? Responsibility for the Public Library Service*, Libri, London (URL: http://www.rwevans.co.uk/libri/Who%27s%20in%20char_e_(as%20printed.pdf), [17.12.2004].

Community Development Foundation(2004), *What is Community Development?* (URL: http://www.cdf.org.uk/html/whatis.html), [20.11.2004].

Community Development Foundation (2004), *Social Inclusion and Community Development Practice* (URL: http://www.cdf.org.uk/html/socinc.html), [19.11.2004].

Community Librarian (2003), 'Through a Glass, Clearly', *Community Librarian*, 30 (Summer), p.14.

Cookman, N., Haynes, D. and Streatfield, D. (2000), *The Use of Volunteers in Public Libraries: A Report to the Library Association*, David Haynes Associates & Information Management Associates, London & Twickenham (URL: http://www.la-hq.org.uk/directory/prof_issues/vols.pdf), [26.8.2005].

Coombes, P.H. and Ahmed, M. (1974), Attacking Rural Poverty. How non-formal Education Can Help, Johns Hopkins University Press, Baltimore, quoted in Smith, M. K. (1999) *Informal Learning: The Encyclopaedia of Informal Education* (URL: http://infed.org/biblio/inf-lrn.htm), [21.11.2004].

Corry, D. and Stoker, G. (no date), *New Localism. Fashioning the Centre-local Relationship*, New Local Government Network, London.

COSLA (1995), *Standards for the Public Library Service in Scotland*, COSLA, Edinburgh.

Countryside Agency (2000), *Not Seen, Not Heard? Social Exclusion in Rural Areas*, Countryside Agency Publications, Wetherby.

Crane, P. (2000), 'Young people and public space: developing inclusive policy and practice', *Scottish Youth Issues Journal*, Vol. 1, No. 1, pp. 105-124.

Creaser, C. and Maynard, S. (2003), *A Survey of Library Services to Schools and Children in the UK 2002-2003*, LISU, Loughborough.

Creaser, C., Maynard, S. and White, S. (2003), *LISU Annual Library Statistics 2003*, LISU, Loughborough.

Creaser, C., Maynard, S. and White, S. (2004), *LISU Annual Library Statistics 2004*, LISU, Loughborough.

CSV (2003), *CSV Reports on Lending Time* (URL: http://www.csv.org.uk/Volunteer/Part-time/Lending+Time/), [25.8.2005].

Culture, Media and Sport Committee (2000), *Culture, Media and Sport- Sixth Report* (URL: http://www.publications.parliament.uk/pa/cm199900/cmselect/cmcumeds/241/24102.htm), [27.11.2004].

Culture, Media and Sport Committee (2004), *Uncorrected Transcript of Oral Evidence Taken Before the Culture, Media and Sport Committee on Tuesday 30 November 2004* (URL: http://www.publications.parliament.uk/pa/cm200405/cmselect/cmcumeds/uc81-i/uc8102.htm), [30.6.2005].

Culture, Media and Sport Committee (2004), *Uncorrected Transcript of Oral Evidence Taken Before the Culture, Media and Sport Committee on Tuesday 14*

December 2004 (URL: http://www.publications.parliament.uk/pa/cm200405/cmselect/cmcumeds/uc81-ii/uc8102.htm), [30.6.2005].

Culture, Media and Sport Committee (2005), *Public Libraries. Third Report of Session 2004-05. Volume 1. Report, together with formal minutes.* (URL: http://www.parliament.the-stationery-office.co.uk/pa/cm200405/cmselect/cmcumeds/ 81/81i.pdf), [22.7.2005].

CyMAL (2004), *CyMAL: Museums, Archives and Libraries Wales Initial Prospectus*, CyMAL, Aberystwyth (URL: http://www.cymal.wales.gov.uk/), [24.08.2005].

CyMAL (2004), *CyMAL: Museums, Archives and Libraries Wales Initial Prospectus*, CyMAL, Aberystwyth (URL: http://www.ncaonline.org.uk/lottsrccymal_museums_archives_and_libraries_wales.html), [2.5.2005].

D'Elia, G., Jörgensesn, D. and Woelfel, J. (2002), 'The Impact of the Internet on Public Library Use: an Analysis of the Current Consumer Market for Library and Internet Services', *Journal of the American Society for Information Science and Technology*, Vol. 53(10), pp. 802-820.

Demos (2003), *Towards a Strategy for Workforce Development*, Demos, London.

Department for Culture, Media and Sport (DCMS) (1999), *Libraries and the Regions: A Discussion Paper*, DCMS, London (URL: http://www.culture.gov.uk/pdf/librariestext.pdf), [22.8.2005].

Department for Culture, Media and Sport (1999), *Libraries for All: Social Inclusion in Public Libraries: Policy Guidance for Local Authorities in England*, DCMS, London (URL: http://www.culture.gov.uk/pdf/socialin.pdf), [28.8.2005].

Department for Culture, Media and Sport (DCMS) (2001), *Comprehensive, Efficient and Modern Public Libraries - Standards and Assessment*, DCMS, London (URL: http://www.culture.gov.uk/PDF/libraries_pls_assess.pdf, [22.08.2005].

Department for Culture, Media and Sport (2001), *Libraries, Museums, Galleries and Archives for All*, DCMS, London (URL: http://www.culture.gov.uk/PDF/libraries_archives_for_all.pdf), [31.8.2005].

Department for Culture, Media and Sport (DCMS) (2003), *Framework for the Future. Libraries, Learning and Information in the Next Decade*, DCMS, London (URL: http://www.culture.gov.uk/global/publications/archive_2003/framework_future.htm), [3.4.2005].

Department of Culture, Media and Sport (DCMS) (2003), *Framework for the Future. Libraries, Learning and Information in the Next Decade*, DCMS, London (URL: http://www.culture.gov.uk/PDF/libraries_pls_assess.pdf), [22.11.2004].

Department for Culture, Media and Sport (2004), *Consultation on the Service Public Library Standards* (URL: http://www.culture.gov.uk/NR/rdonlyres/ecs6j55xhl5uxys3d4mjfreyx3s4rjrhb6eq755tv4oh26cljbvmwnesoua7jqkyzoorjgyuypuk5eq5jhhihdfa2jc/ServiceStandardsconsultationlet.pdf), [22.11.2004].

Department for Culture, Media and Sport (DCMS) (2004), *Culture at the Heart of Regeneration*, DCMS, London (URL: http://www.culture.gov.uk/NR/rdonlyres/AD9F039E-4C09-42B6-98F2-7F88096A11E2/0/DCMSCulture.pdf), [16.08.2005].

Department for Culture, Media and Sport (2004), *Elected Regional Assemblies and the Cultural Sector* (URL: http://www.culture.gov.uk/global/consultations/

2004+current+consultations/default.htm?properties=2004+current+consultations %2C%2C), [18.05.2005].

Department for Culture, Media and Sport (2004), *Libraries and Communities* (URL: http://www.culture.gov.uk/libraries_and_communities/default.htm), [16.5.2005].

Department for Culture, Media and Sport (DCMS) (2004), *Report to Parliament on Public Library Matters*, DCMS, London (URL: http://www.culture.gov.uk/NR/rdonlyres/B07A3589-5C82-496D-9643-A5986B210EBE/0/LibrariesReporttoParliament04.pdf), [18.11.2004].

Department for Culture Media and Sport and MLA (2005), *Efficient Public Libraries* (URL: http://www.mla.gov.uk/documents/fff_efficiency_jointstatement.pdf), [5.8.2005].

Department for Education and Employment (1998), *The Learning Age: A Renaissance for a New Britain*, HMSO, London, Cm. 3790 (URL: http://www.lifelonglearning.co.uk/greenpaper/index.htm), [9.8.2005].

Department for Education and Employment (2001), *Skills for Life: The National Strategy for Improving Adult Literacy and Numeracy Skills*, Department for Education and Employment, London (URL: http://www.dfee.gov.uk/readwriteplus), [9.8.2005].

Department for Education and Skills (2003), *21st Century Skills: Realising Our Potential*, HMSO, London, Cm 5810 (URL: http://www.dfes.gov.uk/skillsstrategy/subPage.cfm?action=whitePaper.default), [16.8.2005].

Department for the Environment, Transport and the Regions (DETR) (1997), *Building Partnerships for Prosperity: Sustainable Growth, Competitiveness and Employment in the English Regions*, DETR, London.

Department for the Environment, Transport and the Regions (1998), *Modern Local Government: in Touch with the People*, DETR, London (URL: http://www.odpm.gov.uk/stellent/groups/odpm_localgov/documents/pdf/odpm_locgov_pdf_605468.pdf), [7.11.2004].

Department of Culture, Arts and Leisure (2002), *Tomorrow's Libraries. Views of the Public Library Sector* (URL: http://www.dcalni.gov.uk/libraries.htm), [18.11.2004].

Department of National Heritage (DNH), *Reading the Future*, DNH, London.

Department of Trade and Industry (1998), *Our Competitive Future: Building the Knowledge Driven Economy*, DTI, London (URL: http://www.dti.gov.uk/comp/competitive/main.htm), [11.6.2005].

Department of Trade and Industry (2002), Press Release: *UK Workers Struggle to Balance Work and Quality of Life as Long Hours and Stress Take Hold* (URL: http://www.dti.gov.uk/work-lifebalance/press300802.html), [23.11.2004].

Disability Rights Commission (2004), *Disability Discrimination Act – What Does it Mean?* (URL: http://www.drc-gb.org/thelaw/thedda.asp), [13.8.2005].

Docherty, I., Goodlad, R. and Paddison, R. (2001), 'Civic culture, community and citizen participation in contrasting neighbourhoods', *Urban Studies*, Vol. 38(12), pp. 2225-2250.

Dodd, C., Baignet, H. and Woodhouse, S. (2002), *NOF ICT Training Programme for Public Library Staff: Interim Survey of Training to Meet Expected Outcomes*

2-8 & Advanced Levels of the Programme, Resource, London (URL: http://www.peoplesnetwork.gov.uk/documents/id598rep.pdf), [22.11.2004].

Doughty, M. (1999), 'A Wide View from a High Place', *Public Library Journal*, Vol. 14(4), pp. 86-90.

Durrani, S. (2001), *Social and Racial Exclusion Handbook for Libraries, Archives, Museums and Galleries*, The Social Exclusion Action Planning Network, Exeter.

Durrani, S. (2002), 'Combating Racial Discrimination in British Public Libraries: the Role of the Quality Leaders Project', *Library Management*, Vol. 23(1/2), pp. 23-52.

Early Years Library Network (2004), *Children's Centres; Guidance for Librarians* (URL: http://www.cilip.org.uk/eyln/archive/news5a.htm), [17.11.2004].

Early Years Library Network (2004), *National Audit of Impact of Library Service on Sure Start Families* (URL: http://www.cilip.org.uk/eyln/archive/news1.htm), [21.11.2004].

Ede, S. (2002), *Snapshot Diagnostic of Data Flow in Relation to the Library Domain*, Resource, London.

Ede, S. (2003), *Full Report of the WILIP Consultation Exercise*, Resource, London.

Education and Employment Committee (2000), *Examination of Witnesses (Questions 380-395)* (URL: http://www.parliament.the-stationery-office.co.uk/pa/cm199900/cmselect/cmeduemp/386/0062104.htm), [08.12.2005].

ELFNI (2001), *Results of an Equality Impact Assessment* (URL: http://www.ni-libraries.net/app/content/docs/Equality Impact Of Electronic Libraries.pdf), [24.8.2005].

Elkin, J. and Kinnell, M. (eds) (2000), *A Place for Children: Public libraries as a Major Force in Children's Reading*, Library Association Publishing, London.

Europa (2003), *Common List of Basic Public Services* (URL: http://europa.eu.int/information_society/eeurope/action_plan/pdf/basicpublicservices.pdf), [23.11.2004].

Eurostat (2004), *Living Conditions in Europe Statistical Pocketbook*, Office for Official Publications of the European Communities, Luxembourg.

Every Child Matters (2003), TSO, Norwich (URL: http://www.everychildmatters.gov.uk/_files/EBE7EEAC90382663E0D5BBF24C99A7AC.pdf), [16.12.2005].

Evangelou, M. and Sylva, K. (2003), *The Effects of the Peers Early Education Partnership (PEEP) on Children's Developmental Progress*, DfES Brief No. RB489 (URL: http://www.dfes.gov.uk/research/data/uploadfiles/RB489.doc), [22.11.2004].

Evans, G. and Shaw, P. (2004), *The Contribution of Culture to Regeneration in the UK: a Review of Evidence* (URL: http://www.mmu.ac.uk/regional/culture/reports/Contributionofculturetoregeneration.pdf), [10.8.2005].

Fine, A. (2002), 'Losing Sight of the Library Child', *68th IFLA Council and General Conference, August 18-24 2002* (URL: http://www.ifla.org/IV/ifla68/papers/165-218e.pdf), [24.11.2005].

Folker, B. and Hafner, A. W. (1993), 'The Canonicity Debate: an Overview for the Librarian', in A. W. Hafner (ed), *Democracy and the Public Library*, Greenwood Press, Westport CT, pp. 45-66.

Fox, K and Rikards, L. (2004), *Sport and Leisure. Results from the Sport and Leisure Module of the 2002; General Household Survey*, The Statistics Office, London (URL: http://www.statistics.gov.uk/downloads/theme_compendia/Sport&Leisure.pdf), [22.11.2004].

Froud, R. and Mackenzie, C. E. (2002), *Government and Public Libraries. Promoting Local and National Agendas*, Bertelsmann Foundation Publishers, Gutersloh (URL: http://www.internationalesnetzwerk.de/en/x_media/pdf/e_government_engl.pdf), [28.11.2004].

Fry, J., Wallis, M. and Southern, J. (2000), *Community and Region: Scale Economies in Public Libraries, Museums and Archives*, Library and Information Commission, London (Library and Information Commission Report 96).

Garcia, J. and Sutherland, S. (1999), *Public Library Administrators in the Political Arena*, Bertelsmann Foundation Publishers, Gütersloh,(URL: http://www.internationalesnetzwerk.de/en/x_media/pdf/public_library_administrators_englisch.pdf), [22.11.2004].

Garcia, J., Knight, T. and Sutherland, S. (2001), *Learning from Others*, Bertlesmann Foundation, Gütersloh (URL: http://www.internationalesnetzwerk.de/en/x_media/pdf/learning_from_others.pdf), [19.11.2004].

Gates Foundation (2004), *Toward Equality of Access: The Role of Public Libraries in Addressing the Digital Divide* (URL: http://www.gatesfoundation.org/nr/Downloads/libraries/uslibraries/reports/TowardEqualityofAccess.pdf), [24.8.2005].

Goulding, A. (1996), *Managing Change for Library Support Staff*, Avebury, Aldershot.

Goulding, A. (2005), 'The public library: a successful public space?', In Turner, P. and Davenport, E. (eds), *Space, Spatiality and Technology*, Springer, Dordrecht, pp. 45-66.

Goulding, A., Bromham, B., Hannabuss, S. and Cramer, D. (1999), *Likely to Succeed: Attitudes and Aptitudes for an Effective Information Profession in the 21st Century*, Library and Information Commission, London (Library and Information Commission Report 8).

Goulding, A. and Kerslake, E. (1996), *Developing the Flexible Library and Information Workforce: A Quality and Equal Opportunities Perspective*, British Library Research and Innovation Centre, London (British Library Research and Innovation Report 25).

Goulding, A. and Kerslake, E. (1996), 'Flexible Working in Libraries: Profit and Potential Pitfalls', *Library Management*, Vol. 17(2), pp. 8-16.

Goulding, A. and Kerslake, E. (1996), 'Flexible Working in UK Library and Information Services: Current Practice and Concerns', *Journal of Librarianship and Information* Science, Vol. 28(4), pp 203-216.

Gray, R. (1998), 'Evolution or Extinction: the Current State of Library Supply', *Public Library Journal*, Vol. 13(5), pp. 70-72.

Great Britain (1964), *Public Libraries and Museums Act 1964. Chapter 75*, HMSO, London.

Greenhalgh, L. and Worpole, K. (1995), *Libraries in a World of Cultural Change*, UCL Press, London.

Gregory, W. (1996), *Informability: the Informability Manual. Making Information More Accessible in the Light of the Disability Discrimination Act*, Blackstone Press, London.
Grindlay, D.J.C. and Morris, A. (2004), 'The Decline in Adult Book lending in UK Public Libraries and its Possible Causes II. Statistical Analysis', Journal of Documentation, Vol. 60(6), pp. 632-657.
Hafner, A. W. and Mick, T. M. (1993), 'Mortimer J. Adler's and Robert M. Hutchins's Vision of the Great Books', in A. W. Hafner (ed), *Democracy and the Public Library*, Greenwood Press, Westport CT, pp. 67-104.
Handy, C. (1991), *The Age of Unreason*, Business Books, London.
Hansard (2004), *Library Service* (URL: http://www.publications.parliament.uk/pa/ld199900/ldhansrd/pdvn/lds04/text/40317-06.htm), [6.5.2005].
Hansard (2004), *Libraries: Libri Report* (URL: http://www.publications.parliament.uk/pa/ld199900/ldhansrd/pdvn/lds04/text/40506-01.htm-40506-01_star0), [12.5.2005].
Harris, K. (1998) *Open to interpretation: community perceptions of the social benefits of public libraries*. London, Community Development Foundation.
Harris, K. and Dudley, M. (2005), *Public Library and Social Cohesion. Developing Indicators*, MLA, London (URL: http://www.mla.gov.uk/documents/id1410rep.pdf), [31.08.2005].
Hartley, J. (2001), *Reading Groups*, Oxford University Press, Oxford.
Hartley, R. (1990), 'The Social and Economic Costs of Low Levels of Literacy', *Australian Public Libraries and Information Services*, Vol. 3(3), pp. 143-148.
Hawkins, M. and Malley, I. (1999), *Joint Service Delivery Arrangements as the Basis of Cooperation Between Library Authorities*, Library and Information Commission, London (Library and Information Commission Report 4).
Hawkins, M., Morris, A. and Sumsion, J. (2001), 'Socio-economic Features of UK Public Library Users', *Library Management*, Vol. 22(6/7), pp. 258-265.
Hedges, G. (2002), 'Should libraries open on Sundays?', *Christian Librarian*, Vol. 26, pp. 59-66.
Heeks, P. (1996), 'Services to Schools', in M. Kinnell and P. Sturges, *Continuity and Innovation in the Public Library: The Development of a Social Institution*, Library Association, London.
Herrera, L. (no date), *Transforming Libraries into Community-Based Partnerships, Perspective Paper no. 5* (URL: http://www.library.ca.gov/LDS/convo/convoc09.html), [31.08.2005].
Hicken, M. (2002), 'Equally good', *Public Library Journal*, Vol. 17(2), pp.51-3.
Hoggart, R. (1958), *The Uses of Literacy*, Penguin, Harmondsworth.
Hoggett, P. (1996), 'New Modes of Control in the Public Service', *Public Administration*, Vol. 74, pp. 3-32, quoted in J. Rouse, 'Performance Management Under New Labour: Really new or merely more of the same'.
Holden, J. (2004), *Creative Reading*, Demos, London (URL: http://www.demos.co.uk/catalogue/creativereading/), [13.8.2005].
Holt, G.E. (1999), *Public Library Partnerships: Mission-driven Tools for 21st Century Success*, Bertelsmann Foundation, Gütersloh (URL: http://www.internationales-netzwerk.de/en/x_media/pdf/holt6en.pdf), [31.08.2005].

Hood, C. (1986), *Administrative Analysis*, Harvester Wheatsheaf, Brighton quoted in C. Needham, *Citizen-consumers: New Labour's marketplace democracy*, Catalyst, London. (URL: http://www.catalystforum.org.uk/pdf/needham.pdf), p. 30, [25.8.2005].

Hutton, W. (2004), *Guardian Unlimited, The Observer: Living on Borrowed Time.* (URL: http://observer.guardian.co.uk/columnists/story/0,12877,1208110,00.html), [20.5.2005].

I&DeA and MLA (2005), *Library Peer Review Programme. Evaluation of Pilots and Phase 1 of the Programme* (URL: http://www.mla.gov.uk/documents/fff_programme_eval_may05_rep.pdf), [22.08.2005].

Institute for Volunteering Research (2002), *Volunteers in the Cultural Sector*, Resource, London (URL: http://www.mla.gov.uk/documents/volunteers.pdf), [26.8.2005].

Jones, B., Sprague, M., Nankivell, C. and Richter, K. (1999), *Staff in the New Library: Skill Needs and Learning Choices*, British Library Research and Innovation Centre, London (British Library Research and Innovation Report 152).

Kearns, A. and Turok, I. (2004), *Sustainable Communities: Dimensions and Challenges*, Office of the Deputy Prime Minister, London.

Kempster, G. (2000), 'The Sunday experience', *Assignation*, Vol. 17, No. 4, pp. 4-6.

Kerr, G. (2001), *Evidence Based Stock Management: the Testing of a New Tool for Librarians*, CPI, Loughborough.

King. R. and Tilley, B. (2001), 'Role model for success', *Public Library Journal*, Vol. 16, No 4, pp. 129-130.

Kinnell, M. (1991), *All Change? Public Library Management Strategies for the 1990s*, Taylor Graham, London.

Kinnell, M. (1996), 'Managing in a Corporate Culture: the Role of the Chief Librarian' in M. Kinnell and P. Sturges (eds.), *Continuity and Innovation in the Public Library: The Development of a Social Institution*, Library Association Publishing, London.

Kirk, W., McMenemy, D. and Poulter, A. (2004), 'Family Learning Services in UK Public Libraries: an investigation of current provision and ongoing development', *New Library World*, Vol. 105 (1200/1201), pp. 176-183.

KPMG and CPI (1995), *DNH study: Contracting-out in Public Libraries*, KPMG, London.

Kranich, N. (2004), 'Libraries: the Information Commons of Civil Society', in D. Schuler (ed), *Shaping the Network Society*, MIT Press, Cambridge, pp. 279-300.

Laird, D. (2004), 'Insight into Blended Learning. The Birmingham Experience', *Library and Information Update*, Vol. 3(4), pp. 40-41.

Larsen, J.I., Jacobs, D.L. and van Vlimmeren, T. (2004), *Cultural Diversity: How Public Libraries Can Serve the Diversity in the Community*. Bertelsmann Foundation, Gütersloh (URL: http://www.internationalesnetzwerk.de/en/x_media/pdf/cultural_diversity_040217.pdf), [22.11.2004].

Lawes, A. (1995), 'Contracting Out', *New Library World*, Vol. 95(1114), pp. 8-12.

Lawes, A. (1995), 'Managing People for Whom One is Not Directly Responsible', *Law Librarian*, Vol. 26(3), pp. 421-3.

Leadbeater (2003). *Overdue. How to Create a Modern Public Library Service*, Demos, London (Laser Foundation Report) (URL: http://www.demos.co.uk/catalogue/default.aspx?id=262), [16.11.2004].

Learning and Skills Council (2003), *Skills in England. Vol. 1*, Department for Education and Skills, London (URL: http://www.lsc.gov.uk/NR/rdonlyres/e6cpkiexyjhgvccqqejg5rdiqyqofijn6hmo2f5vr4f3w2sradzbcfa2zdntztwo52jfapjnjgil5p/SkillsinEnglandVol1.pdf), [7.8.2005].

Leckie, G.J. and Hopkins, J. (2002), 'The Public Place of Central Libraries: Findings from Toronto and Vancouver', *Library Quarterly*, Vol. 72 (3), pp. 326-372.

Library and Information Commission (1997), *New Library: the People's Network*, LIC, London (URL: http://www.ukoln.ac.uk/services/lic/newlibrary/contents.html), [26.8.2005].

Library and Information Commission (1998), *Building the New Library Network*, Library and Information Commission, London (URL: http://www.mla.gov.uk/information/legacy/lic_pubs/policyreports/building) [24.8.2005].

Library and Information Commission (2000), *Empowering the Learning Community*, Library and Information Commission, London (URL: http://www.mla.gov.uk/information/legacy/lic_pubs/policyreports/empower/index.html), [09.12.05].

Library and Information Commission (2000), *Libraries: the Essence of Inclusion* (URL: http://www.mla.gov.uk/information/legacy/lic_pubs/policyreports/inclusion.html), [31.08.2005].

Library and Information Services Council (Wales) (2003), *Mapping Social Inclusion in Publicly-funded Libraries in Wales*, Welsh Assembly Government, Cardiff.

Library and Information Update (2004), 'Deliver, urges Clarke', *Library and Information Update*, Vol. 3(4), p. 3.

Library and Information Update (2004), 'Streamlined for Action?', *Library and Information Update*, Vol. 3(6), p. 4.

Library and Information Update (2004), 'The Good News', *Library and Information Update*, Vol. 3(6), p. 2.

Library Association (2001), *Early Years Advocacy Pack* (URL: http://www.la-hq.org.uk/directory/prof_issues/early01.html), [12.8.2005].

Library Association (2001), *Early Years Survey* (URL: http://www.la-hq.org.uk/groups/ylg/ylr/early.html), [12.11.2004].

Library Association (2001), *Libraries and Lifelong Learning: a Strategy 2002-4*, Library Association, London (URL: http://www.la-hq.org.uk/directory/prof_issues/lls.pdf), [5.8.2005].

Library Association Policy Advisory Group (2001), *Devolution and Regionalism in the UK: Report of the Policy Advisory Group* (URL: http://www.la-hq.org.uk/directory/prof_issues/reg1.html), [22.8.2005].

Liddle, D., Hicks, D. and Barton, D. (1999), *Public Libraries and the Arts: Pathways to Partnerships*, Capital Planning Information Ltd, Stamford.

Linley, R. and Usherwood, B. (1998), *New Measures for the New Library: A Social Audit of Public Libraries*, British Library Research and Innovation Centre, London.

Linley, R. (2004), *New Directions in Social Policy: Communities and Inclusion Policy for Museums, Library and Archives*, MLA, London. Available from: (URL: http://www.mla.gov.uk/documents/ndsp_communities_inclusion.doc), [31.08.2005].

LISU (2003), *Public Library Materials Fund and Budget Survey 2002-4*, LISU, Loughborough.

Literacy Taskforce, *A Reading Revolution: How We Can Teach Every.*

Loader, B.D. and Keeble, L. (2004), *Challenging the Digital Divide? A Literature Review of Community Informatics Initatives*, Joseph Rowntree Foundation, York (URL: http://www.jrf.org.uk/bookshop/eBooks/1859351980.pdf), [24.08.2005].

Local Government Association (2003), *Raising Education Standards in Schools and Beyond*. The Contribution from Cultural Services, Local Government Association, London (URL: http://www.lga.gov.uk/Publication.asp?lsection=0&ccat=28&id=SX6A3-A781CB51), [11.11.2004].

Local Government Association (2004), *Local Government Matters: Facts and Figures About Local Councils 2004-2005*, Local Government Association, London (URL: http://www.lga.gov.uk/Documents/Publication/ localgovmatters04final.pdf), [22.8.2005].

Lomer, M. and Rogers, S. (1983), *The Public Library and the Local Authority*. British Library, London (British Library Research and Development Report 5738).

London Borough of Southwark (1997), *Homework Help Clubs*, London Borough of Southwark Education and Leisure Services Department, unpublished report.

Maynard, S. (2003), *Library & Information Statistics Tables (LIST)*, LISU, Loughborough.

McCabe, R. (2001), *Civic Librarianship. Renewing the Social Mission of the Public Library*, Scarecrow, Folkestone.

McCaskill, K. and Goulding, A. (2001), 'English Public Library Services and the Disability Discrimination Act', *New Library World*, Vol. 102(1165), pp. 192-206.

McElwee, G. (2004), 'It's Never Too Early', *Library & Information Update*, Vol. 3(11), pp. 23-25.

McNicol, S. (2003), 'Dual-use libraries. Do they work?', *Library and Information Update*, Vol. 2, No. 10, pp. 52-53.

McNicol, S. and Dalton, P. (2003), *Public Libraries: Supporting the Learning Process*, CIRT, Birmingham (URL: http://www.ebase.uce.ac.uk/cirtarchive/projects/past/public_libraries.htm), [09.08.2005].

Mellor, W. and Parr, V. (2002), *Government Online: An International Perspective Annual Global Report* (URL: http://tnsofres.com/gostudy2002/), [19.11.2004].

Middleton, S. (2003), *An Introduction to Community Profiles & Social Inclusion for Community Team Librarians* (URL: http://www.seapn.org.uk/resources/communityprofiling.pdf), [31.08.2005].

Ministry of Education (1962), *Standards of Public Library Service in England and Wales (The Bourdillon Report)*, HMSO, London.

MLA (2003), *Inspiring Learning for All* (URL: http://www.mla.gov.uk/action/learnacc/00insplearn.asp), [7.8.2005].

MLA (2004), *Access For All Toolkit: Enabling Inclusion For Museums, Libraries and Archives*, MLA, London (URL: http://www.mla.gov.uk/documents/access_mla_tk.pdf), [31.08.2005].

MLA (2004), *A Quiet Revolution*, MLA, London (URL: http://www.mla.gov.uk/documents/fff_quiet_revolution.pdf), [01.09.2005].
MLA (2004), *Framework for the Future: Action Plan 2004-2006*, MLA, London (URL: http://www.mla.gov.uk/action/framework/framework_03.asp), [20.8.2005].
MLA (2004), *New Funding to Develop Public Libraries* (URL: http://www.peoplesnetwork.gov.uk/news/pressreleasearticle.asp?id=330), [14.11.2004].
MLA (2004), *Public libraries help turn young people into good citizens* (URL: http://www.mla.gov.uk/news/press_article.asp?articleid=739), [13.11.2004].
MLA (2004), Public Libraries Work with Readers – a Shared Vision (URL: http://www.mla.gov.uk/documents/powerpoint/fff_reading_mission.ppt), [16.8.2005].
MLA (2004), The People's Network: evaluation summary, London, MLA (URL;http://www.nof.org.uk/documents/live/8130p__Peoples_network_evaluation_summary.pdf), [24.8.2005].
MLA (2005), *Museums, Libraries, Archives*, MLA, London (URL: http://www.mla.gov.uk/documents/mla_broadsheet.pdf), [31.08.2005].
Molloy, M. (2003), 'Fine Words but False Ideas', *Library and Information Update*, Vol. 2(1), p. 21.
Moor, C. and Whitworth, J. (2001), *All Together Now? Social Inclusion in Rural Communities* (URL: http://www.lga.gov.uk/Documents/Briefing/socialinc.pdf), [31.08.2005].
Moore, N. (1999), 'Partners in the Information Society', *Library Association Record*, Vol. 101(12), pp. 702-703.
Moore, N. (2004), 'Public Library Trends', *Cultural Trends*, Vol. 31, No. 49, pp. 27-57.
Moore, N. (unpub.), 'Recent Trends in English Public Libraries' (Received December 11, 2004).
Mori (2002), *Perceptions of Libraries. Desk Research Conducted for Audit Commission*, Audit Commission, London.
Mori (2003), *Young People's Attitudes Towards Reading*, Nestle UK Ltd, Surrey (URL: http://www.mori.com/polls/2003/pdf/nfm17.pdf), [16.8.2005].
Morris, A. and Brown, A. (2004), 'Siting of Public Libraries in Retail Centres: Benefits and Effects', *Library Management*, Vol. 25(3), pp. 127-137.
Morris Hargreaves McIntyre (2002), *Start With the Child: The Needs and Motivations of Young People*, Morris Hargreaves MacIntyre, Manchester (URL: http://www.mla.gov.uk/documents/re179rep.pdf), [01.09.2005].
Muddiman, D., Durrani, S., Dutch, M., Linley, R., Pateman, J. and Vincent, J. (2000), *Open to All? The Public Library and Social Exclusion*, Resource, London (URL: http://www.mla.gov.uk/action/learnacc/00access_04.asp), [31.08.2005].
Muir, L. (2000), 'Why Should Public Libraries Use Electronic Data Interchange?', *New Library World*, Vol. 101, pp. 222-227.
Muir, L. and Fishwick, F. (2000), *Key Issues in Public Library Book Supply*, Library and Information Commission, London (URL: http://www.bic.org.uk/libsup.doc), [20.8.2005].
Mulholland, H. (2004), *Guardian Unlimited: Regional Government* (URL: http://society.guardian.co.uk/regionalgovernment/story/0,712821,00.html), [20.11.2004].

Mullis, I.V.S., Martin, M.O., Gonzalez, E.J. and Kennedy, A.M. (2003), *PIRLS 2001 International Report: IEA's Study of Reading Literacy Achievement in Primary Schools*, Boston College, Chestnut Hill, MA (URL: http://isc.bc.edu/pirls2001i/PIRLS2001_Pubs_IR.html), [20.8.2005].

National Acquisitions Group (1998), *Public Library Stock Management*, NAG, Leeds.

National Acquisitions Group (2003), *NAG Guidelines for Servicing*, NAG, Leeds.

National Centre for Research in Children's Literature (2001), *Evaluation of the Bookstart Programme*, Booktrust, London.

Needham, C. (2003), *Citizen-Consumers: New Labour's Marketplace Democracy*. Catalyst, London (URL: http://www.catalystforum.org.uk/pdf/needham.pdf), [25.8.2005].

Neighbourhood Renewal Unit (2004), *The Vision for Neighbourhood Renewal* (URL: http://www.neighbourhood.gov.uk/cncl.asp), [21.11.2004].

New Focus (2003), *Libraries Building Communities: Project Information Guide*, New Focus Research Pty Ltd (URL: http://www.libraries.vic.gov.au/downloads/Libraries_Building_Communities_Research__Development_Project_/2582library_boardproject_info_report1final.pdf), [31.08.2005].

Newman, A. and MacLean, F., 'Presumption, Policy and Practice: the Use of Museums and Galleries as Agents of Social Inclusion in Great Britain', *International Journal of Cultural Policy*, Vol. 10, No. 2.

NIACE (2003), *NIACE Evaluation of LSC Funded Family Programmes: Final Report* (URL: http://www.niace.org.uk/Research/Family/LSC_Funded_Family_Progs_Part1.pdf), [15.8.2005].

Niven, A. (1992), 'Introduction', in R. Van Riel (ed), *Reading the Future: a Place for Literature in Public Libraries*, Arts Council, London.

OECD (2000), *Literacy in the Information Age. Final Report of the International Adult Literacy Survey*, OECD, Paris.

Office of the Deputy Prime Minister (2002), *Your Region, Your Choice*, The Stationary Office, London (URL: http://www.odpm.gov.uk/stellent/groups/odpm_regions/documents/pdf/odpm_regions_pdf_607900.pdf), [22.11.2004].

Office of the Deputy Prime Minister (2004), *Tackling Social Exclusion: Taking Stock and Looking to the Future*, ODPM, London (URL: http://www.socialexclusionunit.gov.uk/impactstrends/pdfimptre/tackleSocEx.pdf), [23.11.2004].

Ofsted (2000), *Family Learning: A Survey of Current Practice*, Ofsted, London (URL: http://www.ofsted.gov.uk/publications/index.cfm?fuseaction=pubs.displayfile&id=465&type=pdf), [15.8.2005].

Opening the Book (2004), *Stock Quality Health Check. Adult Fiction and Poetry* (URL: http://www.branching-out.net/branching-out/page2.asp?idno=870), [20.8.2005].

Page, D. (2000), *Communities in the Balance: the Reality of Social Exclusion on Housing Estates*, Joseph Rowntree Foundation, York (URL: http://www.jrf.org.uk/bookshop/details.asp?pubID=330), [31.08.2005].

Pahl, R. (1999), *Social Trends: The Social Context of Healthy Living*, *Policy Futures for UK Health*, No. 6 (URL: http://www.jims.cam.ac.uk/research/health/polfutures/pdf/reports/social.pdf), [18.11.2004].

Parker, S., Banwell, L. and Ray, K. (1998), *LOGOPLUS: the Impact of Local Government Reorganisation on Public Library Users and Staff*, British Library Research and Innovation Centre, London (British Library Research and Innovation Report 153).

Parker, S., Harrop, K., Ray, K. and Coulson, G. (2001), *The Bidding Culture and Local Government: Effects on the Development of Public Libraries, Museums and Archives*. Resource, London (Library and Information Commission Report 103).

Parker, S., Waterson, K., Michaluk, G. and Rickard, L. (2002), *Neighbourhood Renewal and Social Inclusion: The Role of Museums, Archives and Libraries*, Resource, London (URL: http://www.mla.gov.uk/documents/neighbourhood.pdf), [31.08.2005].

Pateman, J. (2004), 'Developing a Needs-based Service', *Library and Information Update*, Vol. 3(5), pp. 34-36.

Pateman, J. (2004), 'PN is Hitting Targets', *Library Association Record*, Vol. 3(7-8), p. 10.

Pateman, J. (2004), 'Structures to Tackle Social Exclusion', *Library and Information Update*, Vol. 3(6), pp. 38-40.

Pateman, J. (1998), 'Public Libraries and Social Exclusion', *LASER Link*, Autumn/Winter, pp. 6-7.

Paul Hamlyn Foundation (2005), *Reading and Library Challenge Fund* (URL: http://www.phf.org.uk/reading.htm), [20.8.2005].

Paxton, W. and Dixon, M. (2004), *The State of the Nation. An Audit of Injustice in the UK*, Institute for Public Policy Research, London (URL: http://www.ippr.org.uk/research/index.php?current=41&project=193), [17.11.2004].

People's Network Computers – Best Value or Expensive Beige Elephants (2003) (URL: http://www.seered.co.uk/peoples_network_computers.htm), [25.8.2005].

Perham, L. (2004), *House of Commons Hansard Debates for 23 June 2004 (pt 4), Column 423WH* (URL: http://www.parliament.the-stationery-office.co.uk/pa/cm200304/cmhansrd/vo040623/halltext/40623h04.htm), [7.8.2005].

PKF (2005), *Public Libraries: Efficiency and Stock Supply Chain Review*, PKF, London (URL: http://www.mla.gov.uk/documents/fff_efficiency_00fullrep.pdf), [5.8.2005].

Policy Action Team 15 (2000), *Closing the Digital Divide: Information and Communication Technologies in Deprived Areas*, DTI, London.

Pollitt, C. (2003), 'Joined-up Government: a Survey', *Political Studies Review*, Vol. 1, pp. 34-49.

Preston-Shoot, M. (2001), 'A Triumph of Hope Over Experience? Modernizing Accountability: The Case of Complaints Procedures in Community Care', *Social Policy and Administration*, Vol. 35(6), pp. 701-715.

PricewaterhouseCoopers (2005), *Libraries Impact Project*, PricewaterhouseCoopers, London (URL: http://www.bl.uk/about/cooperation/pdf/laserfinal6.pdf), [3.4.2005].

Proctor, R., Lee, H. and Reilly, R. (1998), *Access to Public Libraries: The Impact of Opening Hours Reductions and Closure 1986-1997*, British Library Research and Innovation Centre, London (British Library Research and Innovation Report 90).

Product perceptions ltd. (2003), *Inspiring Children. The Impact of the Summer Reading Challenge*, product perceptions ltd, Surrey (URL:

www.readingagency.org.uk/research_files/InspiringChildrenKeyFindings.doc), [13.11.2004].

Raven, D. (2001), 'I Shine Not Burn', *Public Library Journal*, Vol. 16(4), pp. 102-103.

Research Centre for Museums and Galleries (2003), *Measuring the Outcomes and Impact of Learning in Museums, Archives and Libraries*, Resource, London (URL: http://www.mla.gov.uk/documents/insplearn_wp20030501.pdf), [7.8.2005].

Resource (2001), *Building on Success. An Action Plan for Public Libraries (Draft for consultation)*, Resource, London (URL: http://www.mla.gov.uk/documents/bosucc.pdf), [31.08.2005].

Resource, *Renaissance in the Regions: A New Vision for England's Museums*, Resource, London (URL: http://www.mla.gov.uk/documents/rennais.pdf), 2001a, [22.8.2005].

Rikards, L., Fox, K., Roberts, C., Fletcher, L. and Goddard, E. (2002), *Living in Britain. No. 31. Results from the 2002 General Household Survey*, The Stationary Office, London (URL: http://www.statistics.gov.uk/downloads/theme_compendia/lib2002.pdf), [29.0.05].

Rickett, J. (2005), 'The Bookseller', *Guardian Unlimited*, February 12th (URL: http://books.guardian.co.uk/news/articles/0,6109,1411097,00.html), [20.82005].

Rikowski, R. (2003), *Library privatisation: fact or fiction?* (URL: http://www.libr.org/ISC/articles/17-Rikowski-2.html), [8.5.2005].

Roach, P. and Morrison, M. (1998), *Public Libraries, Ethnic Diversity and Citizenship*, British Library Research and Innovation Centre, London, British Library Research and Innovation Report 76.

Roche, B. (2003), 'Tackling Social Exclusion: Achievements, Lessons Learned and the Way Forward', speech by Barbara Roche on 5 March 2003 (URL: http://www.odpm.gov.uk/stellent/groups/odpm_about/documents/page/odpm_about_609013.hcsp), [21.11.2004].

Rouse, J. (2001), *Performance Management Under New Labour: Really New or Merely More of the Same?* (URL: http://www.lss.uce.ac.uk/ppm/ppmodules/pmpso/PM3.pdf), [6.5.2005].

Sainsbury, M. (2005), *Literacy Today: Children's Attitudes to Reading (issue no. 38)*; (URL: http://www.literacytrust.org.uk/Pubs/sainsbury.html), [20.8.2005].

Salmon, H. (2002), 'Social Capital and Neighbourhood Renewal', *Renewal*, Vol. 10(2), pp. 49-55.

Scott, J.W. (1990), 'Deconstructing Equality-versus-Difference' In M. Hirsch and E. Fox Keller (eds), *Conflicts in Feminism*, Routledge, London, pp. 134-149.

Scottish Executive (2000), *Creating Our Future, Minding Our Past*, Scottish Executive, Edinburgh (URL: http://www.scotland.gov.uk/nationalculturalstrategy/docs/cult-00.asp), [3.1.2005].

Scottish Executive (2004), *Working and Learning Together to Build Stronger Communities: Scottish Executive Guidance for Community Learning and Development*, Scottish Executive, Edinburgh (URL: http://www.scotland.gov.uk/library5/housing/segcld.pdf), [8.8.2005].

Scottish Executive (2005), *Cultural Commission Final Report*, Scottish Executive, Edinburgh (URL: http://www.scotland.gov.uk/Resource/Doc/54357/0013577.pdf), [29.9.2005].

Scottish Office (1999), *Communities: Change Through Learning*, The Scottish Office, Edinburgh (URL: http://www.scotland.org.uk/library/documents-w3/cctl-01.htm), [1.11.2004].

SEMLAC (2003), *Realising Our Potential: A Library and Information Development Strategy for the South East 2002-2006*, SEMLAC, Winchester (URL: http://www.semlac.org.uk/library-strategy.html), [26.8.2005].

Sloan, C. and McKay, E. (2000), 'The extra mile', *School Librarian*, Vol. 48, No. 4, p. 183.

Smith, C. (2004), 'The Second Speech', *Man Booker Prize 2004* (URL: http://www.bookerprize.co.uk/2004prize/2004prize.html), [15.8.2005].

Smith, M.K. (1999), 'Informal Learning', *The Encyclopaedia of Informal Education* (URL: http://infed.org/biblio/inf-lrn.htm), [4.11.2004].

Smith, M.K. (2004), 'Learning in the Community and Community Learning', *The Encyclopaedia of Informal Education* (URL: http://infed.org/lifelonglearning/b-edcom.htm), [1.09.2005].

Snape, R. (1995), *Leisure and the Rise of the Public Library*, Library Association Publishing, London.

Social Exclusion Unit (1998), *Bringing Britain Together: A National Strategy for Neighbourhood Renewal*, Social Exclusion Unit, London (URL: http://www.sportdevelopment.org.uk/Bringing_Britain_together.PDF), [31.08.2005].

Social Exclusion Unit (2001), *A New Commitment to Neighbourhood Renewal: National Strategy Action Plan*, Social Exclusion Unit, London (URL: http://www.neighbourhood.gov.uk/formatteddoc.asp?id=89), [31.08.2005].

Social Exclusion Unit, *Bringing Britain Together: A National Strategy for*

Social Exclusion Unit (2001), *Preventing Social Exclusion*, Social Exclusion Unit, London (URL: http://www.socialexclusionunit.gov.uk/publications/reports/html/pse/pse_html/index.htm), [31.08.2005].

Social Exclusion Unit (2004), *Welcome to the Social Exclusion Unit* (URL: http://www.socialexclusionunit.gov.uk/index.htm), [21.11.2004].

Social Inclusion Executive Advisory Group to Cilip (2002), *Making a Difference – Innovation and Diversity* (URL: http://www.cilip.org.uk/advocacy/eags/sereport2.pdf), [21.11.2004].

Solon Consultants (2001), *Survey of Provision for Disabled Users of Museums, Archives, and Libraries*, Resource, London (URL: http://www.mla.gov.uk/action/learnacc/solon00.asp), [31.08.2005].

Sommerlad, E., Child, C., Kelleher, J. and Ramsden, C. (2004), *Competencies and Capabilities: New Paradigms for Workforce Development in the 21st Century*, London, MLA (URL: http://www.mla.gov.uk/documents/ict_full_rep.pdf), [25.8.2005].

Sommerlad, E., Child, C., Ramsden, C., Barkat, S. and Kelleher, J. (2003), *Interim Report: Evaluation of the People's Network and ICT Training for Public Library Staff Programme for the New Opportunities Fund, New Opportunities* Fund, London (URL: http://www.nof.org.uk/documents/live/2636p__ICT_eval.pdf), [26.8.2005].

Sommerlad, E., Child, C., Ramsden, C. and Kelleher, J. (2004), *Books and Bytes: New Service Paradigms for the 21st Century Library*, London, The Big Lottery

Fund (URL: http://www.mla.gov.uk/documents/pn_evaluation_full.pdf), [23.8.2005].

Spacey, R.E. (2003), 'An Evaluation of the New Opportunities Fund ICT Training Programme for Public Library Staff, UK', World Library and Information Congress: 69th IFLA General Conference and Council 1-9 August 2003, Berlin (URL: http://www.ifla.org/IV/ifla69/papers/004e-Spacey.pdf), [26.8.2005].

Spacey, R.E. (2004), *The Attitudes of Public Library Staff to the Internet and Evaluations of Internet Training*, PhD thesis, Department of Information Science, Loughborough University.

Stevens, A. and Wilkie, S. (2004), 'We're All Doing Framework' *Library and Information Update*, Vol. 3(7-8), p. 56.

Streatfield, D., Tibbitts, D., Jeffries, G., Downing, R. and Swan, R. (2000), *Rediscovering Reading. Public Libraries and the National Year of Reading*, Information Management Associates, Twickenham.

Street-Porter, J. (2004), 'No Wonder Our Libraries Are in Crisis', *The Independent*, 29th April.

Sturges, P. and Barr, A. (1992), '"The Fiction Nuisance" in Nineteenth-Century British Public Libraries', *Journal of Librarianship and Information Science*, Vol. 24(1), pp. 23-33.

Suleiman, S. R. and Crosman, I. (eds) (1980), *The Reader in the Text. Essays on Audience and Interpretation*, Princeton University Press, Princeton NJ.

Sure Start (2003), *Sure Start Guidance 2004-6: Delivery Guidance* (URL: http://www.surestart.gov.uk/_doc/index.cfm?Document=326), [9.11.2004].

Sure Start (2003), *Sure Start Guidance 2004-6: Strategic Guidance* (URL: http://www.surestart.gov.uk/_doc/index.cfm?Document=327), [14.11.2004].

The Reading Agency (2004), *A National Public Library Development Programme for Reading Groups* (URL: www.mla.gov.uk/documents/fff_rg_rep.pdf), [20.8.2005].

The Reading Agency (no date), *Final Report of the YouthBOOX Moving On Programme 2003-4* (URL: http://www.readingagency.co.uk/html/download_details2.cfm?e=24&ID=252), [20.8.2005].

The Reading Agency (2004), *Fulfilling Their Potential: A National Development Programme for Young People's Library Services* (URL: http://www.mla.gov.uk/documents/fff_fulfil_potential.pdf), [20.8.2005].

The Reading Agency (2004), *Fulfilling Their Potential: A National Development Programme for Young People's Library Services* (URL: http://www.nya.org.uk/shared_asp_files/uploadedfiles/%7B13BA9DCF-E30D-4A05-9F8E-A1E0B5F122F2%7D_Fulfilling%20Their%20Potential%20Report%20Jul04.pdf), [20.8.2005].

The Reading Agency (2004), *The Reading Agency's Work on Framework for the Future. August 2003 – March 2004* (URL: www.mla.gov.uk/documents/id1233rep.pdf), [2-.8.2005].

The Reading Agency (2005), *Orange Chatterbooks Report 2004* (URL: http://www.readingagency.co.uk/html/download_details2.cfm?e=13&ID=287), [20.8.2005].

Thomas, N. and Cooke, A. (2004), 'The Fleckney Centre: Bringing services to rural communities', *Community Librarian*, No. 13, Winter 2004.

TNS (2003), *Government Online: An International Perspective, Global Summary* (URL: http://www.tnsglobal.com/corporate/Doc/0/JF206RCSIND4H7QIOVKU GST011/21451_Global Report_Final.ppt), [22.11.2004].

Totterdell, B., Bird, J. and Redfern, M. (1976), *The Effective Library: Report of the Hillingdon Project on Public Library Effectiveness*, British Library, London.

Train, B., Chivers, B. and Denham, D. (2000). *The Value and Impact of Homework Clubs in Public Libraries: Library and Information Commission Research Report 34*, Library and Information Commission, London.

Train, B. (2003), *Quick Reads. Reader Development and Basic Skills: An Evaluation Report*, CPLIS, Sheffield (URL: http://cplis.shef.ac.uk/QuickReads%20Report.pdf), [31.08.2005].

Train, B., Usherwood, B. and Brooks, G. (2005), *The Vital Link: An Evaluation Report*, Sheffield, Sheffield University (URL: http://www.literacytrust.org.uk/vitallink/evaluation.html), [01.09.2005].

Tucker, F. and Matthews, H. (2001), '"They don't like girls hanging around there": conflicts over recreational space in rural Northamptonshire', *Area*, Vol. 33, No. 2, pp. 161-168.

Turner, T. (2001), 'Always put this first', *Public Library Journal*, Vol. 16(4), pp. 120-122.

Twist, L., Sainsbury, M., Woodthrope, A. and Whetton, C. (2003), *Reading All Over the World. Progress in International Reading Literacy Study (PIRLS)*, NFER, London (URL: http://www.nfer.ac.uk/research/outcome_popup.asp?theID=PIR), [15.11.2004].

UK Online (2003), *Annual Report 2003* (URL: http://e-government.cabinetoffice.gov.uk/assetRoot/04/00/60/69/04006069.pdf), [21.11.2004].

Usherwood, B. and Pearce, S. (2003), 'Influencing the Politicians', *Public Library Journal*, Vol. 18(4), pp. 83-85.

Usherwood, B., Proctor, R., Bower, G., Coe, C., Cooper, J. and Stevens, T. (2001), *Recruit, Retain and Lead: The Public Library Workforce Study*, Resource, London (Library and Information Commission Research Report 106).

Usherwood, B. and Toyne, J. (2002), 'The Value and Impact of Reading Imaginative Literature', *The Journal of Librarianship and Information Science*, Vol. 34(1), pp. 33 41.

Valentine, P. (2004), *Developing a Vision for Libraries' Work with Readers: Consultation with the Public Libraries Sector. Final Report to the Steering Group* (URL: http://www.readingagency.org.uk/research_files/Visionforlibraries.doc), [20.8.2005].

Vincent, J. (2002), *Library Materials for Socially Excluded People – a Survey of Purchasing Decision-Making: Findings* (URL: http://www.seapn.org.uk/docs/bookscan_report.pdf), [31.08.2005].

Vogt, H. (2004), *Putting the Customer First! Managing Customer Satisfaction*, Bertelsmann Foundation, Gütersloh (URL: http://www.internationales-netzwerk.de/en/x_media/pdf/customer satisfaction_040220.pdf), [23.11.2004].

Wade and Moore (1998), *Bookstart: the First Five Years*, Book Trust, London.

Walker, D. (2002), *In Praise of Centralism: A Critique of the New Localism* (URL: http://www.catalystforum.org.uk/pubs/pub7.html), [3.5.2005].

Wallis, M., Moore, N. and Marshall, A. (2002), *Reading Our Future: Evaluation of the DCMS/Wolfson Public Libraries Challenge Fund 2000-2001*, Library and Information Commission, London (Library and Information Commission Research Report 134) (URL: http://www.mla.gov.uk/action/dcmswolf/00dcmswo.asp), [20.8.2005].

Ward, R. (2003), 'You only live twice. Turning vision into reality', *Public Library Journal*, Vol. 18, No. 3, pp. 51-52.

Welsh Assembly Government (2002), *Creative Future: A Cultural Strategy for Wales, Cymru Greadigol.* (URL: http://www.wales.gov.uk/subiculture/content/creative/creative_home-e.htm), [17.11.2004].

Welsh Assembly Government (2003), *Wales: A Better Country*, Welsh Assembly Government, Cardiff.

Whyte, A. and Macintosh, A. (2003), 'Analysis and Evaluation of E-consultation', *E-service Journal*, Vol. 2, pp. 9-35.

Williams, K. and Green, S. (2001), Literature Review of Public Space and Local Environments for the Cross Cutting Review, DETR, London.

Wills, H. (2003), 'An innovative approach to reaching the non-learning public: the new Idea Stores in London', New Review of Libraries and Lifelong Learning, Vol. 4, pp. 107-120.

Wimmer, M.A. (2002), 'Integrated Service Modelling for Online One-stop Government', *Electronic Markets*, Vol. 12(3), pp. 149-156.

Working Group on Post 16 Basic Skills (The 'Moser Group') (1999), *Fresh Start: Improving Literacy and Numeracy*, DfEE, London (URL: http://www.lifelonglearning.co.uk/mosergroup/index.htm), [9.8.2005].

World Bank (2003), *Lifelong Learning in the Global Knowledge Economy. Challenges for Developing Countries: The World Bank, Washington DC* (URL: http://www-wds.worldbank.org/servlet/WDSContentServer/WDSP/IB/2003/07/08/000094946_03062104054940/Rendered/PDF/multi0page.pdf), [7.8.2005].

Worpole, K. (2004), *21st Century Libraries*, Building Futures, London (URL: http://www.buildingfutures.org.uk/pdfs/pdffile_31.pdf), [25.8.2005].

Index